Judicial Application of International Law in Southeast Europe

Siniša Rodin • Tamara Perišin
Editors

Judicial Application of International Law in Southeast Europe

Springer

Editors
Siniša Rodin
Judge
Court of Justice of the European Union
Luxembourg, European Union

Tamara Perišin
Faculty of Law
University of Zagreb
Zagreb, Croatia

ISBN 978-3-662-46383-3 ISBN 978-3-662-46384-0 (eBook)
DOI 10.1007/978-3-662-46384-0

Library of Congress Control Number: 2015936664

Springer Heidelberg New York Dordrecht London

Printed on acid-free paper

Springer-Verlag GmbH Berlin Heidelberg is part of Springer Science+Business Media (www.springer.com)

Contents

About the Editors

Siniša Rodin, LLM, PhD, is a judge of the Court of Justice of the European Union. Rodin earned his PhD degree from the University of Zagreb, Faculty of Law, Croatia, in 1995, and his LLM degree from the University of Michigan Law School in Ann Arbor, Michigan, in 1992. He specialised in European Law at the European University Institute in Florence, Italy, and in German Constitutional Law at the Max-Planck Institut für ausländisches öeffentliches Recht und Völkerrecht in Heidelberg, Germany. He received the University of Michigan Law School Merit Award and the University of Zagreb Rector's Award. In 2001/2002, he was Fulbright Fellow and Visiting Scholar at Harvard Law School. Judge Rodin is a member of the International Association of Constitutional Law and of the European Communities Studies Association. He is the author of 2 books and more than 50 research papers. Together with Tamara Ćapeta, he co-authored the first textbook on EU law in the Croatian language. Rodin's scientific interests include constitutional interpretation, fundamental rights and constitutional aspects of European integration. His research also focuses on free movement of services. He is a member of the editorial boards of the Croatian Yearbook of European Law & Policy and Zeitschrift für Öffentliches Recht. He is a member of UACES and FIDE. Rodin held *ad personam* the Jean Monnet Chair at the University of Zagreb, Faculty of Law. His teaching has included a general course on EU law and an advanced course on human rights in the EU, and he has supervised students participating in the European Law Moot Court competition and the Central and East European Moot Court. Rodin has taught at CEU San Pablo Madrid and as a Marc and Beth Goldberg Distinguished Visiting Professor at Cornell University Law School. Since 1 July 2013, Rodin has served as the first Croatian judge at the Court of Justice of the European Union.

Tamara Perišin, MJur (Oxon), PhD (Zagreb) is professor of EU and WTO Law at the University of Zagreb - Faculty of Law. She earned her Magister Juris degree in European and Comparative Law as a Chevening Scholar at the University of Oxford, and defended her PhD in Zagreb before an international committee.

Following an internship at Zagreb municipal court, she passed the Croatian Bar exam. During her doctoral and post-doctoral studies, Perišin was a visiting researcher at the TMC Asser Institute, The Hague, a Fulbright Scholar at Georgetown University, Washington DC, and at the University of Michigan Law School, Ann Arbor, a 'visitor-in-the-cabinet' of Advocate General Sharpston, a SOTL fellow at the Central European University, Budapest, a research fellow at the Max Planck Institute, Heidelberg, and a visiting researcher at Harvard Law School. She is the module leader of the Jean Monnet Module 'EU and WTO in a Comparative Perspective' and she co-teaches the Jean Monnet module 'Internal Market Law'. She served as vice dean for International Cooperation and as a member of the working group for Free Movement of Goods in the EU accession negotiating team of the Croatian government. She is on the editorial board of the Croatian Yearbook of European Law and Policy, the Zagreb Law Review and the Southeast European Law School Network Journal. Her scientific interests include EU law, particularly in the area of the internal market, the law of the WTO, and free trade and human rights. She is the author of many articles and of the book 'Free Movement of Goods and Limits of Regulatory Autonomy in the EU and WTO' (TMC Asser Press, 2009).

Contributors

Steven Blockmans PhD, is senior research fellow and head of the EU foreign policy unit of the Brussels-based think tank Centre for European Policy Studies (CEPS). His expertise lies at the crossroads of international and EU law and governance. He has published widely on the Lisbon Treaty structures for EU external action, the Union's role in global governance, norm promotion (inside out) and norm absorption (outside in), CFSP, CSDP, enlargement and ENP. Blockmans has a special knack for issues pertaining to Southeast Europe. He is the author of 'Tough love: the EU's relations with the Western Balkans' (TMC Asser Press/CUP, 2007) and has worked on numerous technical assistance projects in the region. From 2007 to 2009, he served as a long-term expert on legal approximation in the framework of an EU-sponsored project in support for the Ministry of European Integration of Albania. Blockmans is one of the founding members of the Centre for the Law of EU External Relations (CLEER) and a visiting professor at the University of Leuven, where he teaches law of international organisations and European security law. Before joining CEPS, he was head of the department of research at the TMC Asser Institute, an inter-university research centre based in The Hague. From 2005 to 2010, he was a lecturer in the in-service training provided by the European Institute of Public Administration (EIPA) for DG Relex and other external relations DGs of the European Commission. Blockmans holds a PhD in law from Leiden University, where he worked as a lecturer from 1998 until 2002.

Sanja Bogojević DPhil, is associate professor in EU Environmental Law and co-director of the master's programme in European Business Law at Lund University. Bogojević gained her DPhil at the University of Oxford, her LLM from the College of Europe and her LLB with German Law from King's College London and Universität Passau. She has also been a DAAD (Deutscher Akademischer Austausch Dienst) research scholar at the Max Planck Institute for Collective Goods in Bonn, a visiting doctoral Hauser Global Fellow at the New York University School of Law, and Visiting Fellow at the University of New South Wales Australia. Bogojević's research, focusing on environmental markets and their conceptualisation, including by courts, has been published widely in international law journals, and her book 'Emissions trading schemes: markets, states and law' is published by Hart Publishing.

Ivana Božac is head of the Croatian Language Unit at the Court of Justice of the European Union. Previously, she worked as lawyer-linguist at the Court of Justice of the European Union (2013–2014), as European law advisor at the Supreme Court of the Republic of Croatia (2011–2013), as legal advisor at the Constitutional Court of the Republic of Croatia (2010–2011), as judicial advisor at Pula county court (2007–2009), and as judicial trainee also at Pula county court (2006–2007). In 2012, she was appointed as judge at Pula municipal court. She was a trainee lawyer at the European Court of Human Rights, working in a case-processing (legal) division (2009). Božac graduated from the University of Zagreb, Faculty of Law in 2005, and passed her Bar exam in 2007. In 2009, she was admitted to the academic cycle of the initial training for prosecutors and judges at the French National School for the Judiciary (Ecole Nationale de la Magistrature, Bordeaux, France) and was integrated in the intake of the school alongside future French judges (2009–2010). Since 2011, she has been pursuing her PhD studies at the University of Zagreb, Faculty of Law.

Melita Carević LLM, works at the University of Zagreb, Faculty of Law as a research fellow at the Jean Monnet Chair of European Union Public Law and is a PhD candidate in the EU law doctorate programme. Carević graduated *magna cum laude* from the University of Zagreb, Faculty of Law in 2008. During her studies, she was a member of the team of runners-up at the European Law Moot Court competition and received a Special Rector's Award. She earned her master's degree from the University of Michigan Law School in 2011, where she won a University of Michigan Grotius Fellowship. After her graduate studies, Carević briefly worked in a Croatian law office and joined Zagreb Faculty of Law in 2009. She has participated in several international research projects, successfully coached student moot court teams and taught a number of seminars on EU law for legal practitioners, such as judges, members of Bar associations and public prosecutors. Since 2011, Carević has been serving as executive editor of the Croatian Yearbook of European Law and Policy. In 2013, she completed a 9-month judicial internship at several courts in Zagreb and is currently finishing a 4-month internship at the Court of Justice of the European Union. Carević has authored several articles and participated in the development of e-learning materials in general EU law for the Croatian Judicial Academy.

Janja Hojnik PhD, gained university degrees in law (2002) and finances (2003) and her PhD in EU legal studies (2007), all from University of Maribor, Slovenia. She undertook additional professional training at Kingston University (London) and at the Central European University (Budapest). She is assistant professor of EU Law at the University of Maribor Faculty of Law and a visiting lecturer at Luxembourg University. Hojnik has been teaching and researching in the field of

EU law since 2003 and coaching teams for the EU Law Moot Court competition since 2005. She has been a member of national and international research projects (e.g. SEEurope and GoodCOM projects at the European Trade Union Institute, Brussels) and has participated in several international conferences, e.g. the World Jurist Congress in Prague (2011) and the European Law and Policy Conference, organised by Birmingham University (2012). She won the Slovenian Law Societies' award for the most outstanding achievement in the field of law among young lawyers in 2010 and the IUS-INFO award for ten leading lawyers in Slovenia in 2011, based on an open poll organised by a legal website. She has written widely on free movement of goods and on other topics related to the EU internal market. Her main publications include: 'The European company statute: a new approach to corporate governance' (Peter Lang, 2009) (in English, co author); 'Free movement of goods' (2010) (in Slovenian, 830 pp.); 'Decentralisation of the EU internal market (2011) (in Slovenian, 250 pp.); 'The EU internal market' (2009) (in Slovenian, co-author); 'Introduction to EU law' (2011) (in Slovenian, co-author); 'Free movement of goods in a labyrinth: can "Buy Irish" survive the crises?' Common Market Law Review, Vol. 49 (1) 2012.

Mirjana Drenovak Ivanović Mag iur, PhD, is a lecturer in Environmental Law and EU Environmental Policy and Law at the University of Belgrade Faculty of Law. She earned the degree of Magister Juris in Administrative Law and a PhD in Environmental Law at the University of Belgrade Faculty of Law. During her doctoral studies, Drenovak Ivanović was a junior academic visitor at the Faculty of Law, University of Oxford, as a British government Chevening Scholar (Research topic: Comparative and global environmental law), visiting researcher at the Institut für Rechts- und Sozialwissenschaften, Universität Hohenheim in Stuttgart (Research topic: German environmental law), visiting researcher at the Faculté de droit international et européen de l'Université Nice—Institut du Droit de la Paix et du Développement, University of Nice-Sophia Antipolis, as a participant in the Western Balkans ERASMUS MUNDUS programme (Research topics: French environmental law; Court of Justice of the European Union and environmental protection). She has also participated in several international conferences. She was awarded the IASI-IBM Prize for the best paper from young researchers/practitioners providing a contribution to issues related to governance in the twenty-first century (1st edition) at the Annual Conference of the International Association of Schools and Institutes of Administration, Rome, 2011. Her main publications include: 'Access to justice in environmental administrative matters' (Belgrade, 460 pp.) (forthcoming); 'The application of IT and environmental protection', International Review of Administrative Sciences, SAGE, Vol. 78 (4) 2012; 'Implementation of the Aarhus Convention in Serbia', European Energy and Environmental Law Review, Kluwer Law International, Vol. 2 (2) 2011; 'Public participation and environmental impact assessment', RICS Construction and Property, School of the Built Environment University of Salford, 2011; 'Discretionary power in administrative law of Serbia with a comparative analysis of German, French, British and Europe Union administrative law' (Belgrade, 2011, 130 pp.).

Kushtrim Istrefi is visiting fellow at the Graduate Institute of International and Development Studies in Geneva and lecturer in International and European Law at the University of Prishtina. He has been a visiting fellow at the Lauterpacht Centre for International Law of the University of Cambridge, the Max Planck Institute for Comparative Public Law and International Law, and at the University of Graz, where he is completing his PhD. He has lectured and presented in the USA, Switzerland, Spain, Latvia, Germany, Italy, Austria and Albania. Istrefi litigates cases with international law elements. Previously, he worked as legal advisor to the Deputy Prime Minister of Kosovo on secondment from UNDP/Soros and with the USAID justice reform programme. His research interests lie in the fields of UN law, law of treaties, EU external relations law, human rights law, law of statehood, and international law in domestic courts. His main publications include: 'Application of Article 103 of the UN Charter in the European legal order: the quest for regime compatibility on fundamental rights', European Journal of Legal Studies, 2013; 'Think globally, act locally: Al-Jedda's oscillation between the coherence of international law and autonomy of the European legal order', Hague Yearbook of International Law, 2012 (co-author); 'Azemi v. Serbia of the European Court of Human Rights: discontinuity of Serbia's de jure jurisdiction over Kosovo', European Human Rights Law Review, 2014; 'Kosovo's quest for Council of Europe membership', Review of Central and East European Law, 2014; 'Constitutional domestication of international human rights in the Kosovo legal order', Law Journal, 2013. He also contributes to the Oxford Reports on International Law, the EJIL Talk!—Blog of the European Journal of International Law, JURIST of the Pittsburgh Law School, and the Balkans in Europe Policy Blog.

Maja Lukić Mag iur, PhD, is assistant professor in EU Law at the University of Belgrade Faculty of Law. She earned her PhD degree from the same university in 2013 (dissertation title: 'Autonomy of EU law in light of the recent practice of European courts), and an LLM degree from University Paris 1, Panthéon-Sorbonne, Department of International Law and International Organizations in 2002 (thesis title: 'Admissibility of reservations to international treaties'). Lukić completed her traineeship for the practice of law in France with the law firm Cabinet De Guillenchmidt & Baillet, in its Paris office, as well as for the practice of law in Serbia with the law firm Dražić & Beatović. She passed the Serbian Bar exam in 2006, and was licensed to practise law in Serbia from 2006 until 2009 as a senior associate of the international law firm Gide Loyrette Nouel. From 2009 until 2011, she worked in 'of counsel' capacity in the global law firm DLA Piper. She teaches several courses at bachelor, master and doctoral levels, including a general course on EU law, international relations of the EU, immigration and asylum policy of the EU and the EU common agricultural policy (within the Master in EU Law programme). In 2014, Lukić started teaching a master programme at the University of Belgrade Faculty of Philology. She has presented papers at numerous international conferences and seminars. She participated, *inter alia*, in the second workshop of the Institute for Global Law and Policy (IGLP) at Harvard Law School in

2011. Her research interests include the law of international treaties, EU institutional law, and the regulation of financial services at the EU level. She has published scholarly articles in English, French and Serbian.

Mislav Mataija PhD, is a member of the legal service of the European Commission, where he works in the WTO & Trade Policy team. Previously, he was employed at the Jean Monnet Department of European Public Law at the University of Zagreb, Faculty of Law as lecturer and researcher. He graduated from the University of Zagreb, Faculty of Law in 2007. He obtained his LLM in 2009 as a Fulbright Scholar at Columbia Law School in New York, where he was named James Kent Scholar in recognition of his academic achievement. He defended his PhD thesis titled 'Private regulation, competition and free movement' at the European University Institute in Florence in 2013. He has been a team member and coach in several top-placed European Law Moot Court competitions. He has authored numerous papers and book chapters on various issues of EU constitutional, internal market and competition law and has acted on three occasions as FIDE (Fédération Internationale pour le Droit Européen) national rapporteur for various EU law topics. He has worked on a number of national and international training and research projects with judges, attorneys, parliamentarians, civil servants and journalists. His research interests include internal market law, competition law and international trade law.

Zlatan Meškić PhD, earned his degree of Magister Juris at the University of Vienna Faculty of Law in 2006, with an additional degree in the field of International Law and International Relations. His thesis embraced, in the field of European Union Law, the topic 'Missbrauch einer marktbeherrschenden Stellung gem. Art 82 EG: Rs IMS Health' and, in the field of Public International Law, the topic 'State responsibility and individual responsibility for genocide committed in Bosnia and Herzegovina'. In Vienna, he completed his doctoral studies in the field of European and Private International Law in 2008. He defended his dissertation on the topic 'Europäisches Verbraucherrecht unter besonderer Berücksichtigung des Grünbuchs 2007'. Meškić is professor of European Union Law, European Private Law and Private International Law in the Departments for Civil Law and State and International Law at the University of Zenica, Bosnia and Herzegovina. He is vice dean for scientific research at the University of Zenica Faculty of Law and editor-in-chief of the journal 'Annals of the Law Faculty University of Zenica'. He is member of the editorial board of the journal 'Nova pravna revija' (Sarajevo) and the 'SEE Law Journal' (Skopje). He is a scholarship holder of the Max-Planck Institute for Foreign and Private International Law (Hamburg, 2011). His works are published in English, German and Bosnian/Croatian/Serbian. He is the author of two books and several articles and has contributed to international projects published in Austria, Serbia, Croatia, FYR Macedonia, and Bosnia and Herzegovina.

Kristina Miševa LLM, has been working since 2007 at the University 'Goce Delčev', Stip, Faculty of Law. In 2003, she graduated in legal studies at the Faculty of Law "Iustinianus Primus", University "Ss. Cyril and Methodius", Skopje, Macedonia, and later she obtained her LLM degree at the Business Law Department at the same faculty defending her thesis 'Investment funds—legal aspects'. She is currently a PhD candidate at the Faculty of Law 'Iustinianus Primus', University 'Ss. Cyril and Methodius', Skopje, Macedonia. From May 2003 to July 2004, Miševa volunteered at the primary court of law in Stip, and from 2004 to 2006 she was a member of the jury at the same court. From June 2004 to July 2007, she worked at Komecijalna Banka AD Skopje, Stip branch. In 2006, she successfully passed the Bar exam. Her main academic interest and research activities lie in the following areas: national, European and international company law; domestic and international finance law; EU law, particularly the internal market; the capital market; and transposition of the EU acquis into national law. Miševa is the author of several research papers and has actively participated in many domestic and international conferences. As a student, she was active in many student and non-governmental organisations. Currently, she is member of several faculty commissions at 'Goce Delčev' University.

Visar Morina PhD, holds a bachelor's and master of science degree from Prishtina University, Kosovo, and a PhD degree in law from Linz University, Austria. For the last 10 years, he has taught in the areas of constitutional law and human rights at universities in Kosovo and Albania and has conducted research and scholarly programmes at the University of Graz (Austria), University of Trento (Italy) and Oxford University (UK). His PhD research, carried out at the Johannes Kepler University in Linz from 2003 to 2007, focused on the challenges and perspectives of constitutional justice in countries in transition: the case of Albania. From March 2002 until present, Morina has worked as lecturer at Prishtina University in the Faculty of Law at bachelor and master level. He has published an article titled 'The newly established Constitutional Court in post-status Kosovo: selected institutional and procedural concerns' in the Review of Central and East European Law. He also co-authored an article on the relationship between international law and national law in the case of Kosovo published in the International Journal of Constitutional Law. Morina has acted as legal advisor in the Ministry of Public Administration and in the Ministry of Environment of the government of Kosovo. He has also acted as legal advisor for internationally accredited missions in Kosovo, including the United Nations Mission in Kosovo and the Organization for Cooperation and Security in Europe. He has participated in the capacity of external expert in the drafting of the 2008 Kosovo Constitution and the Law on the Constitutional Court in Kosovo. Morina is currently working on justice reform as senior legal advisor with the United States Agency for International Development—The Effective Rule of Law Programme in Kosovo.

Lana Ofak PhD, is assistant professor at the University of Zagreb, Faculty of Law. From 2004 to 2006, she worked for the United Nations Development Programme in Zagreb. Since 2006, she has been employed at the Faculty of Law in Zagreb in the Chair of Administrative Law where she teaches Administrative Law,

Administrative Procedural Law and Environmental Law. She earned her PhD in Public Law and Public Administration from the Faculty of Law in Zagreb in 2012. She is a member of the Avosetta Group, the advisory board of Justice and Environment, the Environmental Law Network International, and the European Environmental Law Forum. She is also a member of the Croatian Academy of Legal Sciences. In 2012, she won the 'Junior Faculty Development Program' fellowship that enabled her to spend the 2013 spring semester at Florida State University College of Law (Environmental, Energy and Land Use Law Program) as a visiting scholar.

Dušan Rakitić Mag iur, LLM, is assistant lecturer at the University of Belgrade Faculty of Law. During the mandate of the first democratically elected government of Serbia after WWII (2001–2003), he was one of the two experts who designed the framework for the restoration of religious instruction in public schools, as well as one of the three experts who designed specific property rights on construction land, enacted in the Law on Planning and Construction of 2003. He participated in designing a two-tier model of registration of religious communities, which has been followed by several Central European countries since its presentation in 2001/2002. From 2001 until 2011, he advocated restitution in kind as a primary model of denationalisation, which has significantly contributed to the adoption of that model in the Law on Restitution of 2011. Dušan Rakitić earned LLM degrees from Harvard Law School and from the University of Belgrade Faculty of Law. His publications include: 'Envisaging a legal framework for ensuring sustainable preservation of holy places with regard to the case of Kosovo and Metochia', in S Ferrari and A Benzo (eds) *Between cultural diversity and common heritage: legal and religious perspectives on the sacred places of the Mediterranean* (Ashgate Publishing Ltd., 2014); 'Understanding secularity in a post-communist state: the case of Serbia', co-author with Sima Avramović, Oesterreichisches Archiv fuer Recht und Religion, 2/2012; 'Analysis of principal elements of the general restitution statute of Serbia from the perspective of the European Court of Human Rights case-law' [in Serbian], Annals of the Belgrade University Law School, 2/2011, 212–234; 'Historische und gegenwaertige Aspekte des neuen Gesetzes ueber die Kirchen und Religionsgemeinschaften in Serbien', Oesterreichisches Archiv fuer Recht und Religion, Heft 3, 2003, 461–484; 'Achievements and future goals of the government of Serbia in the field of religious freedom', Brigham Young University Law Review, 2003, 625–636.

Marija Risteska PhD, holds her PhD in Political Science. She is the founder and senior analyst at the Centre for Research and Policy Making in Skopje, Macedonia. Her research work lies in the area of public administration reform, public management, good governance, policy transfer and European integration. She teaches public policy courses at FON University in Skopje. She has contributed to four specific public sector reforms in Macedonia on public policy development, strategic planning, and better regulation. Risteska has 10 years of consulting experience with the EU and all UN agencies. In the past, she has managed the World Bank education portfolio in Macedonia. In the area of European Integration, she has co-authored a book on 'European law for small and medium enterprises' (Zahorka, Dimovska, 2004), and several book chapters: 'Macedonian EU accession' in Kral and others (eds) 'The future of EU enlargement: on track or derailed? Debates in new member states, candidates and neighbours' (2007); 'The Macedonian experience with cross-border cooperation programs' in 'EU assistance programs—INTERREG initiatives in Albania, Croatia and Macedonia' (AIIS, 2007); 'Internationalization of Macedonian SMEs' in Dana and others (eds) 'A theory of internationalization for European entrepreneurship' (Edward Elgar, 2007). Risteska has published several articles in peer-reviewed journals: 'The EU role in the promotion of good governance in Macedonia: between state building and democracy building', Nationalities Papers, 6/2012; 'The effects of the Lisbon Treaty on Accession Countries', Turkish Policy Quarterly, Vol. 9 (3), Fall 2010—Viewpoints collide: shifts in Turkey and its neighborhood. Risteska has edited the book 'Mapping the leaders in Macedonia and Albania: can elites promote positive social change?' (2010) and co-edited the books 'The Macedonian question: 20 years of political struggle into European integration structures" (2012) and "Ten years after the Ohrid Framework Agreement: lessons (to be) learned" (2011).

Semir Sali LLM, works as a legal officer at the Supreme Court of the Republic of Albania, Criminal Law Bench. Sali previously completed legal internships at the International Criminal Tribunal for the former Yugoslavia (both Appeals and Trial Chamber III), at the Association for International Arbitration, and at the North Atlantic Treaty Organization Headquarters, Office of the Legal Adviser. In 2010, he attended The Hague Academy of International Law. He is a case reporter for the Oxford Reports on International Law, International Criminal Law Module, a member of the International Law Association, Albanian branch, and is managing editor of the Albanian Journal for Legal Studies. Sali is a graduate of Leiden University, the Netherlands (LLM in Public International Law) and of the University of Turin, Italy (*Laurea Specialistica, cum laude*).

Darko Samardžić PhD, finished his First State Board Examination in Law at the University of Hamburg (Germany) in 2002 with a focus on European and International Law and his Second State Board Examination in Law (Germany) in 2007. He earned his PhD in 2009 (Hamburg, Germany) in the field of Constitutional and European Law focusing on the role of political parties and parliamentary rights, campaigns and elections. Samardžić is professor of European Union Law at the Department for State and International Law at the University of Zenica, Bosnia and Herzegovina. From 1999 to the end of 2005, he worked as an assistant officer in the Hamburg Parliament, Germany. From 2005 to 2007, he worked as assistant to the professor of Public Law/Eastern European Law, University of Hamburg, and was a lecturer in European and International Law at the 'Repetitorium Jura Intensiv' (Hamburg, Germany). Since 2007, he has been working as a company lawyer and auditor at Continental AG (an international automotive supplier) with a focus on mergers & acquisitions and compliance. Additionally, he has been leading various projects in the field of European Union law and its business implementation. Samardžić is editor for European and international law in the European Law Review (Kragujevac, Serbia). His publications embrace current issues of European and constitutional law, and he has participated in several international conferences in Germany, Serbia, Montenegro, Bosnia and Herzegovina.

Gentian Zyberi PhD, is associate professor of International Law at the Norwegian Centre for Human Rights, University of Oslo. Over the last 11 years, he has researched and published, and prepared and taught courses on international human rights, humanitarian law, international criminal law and public international law at different universities in the Netherlands, the USA, China and Albania. In 2008, Tilburg University and the Netherlands School of Human Rights Research awarded him second prize of the prestigious Max van der Stoel Human Rights Award for his PhD dissertation on the contribution of the International Court of Justice (ICJ) to human rights and humanitarian law. Zyberi's edited book volume titled 'An institutional approach to the responsibility to protect' was the first to examine the responsibility to protect doctrine from an institutional perspective (CUP, 2013). He has worked as legal assistant and interpreter for the defence at the International Criminal Tribunal for the former Yugoslavia (ICTY) in two cases, namely *Prosecutor v. Limaj et al.* and *Prosecutor v. Haradinaj et al.*, and has served as *pro bono* co-counsel for post-conviction issues for Mr Haradin Bala. Throughout 2009, he acted as legal adviser and coordinator of the Albanian legal team in the *Kosovo Declaration of Independence* case before the International Court of Justice. His areas of interest include international courts and tribunals, community interests in international law, responsibility to protect, and transitional justice with a focus on the Balkans.

Part I
Introduction

Application of International Law as a Litmus Test for the Application of EU Law in Southeast Europe

Siniša Rodin and Tamara Perišin

Southeast Europe (SEE) is an area towards which the European Union (EU) has been gradually enlarging. Slovenia joined the EU in 2004; Croatia in 2013; Albania, Macedonia, Montenegro and Serbia are candidate countries; and Bosnia and Herzegovina and Kosovo have the status of potential candidate countries (Table 1).[1] As was the case with other enlargements, the advantages would go beyond the classic economic benefits of a greater market. On the current map of the EU, SEE countries which are not EU members seem like an enclave, so enlargement to this area is also relevant for many political and security reasons.

For the countries of the SEE and for the EU as a whole, it is relevant to know, when they accede, whether these countries will be able to fully function as part of the EU. Some of the previous enlargements have shown that not all new members were equally prepared for EU accession. The extent of their readiness was visible in many areas such as the translation of the *acquis communautaire*, including the decisions of the Court of Justice (CJEU), the use of EU structural funds, interest in EU politics, participation in elections for the European Parliament, etc.

This volume focuses on national courts in SEE countries. Our interest in the judicial branch derives from the fact that the courts of the EU Member States are essential for the life of EU law. Unlike in the federal model of the United States, where the application of federal law is in the hands of federal, and not state, courts ('horizontal federalism'), the EU relies on state courts to serve as European courts

[1] European Commission, European Neighbourhood Policy and Enlargement Negotiations. http://ec.europa.eu/enlargement/countries/check-current-status/index_en.htm#pc. Accessed 25 November 2014.

S. Rodin (✉)
Judge, Court of Justice of the European Union, Luxembourg, European Union
e-mail: srodin@gmx.com

T. Perišin
Faculty of Law, University of Zagreb, Zagreb, Croatia
e-mail: Tamara.perisin@pravo.hr

S. Rodin, T. Perišin (eds.), *Judicial Application of International Law in Southeast Europe*, DOI 10.1007/978-3-662-46384-0_1

Table 1 Overview of non-EU SEE countries' relations with the EU[a]

SEE country	Signing of the SAA	Entry into force of the SAA	Potential candidate country status	Candidate country status	Scheduled EU accession
Albania	June 2006	April 2009	June 2003	June 2014	–
Bosnia and Herzegovina	June 2008	–	June 2003	–	–
Kosovo	–	–	June 2003	–	–
Macedonia	April 2001	April 2004	June 2003	December 2005	–
Montenegro	October 2007	May 2010	June 2003	December 2010	–
Serbia	April 2008	September 2013	June 2003	March 2012	–

[a]European Commission, European Neighbourhood Policy and Enlargement Negotiations. http://ec.europa.eu/enlargement/countries/check-current-status/index_en.htm#pc. Accessed 25 November 2014. Kosovo's SAA negotiations were concluded in 2014. At the time of the EU-Western Balkans Summit in Thessaloniki in June 2003 which recognised Western Balkan countries as potential candidate countries, Kosovo was part of Serbia and Montenegro. It declared independence in February 2008. At the time of the Thessaloniki Summit, Montenegro was part of Serbia and Montenegro. It declared independence in June 2006

('vertical federalism').[2] Namely, European law entrusts national courts to apply EU law directly (direct effect),[3] to interpret national law in the light of EU law (indirect or interpretative effect),[4] to adjudicate damages caused to an individual by a Member State acting contrary to EU law,[5] to communicate with the Court of Justice concerning the appropriate interpretation and validity of EU law,[6] etc. Significant parts of EU law have actually been developed thanks to the preliminary references of national courts. The ECJ established some of the most important principles of EU law, such as mutual recognition,[7] observance of fundamental rights,[8] or equal pay

[2] On the role of the judiciary in horizontal and vertical federal systems, see Halberstam (2010).

[3] Case 26/62 *NV Algemene Transport- en Expeditie Onderneming van Gend & Loos v Netherlands Inland Revenue Administration* [1963] ECR 1.

[4] Case 14/83 *Sabine von Colson and Elisabeth Kamann v. Land Nordrhein-Westfalen* [1984] ECR 01891; Case C-282/10 *Maribel Dominguez v. Centre informatique du Centre Ouest Atlantique and Préfet de la région Centre* [2012] ECR I-000.

[5] Joined cases C-6/90 and C-9/90 *Andrea Francovich and Danila Bonifaci and others v. Italian Republic* [1991] ECR I-05357.

[6] Article 267 TFEU (ex Article 234 TEC).

[7] Case 120/78 *Rewe-Zentrale AG v. Bundesmonopolverwaltung fur Branntwein* [1979] ECR 649 (*Cassis de Dijon*).

[8] Case 11-70 *Internationale Handelsgesellschaft mbH v. Einfuhr- und Vorratsstelle für Getreide und Futtermittel* [1970] ECR 01125; Case 4-73 *J. Nold, Kohlen- und Baustoffgroßhandlung v. Commission of the European Communities* [1974] ECR 00491.

for work of equal value,[9] precisely in response to a question raised by a national court.

The aim of this book is to tease-out how prepared the national courts of SEE countries are for these functions. The underlying premise is that the courts' readiness to apply EU law lies in correlation to their application of international law. In *Van Gend en Loos*, the European Court of Justice famously held that 'the Community constitutes a new legal order of international law'[10] and since then EC/EU law has evolved into a unique supranational legal order.[11] Still, the EU functions within the international legal order and many parts of international law are vital for the operation of the EU. From the perspective of the SEE countries, accepting certain parts of international law is even a prerequisite for developing closer ties with the EU (e.g. cooperation with international criminal tribunals, observing fundamental rights treaties such as the European Convention for Human Rights (ECHR), and for becoming a member of the World Trade Organization (WTO)). The EU also uses agreements such as the Stabilisation and Association Agreement (SAA) for strengthening cooperation.

The book has two central parts (Parts II and III), corresponding to the two parts of the research.

Part II of the book contains horizontal chapters looking at the application of specific parts of international law in all SEE countries. These chapters are relatively narrow in terms of subject matter in the sense that they examine only one area of international law, but are broad in their jurisdictional coverage in that they deal with judicial behaviour in all eight countries.

Three areas of international law are taken as representative to serve as comparators in projecting preparedness for the application of EU law: WTO law, the SAAs, and the Aarhus convention.[12] First, concerning WTO law, membership in this organisation has in several instances been seen as a precondition for entering into other agreements with the EU. Typically, SEE countries (with the exceptions of Bosnia & Herzegovina and Serbia) first became WTO members, and only afterwards did they conclude an SAA with the EU. This kind of approach leads to gradual trade liberalisation—first, through the WTO, then through the SAA, all contributing to the country's preparedness for being a part of the EU internal market. Second, regarding the judicial application of the SAAs, while these agreements can be seen as part of EU law, in the SEE countries that are not EU members, the SAAs have the status of international law. Nevertheless, they are a tool for the

[9] Case C-127/92 *Dr. Pamela Mary Enderby v. Frenchay Health Authority and Secretary of State for Health* [1993] ECR I-05535.

[10] *Van Gend en Loos*, supra n. 3.

[11] There has been vast scholarship on whether the EC/EU legal order is unique and on what makes it different from international law. Some of the most influential work in this regard include: Stein (1981), p. 1; Weiler (1991), p. 2403; Wyatt (1982), p. 147.

[12] Convention on Access to Information, Public Participation in Decision-Making and Access to Justice in Environmental Matters. United Nations Economic Commission for Europe, Denmark, 25 June 1998.

SEE countries to approximate their national laws to EU law and they create obligations for all branches of government, including the courts. Third, the Aarhus Convention is taken as an example of an international agreement to which both the EU and all its Member States as well as all SEE countries (except Kosovo) are parties.

Part III of the book consists of country reports from eight SEE countries: Albania, Bosnia & Herzegovina, Croatia, Kosovo, Macedonia, Montenegro, Slovenia and Serbia. These reports give a detailed and broad insight into the application of different types of international law by all the types of national courts in one country. Attention is paid not only to the application of general international law, but special and specific focus is placed, where appropriate, on the law of the European Convention on Human Rights and Fundamental Freedoms (ECHR); the law of the Central European Free Trade Agreement (CEFTA); international criminal law, particularly in connection to the work of the International Criminal Tribunal for the former Yugoslavia (ICTY). The chapters also seek to explore substantive standards and how they are interpreted by national courts.

The main research questions for all country reports were the following.

1. What is the constitutional status of international law in the national legal order of your country? Does your constitution distinguish between international treaties and other sources of international law (e.g. customary international law)? Does your constitution grant any specific legal force to international law?
2. Does the constitution allow self-executing effect of international treaties? Does it differentiate between different categories of international treaties (e.g. human rights treaties. etc.)? Are there any other national sources of law (other than the Constitution) that address these issues? Has there been any evolution concerning these questions?
3. How does the Constitution (and/or other legislation) address the legal status of secondary acts adopted under international treaties (e.g. decisions of the Stabilisation and Association Council)? Can such secondary acts have direct effect in national law?
4. Describe briefly how ordinary courts in your country are organised. Do they have legal authority to apply international law directly? If they do, what is the source of that authority? Does this apply to courts of all levels and jurisdictions (e.g. ordinary courts of first instance, courts of appeal, the Supreme Court, administrative courts, etc.)? If there is specific legislation applicable, please refer to it. Are there any specific procedural rules applicable? Please do not refer to private international law rules, since these are not subject of our study!
5. Do national courts apply international law? If so, quote cases and describe circumstances in which they do so. Differentiate between the application of international treaties and the application of customary international law, the practice of international courts and other sources. If possible, differentiate different categories of international law (e.g. human rights treaties, free trade agreements, etc.). In cases where national courts apply international law, is it of

their own motion (*ex officio*) or is it because attorneys have brought the argument before the court and have insisted on it?

6. Do national courts refer to the case law of the European Court of Human Rights and other international courts? Do they quote other national courts, e.g. the German Federal Constitutional Court? Please give examples. Are such references coherent?
7. Do national courts interpret national law in accordance with international law (Völkerrechtsfreundliche Auslegung)? Is there an explicit legal basis for such interpretation in national law? Please give examples!
8. Are there any substantial differences in interpretation between national and international courts? For example, do they interpret the freedom of expression, a fair trial within a reasonable time and other concepts differently? How do you explain those differences where they exist?
9. How do national courts interpret so-called 'mirror provisions' (provisions of Stabilisation and Association Agreements that reproduce the text of the Treaty on the Functioning of the EU, e.g. provisions on free movement of goods etc.)?
10. When answering the questions above, are there any differences in the practice of the Constitutional Court and ordinary courts, especially the Supreme Court?
11. Is the case law of national courts regularly published and accessible on the internet? Please explain how and where. Do judges have internet access which makes it possible to search foreign sources of law, e.g. CELEX, HUDOC, etc? How does the accessibility of court practice affect the application of law?
12. To what extent is international law part of the legal education of judges and other legal professionals? At law school level and in professional education before and after the bar exam? Does the bar exam include an examination of international law? Are there forms of lifelong learning that include international law?
13. What is the role of the highest courts in creating awareness of international law in the national legal system? Constitutional Court, Supreme Court, possibly other high courts? Do these courts act as a progressive or as a conservative force? Explain why. How will the judicial hierarchy affect developments in the application of international law? Will lower courts be intimidated into adopting a new line of practice?
14. Can the Constitutional Court review legislation regarding its compatibility with international treaties (abstract constitutional review)? Has there been any such practice? Does the Constitutional Court apply international treaties as a standard of review in the constitutional complaint procedure (accessory constitutional review)? If so, please clarify.
15. Are preliminary references of constitutionality possible in your legal system, and if so are they frequent in practice? How do you imagine the courts will deal with future preliminary references once your country joins the EU? What legislative changes will be needed, if any?
16. On the grounds of existing practice, can you give an assessment of whether legislative changes will be required in order to enable the courts to apply EU law and the law of Stabilisation and Association Agreements? What kinds of

changes? Would change of judicial practice suffice, or are constitutional and legislative amendments needed? Please focus on the requirements of the supremacy and direct effect of EU primary and secondary law. Also consider whether EU and SAA law is or should be treated in the same or in a different manner from general international law.

As seen from these questions, we consider that in determining whether and how the SEE countries apply international law, it is vital to go beyond the formal rules governing judicial decision-making. Constitutional and statutory provisions stipulating how the courts should apply international law are only taken as a starting point. Our research then continues to look at practice, i.e. national case law. Such research brings a fresh perspective to the role of the judiciary in SEE, especially since significant parts of the case law are not published. The authors have sought to investigate the judicial practice of ordinary courts of all levels, constitutional courts and specialised courts (e.g. war crimes tribunals), where they exist. In some instances, the authors also looked at administrative practice, although this was not our primary focus of interest.

The book seeks to present the state-of-the-art of law in SEE as it stands today. However, where appropriate, the authors have also presented the evolution of law and described specific developments triggered both by legislative developments and the developments of judicial practice. Research has also been undertaken to examine whether the judicial approach to international law could change in the foreseeable future. It was thus necessary to look at legal education, in particular at whether there is any continuous education of judges in the field of international law and at whether law students are being educated in specialised fields of international law.

By highlighting the strengths and weaknesses in the application of international law by the courts in SEE, this book indicates potential problems in the application of EU law. These are issues that could be addressed in the Stabilisation and Association processes as well as in accession negotiations to ensure that the judiciary in SEE countries will be able to function properly as EU courts on gaining EU membership.

References

Halberstam D (2010) Comparative federalism and the role of the judiciary. In: Whittington KE, Kelemen RD, Caldeira GA (eds) The Oxford handbook of law and politics. Oxford University Press, Oxford

Stein E (1981) Lawyers, judges and the making of the transnational constitution. Am J Int Law 75:1

Weiler JHH (1991) The transformation of Europe. Yale Law J 100:2403

Wyatt D (1982) New legal order, or old? Eur Law Rev 7:147

Part II
Judicial Application of Specialised Fields of International Law in Southeast Europe

The Unfulfilled Potential of Stabilisation and Association Agreements Before SEE Courts

Mislav Mataija

1 Introduction

Stabilisation and association agreements have been a vital part of the EU's enlargement policy toward SEE countries. Building on and to a large extent replicating the provisions of the so-called 'Europe agreements' concluded with the CEE states that joined the EU in 2004,[1] SAAs have so far been signed with Macedonia and Croatia (2001), Albania (2006), Montenegro (2007), Serbia and Bosnia and Herzegovina (2008), and negotiations on an SAA with Kosovo opened in 2013.[2] Of those that have been signed, the Macedonian (2004), Croatian (2005), Albanian (2009),

Member of the Legal Service, European Commission. At the time of writing, I was Senior Assistant, University of Zagreb Faculty of Law. Thanks are due to all the chapter authors, especially the authors of the national reports, and to all the members of the Jean Monnet Department of European Public Law at the University of Zagreb Faculty of Law, for their helpful comments. All views are personal.

[1] Blockmans and Lazowski (2006), p. 3.

[2] Stabilisation and Association Agreement between the European Communities and their Member States, of the one part, and the former Yugoslav Republic of Macedonia, of the other part [2004] OJ L84; Stabilisation and Association Agreement between the European Communities and their Member States, of the one part, and the Republic of Croatia, of the other part [2005] OJ L26; Council of the European Union, Stabilisation and Association Agreement between the European Communities and their Member States, of the one part, and Bosnia and Herzegovina, of the other part (6.6.2008) 8226/08; Stabilisation and Association Agreement between the European Communities and their Member States, of the one part, and the Republic of Albania, of the other part [2009] OJ L107; Stabilisation and Association Agreement between the European Communities and their Member States, of the one part, and the Republic of Montenegro, of the other part [2010] OJ L108; Stabilisation and Association Agreement between the European Communities and their Member States of the one part, and the Republic of Serbia, of the other part [2013] OJ L278.

M. Mataija (✉)
Faculty of Law, University of Zagreb, Zagreb, Croatia
e-mail: mislav.mataija@gmail.com

S. Rodin, T. Perišin (eds.), *Judicial Application of International Law in Southeast Europe*, DOI 10.1007/978-3-662-46384-0_2

Montenegrin (2010) and Serbian (2013) SAAs have entered into force. The SAA for BiH has been ratified by Bosnia and Herzegovina as well as by all the EU Member States, but not by the EU itself.

Within the EU's enlargement policy, SAAs are seen as a way of imposing conditionality on potential candidates, based on the idea that the '*tangible* prospect of EU membership is the key instrument for transformation of the Western Balkans'.[3] They have been used to encourage reforms in a wide range of areas, including regional cooperation and human rights protection, by giving association countries access to the EU market and, even more importantly, by giving a concrete shape to their EU membership aspirations.

There is a wealth of literature on these systemic aspects of the SAAs.[4] This chapter will look at a different issue, however: the use of SAAs by courts in legal disputes. There has been a certain amount of EU case law on the effects of similar instruments in the legal orders of the EU Member States.[5] In addition, we know that the Europe agreements in particular were read by the high courts of some of the Member States that joined in 2004 as imposing wide-ranging interpretative duties, in effect creating a 'back door' for the application of EU law even before accession.[6] What we do not know, at least not in a systematic fashion, is whether the same has been true in the SEE countries, i.e. with respect to the SAAs. Looking at their content, the SAAs should provide at least as much material for judicial application as the Europe agreements. At least some of their provisions are capable of having direct effect under EU standards. Besides, like the Europe agreements, they contain provisions on the approximation of laws that could be read as imposing a duty on SEE courts to interpret national law in the light of EU law even before accession.

This chapter will argue that, despite these similarities, the evidence seems to show the SAAs have, by and large, not been relied upon to impose broad interpretative duties in the SEE states, such as the duty to interpret national law in the light of EU law. In addition, they have rarely been relied upon directly before national courts in order to disapply national law. They have, however, had a more practical

[3] Blockmans (2006), p. 315.

[4] See e.g. Blockmans (2007); Elbasani (2008); Kellermann et al. (2001); Kellermann et al. (2006); Noutcheva (2009), p. 1065; Phinnemore (2003), p. 77; Renner and Trauner (2009), p. 449.

[5] See, among others, Case 270/80 *Polydor Ltd. and RSO Records Inc v. Harlequin Record Shops Ltd. and Simons Records Ltd 2* [1982] ECR 329; Case 104/81 *Hauptzollamt Mainz v. C.A. Kupferberg & Cie KG a.A* [1982] ECR 3641; Case C-192/89 *S.Z. Sevince v. Staatssecretaris van Justitie* [1990] ECR 3461; Case C-63/99 *The Queen v. Secretary of State for the Home Department, ex parte Wieslaw Gloszczuk and Elzbieta Gloszczuk* [2001] ECR I-6369; Case C-268/99 *Aldona Malgorzata Jany and Others v. Staatssecretaris van Justitie* [2001] ECR I-08615; Case C-438/00 *Deutscher Handballbund eV v. Maros Kolpak* [2003] ECR I-4135; Case C-265/03 *Igor Simutenkov v. Ministerio de Educación y Cultura and Real Federación Española de Fútbol* [2005] ECR I-02579; and Case C-101/10 *Gentcho Pavlov and Gregor Famira v Ausschuss der Rechtsanwaltskammer Wien* [2011] ECR I-5951.

[6] See Sect. 3.2 below, as well as the national reports on the Member States with Europe agreements in Kellermann et al. (2006).

effect in areas where the SAA makes a specific reference to the EU *acquis*—notably in competition law.

This chapter attempts to cover all the association countries that are signatories to the SAAs. Slovenia, as one of the 2004 Member States and party to a 'Europe agreement' rather than an SAA, is covered only in passing. For Croatia, the judgments mentioned in the text were collected by way of a search of various case-law databases. For the other SEE states, the chapter relies on information given either in the national reports or by their authors.

2 The Basic Elements of the SAAs

The SAAs, based on today's Article 217 TFEU,[7] are examples of so-called mixed agreements that impact areas of exclusive Member State competence and therefore require ratification by all of the Member States as well as the EU and the association country. While based on the Europe agreements concluded with the CEE countries, they have been adapted in several respects for the states of the Western Balkans. Thus, for example, unlike the Europe agreements, the preambles of the SAAs do not mention accession, but only the EU's 'readiness to integrate' the association countries 'to the fullest possible extent' and their status as 'potential candidates' for EU membership. In addition, the objectives of the SAAs—and thus also the kind of 'conditionality' that these instruments promote[8]—are somewhat broader, referring to respect for democratic principles, human rights, international law and the rule of law[9] as well as to intra-regional cooperation.[10] The 'operative' provisions of the SAAs, however, are largely similar to those of the Europe agreements. This is certainly true of the provisions that are most likely to be applied by a court, such as those on free movement of goods or competition.

In broad terms, all of the SAAs share the following features.

Firstly, all of them require the association countries to gradually approximate their legislation to the EU *acquis* by the expiry of a transitional period, the duration of which differs (5 years after the SAA's entry into force for Montenegro, six for BiH, Croatia and Serbia, and ten for Albania and Macedonia). They also require the approximation to initially focus on certain areas, mostly those that are relevant for the internal market. The precise priorities differ to some extent (e.g. in the case of Serbia and Montenegro, justice, freedom and security is also mentioned as a priority

[7] The Article states: 'The Union may conclude with one or more third countries or international organisations agreements establishing an association involving reciprocal rights and obligations, common action and special procedure.'

[8] Rodin (2006), p. 357.

[9] See Art 2 of all the SAAs.

[10] Art 11 SAA Croatia and SAA Macedonia; Art 12 SAA Albania; and Art 14 SAA Serbia, SAA Montenegro and SAA BiH.

area, while SAA Albania contains a more detailed list of substantive policy priorities[11]). There are also more specific harmonisation clauses requiring the association states to gradually implement the EU *acquis* in areas such as intellectual property, standardisation and consumer protection.[12]

Secondly, they contain trade liberalisation provisions modelled on the TFEU free movement and competition rules. The provisions on customs duties are asymmetrical, giving preferential access to EU markets to the association countries immediately while allowing them to temporarily maintain protectionist measures.[13] Some provisions, notably those on the free movement of goods and competition, can be described as 'mirror provisions' whose content is almost identical to equivalent Treaty rules, while others, such as those on workers or services, do not go as far. The SAAs contain, among other things:

- standstill clauses (prohibitions of new or higher tariffs);
- prohibitions of quantitative restrictions on imports and measures of equivalent effect;
- prohibitions of fiscal discrimination;
- rules on non-discrimination of workers and the access of their spouses and children to the labour market;
- rules on the freedom of establishment;
- rules on the 'supply' of services;
- rules on current payments and the movement of capital;
- provisions on public-policy justification of restrictive measures;
- provisions on competition (agreements, abuses of dominant position, state aids[14]);
- specific rules on public contracts, intellectual property protection, standardisation and consumer protection.

These rules had already largely been taken over by the so-called interim agreements, the purpose of which was to implement the SAA trade liberalisation provisions even before the entry into force of the SAAs.[15]

---

[11] Art 70 SAA Albania and BiH; Art 69 SAA Croatia; Art 68 SAA Macedonia; Art 72 SAA Montenegro and SAA Serbia.

[12] See, for example, Arts 71, 73 and 74 SAA Croatia.

[13] Arts 17–20 SAA Albania; Arts 19–21 SAA BiH, Montenegro, Serbia; Arts 16–18 SAA Croatia; Arts 16–19 SAA Macedonia.

[14] In this respect, all of the SAAs except SAA Macedonia go farther than the Europe agreements in that they require the association states to not only establish an independent competition agency, but to empower it to order the recovery of unlawfully granted aid (para 4 of the relevant SAA competition provision).

[15] See, for example, the Interim Agreement on trade and trade-related matters between the European Community, of the one part, and Bosnia and Herzegovina, of the other part (2008) OJ L169, which is currently in force.

Thirdly, the SAAs contain provisions on justice and home affairs and on cooperation in various policy areas.[16] While important, these elements of the SAAs seem to be less amenable to judicial application. Indeed, the judgments reported below deal only with the provisions of trade liberalisation and approximation of laws.

Fourthly, they contain financial and institutional provisions. Most importantly, they create Stabilisation and Association Councils that supervise the application of the agreements and have the power to adopt various decisions or delegate them to a Stabilisation and Association Committee.[17]

Finally, the SAAs allow rather ill-defined sanctions for non-compliance with various provisions. Most importantly, they allow the EU as well as the association countries to 'take appropriate measures' in the case of a breach of the agreement.[18]

3 Applying the SAAs in Legal Disputes

The SAAs could be applied by SEE courts in two main ways. Firstly, courts can apply the SAA itself, either directly or indirectly. In practical terms, the consequence of applying the SAA directly would usually be to disapply or annul (where this is possible) a conflicting national measure. Courts could also apply the SAA as such indirectly, by interpreting national law in the light of its provisions.

Secondly, the SAA could trigger the consistent interpretation of national rules with the EU *acquis*, beyond the provisions of the SAA itself. The most interesting aspect of this second option is its ability to introduce the rules of EU law through a 'back door' of sorts: arguably, at least in some cases, the SAAs require national courts to apply national rules in accordance with the requirements of EU law, including CJEU case law. It seems that the SEE legal orders examined in this book recognise this to some extent. Not even within particular states, however, is there agreement on how far this obligation can go.

The second option is different from the first in that the courts apply EU law (legislation, case law or even soft law) that is not contained in the SAA itself, and perhaps not even directly referred to in the SAA. This distinction may not be as significant as it seems. We can take the example of a court that is applying—whether directly, by refusing to apply a conflicting provision of national law, or indirectly, by interpreting national law in the light of the SAA—an SAA provision on restrictions on imports of goods. Let us imagine, quite realistically, that the court would wish to inform its interpretation of the SAA provision by looking at the

[16] See, for example, Titles VII and VIII of SAA Croatia.

[17] The role of these bodies varies in different states. The Croatian implementing legislation, for example, made the decisions of the Stabilisation and Association Committee subject to parliamentary approval, thus stripping this provision of much practical value.

[18] See e.g. Art 120/2 SAA Croatia.

CJEU case law on the equivalent provisions of the founding Treaties, perhaps even citing it in the judgment. What is the 'legal source' or legal authority in this case: the SAA as such, or EU law beyond the SAA? The answer is not perfectly clear, but it is probably not important either, as long as we accept the possibility that courts may support their chosen interpretation of law by something other than formally binding, *ex ante* identifiable 'sources of law' (more on this below). There is a problem, however, if one believes that a legal provision, even one as open-ended as a prohibition of 'measures having equivalent effect to quantitative restrictions on imports', can or should be applied by only looking at the text of the provision itself. From that point of view, to inform the interpretation of the provision by anything other than its text would be to *apply* another source of law, which could be described as illegitimate.

The second option may not, therefore, be as different from the first option as it seems. Within the second option, however, there is a practically important distinction between two forms of consistent interpretation. The first and more obvious form is to rely on the provisions of the SAAs that explicitly require or allow the use of various EU law interpretative mechanisms, such as case law or Commission decisions. This is the case with the SAA provisions on competition law. While there is some controversy in using this sort of consistent interpretation, it has nevertheless by and large been accepted in the SEE states.

The second form of consistent interpretation, however, has so far found little fertile ground. This is the possibility of invoking general clauses that require the SEE countries to approximate their legal rules to EU law. According to some authors, since the harmonisation clauses are addressed to the State as a whole, they should also be relevant for courts. The way courts should implement this duty is to interpret national rules, in areas where this is relevant, with the requirements of EU legislation and case law.

In the following sections, I will look at whether and how these options (the direct application of SAA provisions, the application of EU law through general harmonisation clauses and through explicit SAA references in competition law) have been used by the SEE courts.

3.1 Direct Application of SAA Provisions

The most important prerequisite for applying SAA provisions before national courts is that the constitution allows for the direct effect of international treaties. In order to deal with conflicts with domestic rules, the constitution should also specify that treaties are hierarchically superior.

These prerequisites are to a large extent fulfilled in all the analysed SEE States. International agreements have both direct effect and supremacy over national law in Albania, Croatia, Macedonia, Montenegro, Serbia and Slovenia. Bosnia and Herzegovina seems to be a more complex case: a clear constitutional provision on the direct effect of international agreements and their relationship with conflicting national laws only exists in relation to treaties explicitly listed in the Constitution, which does not include the SAA. The national report, however, concludes that the SAA should, upon its entry into force, also be recognised as having direct effect and as being superior to domestic laws.[19] Similarly to Bosnia and Herzegovina, the constitutional approach to the application of international law in Kosovo is also rather complex, granting priority to the rather unclear category of 'legally binding norms of international law' and a set of human rights conventions, including the ECHR. As for a future SAA for Kosovo, it seems that it would fall under a constitutional provision that pronounces ratified international agreements to be 'part of the internal legal system ... directly applied except for cases when they are not self-applicable and the application requires the promulgation of a law'.[20]

The national reports reveal only a small number of cases where the SAAs were directly applied against a provision of national law or a measure adopted by national authorities. Thus, the Albanian Constitutional Court invoked the SAA standstill clause, prohibiting the introduction of new or more restrictive quantitative restrictions on imports and measures having equivalent effect, against a decision of the Albanian Council of Ministers. The decision treated domestically produced diesel oils more favourably than imports and imposed a ban on importing a particular type of diesel oil. The Constitutional Court concluded that the decision violated the SAA standstill clause, as well as its provision on measures that 'constitute a means of arbitrary discrimination or a disguised restriction on trade'.[21]

In *Makpetrol v. Ministry of Finance Customs Office*, the First Skopje Basic Court similarly disapplied two by-laws imposing customs duties in violation of the Macedonian SAA and interim agreement. This judgment is the only example found for the purposes of this book of an ordinary court disapplying a provision of national law on the basis of the SAA. The court even made a declaratory finding that the provisions were 'no longer in force' because they conflicted with the SAA and the interim agreement.[22]

On the other hand, there seem to be no examples of indirect application of an SAA (re-interpreting a provision of national law in the light of an SAA provision). Similarly, neither has the direct application of an SAA provision led to more extensive reliance on EU law beyond the SAA itself. When SEE courts directly apply a substantive provision of an SAA (i.e. not in cases when they rely on SAA

[19] See the chapter by Zlatan Meškić and Darko Samardžić, Application of International and EU Law in Bosnia and Herzegovina.

[20] On these issues, see Art 122 of the Albanian Constitution; Art II of the Constitution of Bosnia and Herzegovina; Art 141 of the Croatian Constitution; Art 19.1 of the Constitution of Kosovo; Art 118 of the Macedonian Constitution; Art 9 of the Montenegrin Constitution; Arts 16 and 94 of the Serbian Constitution; Art 8 of the Slovenian Constitution. For more details, see the respective national reports.

[21] See the chapter by Gentian Zyberi and Semir Sali, The Place and Application of International Law in the Albanian Legal System.

[22] See the chapter by Marija Risteska and Kristina Miševa, Application of International Law in Macedonia.

provisions on the approximation of laws, which raise their own consistent interpretation issues which will be discussed below), it might seem quite likely that they would also take into account EU law outside the confines of the SAA itself, such as CJEU case law. Indeed, at least with the so-called 'mirror provisions' which are almost identical in content and similar in aims to the provisions of EU Treaties, common sense dictates that the SAA cannot be adequately understood without considering EU case law or other parts of the *acquis*. This does not mean that SEE courts would be bound by CJEU case law, in the sense that they should achieve the same outcome. The CJEU has, for its part, found that the interpretation of mirror provisions can be different from the interpretation of equivalent Treaty provisions due to the less ambitious nature of the legal documents in which they are contained. As a consequence, the level of protection of SAA rights can in some cases be lower than in equivalent intra-EU cases.[23]

It is questionable whether SEE courts would openly follow such an approach. This may be explained by a general reluctance to openly discuss interpretative choices.[24] Most of the cases analysed in this chapter seem to follow an all-or-nothing logic: EU law is either followed to the letter, or not at all. Adapting the interpretation of a similarly worded legal instrument, depending on the context, could prove to be an unnatural exercise for SEE courts, which seem to be accustomed to viewing legal texts either as binding 'sources of law' or as largely irrelevant. For most SEE courts, the use of foreign law, international law, scholarly writings or other sources in support of a particular argument, much less as so-called 'persuasive authority',[25] is uncommon. There are exceptions to this, in particular constitutional courts, which do frequently refer to international or transnational law, but this is almost exclusively limited to the ECHR and the decisions of the European Court of Human Rights.[26]

The conclusion is that an SEE court disinclined to apply an SAA provision would be more likely to find it wholly inapplicable or not to have direct effect rather than to contrast it with CJEU case law and show why the SAA contextually warrants a lower level of protection, because the latter strategy would require a shift in the usual mode of argumentation applied by those courts.

---

[23] See, in particular, *Polydor* (paras 14–21) and the other judgments cited in n 5.

[24] For a similar conclusion regarding the CEE states, see Kühn (2005a), p. 563; Kühn (2005b), pp. 55, 63. In the Croatian context, see Ćapeta (2005), p. 23 and Rodin (2005), p. 1. As Bobek points out, of course, this may not be an issue for SEE or CEE judges alone, and one should not be overly optimistic about either the desirability or the capacity of ordinary courts in general to adopt broad principle-based legal interpretations. See Bobek (2006), p. 265.

[25] On the difference between 'binding' and 'persuasive' authority, as well as on the oft-noted contradiction of describing an authority as 'persuasive', see Schauer (2008), p. 1931.

[26] In the case of Croatia, extensive citation of ECtHR case law by the Constitutional Court has become commonplace, while at the same time it remains very rare in the decisions of any other courts, even the Supreme Court. Cf. Ćapeta (2005), p. 37. In Montenegro, the ECHR is also the most frequently cited source of international law, most notably in the decisions of the Supreme and Constitutional courts (see the chapter by Dušan S. Rakitić, Judicial Application of International Law in Montenegro).

There are judgments that lend support to this conclusion. The Croatian Constitutional Court, for example, rejected a complaint related to a customs procedure during which imported goods were reclassified under a higher tariff heading. The applicant claimed that the decision of the customs authority violated the 'general principles' of the SAA, including the 'duty of the Republic of Croatia to ensure the application of legal rules aligned [with EU law] in administrative and judicial practice'. This rather abstract argument seemed to be based on Article 73 of the Croatian SAA, requiring Croatia to 'take the necessary measures in order to gradually achieve conformity with Community technical regulations' and 'start at an early stage' to 'promote the use of Community technical regulations and European standards, tests and conformity assessment procedures.'

The Constitutional Court rejected this argument out of hand, finding that the provision 'does not give rise to any rights for individuals' and therefore 'cannot be the basis for the provision of constitutional protection to the applicant'.[27]

Looking at the facts of the case, the decision not to rely on the SAA may have been unsurprising. Indeed, it is unclear from the judgment how customs reclassification procedures would be affected by European technical regulations and standards or why the decision to reclassify was contrary to them. What is remarkable, however, is the broad rejection of the use of SAA harmonisation provisions as a basis for the protection of individual rights. This particular issue will be examined in more detail in the following section.

3.2 Mandatory or Optional Application of EU Law Through Harmonisation Clauses

In the CEE states that acceded in 2004, there were a number of examples of using the harmonisation clauses contained in their 'Europe agreements' as a basis for interpreting national law in conformity with EU law. Thus, in 1997 the Polish Constitutional Tribunal found that the agreement's general harmonisation clause creates a duty for Polish courts to interpret existing legislation so as to ensure conformity with EU law as much as possible.[28] The Czech Constitutional Court found in 2001 that primary EU law is 'not foreign law' and that it should be applied by courts, especially when it comes to 'general principles of law'.[29] The Slovenian case also seems to prove the point; in her report, Hojnik points out that it was generally accepted that Slovenian courts should, on the basis of the SAA, '*mutatis mutandis* apply the case law of the Court of Justice of the European Union in cases concerning mirror provisions of the Treaty establishing the European

[27] U-III/4961/2005 (NN 47/08), judgment of 2 April 2008, para 9.

[28] Case K. 15/97 (OTK 19/1997). For more details and other related judgments, see Kühn (2005b), pp. 61–63.

[29] The Milk Quota case (410/2001 Sb.). See Kühn (2005b), p. 66.

Community'.[30] Even the Hungarian Constitutional Court, in its 'Europe agreement' judgment which is otherwise not at all 'friendly' towards the pre-accession reliance on EU competition rules, found that national law can in principle be interpreted in the light of the SAA obligations on a non-mandatory basis.[31]

As already outlined, the SAAs contain clauses similar to the clauses of Europe agreements that led CEE courts to read interpretative duties (or, at least, interpretative possibilities) into national law. Article 69 SAA Croatia, just to give one example, provides that 'Croatia shall endeavour to ensure that its existing laws and future legislation will be gradually made compatible with the Community *acquis*', starting on the date of signature of the SAA and gradually extending 'to all the elements of the Community *acquis* referred to in this Agreement' within 6 years after its entry into force—i.e. by 1 February 2011. In addition, there are similar, more specific harmonisation clauses for areas such as intellectual property (Art 71), technical regulations, standardisation and normisation (Art 73, as referenced above), statistical cooperation (Art 83), cross-border broadcasting (Art 97), electronic communications (Art 98) and energy (Art 101).

Given the experience of the CEE states, it might be expected that these SAA provisions would have a similar impact on courts. This was also advocated in the local legal literature.[32] Under this view, for example, a party could indirectly invoke CJEU case law on electronic communications or a directive on energy markets liberalisation as an argument in favour of a particular 'EU-friendly' reading of national law, on the basis of the SAA harmonisation clause, even before accession. The reasoning behind this is that courts are also charged with the duty of (gradual) alignment with EU law, especially if one takes into account the rather obvious point that alignment with the *acquis* is not and cannot be simply a formal process of legislative adoption. Alignment has to relate to the actual implementation of the *acquis*, and that question is clearly one for the courts.[33]

Thus, courts should at least have the option to take EU law into account when deciding how national law should be interpreted. Ćapeta has gone even further and argued that Article 69 of the Croatian SAA not only allows, but requires, such a consistent interpretation—at least when applying legislation that is specifically intended to harmonise Croatian law with the *acquis*.[34]

Practice, however, has by and large not followed this approach. While SEE courts have at times dealt with various sources of EU law, there has been no consensus in any of the analysed states (apart from Slovenia, apparently) that there is a general duty to interpret national law consistently with EU law pre-accession. Some judgments that went in that direction were rebuked by subsequent

---

[30] See the chapter by Janja Hojnik, Judicial Application of International and EU Law in Slovenia.

[31] 'Europe Agreement Judgment', judgment No. 30 of 25 June 1998, VI.3. See also Volkai (1999), p. 25, as well as Harmathy (2001), p. 315.

[32] Ćapeta (2006), p. 1443.

[33] Ibid, pp. 1475–1479.

[34] Ibid, pp. 1482–1483.

practice, and there have been no straightforward decisions of a high court, such as a constitutional or supreme court, imposing that duty, unlike the Polish and other examples above. In fact, if we disregard the special case of competition law (see below), even the non-mandatory use of EU materials in adjudication has been considered problematic at times.

This is not to say that international or EU law is never cited by SEE courts. Curiously, national courts have on occasion made use of EU law in a completely amorphous way—without clarifying why it is pertinent or what its effect is. One example of this is the Albanian Constitutional Court's judgment in *Instituti i Ekspertëve Kontabël të Autorizuar*. The Court invoked Directive 2006/43 on statutory audits of annual accounts and consolidated accounts[35] as support in order to reject a claim that the national law on auditing was unconstitutional. It found, for example, that State supervision of auditors did not violate the independence of the profession, *inter alia* because such supervision is required by the Directive. Thus, hypothetical conformity with EU law was used as an argument for the actual conformity of the law with the Albanian constitution, though without clarifying the precise basis on which EU law was taken into account.[36]

The Serbian Supreme Court of Cassation similarly supported its findings in a family law dispute by referring, in general terms, to the provisions on the right to family life and children's rights of the EU Charter of Fundamental Rights—again, without explaining why the Charter was a relevant legal source.[37] In Croatia, Zagreb County Court dealt with a collective claim raised by a group of NGOs against the discriminatory statements of a football official about homosexuals. The plaintiffs invoked the ECJ judgment *Firma Feryn*,[38] in which an executive's general statements against hiring immigrants were considered discriminatory. The County Court distinguished between the two cases because they dealt with different discriminatory grounds—a distinction which seems rather irrelevant. The key point, however, is that EU law was taken into account and discussed almost as if it was binding on Croatian courts—without explaining why or on what basis.[39]

These cases could, of course, be just random examples that show no general trend. On the other hand, they do suggest that, on occasion, invoking EU law in a general, non-specified manner can be a helpful strategy for litigants. As will be discussed, however, when the argument is based more closely on the SAA or

[35] Directive 2006/43/EC of the European Parliament and of the Council of 17 May 2006 on statutory audits of annual accounts and consolidated accounts, amending Council Directives 78/660/EEC and 83/349/EEC and repealing Council Directive 84/253/EEC [2006] OJ L157/87.

[36] See the chapter by Gentian Zyberi and Semir Sali, The Place and Application of International Law in the Albanian Legal System.

[37] Judgment of the Appellate Court in Belgrade, Rev. 2401/2010 of 28 April 2010. See the chapter by Mirjana Drenovak Ivanović and Maja Lukić, Judicial Application of International Law in Serbia.

[38] Case C-54/07 *Centrum voor gelijkheid van kansen en voor racismebestrijding v. Firma Feryn NV* [2008] ECR I-5187.

[39] Zagreb County Court, judgment 15 Pnz-6/10-27 of 6 April 2011.

framed in terms of a legal obligation, courts seem to take a more conservative approach—often saying that unless an EU act or decision is formally recognised as a source of law, it cannot be used. If this suggestion is true, a paradox seems to be at play: the more a plaintiff invests in explaining why 'foreign' sources should be used, the less likely he or she is to succeed. The paradox could be explained, however, by the frequent all-or-nothing attitude of SEE courts to using legal materials: if something is presented (explicitly or even tacitly, as was perhaps the case in the three judgments just cited) as a 'source of law', it must be applied and followed, and if it is presented as something less than that, it must be rejected. Another, simpler, explanation could lie in the fact that these three cases dealt with EU legislation. Even though EU legislation is no more binding prior to accession than, for example, CJEU decisions, it could be the case that courts accustomed to using only legislation as a legal source are more likely to accept references to non-binding legislation than to non-binding case law or soft law.

In any event, there are a number of examples of SEE courts refusing to interpret domestic law in the light of EU sources. One of them is the Serbian Constitutional Court judgment in *ERC Commerce Computers*, a customs classification case. While the judgment did not turn on SAA obligations, it had to do with an even more persuasive 'back door' for the application of EU law: a provision of the Customs Tariff Act requiring the mandatory application of customs classification decisions published in the Official Journal of the EU. The applicants, having lost their case before the customs authorities and the Administrative Court, attempted to invoke *Kamino International Logistics*,[40] a judgment in which the CJEU dealt with the classification of products similar to those at stake in the Serbian case.

Regardless of the merits of the case, it seems quite clear that, in order to properly apply EU legal acts, one should interpret them in the way that they are interpreted in the EU, and this means having a look at ECJ case law. The applicant's plea asking the Constitutional Court to do so was, however, rejected 'because the... Customs Tariff Act provides that only decisions on the classification published in the Official Journal of the European Union are legally binding'.[41]

Some Croatian courts also seem to follow this approach. The High Commercial Court, in a 2007 ruling, rejected a party's attempt to use the SAA as a basis for relying on the Treaty rules on free movement of goods and the corresponding ECJ case law in a case on parallel imports and the trade mark exhaustion of rights principle. The Court's view was that reliance on EU law beyond the confines of the SAA is not permitted, the sole exception to this being the SAA provision on competition law which explicitly refers to 'criteria arising from the application of

---

[40] C-376/07 *Staatssecretaris van Financiën v. Kamino International Logistics BV* [2009] ECR I-1167.

[41] Decision of the Constitutional Court of the Republic of Serbia, Už-4787/2011 of 24 November 2011. See, similarly, the Constitutional Court's decision on the Judges Act, where arguments based on various non-binding international documents were rejected as these are not 'formal sources of law' under the Constitution. See further the chapter by Mirjana Drenovak Ivanović and Maja Lukić, Judicial Application of International Law in Serbia.

the competition rules applicable in the Community'. The SAA rules on IP, the Court reasoned, only require Croatia to achieve 'a level of protection of intellectual, industrial and commercial property rights similar to that existing in the Community', which means that, in the area of trademarks, 'Croatia will only be bound to respect the interpretations given by the European Court of Justice when it becomes a full member of the EU'.[42]

This was a kind of pigeon-holing: because Croatia is not an EU Member State, this case is not about quantitative restrictions, but only about the exercise of trademark rights. Therefore, the Court looked only at the SAA provision dealing with IP, and not the one prohibiting quantitative restrictions—which would have been much more on point. The case could have been simply distinguished on the facts (the allegedly infringing goods were imported from Turkey, and not from the EU), or perhaps dealt with in a more nuanced way, acknowledging the application of EU law through the SAA 'back door' but reading it in a more flexible way than required under Article 34 TFEU (see above). Instead, the High Commercial Court suggested that EU law was irrelevant to such cases as a matter of principle.

Similarly, the Croatian Administrative Court in 2010 overturned a Competition Agency state aids decision partly because of its reliance on the Community guidelines on state aid for rescuing and restructuring firms in difficulty, a non-binding Commission document. The Court cited the constitutional provision allowing for the direct application of international agreements, concluding that:

> the [SAA and the Interim Agreement] could have therefore been applied in this case, while the criteria, standards and interpretative instruments of the European Community relied upon by the defendant institution which are not contained in the text of those agreements, nor are they taken over and published in any other Croatian law or legal rule, cannot be a source of law.[43]

Interestingly, this ruling was adopted in spite of the well-established case law of the Constitutional Court that allows the interpretative use of EU law in competition cases (see below).

There are also some opposite examples. In three related judgments on trademarks from 2006, the Croatian High Commercial Court seemed quite open to reading the SAA as imposing a duty to interpret national rules consistently with EU law. Thus, it drew support from the Trade Marks Directive 89/104 to prevent a

---

[42] Judgment of the High Commercial Court of the Republic of Croatia Pž 5155/07-3 of 11 December 2007.

[43] Judgment of the Administrative Court of the Republic of Croatia Us-5362/2007-10 of 3 November 2010. Curiously, the Croatian Supreme Court—the highest Croatian court if we disregard the special case of the Constitutional Court, and in charge of harmonising the case law of all courts below—has largely been absent from the debate. To my knowledge, it has referred to the SAA in only two judgments. Neither of those cases had much of a connection to the SAA (they were deposit payment disputes), it was not clear why the plaintiffs were invoking it, and the Supreme Court's only finding was that the SAA could not be applied given that it had not yet entered into force at the material time (judgment 1301/2007-2 of 21 February 2008 and judgment 796/2007-2 of 7 October 2008).

trade mark owner from relying on the mark against a third party that had been using it as his own name in the course of trade. In the first judgment, the Court reasoned that the Directive can be used due to the entry into force of the SAA, 'under which the Republic of Croatia and the courts of the Republic of Croatia are bound to interpret existing legal rules in a way that conforms with the *acquis*'.[44] In the second and third judgments, the Court was even more detailed, finding explicitly that Article 69 of the SAA (the general harmonisation clause) 'creates a duty not only for the Croatian legislative and executive authorities to harmonise future legal rules with the *acquis* of European law, but also for courts to interpret existing legal rules in a way that conforms with the *acquis*'.[45] While these statements seem to go quite far, their value is rather limited. The first reason for this is that the 2007 judgment by the same chamber of the same court, as described above, goes in an entirely opposite direction.[46] Secondly, as in the cases where EU law was referred to without a clear legal basis, the openness of the court to consistent interpretation in these cases could be explained by the fact that a legislative text—a Directive—was at stake. Whether this would hold, for example, if an important CJEU judgment on trademarks was invoked, is questionable. The final reason is the fact that there was never clear support for this view in the case law of either the Croatian Constitutional Court or the Supreme Court (whose task is to ensure conform interpretation in the judicial branch).

As an interim conclusion, while it is still early days for many of the SAAs, the overall picture shows very little evidence of the pre-accession use of EU law on the basis of an interpretative duty imposed by the SAAs. To some extent, however, an exception can be made in the area of competition law, the subject of the next section.

3.3 Privileged Areas: Competition Law

Competition law, including the rules on state aids, is a more promising avenue for pre-accession reliance on EU law. This is because of explicit SAA provisions requiring national courts and competition agencies to assess restrictive agreements,

[44] Judgments of the High Commercial Court of the Republic of Croatia Pž 639/06-3 of 23 February 2006 and Pž 8064/04-3 of 17 May 2006.

[45] Judgment Pž 2330/05-3 of 13 June 2006. Curiously, the Court also added that, as a consequence of the SAA's entry into force, 'where a rule of national law is not in accordance with European law, and European law has greater legal force than national law, we are bound to apply the rule of European law'. It is not clear if this was meant purely as an *obiter dicta* or if it is simply unfortunate drafting. It is doubtful that the High Commercial Court actually meant to say that the SAA's entry into force immediately requires EU law in general to be applied directly and trump national rules. In any event, this would clearly not have been necessary for the resolution of the trade mark disputes.

[46] It could perhaps also be added that the composition of the chamber deciding all four of the judgments was identical, except for the first 2006 case in which one of the members of that chamber was deciding as an individual judge.

abuses of a dominant position and state aids[47] 'on the basis of criteria arising from the application of the competition rules applicable in the Community, in particular from Articles [101, 102, 106 and 107 TFEU] and interpretative instruments adopted by the Community institutions'.[48] These 'criteria' and 'interpretative instruments' include legislation, various soft law measures such as Commission Guidelines and Notices, the case law of the Court of Justice and the General Court of the EU, as well as Commission decisions in competition cases.

On the face of it, this duty only relates to anticompetitive behaviour that 'may affect trade' between the SEE state involved and the EU. This excludes behaviour that does not affect cross-border trade and would therefore, in the EU context, only fall under national competition law. Nevertheless, national legislation and practice do not always take the borderline between the two very seriously. Thus, the Croatian Competition Act provides, rather loosely, that Croatian authorities will 'in accordance with [Art 70 of the SAA], particularly in the case of legal voids and uncertainties relating to the interpretation of competition rules, accordingly apply the criteria arising from the application of the competition rules applicable in the European Community'.[49] This can be read as imposing an interpretative duty even in cases that do not affect trade with the EU, and it seems that this is what happens in practice. The Croatian Competition Agency has relied on EU materials whenever they seemed pertinent in terms of subject matter. From the EU's point of view, this reliance on EU competition law solutions even in areas where those rules cannot apply is not problematic: indeed, the Court of Justice has recently accepted jurisdiction in a preliminary reference where the national court explicitly said that there was no effect on trade, but claimed that national competition law nevertheless requires courts to take EU law into account.[50]

The interesting question for the purposes of this chapter is whether courts accept this wide-ranging use of EU law in pre-accession competition cases, and how that compares with the pre-accession use of EU law in other areas. The general answer—based, it should be said, on a relatively limited body of judgments—is that competition law cases are indeed different. SEE appellate courts have been more open to the use of EU law in these cases than elsewhere, albeit not without controversy.

---

[47] The SAAs do not refer to concentrations, but national competition laws may extend this duty to follow EU law to that area as well (as was the case in Croatia, for example).

[48] Art 70 SAA Croatia.

[49] Zakon o zaštiti tržišnog natjecanja (NN 79/09, 80/13), Art 74. A translation of the 2009 version of the act can be found at http://www.aztn.hr/uploads/documents/eng/documents/COMPETITION_ACT_2009.pdf. The State Aid Act of 2005, as amended in 2011 (NN 140/2005, 49/2011), contained a similar provision (Art 6/4), requiring the Croatian Competition Agency to apply these 'criteria' accordingly, in line with Art 70 SAA. The 2013 State Aid Act (NN 72/2013, 141/2013) removes this provision, as part of an overall simplification required by EU accession and the shift of authority to the Commission in state aid decisions.

[50] Case C-32/11 *Allianz Hungária Biztosító Zrt. and Others v. Gazdasági Versenyhivatal* (14 March 2013, nyr).

So far, apart from Croatia, there is only one such case in the national reports: the *ASA Auto*[51] judgment of the Court of Bosnia and Herzegovina. Even though the SAA of BiH had not, and still has not, entered into force, the Competition Act—adopted even before the ratification of the SAA—contains a provision enabling the Competition Authority to 'take into account the practice of the ECJ and the decisions of the European Commission' when deciding a case. In *ASA Auto*, the Court found an abuse of a dominant position following the legal test laid down by the ECJ in its *IMS Health*[52] judgment. While the judgment itself was not cited, the Court of BiH referred both to the provision of the Competition Act allowing for the use of EU law and, in general terms, to the case law of the ECJ. It seems that this reliance on EU law raises no constitutional issues in BiH.[53]

In Croatia, a fairly extensive body of case law has developed on these issues. The debate was launched by the Administrative Court,[54] charged with reviewing Competition Agency decisions. In three judgments from 2006, it took different positions on whether EU law can be used by the Agency. In October 2006, it held that:

> the [SAA and the Interim Agreement] could have been applied in this case, while the criteria, standards and interpretative instruments of the European Community relied upon by the defendant institution which are not contained in the text of those agreements, nor are they taken over and published in any other Croatian law or legal rule, cannot be a source of law.[55]

Only a month later, however, a different chamber of the same court found in two related judgments that the Agency was wholly justified in relying on EU legal sources as well as soft law, not just because that is required by the provisions of the SAA, the Interm Agreement and the Competition Act, but also because it helps improve the predictability and clarity of the legal standards that the Agency will apply. In addition, the judgments found that EU law can be relied upon in this way even in the case of anticompetitive agreements concluded before the entry into force of the interim agreement, given that the purpose of the interim agreement and the SAA is to eliminate existing restrictions of competition.[56]

Deciding on a constitutional complaint against one of the latter judgments, the Constitutional Court broadly agreed. In response to the argument that 'criteria,

---

[51] Court of BiH, decision No. S1 3 U 005412 10 Uvl of 15.3.2012, M.R.M. Ljubuški/ASA Auto d.o.o. Sarajevo (*ASA Auto*). See the chapter by Zlatan Meškić and Darko Samardžić, Application of International and EU Law in Bosnia and Herzegovina.

[52] Case C-418/01 *IMS Health GmbH & Co. OHG v. NDC Health GmbH & Co. KG* [2004] ECR I-5039.

[53] See the chapter by Zlatan Meškić and Darko Samardžić, Application of International and EU Law in Bosnia and Herzegovina.

[54] At the time, this was the only administrative court in Croatia. Today, there are four administrative courts and a High Administrative Court.

[55] Judgment of the Administrative Court of the Republic of Croatia Us-5438/2003-7 of 26 October 2006.

[56] Judgment Us-555/2003-4 of 9 November 2006 and judgment Us-4832/2003-6 of 9 November 2006.

standards and interpretative instruments' of EU law cannot be applied unless they are taken over and published as Croatian law, the Court considered that these materials are not 'primary sources of law' but only an 'auxiliary interpretative tool'. In a sense, the Court played down the role of EU law as one of merely 'filling in legal voids' in a way that 'conforms to the spirit of national law'.[57]

This distinction between 'primary' and 'interpretative' sources of law can be challenged as a matter of principle.[58] More to the point, it is highly questionable whether what the SAA requires falls into the latter category. After all, the SAA does not merely allow Croatian authorities to refer to EU materials, but it requires them to apply national competition law in line with them. To give one example, following the SAA, in a case that affects trade between the EU and Croatia, the Competition Agency would almost certainly not be at liberty to depart from the interpretation provided by CJEU case law. The SAA therefore intends precisely for EU law to bind national authorities and to be used in a way that affects the outcome. The fact that the various legal materials referred to by Article 70 of the SAA are not formal sources of law, for instance in the sense of independently giving rise to a cause of action, seems irrelevant given that they fundamentally affect the actual content of the legal rules as applied by the authorities. The Constitutional Court's talk of 'auxiliary interpretative tools' was therefore rather misleading, since it could lead to the conclusion that Croatian institutions are free to follow the EU competition law *acquis* or not, even though the SAA as well as national competition law clearly require them to do so.[59]

In a subsequent judgment, the Constitutional Court repeated the 2008 ruling on this point. Interestingly, however, it completed the citation by stating: 'Croatian competition bodies are authorised and obliged to apply the criteria' arising from EU law.[60] Adding the word 'obliged' would seem to go against the notion that EU law is not used as a 'primary source of law', but only as a gap-filling mechanism that does not contradict Croatian law.

Regardless of these quibbles, the Constitutional Court judgments were a win for the Competition Agency, legitimising its reliance on EU law. An interesting question, however, is whether they go farther than that. Specifically, in the 2008 judgment the Court supported its findings by adding that the competition law harmonisation clause (Art 70 SAA) should be viewed in the context of Croatia's duty to align itself with the *acquis*. This meant that 'when applying legislation that has been aligned in this way, it is the duty of State authorities to do so as it is done in the European Communities, i.e. according to the meaning and spirit of the legal rules on the basis of which the alignment was performed'.

---

[57] For an extensive commentary of this decision, see Stanić (2008), p. 247.

[58] See e.g. Schauer (2008), p. 1931.

[59] In that sense, the Europe Agreement judgment of the Hungarian Constitutional Court, declaring a decree on the implementation of the Europe agreement to be unconstitutional because it required the application of EU competition law criteria, was more honest. See n 32.

[60] Judgment U-III/4082/2010 (NN 28/11) of 17 February 2011 para 7.1.

This statement is so general that it could be read as applying not only to Article 70 SAA and the competition rules, but also to all other areas where alignment with EU law took place, i.e. wherever the general SAA harmonisation clause is relevant. Whether the Constitutional Court actually meant to go that far is an open question, and so far we do not know if this has been (or will be, in the limited subset of cases in which the Croatian SAA may still be relevant) taken up by other courts. The cases referred to in Sects. 3.1 and 3.2, where courts have not always been friendly to reliance on EU law, mostly predate the judgment of the Constitutional Court. There is, however, no subsequent case law showing more openness to consistent interpretation. If anything, the 2010 Administrative Court judgment, rejecting the use of EU law even in a clear-cut competition case (see Sect. 3.2), shows that the message has not come across.

4 Conclusion

This chapter has covered the judgments in which either the SAAs, or EU law in general, were invoked or applied prior to EU accession in the states covered in this book. Admittedly, the sample is limited to what could be found in various case law databases (the case of Croatia) and to what was reported by the authors of the other national reports. It is possible that some relevant cases were missed.

With that *caveat*, several tentative conclusions can be made.

Firstly, the SAAs and EU law in general can be applied in a number of ways. Some of these seem to have been followed more frequently than others. The following table lists them, along with some examples (Table 1).

Overall, the SAAs seem to have had rather limited effect. None of the SEE states have been particularly open to applying the SAAs or to imposing extensive pre-accession interpretative duties. For example, unlike the case in some of the Member States that joined the EU in 2004, there have been no conclusive judgments of the high courts of the SEE states that make it clear that the SAAs impose a general duty to interpret national law in line with EU law. Some judgments found that such a duty exists, but they were contradicted by later judgments of the same court or other courts.

Table 1 Overview of different ways of applying the SAAs or EU law pre-accession

Ways of applying SAAs/EU law	Legal basis for applying SAAs/EU law
Application of the SAA itself	Direct application (e.g. *Makpetrol*)
	Indirect application (no examples found)
Application of the EU *acquis* on the basis of the SAA	General harmonisation clauses (the Croatian High Commercial Court judgments of 2006)
	Specific interpretative duties or references to EU law, such as in competition law (e.g. *ASA Auto*; the Croatian Constitutional Court judgments of 2008 and 2010)
Amorphous citation of EU/-international law	Unclear (e.g. the Croatian NGOs case)

In addition, there are very few cases where the SAAs were applied directly or where a conflicting provision of national law was disapplied. In Croatia, for example, it seems there were no such cases in the eight years in which the SAA was in force prior to accession. In addition, there seem to have been no cases anywhere in which national law was (re-)interpreted in light of the provisions of the SAA itself, or where a court conducted a *Polydor*-like analysis of 'mirror provisions', comparing the interpretation that should be given to an SAA provision to that given to an equivalent Treaty provision by the CJEU.

The only exception to this rather limited role of EU law prior to accession has been competition law, where the SAAs make an explicit reference to the 'criteria' and 'interpretative instruments' of EU law. This 'back door' for the application of EU law has been grudgingly accepted, despite some controversy (see, for example, the 2006 case law of the Croatian Administrative Court, as well as the 2010 judgment of that court that again refuses the application of EU law, in contrast to the Constitutional Court).

Finally, in some cases international or EU law has been used in a non-specified way, without clarifying its relevance or the basis for citing it. Paradoxically, SEE courts seem to be willing to rely on EU law, especially EU legislation, as long as no one raises the question of *why* they should do so. If that question is raised, however, they are more likely to take a conservative stance and refuse to take EU law into account, given that it is not a binding 'source of law'. This response is given not only when EU law is claimed to be binding authority (meaning that national law *has* to be interpreted in the light of EU law), but even in some cases where it is invoked as persuasive authority or merely as a supporting argument (i.e. an interpretative choice that the court *can*, but need not, make).

I have suggested that the reasons for this paradox are similar to those that explain the general reluctance to rely on EU or international law. SEE courts seem to build their decisions by either fully relying on something as a 'source of law' or by simply refusing to apply it (finding, for example, that a provision has no direct effect or that it is irrelevant to the case at hand). Adapting the interpretation of a legal source in the light of other legal or non-legal material, including EU law, is not a part of the toolbox with which judges usually approach cases. Thus, EU law can be applied if it is somehow recognised *ex ante*—not necessarily on the basis of an explicit discussion—as a 'source of law'. If, however, it is invoked in the context of a general duty to re-interpret another source of law, it may encounter resistance. This is also why explicit legislative or Treaty references to EU law, as in the case of the SAA provisions on the EU competition *acquis*, make it much more likely (but not certain) to have an impact.

References

Blockmans S (2006) Western Balkans (Albania, Bosnia-Herzegovina, Croatia, Macedonia and Serbia and Montenegro, Including Kosovo). In: Blockmans S, Lazowski A (eds) The European

Union and its neighbours: a legal appraisal of the EU's policies of stabilisation, partnership and integration. TMC Asser Press, The Hague, p 315
Blockmans S (2007) Tough love: the European Union's relations with the Western Balkans. TMC Asser Press, The Hague
Blockmans S, Lazowski A (2006) The European Union and its neighbours: questioning identity and relationships. In: Blockmans S, Lazowski A (eds) The European Union and its neighbours: a legal appraisal of the EU's policies of stabilisation, partnership and integration. TMC Asser Press, The Hague, p 3
Bobek M (2006) A new or a non-existent legal order? Some (early) experience in the application of EU law in Central Europe. Croat Yearb Eur Law Policy 2:265
Ćapeta T (2005) Courts, legal culture and the enlargement of the EU. Croat Yearb Eur Law Policy 1
Ćapeta T (2006) Interpretativni učinak europskog prava u članstvu i prije članstva u EU. Zbornik Pravnog fakulteta u Zagrebu 56(5)
Elbasani A (2008) The stabilisation and association process in the Balkans: overloaded agenda and weak incentives? EUI WP SPS 2008/03
Harmathy A (2001) Constitutional questions of the preparation of Hungary to accession to the European Union. In: Kellermann AE, de Zwaan JW, Czuczai J (eds) EU enlargement: the constitutional impact at EU and national level. TMC Asser Press, The Hague. pp 315
Kellermann AE, de Zwaan JW, Czuczai J (eds) (2001) EU enlargement: the constitutional impact at EU and national level. TMC Asser Press, The Hague
Kellermann AE, Czuczai J, Blockmans S, Albi A, Douma WT (eds) (2006) The impact of EU accession on the legal orders of new EU Member States and (pre-)candidate countries: hopes and fears. TMC Asser Press, The Hague
Kühn Z (2005a) The application of European law in the new Member States: several (early) predictions. Ger Law J 6(3):563
Kühn Z (2005b) European law in the empires of mechanical jurisprudence: the judicial application of European law in Central European candidate countries. Croat Yearb Eur Law Policy 1
Noutcheva G (2009) Fake, partial and imposed compliance: the limits of the EU's normative power in the Western Balkans. J Eur Public Policy 16:1065
Phinnemore D (2003) Stabilisation and association agreements: Europe agreements for the Western Balkans? Eur Foreign Aff Rev 8:77
Renner S, Trauner F (2009) Creeping EU membership in south-east Europe: the dynamics of EU rule transfer to the Western Balkans. J Eur Integr 31:449
Rodin S (2005) Discourse and authority in European and post-communist legal culture. Croat Yearb Eur Law Policy 1:1
Rodin S (2006) Croatia. In: Blockmans S, Lazowski A (eds) The European Union and its neighbours: a legal appraisal of the EU's policies of stabilisation, partnership and integration. TMC Asser Press, The Hague, p 357
Schauer F (2008) Authority and authorities. Va Law Rev 94:1931
Stanić B (2008) The interpretative effect of European law in the judgment of the Croatian Constitutional Court No U-III-1410/2007. Croat Yearb Eur Law Policy 4:247
Volkai J (1999) The application of the Europe agreement and European law in Hungary: the judgment of an activist Constitutional Court on activist notions. Harvard Jean Monnet working paper 8/99

Judicial Application of WTO Law in Southeast Europe

Tamara Perišin

1 Introduction

This chapter deals with the application of the law of the World Trade Organization (WTO) in eight countries of Southeast Europe (SEE): Albania, Bosnia and Herzegovina, Croatia, Kosovo, Macedonia, Montenegro, Serbia and Slovenia. Five of these countries, Albania, Croatia, Macedonia, Montenegro and Slovenia, are WTO members[1]; two countries, Bosnia and Herzegovina and Serbia, have observer status and their accession is in progress; Kosovo has yet to start these processes. The WTO membership of Slovenia is specific since this country is an EU Member State so a large share of the competence in the field of WTO law is conferred on the EU and the status of WTO law is largely governed by EU law. The same is true for Croatia following the country's accession to the EU on 1 July 2013, but this chapter entails research on the application for WTO law prior to EU accession.

The chapter has two main parts. The first deals with the effects that WTO law is aimed to produce in general, and within the EU legal order in particular. The effects of WTO law in the EU are taken as relevant because all SEE countries see their future there, so they might be willing to recognise such effects even before EU accession. The second part looks at the effects that WTO law has so far had in SEE countries. It shows that WTO law has only rarely been applied in SEE countries and that in most of them there has not been a single case where a national court has relied on WTO law or where parties have cited WTO law to support their claims. The concluding part looks at reasons for the poor application of WTO law in SEE.

Research for this paper was completed in June 2013.

[1] The dates of their accession are as follows: Albania—8 September 2000; Croatia—30 November 2000; Macedonia—4 April 2003; Montenegro—29 April 2012; Slovenia—30 July 1995.

T. Perišin (✉)
Faculty of Law, University of Zagreb, Zagreb, Croatia
e-mail: Tamara.perisin@pravo.hr

S. Rodin, T. Perišin (eds.), *Judicial Application of International Law in Southeast Europe*, DOI 10.1007/978-3-662-46384-0_3

2 WTO Law and Its Effect

It is well known that the WTO was established in 1995 as an umbrella organisation covering a large number of diverse agreements on trade in goods, services, intellectual property, dispute settlement, and trade policy reviews. All WTO members must be parties to all multilateral agreements which are covered by the WTO umbrella, but there is also a smaller number of plurilateral agreements which are optional.

The WTO is an international, not a supranational, organisation, so its treaties have the legal effect of general international law. The idea that WTO law should *per se* have direct effect in all its member states (similarly to the effect of EU law) was explicitly rejected during the Uruguay round, and, for example, the Panel in *US—Sections 301–310 of the Trade Act of 1974* explicitly mentioned how neither the GATT nor any part of WTO law was ever interpreted as having direct effect.[2] However, this Panel held:

> [t]he fact that WTO institutions have not... construed any obligations as producing direct effect does not necessarily preclude that in the legal system of any given Member, following internal constitutional principles, some obligations will be found to give rights to individuals. [The Panel's]... statement of fact does not prejudge any decisions by national courts on this issue.[3]

This means that the effect of WTO law in WTO members depends on their own constitutional principles, primarily on whether the country is monist or dualist.

Within the EU legal order, the European Court of Justice (ECJ) took very early on the position that the General Agreement on Tariffs and Trade (GATT) had no direct effect. In *International Fruit Company*, it considered that the characteristics of the GATT, primarily the 'great flexibility of its provisions, in particular those conferring the possibility of derogation' and the possibility to unilaterally suspend, withdraw or modify its concessions made it impossible for this agreement to have direct effect.[4] Later, when the WTO was established, new litigants tried persuading the Court that this new legal system was such that its agreements should have direct effect within the EU. The Court rejected this possibility. In *Portugal v Council*, it held that 'having regard to their nature and structure, the WTO agreements are not in principle among the rules in the light of which the Court is to review the legality of measures adopted by the Community institutions' and that 'by its nature, the Agreement establishing the World Trade Organisation, including the Annexes thereto, is not susceptible to being directly invoked in Community or Member State courts'.[5]

However, the Court did (both before and after the establishment of WTO law) allow for some narrow exceptions under which WTO law could be invoked by

---

[2] United States—Sections 301–310 of the Trade Act of 1974, WT/DS152/R, 22 December 1999, para 7.72.

[3] Ibid, fn. 661.

[4] Case 21–24/72 *International Fruit Company NV and others v. Produktschap voor Groenten en Fruit* [1972] ECR 01219 paras 21, 26, 27.

[5] Case C-149/96 *Portuguese Republic v. Council of the European Union* [1999] ECR I-08395, paras 47, 48.

individuals and used to assess the validity of EC/EU law. These were situations where the EU measure expressly referred to precise provisions of WTO agreements (*Fediol*)[6] or where the EU measure was intended to implement a particular WTO obligation (*Nakajima*).[7] The Court has also allowed WTO law to have interpretative effect, so both European and national legislation must be interpreted in its light.[8]

3 Application of WTO Law in SEE

The analysis of the application of WTO law in eight SEE countries is based on national reports containing answers to a questionnaire inquiring about various aspects of WTO accession, the application of WTO law, and education in the field. These answers were provided by rapporteurs in charge of national reports to this book and by other contributors, who are all academics dealing with EU and international law issues, well acquainted with their country's legal order, the functioning of national institutions, including the judiciary, and domestic legal education.[9]

3.1 *Status and Availability of WTO Law in SEE*

The first part of the questionnaire dealt with the status and availability of WTO law in SEE. The reports confirmed that all eight SEE countries covered by this research have a monistic understanding of the relationship between national and international law. The Constitutions of Albania,[10] Croatia,[11] Kosovo,[12] Macedonia,[13]

[6] Case 70/87 *Fédération de l'industrie de l'huilerie de la CEE (Fediol) v. Commission of the European Communities* [1989] ECR 01781 paras 19, 21.

[7] Case C-69/89 *Nakajima All Precision Co. Ltd v. Council of the European Communities* [1991] ECR I-02069 para 31.

[8] See ECJ cases C-61/94, *C* v. *Germany* [1996] ECR I-03989, para 52 on the interpretative effect of international agreements; and C-53/96 *Hermès International* v. *FHT Marketing Choice BV* [1998] ECR I-03603, the interpretative effect of WTO law.

[9] The rapporteurs on the application of WTO law were the following: Semir Sali and Gentian Zyberi—Albania; Zlatan Meškić, Aida Mulalić and Darko Samardžić—Bosnia and Herzegovina; Tamara Perišin—Croatia; Kushtrim Istrefi and Visar Morina—Kosovo; Marija Risteska and Kristina Miševa—Macedonia; Dušan Rakitić—Montenegro; Mirjana Drenovak Ivanović, Maja Lukić—Serbia; Janja Hojnik—Slovenia.

[10] Art. 122 of the Constitution of Albania. http://www.km.gov.al/skedaret/1231927768-Constitution%20of%20the%20Republic%20of%20Albania.pdf. Accessed 3 June 2013.

[11] Art. 141 of the Constitution of the Republic of Croatia, NN 85/10.

[12] Art. 19 of the Constitution of the Republic of Kosovo. http://www.assembly-kosova.org/common/docs/Constitution1%20of%20the%20Republic%20of%20Kosovo.pdf. Accessed 3 June 2013.

[13] Art. 118 of the Constitution of the Republic of Macedonia. http://www.sobranie.mk/en/?ItemID=9F7452BF44EE814B8DB897C1858B71FF. Accessed 3 June 2013.

Montenegro,[14] Serbia[15] and Slovenia[16] expressly state that international agreements which have been properly ratified and published in the official journal are a part of the country's internal legal order and that they enjoy priority over national laws. The Constitution of Bosnia and Herzegovina is silent on the legal status of international agreements in general,[17] but its Article 2(2) expressly states that the European Convention on Human Rights (ECHR) is directly applicable and hierarchically superior to other national laws,[18] and the Constitution's Annex I lists some other agreements for the protection of fundamental rights which also appear to be self-executing.[19] All this suggests that WTO treaties to which SEE countries are parties are also a part of the internal legal order of these countries (except perhaps in Bosnia and Herzegovina), and that they are hierarchically superior to national laws.

However, while formally there should be no problems in the application of WTO treaty texts, a practical problem derives from the fact that WTO law is mostly unavailable in the official languages of the SEE countries. The situation of Slovenia and Croatia is special in this respect, as the WTO Agreement and all of its annexes are available in their official languages through the EU database EUR-Lex.[20] As regards other SEE countries which are not EU members, data collected through questionnaires reveals Macedonia is the only one which has translated the WTO Agreement with its annexes into Macedonian.[21] In Croatia and Montenegro, there are official translations of the countries' accession protocols with some schedules of concessions.[22] In Serbia, a commercial database offers a translation of TRIPS into

[14] Art. 9 of the Constitution of Montenegro. http://www.dri.co.me/1/index.php?option=com_wrapper&view=wrapper&Itemid=51&lang=en. Accessed 3 June 2013.

[15] Arts. 16 and 194 of the Constitution of the Republic of Serbia, Official Gazette of the Republic of Serbia No. 98/2006. http://www.ustavni.sud.rs/page/view/en-GB/235-100028/constitution. Accessed 3 June 2013. These provisions do not mention publication in the official journal as a condition for international treaties to become a part of the internal legal order.

[16] Art. 8 of the Slovenian Constitution, Official Gazette RS, Nos. 33/91-I, 42/97, 66/2000, 24/03, 69/04 and 68/06. http://www.us-rs.si/en/about-the-court/legal-basis/constitution/. Accessed 3 June 2013.

[17] Ustav Bosne i Hercegovine http://www.ccbh.ba/pblic/down/USTAV_BOSNE_I_HERCEGOVINE_bos.pdf. Accessed 3 June 2013.

[18] Ibid.

[19] Ibid.

[20] E.g. http://eur-lex.europa.eu/LexUriServ/LexUriServ.do?uri=CELEX:21994A1223(01):EN:NOT. Accessed 11 November 2014.

[21] According to the national report, the Macedonian Official Gazette contains the Macedonian Protocol of Accession to the WTO in the Macedonian language (Zakon za ratifikacija na protokolot za pristapuvanje na Republika Makedonija kon Svetskata trgovska organizacija; Služben vesnik na Republika Makedonija- megunarodni dogovori br.7/03 od 24.01.2003). There is also a book which contains the WTO Agreement with all the annexes translated into Macedonian: Dimitrovski et al. (2003).

[22] For Croatia, see Zakon o potvrđivanju Protokola o pristupanju Republike Hrvatske Marakeškom ugovoru o osnivanju Svjetske trgovinske organizacije, NN-MU 13/00; for Montenegro, see Law No. 30-1/12-1/4 EPA 778, 27 February 2012.

Serbian.[23] The situation is even worse when it comes to WTO case law, as neither full cases nor even case excerpts are available in any of the SEE languages. Only the Macedonian rapporteurs reported that information on WTO law which includes excerpts from selected cases can be obtained in Macedonian through translations in certain books and textbooks.[24]

3.2 *Attitude of SEE Countries' Legislative and Executive Branches Towards WTO Law*

The second part of the questionnaire inquired about the attitudes of the SEE countries' legislative and executive branches towards WTO accession and WTO law. For all eight SEE countries covered by this survey, WTO accession was or is among the governments' priorities. This is visible in various documents, most frequently from WTO working party reports containing official government statements.[25]

However, in SEE countries, WTO accession is not considered very important *per se*. Countries do not show great interest in what WTO rules have to offer in terms of trade liberalisation and benefits for imports and exports. These countries do not expect to achieve significant trade at the global level because the circle of their trading partners is relatively narrow. The lion's share of SEE countries' trade is within the region and with the EU,[26] and these trade relations have been liberalised through special agreements going beyond WTO obligations. For example, all of the SEE countries (with the exception of Slovenia) are parties to the Central European Free Trade Agreement (CEFTA) which liberalises trade between them (and with Moldova).[27] Furthermore, all of the SEE countries (except Slovenia which has had a Europe Agreement since 1996)[28] have concluded Stabilisation and

[23] Paragraf Lex. www.paragraf.rs/. Accessed 3 June 2013.

[24] E.g. Dimitrovski et al. (2003), Macušita et al. (2009), Krugman and Obstfeld (2009) and Kikerkova (2008).

[25] E.g. Report of the Working Party on the Accession of the Former Yugoslav Republic of Macedonia, WT/ACC/807/27, 26 September 2002, para 6; Report of the Working Party on the Accession of Montenegro to the World Trade Organization, WT/ACC/CGR/38, WT/MIN(11)/7, 5 December 2011, para 4; Report of the Working Party on the Accession of Albania to the World Trade Organization, WT/ACC/ALB/51, 13 July 2000, para 4.

[26] See e.g. EU DG Trade Statistics: Croatia—EU Bilateral Trade and Trade with the World, 26 April 2013. http://trade.ec.europa.eu/doclib/docs/2006/September/tradoc_113370.pdf. Accessed 3 June 2013.

[27] http://www.cefta2006.com/. Accessed 3 June 2013. Zakon o potvrđivanju ugovora o izmjeni i dopuni i pristupanju Srednjoeuropskom ugovoru o slobodnoj trgovini, NN-MU 6/2007.

[28] Europe Agreement establishing an association between the European Communities and their Member States, acting within the framework of the European Union, of the one part, and the Republic of Slovenia, of the other part, OJ L 51, 26.2.1999, pp. 3–195.

Association Agreements (SAA) with the EU.[29] Croatia's relations with the EU were regulated by an SAA until its EU membership, and currently the SAAs of Albania, Macedonia and Montenegro are in force, while Bosnia and Herzegovina and Serbia have interim agreements[30] pending completion of the SAAs' ratification process in all EU Member States. Kosovo is currently the only SAA country which has not yet concluded an SAA, but the first steps are being taken in that direction.[31] Consequently, SEE countries have achieved significant trade liberalisation with their major trading partners through means other than WTO membership. CEFTA and the SAAs thus make WTO accession less important in terms of trade liberalisation benefits.

Nevertheless, for SEE countries, WTO accession was or is important for political reasons, especially since it is one of the prerequisites for EU membership. The political (rather than trade) dimension of WTO membership can be detected from the comments of Montenegrin officials where WTO accession is put in the broader political context of integration with non-trade related organisations, as heard, for example, in the statement that WTO accession is the "third most important integration process after the EU and NATO accession goals".[32]

The consequence of this political rather than economic importance of WTO membership is that SEE countries will always want to appear to be acting in a WTO compatible manner, but they might not want to invest real effort into screening their rules for WTO noncompliance and removing WTO incompatible measures so as to achieve greater economic efficiency. In practice, this means that legislative acts might invoke WTO law,[33] and government representatives may claim that certain

---

[29] In order of entry into force: Stabilisation and Association Agreement between the European Communities and their Member States, of the one part, and the former Yugoslav Republic of Macedonia, of the other part, OJ L 84, 20.3.2004, pp. 1–197; Stabilisation and Association Agreement between the European Communities and their Member States, of the one part, and the Republic of Croatia, of the other part, OJ L 26, 28.1.2005, pp. 3–220; Stabilisation and Association Agreement between the European Communities and their Member States, of the one part, and the Republic of Albania, of the other part, OJ L 107, 28.4.2009, pp. 166–502; Stabilisation and Association Agreement between the European Communities and their Member States, of the one part, and the Republic of Montenegro, of the other part, OJ L 108, 29.4.2010, pp. 3–354.

[30] In order of entry into force: Interim Agreement on trade and trade-related matters between the European Community, of the one part, and Bosnia and Herzegovina, of the other part, OJ L 169, 30.6.2008, pp. 13–807; Interim Agreement on trade and trade-related matters between the European Community, of the one part, and the Republic of Serbia, OJ L 28, 30.1.2010, pp. 2–397.

[31] Communication from the Commission to the European Parliament and the Council on a Feasibility Study for a Stabilisation and Association Agreement between the European Union and Kosovo, SWD (2012) 339 final, Brussels, 10.10.2012, COM (2012) 602 final.

[32] Statement of the Montenegrin Minister of Economy, Mr. Kavarić, in 'Montenegro breaks deadlock in WTO-accession negotiations with Ukraine', Government of Montenegro Homepage. www.gov.me/en/News/108761/Montenegro-breaks-deadlock-in-WTO-accession-negotiations-with-Ukraine.html. Accessed 3 June 2013.

[33] E.g. Trademark Laws of Montenegro, OG MNE No. 72/10 (e.g. in Art. 3) and of Croatia, NN 173/03, 54/05, 76/07, 30/09, 49/11, (e.g. in Art. 19) explicitly mention the WTO.

parts of the legal system have been made compliant with WTO rules.[34] However, WTO noncompliance is never mentioned, even for measures that remained in force from before WTO membership. One can guess that there are WTO incompatible measures in all SEE countries (as generally in any WTO member), but since there have been no challenges against these measures, they could remain in force indefinitely (see below Sect. 4).

3.3 Application of WTO Law by National Courts in SEE Countries

The third part of the questionnaire concerned the judicial application of WTO law in SEE. The survey showed that WTO law has almost never been applied by the courts of SEE. This is despite the fact that these countries have monist systems. However, there are some differences between the countries.

It seems that Croatian courts have been the most active in the region in applying WTO law, but the total number of decisions citing WTO law which are available online (through a commercial database[35]) barely reaches double figures. The most prominent case concerns a foreign law firm wanting to set up a branch in Croatia on the basis of the General Agreement on Trade in Services (GATS). The Zagreb Commercial Court (ZCC) decided on the law firm's request for registration three times, and each time its decision to allow the registration was appealed by the Croatian Bar Association—in the first two appeals the High Commercial Court (HCC) annulled the decision of the ZCC and remanded it for new proceedings.[36] In the view of the HCC, the first two requests for registration and the ZCC decisions allowing registration were too broad and went beyond the obligations which Croatia took in its GATS schedule of commitments.[37] Namely, according to the HCC, Croatia had not liberalised the sector of legal services in a way which would allow foreign companies to operate in the same way as domestic ones, e.g. to represent clients before courts, to consult on matters of Croatian law, etc. In the view of the HCC, the registration of a foreign company's branch was only permissible for the activity of consultancy related to the service provider's home country law, and foreign and international law.[38] Other types of legal services were strictly

[34] E.g. according to the Montenegrin representative in WTO accession negotiations, the Montenegrin intellectual property rules are compliant with the TRIPS. Report of the Working Party on the Accession of Montenegro to the World Trade Organization, WT/ACC/CGR38, WT/MIN(11)7, of 5 December 2011, 55.

[35] www.iusinfo.hr/. Accessed 3 June 2013.

[36] See decisions of the Croatian High Commercial Court Pž 1406/05-6, 14.06.2005; Pž 4219/06-3, 18.07.2006; and Pž 5819/07-3, 15.01.2008.

[37] Decisions of the Croatian High Commercial Court Pž 1406/05-6, 14.06.2005 and Pž 4219/06-3, 18.07.2006.

[38] Ibid.

regulated by Croatian law and conducting them required membership of the Croatian Bar Association.[39] Ultimately, on the basis of the GATS, the foreign company's branch was registered (albeit for limited types of legal services).[40] The Croatian Bar Association challenged this before the Croatian Constitutional Court which decided that the challenge was unfounded, and in its decision it cited WTO law.[41] References to WTO law before the Croatian courts have also been made in several other cases.[42]

For Slovenia, the national report states that TRIPS is the only part of WTO law which has been applied by regular courts and the Constitutional Court. For example, TRIPS was invoked by a wine producer challenging Slovenian rules concerning wine with the indication of the recognised traditional name—Cviček—before the Slovenian Constitutional Court which determined that neither the TRIPS nor the Slovenian Constitution had been breached.[43] The national rapporteur reported finding no case law applying other WTO agreements, although in some cases these agreements were mentioned, but then not applied to the facts of the case.[44]

In Albania, WTO law was once invoked before the Constitutional Court.[45] The national report states that a private company invoked WTO law and the Albanian Stabilisation and Association Agreement arguing that these had been violated by Albanian rules giving preferential treatment to domestically produced diesel fuel.[46] The Albanian Constitutional Court established that there had indeed been a breach of the SAA, but it did not analyse the compatibility of the measures with WTO rules.[47]

The reports from Macedonia and Montenegro stated that no national court has ever applied WTO law or made any reference to it, and that they are not aware of any instance where the application of WTO law was sought by the parties. In both

[39] Ibid.

[40] Decision of the Croatian High Commercial Court Pž 5819/07-3, 15.01.2008.

[41] Decision of the Croatian Constitutional Court U-III/1337/2008, 20.05.2009.

[42] E.g. in decisions of the Croatian Administrative Court Us-624/2000-8, 30.01.2002; Us-1702/2007-11, 24.03.2010; Us-9440/2006-6, 07.10.2010.

[43] Decision of the Slovenian Constitutional Court No. U-I-228/00, 8 November 2001, Official Gazette RS, No. 101/00, Official Gazette RS, No. 96/01 and OdlUS X, 182. http://odlocitve.us-rs.si/usrs/us-odl.nsf/o/82B4DD99BBFF9458C125717200288B3B. Accessed 3 June 2013.
English abstract at: http://odlocitve.us-rs.si/usrs/us-odl.nsf/o/9F68BC0DA0B0C902C125717200280AF6. Accessed 3 June 2013.

[44] See e.g. the decision of the Slovenian Constitutional Court U-I-148/93, 20.01.1994. http://odlocitve.us-rs.si/usrs/us-odl.nsf/o/A63AAA295D32311DC12571720028877E. Accessed 3 June 2013; U-I-368/98, 08.07.1999. http://odlocitve.us-rs.si/usrs/us-odl.nsf/o/3D7E365D4CDADF96C125717200280E64. Accessed 3 June 2013.

[45] *Shoqata e Shoqërivetë Hidrokarbureve v. Këshilli i Ministrave*, judgment of the Albanian Constitutional Court, No. 24, 24. 07. 2009.

[46] Ibid.

[47] Ibid.

countries, judgments of the national courts are freely available online[48] so if WTO law was applied, it would be relatively simple to determine this.

Finally, for three SEE countries which are not WTO members, Bosnia and Herzegovina, Serbia and Kosovo, reports logically do not mention any cases where WTO law was applied or invoked before a national court.

3.4 *Education and Expertise on the WTO*

The application of WTO law by national courts and other institutions correlates with legal education in the field. The fourth part of the questionnaire was thus aimed at determining whether judges, practising attorneys and other lawyers have the opportunity or duty to learn about WTO law within their basic or advanced legal education or when preparing for professional exams.

The national reports revealed that in most SEE countries there is not a single course with a dominant focus on WTO law. The only exception is Croatia where the Faculty of Law, University of Zagreb, offers a Jean Monnet module "EU and WTO in a comparative perspective".[49] In some of the SEE countries, the WTO is briefly covered within broader courses at faculties of law or of economics (e.g. within courses on international law, international business, international economic relations, etc.).

WTO law is also not a part of any courses organised for judges, public prosecutors, public defenders, private lawyers, and it is not examined within the bar exam. However, there has been some training for civil servants and diplomats working on WTO-related issues (e.g. in Montenegro[50] and in Serbia[51]).

[48] In Montenegro through 'The Courts of Montenegro'. Portal http://sudovi.me. Accessed 3 June 2013; and in Macedonia through www.pravda.gov.mk/novost_detail.asp?lang=mak&id=406 or directly on the website on the particular court: www.vsrm.mk; www.asskopje.mk/; www.asbitola.mk/; www.asstip.mk/; www.asgostivar.mk/; www.osskopje2.mk/; www.osskopje1.mk/. All sites accessed 3 June 2013.

[49] The course is taught be the author of this chapter.

[50] See e.g. Questionnaire on information required from the Government of Montenegro by the European Commission for the purpose of preparing the Opinion on the Application of Montenegro for European Union membership, Additional Questions, Government of Montenegro, Ministry of Economy, 12 April 2010, Section 30, External Relations, 8. www.upitnik.gov.me/. Accessed 3 June 2013.

[51] E.g. www.mfa.gov.rs/sr/index.php/diplomatska-akademija/program-diplomatske-obuke?lang=lat. Accessed 3 June 2013.

4 Concluding Remarks: Reasons for the Lack of Application of WTO Law in SEE

The survey demonstrated that there is hardly any judicial application of WTO law in SEE countries. There are several possible explanations for this.

First, it is theoretically possible that all the national rules in all SEE countries comply with WTO law so that it was never necessary to directly apply WTO law itself in any dispute. This is an improbable reason for the non-application of WTO law.

Second, it is highly relevant that there have not been any WTO disputes involving an SEE country as a complainant, respondent or a third party. The only exception is Croatia, against whose measures affecting imports of live animals and meat products[52] Hungary requested consultations in 2003,[53] but Croatia changed its measure[54] so WTO bodies were never required to decide on the matter. The reason for almost no challenges against SEE countries' measures cannot be due to perfect compliance with WTO rules, but rather to the specificities of the countries involved. Perhaps most importantly, all of the SEE countries are relatively small (ranging from the smallest SEE country of Montenegro with an estimated population of 630,261, to the largest SEE country Serbia with an estimated population of 7,258,745[55]) and have small markets. This means that for other WTO members which might be interested in exporting to an SEE country it is simply too costly to go through a WTO dispute in order to improve its access to such a small market. Furthermore, in all SEE countries there are other significant problems facing exporters, making business activities there less attractive. These problems are related to corruption,[56] long bureaucratic procedures, outdated laws and in general a business unfriendly climate.[57] These are the kind of problems that the WTO cannot address, so other WTO members might not be interested in litigating to

[52] Naredba o zabrani uvoza u Republiku Hrvatsku živih životinja i proizvoda životinjskog podrijetla radi sprječavanja unošenja u Republiku Hrvatsku transmisivnih spongiformnih encefalopatija, NN 89/2003; Naredba o zabrani uvoza u Republiku Hrvatsku goveda, proizvoda od goveda, kao i krmiva animalnog podrijetla radi sprječavanja unošenja u Republiku Hrvatsku transmisivnih spongiformnih encefalopatija, NN 89/2003.

[53] Croatia—Measure Affecting Imports of Live Animals and Meat Products—Request for Consultations by Hungary, G/L/636 G/SPS/GEN/411 WT/DS297/1.

[54] Naredbe o zabrani uvoza u Republiku Hrvatsku živih životinja I proizvoda životinjskog podrijetla radi sprječavanja unošenja u Republiku Hrvatsku transmisivnih spongiformnih encefalopatija, Narodne novine 96/2003, 100/2003, 121/2003, 141/2003, 7/2004.

[55] Data taken from the World Bank website: http://data.worldbank.org/indicator/SP.POP.TOTL. Accessed 3 June 2013.

[56] See Transparency International data: http://cpi.transparency.org/cpi2012/results/. Accessed 3 June 2013.

[57] See European Bank for Reconstruction and Development data http://www.ebrd.com/pages/research/economics/data/macro.shtml#ti. Accessed 3 June 2013.

remove a WTO-incompatible measure when they know that exports would remain very difficult even without that measure.

Third, foreign companies that do manage to conduct their business in an SEE country are also not very keen to push their governments to start a WTO dispute or to go before a national court and seek the application of WTO law. It seems that interested companies try to resolve the issue with national authorities without entering any dispute (even when that means sustaining some losses). So, the vigilance of individuals does not operate in the same way as with the enforcement of EU law or of fundamental rights and freedoms guaranteed by the ECHR.

Finally, the average level of knowledge about WTO law in the legal profession in SEE countries is low. In all SEE countries (except Croatia), there is no university law course focusing on WTO law, there are no professional courses on this topic organised for practising lawyers or judges, and WTO law is not part of the bar exams. In contrast, for other areas of international/supranational law such as the ECHR or EU law which were equally new for these countries, there have been numerous types of educational activities and projects targeted at the legal profession throughout the region. The lack of education in the field is probably one of the reasons why practising lawyers do not rely on WTO law.

References

Dimitrovski D et al (trs) (2003) Rezultati od Urugvajskata runda na multulateralni trgovski pregovori: pravni tekstovi; Svetska trgovska organizacija. USAID, Makedonija

Macušita M, Šonbaum TĐ, Mavroidis PC (2009) Svetska trgovska organizacija, pravo, praktika i politika. Prosvetno delo AD, Skopje

Krugman PR, Obstfeld M (2009) Megunarodna ekonomija: Teorija i politika. Data Pons, Skopje

Kikerkova I (2008) Nadvorešna trgovija. UKIM, Ekonomski fakultet, Skopje

Application of the Aarhus Convention in Southeast Europe

Lana Ofak

1 Introduction

The United Nations Economic Commission for Europe (UNECE) Convention on Access to Information, Public Participation in Decision-making and Access to Justice in Environmental Matters was adopted on 25 June 1998 in Aarhus, Denmark, at the Fourth Ministerial Conference in the 'Environment for Europe' process. It came into force on 30 October 2001.

The Aarhus Convention is generally considered as a new kind of international agreement in the field of environmental protection that links environmental rights and human rights.[1] For the first time in a legally binding international agreement adopted in Europe, the right to a healthy environment is stated as a human right:

> In order to contribute to the protection of the right of every person of present and future generations to live in an environment adequate to his or her health and well-being, each Party shall guarantee the rights of access to information, public participation in decision-making, and access to justice in environmental matters in accordance with the provisions of this Convention. (Article 1 on the objective of the Convention).

Although the Convention does not expressly guarantee the right to a healthy environment, it does refer to it as an accepted fact.[2] The rights of access to information, public participation in decision-making, and access to justice in environmental matters, in literature often considered as procedural environmental

[1] United Nations Economic Commission for Europe (2013a), p. 1.

[2] Ibid, p. 31.

L. Ofak (✉)
Faculty of Law, University of Zagreb, Cirilometodska 4, 10000 Zagreb, Croatia
e-mail: lana.ofak@pravo.hr

S. Rodin, T. Perišin (eds.), *Judicial Application of International Law in Southeast Europe*, DOI 10.1007/978-3-662-46384-0_4

rights, are not an end in itself, but represent a meaningful instrument for the realisation of the substantive right to a healthy environment.[3]

As of 30 June 2013, there were 46 Parties to the Aarhus Convention. The dates of ratification and accession of the seven countries of Southeast Europe that are parties to the Convention are as follows: Albania—27 June 2001, Bosnia and Herzegovina—1 October 2008, Croatia—27 March 2007, Macedonia—22 July 1999, Montenegro—2 November 2009, Slovenia—29 July 2004, Serbia—31 July 2009.[4] Kosovo is not a party to the Convention.

A Protocol on Pollutant Release and Transfer Registers to the Aarhus Convention was adopted at the Extraordinary Meeting of the Parties held in Kiev from 21 to 23 May 2003. Out of seven countries of Southeast Europe, Bosnia and Herzegovina and Montenegro signed the Protocol but have not ratified it yet. Another five countries are parties to the Protocol.[5] The application of the Protocol will not be discussed in this chapter.

Genetically modified organisms (GMOs) were one of the most controversial topics during the negotiations over the draft of the Aarhus Convention.[6] The provisions of the Convention that guarantee public participation in decision-making apply to decisions on whether to permit the deliberate release of GMOs into the environment only 'to the extent feasible and appropriate' (Article 6/11 of the Convention). At the second meeting of the Parties held in Almaty, Kazakhstan, from 25 to 27 May 2005, the Parties adopted the Amendment to the Aarhus Convention that introduced a new Article 6 bis and Annex I bis with the aim to strengthen public participation in decision-making on GMOs. The amendment will enter into force when it has been ratified by at least three-quarters of the Parties that were party to the Convention at the time the amendment was adopted (i.e. it must be ratified by 27 of the 35 Parties that were party to the Convention at the time the amendment was adopted). As of 30 June 2013, the amendment has been ratified by 27 Parties, 22 of which were party to the Convention at the time the amendment was adopted. This means a further five ratifications are required. Slovenia is the only country in Southeast Europe that has ratified the GMO amendment.[7] Albania and Macedonia are among the parties that were parties to the Convention at the time the amendment was adopted but are yet to ratify the amendment.

---

[3] For a discussion on substantive and procedural environmental rights, see e.g. Pallemaerts (2004); UNEP. http://www.genevaenvironmentnetwork.org/?q=en/system/files/human_rights_env_report.pdf. Accessed 30 June 2013; Pedersen (2008), pp. 73–111. http://ssrn.com/abstract=1122289. Accessed 30 June 2013; May and Daly (2009); Widener Law School Legal Studies Research Paper No. 09–35. http://ssrn.com/abstract=1479849. Accessed 30 June 2013.

[4] UN Treaty Collection. Status of ratification. http://treaties.un.org/Pages/ViewDetails.aspx?src=TREATY&mtdsg_no=XXVII-13&chapter=27&lang=en. Accessed 30 June 2013.

[5] UN Treaty Collection. Status of ratification. http://treaties.un.org/Pages/ViewDetails.aspx?src=TREATY&mtdsg_no=XXVII-13-a&chapter=27&lang=en. Accessed 30 June 2013.

[6] Wates (2011), p. 14.

[7] UN Treaty Collection. Status of ratification. http://treaties.un.org/Pages/ViewDetails.aspx?src=TREATY&mtdsg_no=XXVII-13-b&chapter=27&lang=en. Accessed 30 June 2013.

Public authorities might tend to discriminate against non-citizens or non-residents in determining whether they have a recognisable interest regarding the right to initiate administrative and/or judicial procedures on the basis of Article 9 of the Convention, and might also tend to omit non-citizens and non-residents in decision-making on environmental matters.[8] Prohibition of discrimination is one of the main principles of the Aarhus Convention. Within the scope of the relevant provisions of this Convention, the public will have access to information, have the possibility to participate in decision-making and have access to justice in environmental matters without discrimination as to citizenship, nationality or domicile and, in the case of a legal person, without discrimination as to where it has its registered seat or effective centre of activities (Article 3(9)). This provision establishes that all persons, regardless of their citizenship, nationality or domicile, have the same rights under the Convention as citizens of the Party concerned.

Pursuant to Article 17 of the Convention that allows regional economic integration organisations constituted by sovereign UNECE Members States to become its parties, the European Community signed the Convention on 25 June 1998 in Aarhus. The Convention was concluded by the Council of the European Union on 17 February 2005.[9] Agreements concluded by the Union are binding upon the institutions of the Union and on its Member States (Article 216(2) of the Treaty on the Functioning of the European Union). In addition, all EU Member States ratified the Aarhus Convention. Its provisions are, therefore, binding on them in two ways: firstly, as its direct Parties, and secondly as the Member States of the EU that are committed to respect obligations under the Treaties.

The European Union is also a Party to the Protocol on Pollutant and Transfer Registers and to the GMO Amendment to the Aarhus Convention.

2 Status of the Aarhus Convention Within the Domestic Legal System

In the countries of Southeast Europe, ratified international treaties form an integral part of the domestic legal order and have primacy over domestic law.[10] Therefore, the status of the Aarhus Convention is superior to all laws and other general legal acts. The only exception is Macedonia where international treaties have equal rank to domestic laws, but cannot be changed or derogated by law.[11]

---

[8] See similar: United Nations Economic Commission for Europe (2013a), p. 65.

[9] Council Decision 2005/370/EC, OJ 2005 L 124, p. 1.

[10] See Article 116(1) of the Albanian Constitution (Law No. 8417 as modified by Law No. 9675 and by Law No. 9904), decision U 5/09 of the Constitutional Court of Bosnia and Herzegovina, Article 141 of the Croatian Constitution (*Narodne novine* (NN) No. 85/10—consolidated text), Article 9 of the Montenegrin Constitution (*Službeni list CG* no. 1/07), Article 8 of the Slovenian Constitution (*Uradni list RS* no. 33/1991 (as am.)) and Article 194 of the Serbian Constitution (*Službeni glasnik RS* no. 98/06).

[11] Risteska and Miševa (2013).

Constitutional courts exist in all the countries of Southeast Europe. They have the competence to determine the conformity of domestic laws with international treaties to which the State is a party,[12] with the exception of the Macedonian Constitutional Court.[13] In principle this means that there is the possibility to initiate before constitutional courts a procedure of review on whether the provisions of domestic law are in concordance with the provisions of the Aarhus Convention.

In Croatia, Macedonia, Montenegro and Serbia any person has the right to submit an initiative for commencing a procedure of assessing the constitutionality of a law or the constitutionality and legality of other regulations.[14] The submission of an initiative in these countries is not conditioned by the existence of legal interest.

A very different situation exists in Albania and Bosnia and Herzegovina. In Albania, individuals do have the right to initiate proceeding before the Albanian Constitutional Court, but only for issues related to their interests. Since

> …every normative act is, technically speaking, abstract in nature and has general effects, [so] it would be quite hard to argue that an individual may have a personal interest in their compatibility with the Constitution or international treaties. If a law is incompatible with the Constitution, it would first have to be applied to the concerned individual, who in turn could file a lawsuit with a district court and claim such incompatibility. In such case, it would be the court to formally seize the Constitutional Court (incidental proceedings ex art. 145(2)[15]), not the individual.[16]

---

[12] Article 131 of the Albanian Constitution, Article VI(3) of the Constitution of Bosnia and Herzegovina, Article 149 of the Montenegrin Constitution, Article 160 of the Slovenian Constitution and Article 167 of the Serbian Constitution. The Croatian Constitution does not explicitly empower the Constitutional Court to review the conformity of an act with international treaties; however, the Constitutional Court has accepted the competence of reviewing the conformity of domestic acts with international treaties which have been ratified in Croatia (see e.g. U-I-745/1999 (NN No. 112/00)).

[13] The Macedonian Constitutional Court is empowered to review the conformity of laws with the Constitution and the conformity of collective agreements and other regulations with the Constitution and laws (see Article 110 of the Macedonian Constitution). The Macedonian Constitution does not expressly empower the Constitutional Court to review the conformity of laws with international treaties. Nevertheless, the Constitutional Court has the authority to repeal the provisions of domestic laws that are contrary to the ratified international agreements. (Miševa K. Email correspondence with the author (1 July 2013). Many thanks to Kristina Miševa for her explanation of the competence of the Macedonian Constitutional Court.)

[14] See Article 38(1) of the Constitutional Act on the Constitutional Court of the Republic of Croatia (NN No. 49/02—consolidated text), Article 12 of the Rules of Procedure of the Constitutional Court of the Republic of Macedonia (*Службен весник на РМ* No. 70/1992), Article 150 (1) of the Montenegrin Constitution and Article 168(2) of the Serbian Constitution.

[15] Article 145(2) of the Albanian Constitution reads as follows: 'If judges believe that a law is unconstitutional, they do not apply it. In this case, they suspend the proceedings and send the question to the Constitutional Court. Decisions of the Constitutional Court are binding on all courts'.

[16] Sali S. Email correspondence with the author (26 June 2013). Many thanks to Semir Sali and Gentian Zyberi for their explanation of the right of individuals to submit an initiative before the Albanian Constitutional Court.

Something similar is prescribed by the Constitution of Bosnia and Herzegovina. The Constitutional Court has jurisdiction over issues referred by any court in Bosnia and Herzegovina concerning whether a law, on whose validity its decision depends, is compatible with the Constitution, with the European Convention for Human Rights and Fundamental Freedoms and its Protocols, with the laws of Bosnia and Herzegovina, or concerning the existence of or the scope of a general rule of public international law pertinent to the court's decision.[17] In conclusion, individuals do not have direct access to the Constitutional Court to challenge the compatibility of domestic laws with the Aarhus Convention, as they do in Croatia, Montenegro and Serbia.

In Slovenia, the right to submit a petition to initiate a procedure for the assessment of the constitutionality or legality of regulations or general acts is connected with the existence of the legal interest of the person who submits it.[18] Legal interest is deemed to be demonstrated if a regulation or general act issued for the exercise of public authority whose review has been requested by the petitioner directly interferes with his rights, legal interests, or legal position (Article 24(2) of the Constitutional Court Act). In instances in which regulations or general acts issued for the exercise of public authority have direct effects and interfere with the rights, legal interests, or legal position of the petitioner, a petition may be lodged within 1 year after such an act enters into force or within 1 year after the day the petitioner learns of the occurrence of harmful consequences (Article 24(3)).

The only case of repealing domestic laws due to their incompatibility with the Aarhus Convention can be found in Slovenia.

2.1 A Case of Review of Conformity of Domestic Law and Regulation with the Aarhus Convention in Slovenia

The Society for the Liberation of Animals and their Rights (*Društvo za osvoboditev živali in njihove pravice*) lodged a petition for the initiation of a procedure for the review of the constitutionality and legality of the Regulation amending the Regulation on Protected Wild Animal Species and the Ordinance on the withdrawal of the brown bear. The Society based its legal interest on the fact that it operates in the public interest. However, the Constitutional Court did not consider that such a status was sufficient for the recognition of legal interest. The legal interest of the petitioner was rather established on the fact that, as a member of the public concerned, the Society was not able to participate in the drafting of legally binding rules that regulate the protection of the area in which it operates.[19]

[17] Article VI/3(c) of the Constitution of Bosnia and Herzegovina.

[18] See Article 24 of the Constitutional Court Act (*Uradni list RS* No. 64/07—consolidated text).

[19] Decision of the Slovenian Constitutional Court, U-I-386/06-32, paras 3 and 4.

The petitioner claimed that the procedure of adopting the contested Regulation and Ordinance was not carried out in accordance with Article 8 of the Aarhus Convention that addresses public participation in the preparation of executive regulations and other generally applicable legally binding rules that may have a significant effect on the environment. The Constitutional Court agreed with this argument and went even further and repealed the Nature Protection Act. Although Articles 26(1) and 81(1) of the Nature Protection Act[20] provide legal foundations for passing implementing regulations in the material field of its application, this Act lacked provisions that guarantee public participation in the preparation of such regulations. Thus, the Nature Protection Act was not in conformity with Article 8 of the Aarhus Convention.[21]

The Constitutional Court found that the Act is unconstitutional for the very reason that it did not regulate public participation in the preparation of subordinate legislation governing the protection of flora and fauna (i.e. implementing regulations that are adopted by the executive branch of government). In view of the fact that Slovenia is obliged to implement the Aarhus Convention, the legislature had the obligation to prescribe in the Act procedural rules for effective public participation in the preparation of these regulations. Since the Nature Protection Act, whose provisions provide a basis for the adoption of implementing regulations in this area, does not regulate public participation in the process of their preparation, it is inconsistent with the Aarhus Convention, and thus in conflict with the Constitution.[22]

The Slovenian legislature (*Državni zbor*) was instructed by the Court to correct the omission of public participation provisions within 3 months of the date of publication of the decision of the Constitutional Court in the Official Journal of the Republic of Slovenia. The Constitutional Court considered the deadline of 3 months to be adequate for rectifying the unconstitutionality, since the Nature Protection Act could be amended with minor changes.[23]

The contested Regulation amending the Regulation on Protected Wild Animal Species and the Ordinance on the withdrawal of the brown bear were adopted on the basis of the Nature Protection Act that was determined to be inconsistent with the Constitution. Since the Regulation was passed in a procedure that was, unconstitutionally, not regulated by the Act, the Constitutional Court found that this implementing regulation was in conflict with the Constitution and repealed it. The Ordinance was also repealed, with the explanation that it was adopted under the provisions of the Regulation which had just been invalidated by the Constitutional Court.[24]

---

[20] *Uradni list RS* No. 56/99, 31/200—popr., 119/02, 41/04 in 96/04—ur. p. b.

[21] Decision of the Slovenian Constitutional Court, *supra* note 19, para 9.

[22] Article 153(2) of the Slovenian Constitution prescribes that 'Laws must be in conformity with generally accepted principles of international law and with valid treaties ratified by the National Assembly, whereas regulations and other general legal acts must also be in conformity with other ratified treaties'.

[23] Decision of the Slovenian Constitutional Court, *supra* note 19, para 11.

[24] Ibid, paras 12–14.

The importance of this decision of the Slovenian Constitutional Court for the region of Southeast Europe is twofold. Firstly, it demonstrates that, pursuant to the hierarchy of legal norms, all laws and subordinate legislation must be in conformity with the Aarhus Convention and, in the case of conflict, their provisions can be challenged before the Constitutional Court in a procedure of assessment of their constitutionality. The only dissimilarity between the countries refers to different regulation of the right to submit an initiative for reviewing the constitutionality before the Constitutional Court (as noted *supra*). Secondly, although Article 8 of the Aarhus Convention, instead of mandatory wording, requires that the Parties 'strive to promote effective public participation', the Constitutional Court interpreted this phrase as obliging Slovenia to take concrete measures to fulfil the objectives of the Convention. Since there were neither legislative guarantees nor efforts on the side of Slovenian legislature to promote effective public participation in the preparation of implementing regulations, the absence of such guarantees in the Nature Protect Act represented a violation of the Aarhus Convention.

3 Direct Application of the Aarhus Convention by the Courts

In Albania, Croatia, Macedonia, Montenegro, Serbia and Slovenia international treaties are directly applicable by the courts.[25] Recognition of the direct application of international agreements in Bosnia and Herzegovina arises from the interpretation of Articles 28 and 29 of the Law on the Procedure for the Conclusion and Execution of International Treaties.[26]

One of the main features of a monistic relationship between national and international law is the obligation of the national authorities of a Contracting State to interpret and apply domestic legislation in a manner that their decisions are not contrary to the international obligations their State has committed itself to by the ratification of a treaty.[27] In addition, ratified rules of international law become directly applicable before the national courts and other public authority bodies without the need for any additional regulatory activity of the parliament or the government.[28] However, Article 3(1) of the Aarhus Convention requires the Parties to establish and maintain a clear, transparent and consistent framework for its implementation. Moreover, certain provisions of the Convention often contain

---

[25] See Article 122(1) of the Albanian Constitution; Article 118(3) of the Croatian Constitution; Article 98(2) of the Macedonian Constitution; Article 9 of the Montenegrin Constitution; Article 16(2) of the Serbian Constitution; Article 8(2) of the Slovenian Constitution.

[26] See the chapter of Meškić and Samardžić in this book.

[27] Omejec (2009), pp. 7–8. http://www.venice.coe.int/webforms/documents/?pdf=CDL-JU(2009)035-e. Accessed 30 June 2013.

[28] Ibid, p. 8.

the phrase 'within the framework of its national legislation'. This suggests that the Parties have the duty to adopt detailed provisions in their legislation to allow the implementation of the Convention. Therefore, direct application of the Convention by the national authorities may not be enough to fulfil the obligations that the Parties have undertaken.[29]

This issue was addressed by the Aarhus Convention Compliance Committee in its Report to the second Meeting of the Parties.[30] It was noted that some Parties, with legal systems that allow for ratification of an international treaty without prior transposition of its requirements into the domestic system, sometimes make inadequate institutional arrangements for the implementation of the Convention, relying on its direct applicability.[31] Although the Convention in these cases becomes a part of the domestic legal system, in many of its provisions it represents only a framework without clear requirements. These can lead to findings of the Compliance Committee that the Party concerned failed to take sufficient measures to establish a proper framework to implement the provisions of the Convention, regardless of the fact that national courts have the obligation to directly apply international treaties.[32]

In principle, courts deny the possibility of the direct application of rules of international treaties that are formulated in such a vague way that they could not be considered as self-sufficient and directly applicable.[33] If a provision of an international treaty is formulated in such a way that it is necessary to adopt other legal norms to enable its implementation, due to the clear principle of separation of powers, judges cannot create a new norm, and, as a consequence, they cannot apply the provisions of the international treaty. Despite its vagueness, the norm of an international treaty is still binding upon a Party and creates obligations. Even in the event that individuals cannot invoke provisions that do not have a self-executing character before the national courts, the State can still be held responsible for non-compliance with the international treaty.

Are the provisions of the Aarhus Convention formed in a sufficiently clear way that enables the national courts to directly apply them in the case of a lack or deficiency of national norms? An explicitly affirmative answer in relation to all the provisions of the Convention certainly cannot be given. However, in my opinion the courts should be wary of declaring a lack of clarity of certain norms of the Convention and denying their direct application. Specifically, lack of clarity in

[29] For the interpretation of the term 'within the framework of its national legislation' see United Nations Economic Commission for Europe (2013a), pp. 32–34.

[30] ECE/MP.PP/2005/13, 11 March 2005. http://www.unece.org/fileadmin/DAM/env/documents/2005/pp/ece/ece.mp.pp.2005.13.e.pdf, paras 36–38. Accessed 30 June 2013.

[31] Ibid, para 36.

[32] Ibid.

[33] For the restrictive case law of the French State Council (*Conseil d'Etat*) in providing direct effect of the norms of international treaties, see Betaille (2009), pp. 63–73. For a similar restrictive case law of the Czech Supreme Administrative Court (Nejvyšší správní spoud), see Passer (2001), pp. 41–48.

the application of norms of international treaties is comparable to the situation of the interpretation of domestic legal norms. Certain ambiguities in legal norms do not necessarily mean that the norm automatically becomes inapplicable, since courts are bound to apply the law, including international treaties. National courts should interpret the relevant national norms in accordance with the requirements of the Aarhus Convention and in many cases this should be sufficient to fulfil its goals of providing access to information, public participation in decision-making and access to justice in environmental matters.[34]

How does a court deal with a case of conflict between national norms and the Aarhus Convention? Taking into consideration that the Aarhus Convention is part of the *acquis communautaire*, the answer to this question depends on whether the country concerned is an EU Member State or not. In EU Member States, if the provisions of domestic law are incompatible with or contrary to the Convention (for example, due to the incorrect implementation of the provisions in national legislation or the retaining of existing national norms that are contrary to the Convention), national authorities should, in line with the principles of direct effect and supremacy of EU law, directly apply the provision of the Aarhus Convention that is clear, precise and unconditional. If an issue is regulated by a provision of the Convention which is not sufficiently clear and precise to have direct effect and the relevant provisions of national law are incompatible with the Convention or there is no adequate provision of domestic law, the national authorities must, as far as possible, interpret domestic law in line with the objectives of the Convention. With respect to the Aarhus Convention, this obligation was established by the Court of Justice of the EU in judgment C-240/09 *Lesoochranárske zoskupenie VLK*. In this case of reference for a preliminary ruling by the Slovakian Supreme Court, the Grand Chamber of the CJEU ruled that:

> Article 9(3) of the Convention on access to information, public participation in decision-making and access to justice in environmental matters ... does not have direct effect in European Union law. It is, however, for the referring court to interpret, to the fullest extent possible, the procedural rules relating to the conditions to be met in order to bring administrative or judicial proceedings in accordance with the objectives of Article 9(3) of that convention and the objective of effective judicial protection of the rights conferred by European Union law, in order to enable an environmental protection organisation, such as the *Lesoochranárske zoskupenie*, to challenge before a court a decision taken following administrative proceedings liable to be contrary to European Union environmental law.

The requirement to interpret national law in conformity with Union law is called the principle (doctrine) of consistent interpretation.[35]

In countries that are not EU Member States, if a court in its proceedings determines that the law to be applied, or some of its provisions, are not in accordance with ratified international treaties, it shall stop the proceedings and

[34] For the same opinion, see Černý (2009).

[35] For judicial application of the doctrines of direct effect and consistent interpretation in the field of EU environmental law, see Jans et al. (2013).

initiate a review of the constitutionality of the law before the Constitutional Court.[36]

In our search for cases of direct application of the Aarhus Convention by courts in Southeast Europe, we have not been able to find many examples.[37] There are many possible explanations for the rare application of the Convention. The European Union has adopted several legal instruments, binding on its Member States, that include rules on access to information, public participation in decision-making and access to justice in environmental matters (e.g. Directives 2003/4/EC, 85/337/EEC, 2001/42/EC, 2003/35/EC, 2004/35/EC). In the process of harmonisation with the *acquis*, EU candidate countries must align their legislation with the EU directives. In most of the countries of Southeast Europe, implementation of the Aarhus Convention was part of such a process of harmonisation with EU law. Therefore, in situations where the provisions of the Aarhus Convention are relevant to the merits of the case, the courts will apply the corresponding norms of domestic legislation rather than the provisions of an international treaty. There is another restrictive factor for the direct application of the Convention in environmental cases. The Convention does not contain any provisions that prescribe the level of the quality of the environment (e.g. levels of air or water quality) that should be protected, since it only covers procedural environmental rights (access to information, public participation and access to justice). Thus, in many environmental cases the provisions of the Convention will not be relevant for the adjudication of the dispute.[38] The failure of a State to ensure a certain standard of the right to a healthy environment will not constitute a breach of the Aarhus convention, provided that all the procedural rights guaranteed by the Convention have been respected.

---

[36] See Article 145(2) of the Albanian Constitution, Article VI.3(c) of the Constitution of Bosnia and Herzegovina, Article 44 of the Act on Constitutional Court of Montenegro (*Sl. list Crne Gore* No. 64/08) and Article 63 of the Serbian Act on the Constitutional Court (*Sl. glasnik RS* No. 109/2007, 99/2011 and 18/2013). To my knowledge, the Rules of Procedure of the Macedonian Constitutional Court do not contain similar provisions.

[37] To my knowledge, and also based on the information received from other authors of this book, no cases have been reported in Bosnia and Herzegovina, Macedonia, Montenegro and Serbia. There have been very few cases in Slovenia and Croatia where the Aarhus Convention was mentioned in judgments but not directly applied (in Slovenia: Judgment of the Administrative Court, I U 2/2010; in Croatia: Judgment of the Administrative Court, Us-7555/2004-5, Judgment of the Misdemeanour Court in Zagreb, VI-G-2047-09).

[38] Examples where the court found that the Aarhus convention was not relevant for the merits of the case were found in Slovenia (Judgment of the Administrative Court, I U 2/2010), and Macedonia (*Citizens of Veles v. Republic of Macedonia*). The Slovenian case concerned the issuance of an environmental permit. In this case, the court determined that the '...Aarhus Convention invoked by the plaintiff does not contain provisions that can be directly taken into account in the procedure...'. In the case before the Macedonian courts, the basic court in Veles and the appellate court in Skopje applied the EC Directive 2004/35/EC and not the provisions of the Aarhus Convention.

3.1 A Case of the Direct Application of the Aarhus Convention in Croatia

Since the Aarhus Convention came into force in respect of Croatia, there has only been one judgment of the Administrative Court of Republic of Croatia in which the provisions of the Aarhus Convention were directly applied.[39]

The Croatian Society for Bird and Nature Protection submitted a request to make copies of the complete environmental impact assessment (EIA) study for the project ‘Control works on the River Drava from 0 +000 to 56 +000 rkm’. The Ministry of Environmental Protection allowed access to the entire study. However, the request for making copies of the study was rejected because it might reasonably be expected this would endanger the intellectual property of the author of the study. The Society appealed without success. The Society then brought an action against the second-instance decision before the Administrative Court. The Administrative Court dismissed the lawsuit (Judgment of 23 October 2009, Us-5235/2009-5). In my opinion, the Administrative Court wrongly interpreted the relevant provisions of the Convention in several important points.

The first error was that the Administrative Court did not examine whether the study was really protected by copyright, but it held this to be indisputable. The Court only found that, pursuant to Art. 4(4), a request for environmental information may be refused if the disclosure would adversely affect, among other things, intellectual property rights. It did not give any reasons for the opinion that copying the EIA study was forbidden on the grounds of intellectual property law. It also did not explain why copying the study would adversely affect intellectual property rights. The plaintiff noted that he had never abused anyone’s intellectual property rights. He never intended to become an authorised developer of environmental studies. Therefore, there was not even a theoretical risk of abuse of intellectual property rights.

There are also cases from EU Member States where administrations have refused public access to EIA studies with the argument that the studies are protected by copyright or intellectual property provisions.[40] The Aarhus Convention Compliance Committee in its report with regard to communication ACCC/C/2005/15 concerning compliance by Romania raised doubts that intellectual property rights could ever be applicable in connection with EIA documentation:

> Even if it could be, the grounds for refusal are to be interpreted in a restrictive way, taking into account the public interest served by disclosure. Decisions on exempting parts of the information from disclosure should themselves be clear and transparent as to the reasoning for non-disclosure. Furthermore, disclosure of EIA studies in their entirety should be considered as the rule, with the possibility for exempting parts of them being an exception to the rule.[41]

---

[39] This chapter contains parts of my article: Ofak (2012), pp. 16–17.

[40] Krämer (2011), p. 34.

[41] Report by the Compliance Committee, Addendum, Compliance by Romania with its obligations under the Convention, ECE/MP.PP/2008/5/Add.7, 16 April 2008, para 30.

The Administrative Court held that the right of the plaintiff had not been violated since he had been granted access to the complete study. He was only deprived of the right to copy it. However, the right to copy information is an integral part of the right of access to information.

Public authorities must make information available to the public, including, where requested, copies of the actual documentation containing or comprising such information (Art. 4(1)). A copy of the document, i.e. receiving information in the form requested, can be denied if it is reasonable for the public authority to make it available in another form, in which case reasons shall be given for making it available in that form, or if the information is already publicly available in another form (Art. 4(1)). Since the Ministry of Environmental Protection published a summary of the study on an official website, the Administrative Court considered that Art. 4(1) was respected in this case. In my opinion, this is not a valid interpretation of Art. 4(1). The Society requested a copy of the entire study. Another form in which information is made available must constitute the functional equivalent of the form requested, not just the summary. The information should be available in its entirety.[42]

Although this is only one judgment in which the court directly applied the provisions of the Aarhus Convention, it is evident that it did not comply with the role of protector of the rights guaranteed by the Convention. It is not enough to read what the norm of the Convention prescribes, but to understand its true meaning.

In order to understand the provisions of the Convention which, especially in Article 9, use expressions that are subject to interpretation (e.g. effectiveness, timeliness, fairness, equitability, etc.), it is important to take into consideration the findings of the Aarhus Convention Compliance Committee (ACCC) in cases that were brought before it. Non-compliance or misapplication of the Convention in domestic practice can be avoided by being acquainted with the case law of the Compliance Committee. In addition, cases of non-compliance with the Convention of other Parties can be used in the formulation of proposals for amendments to the same or similar national legislation and/or practices that were determined to be contrary to the Convention. The impediment to broader knowledge of the case law of the Compliance Committee is that its Reports are not accessible in official/national languages. Moreover, judges do not have access to information on relevant ACCC case law through specific departments at the court or at the Ministry of Justice. On the other hand, States have responsibility to provide training for judges in cases which involve protection of rights guaranteed by international treaties. It seems that the Parties have recognised the importance of providing courses for judges on the topic of the Aarhus Convention.[43]

[42] United Nations Economic Commission for Europe (2013a), p. 75.

[43] Some examples are: 'In January 2013, the Judicial Training Institute organized a training seminar for judges on implementing the Access to Justice Pillar of Aarhus Convention. It is a part of a program Capacity Building to Put the Aarhus Convention into Action and Support Development of PRTR Systems in Serbia'. (Drenovak Ivanović and Lukić (2013)); in Macedonia, the Academy for Judges offers a course on criminal cases and misdemeanours against the

4 Aarhus Convention Compliance Committee Case Law Related to the Countries of Southeast Europe

Article 15 of the Aarhus Convention on review of compliance requires a Meeting of the Parties to establish optional arrangements of a non-confrontational, non-judicial and consultative nature for reviewing compliance with the provisions of the Convention. One of the particularities of the Aarhus Convention is that it has opened the way for the establishment of a control mechanism that will be available not only to Parties, but also to individuals. At the first meeting of the Parties to the Convention in October 2002, Decision I/7 on Review of Compliance[44] was adopted and the first members of the Compliance Committee were appointed. The compliance mechanism enables individuals to refer to the Committee cases of non-compliance, and the Committee in turn can provide expert assistance to Parties to the Convention for the harmonisation of their legislation and/or practice with the Convention.[45] Specifically, a review of compliance may be triggered in four ways:

(1) a Party may make a submission about compliance by another Party (so far, there has been only one case initiated by Romania about compliance by Ukraine (ACCC/S/2004/1));
(2) a Party may make a submission concerning its own compliance (no submissions yet);
(3) the secretariat may make a referral to the Committee (to date, no referrals have been made by the secretariat);
(4) members of the public may make communications concerning a Party's compliance with the convention (83 communications as of 30 June 2013).

In its Report submitted to the second Meeting of the Parties, the Committee noted that the compliance procedure is designed to improve compliance with the Convention and is not a redress procedure for violations of individual rights.[46] The competence of the Committee is limited by the fact that the Meeting of the Parties is the main decision-making body in respect of non-compliance. The Committee, as a rule, holds meetings four times a year, and Meetings of Parties are held every 3 years. Since 3 years is a relatively long period of time, the Committee may, for the

environment and nature that provides an introduction to the provisions of the Aarhus Convention (Risteska and Miševa 2013); in 2013 education for judges on the Aarhus Convention is also being provided in Bosnia and Herzegovina (Meškić and Samardžić 2013); in Croatia, the Judicial Academy, in cooperation with non-governmental organisations Green Istria and GONG, organised training for judges on the Aarhus Convention in September 2011.

[44] http://www.unece.org/env/pp/documents/mop1/ece.mp.pp.2.add.8.e.pdf. Accessed 30 June 2013.

[45] For ACCC case law and procedures, see, for instance: Jendrośka (2011), pp. 91–147; Andrusevych et al. (2011); Koester (2007), pp. 83–96.

[46] Report to the second Meeting of the Parties, *supra* note 30, para 13.

purpose of resolving cases without delay, take certain measures if it finds non-compliance with the Convention in the period between the Meetings of the Parties. These measures are subject to subsequent review by the Meeting of the Parties, and include:

a) providing advice and facilitating assistance to individual Parties regarding the implementation of the Convention;
b) making recommendations to the Party concerned;
c) requesting the Party concerned to submit a strategy, including a time schedule, to the Compliance Committee regarding achieving compliance with the Convention and reporting on the implementation of this strategy;
d) In cases of communications from the public, making recommendations to the Party concerned on specific measures to address the matter raised by the member of the public.[47]

Measures under b) and d) may be taken only if the Party concerned gives consent. Koester Veit, former Chairperson of the Committee (2002–2011), noted that so far the Committee has managed to persuade the Parties to agree to the recommendations, pointing out to them that, in the event of their non-compliance, it would submit a decision to the Meeting of the Parties. However, if the Party agrees to the recommendations of the Committee, and if it shows some improvement in compliance, the Committee will not submit a separate decision on its non-compliance at the next Meeting of the Parties, but it will only mention the case in its report.[48]

In the case of non-compliance, the Committee may propose to the Meeting of the Parties that it undertake one or more of the following measures:

a) provide advice and facilitate assistance to individual Parties regarding the implementation of the Convention;
b) make recommendations to the Party concerned;
c) request the Party concerned to submit a strategy, including a time schedule, to the Compliance Committee regarding the achievement of compliance with the Convention and to report on the implementation of this strategy;
d) in cases of communications from the public, make recommendations to the Party concerned on specific measures to address the matter raised by a member of the public;
e) issue declarations of non-compliance;
f) issue cautions;
g) suspend, in accordance with the applicable rules of international law concerning the suspension of the operation of a treaty, the special rights and privileges accorded to the Party concerned under the Convention;

[47] See United Nations Economic Commission for Europe (2013b).

[48] Koester (2007), p. 87.

h) take such other non-confrontational, non-judicial and consultative measures as may be appropriate.[49]

Since the powers of the Committee have a consultative character, the Meeting of the Parties is not required to adopt its recommendations. However, so far, the Meeting of the Parties has confirmed all the findings of non-compliance and adopted most of the recommendations of the Committee.

Out of 83 communications, only four cases have been triggered by members of the public concerning compliance with the Convention with regard to the countries of Southeast Europe (two concerning Albania and two concerning Croatia).[50]

4.1 The Review of Compliance by Albania

The first case of review of compliance by Albania with its obligations under the Convention was initiated in response to a communication (ACCC/C/2005/12) from the Alliance for the Protection of the Vlora Gulf concerning public access to information and participation in decision-making on the construction of an industrial park and a thermal electric power station in Vlora, Albania. The Alliance claimed that the public concerned was neither properly notified nor consulted in decision-making on the planning of an industrial park including oil and gas pipelines, storage of petroleum, thermal power plants and a refinery on a site of 560 ha inside a Protected National Park.

With respect to the proposed industrial and energy park, the Committee found that the decision by the Council of Territorial Adjustment of the Republic of Albania to allocate territory for the Industrial and Energy Park of Vlora fell within the scope of Article 7 (i.e. public participation during the preparation of plans and programmes relating to the environment). Albania failed to implement the requirements in the relevant decision-making process and thus was not in compliance with Article 7. With respect to the decision by the Council of Territorial Adjustment on the siting of the thermal electric power station near Vlora, the Committee found that, although some efforts were made to provide for public participation, these largely took place after the crucial decision on siting and were subject to some qualitative deficiencies. Thus, the Party concerned failed to comply fully with the requirements of the Aarhus Convention in question (Article 6, paragraphs 3, 4 and 8). By failing to establish a clear, transparent and consistent framework to implement the provisions of the

[49] United Nations Economic Commission for Europe (2013b), p. 7.

[50] Two of those procedures were stopped (dismissed). One case regarding Albania (ACCC/C/2008/25) was stopped due to lack of information and because the issues resembled those related to the Vlora Power Plant for which the Committee had reached its findings. The other case concerning Croatia (ACCC/C/2013/80) was also dismissed due to a lack of corroborating information.

Convention in Albanian legislation, the Committee also found that Albania was not in compliance with Article 3(1) of the Convention.[51]

On the third meeting held in Riga in June 2008, the Meeting of the Parties approved the findings of the Compliance Committee as regards Albania's failure to comply with the Convention.[52] Albania was requested to annually submit progress reports to the Compliance Committee with regard to the implementation of the Committee's recommendations. These recommendations referred to ensuring early and adequate opportunities for public participation in decision-making in environmental matters. In its Report from the meeting held in February 2011, the Committee noted with appreciation that Albania had seriously and actively engaged to follow the recommendations and that it was no longer in a state of non-compliance with the provisions of the Aarhus Convention.[53]

This case shows the positive outcome that can be reached by initiating the compliance mechanism. After the Meeting of the Parties decided in 2008 that it was in non-compliance, Albania had the obligation to regularly report what progress had been made regarding improvement of the existing legal framework. Finally, the Compliance Committee in 2011 decided that Albania had solved its compliance problems.

4.2 *The Review of Compliance by Croatia*

On 24 January 2012, a Croatian Association for Nature, Environment and Sustainable Development 'Sunce' submitted a communication alleging non-compliance with the Convention by Croatia. They claimed that waste management plans were adopted in a number of towns in Croatia without inspection control and public participation, as provided under the Environmental Protection Act. This, according to the communication, constitutes non-compliance with Article 7 of the Aarhus Convention. A discussion before the Compliance Committee was held in December 2012. Draft findings and recommendations have not been adopted yet by the Committee. Hopefully, this case will clarify the obligation of the public authorities to provide public participation in the preparation of waste management plans.

---

[51] Report of the Compliance Committee on its sixteenth meeting. Addendum. Findings and recommendations with regards to compliance by Albania, ECE/MP.PP/C.1/2007/4/Add.1, 31 July 2007, para 92. http://www.unece.org/fileadmin/DAM/env/documents/2007/pp/ECE_MP.PP_C_1_2007_4_Add_1.pdf. Accessed 30 June 2013.

[52] Decision III/6a of the Meeting of the Parties on compliance by Albania with its obligations under the Convention, ECE/MP.PP/2008/2/Add.9, 26 September 2008. http://www.unece.org/fileadmin/DAM/env/pp/compliance/MoP3decisions/Albania/ece_mp_pp_2008_2_add_9_e_Albania%20ODS.pdf. Accessed 30 June 2013.

[53] Report of the Compliance Committee on its 31st meeting. Addendum. Compliance by Albania with its obligations under the Convention, ECE/MP.PP/C.1/2011/2/Add.1, April 2011, para. 22. http://www.unece.org/fileadmin/DAM/env/pp/compliance/CC-31/ece_mp.pp_c.1_2011_2_add.1_adv%20edited.pdf. Accessed 30 June 2013.

5 Other Complaint Mechanisms with Regard to Projects Which May Have a Significant Effect on the Environment

Since major projects that have a significant effect on the environment require substantial funds, in many cases their execution would not be possible without financial loans. One of the institutions that often provides such loans to the countries of Southeast Europe is the European Bank for Reconstruction and Development.

In 2012, the national electricity company (*Hrvatska elektroprivreda d.d.*—HEP) started to implement a plan to construct the Ombla underground hydropower plant based on an environmental impact assessment that was conducted in 1999. On the day of Croatia's accession to the EU, the location of Ombla was due to enter the ecological network Natura 2000. In 2008, the Croatian State Institute for Nature Protection declared the project 'unacceptable for nature'. In addition, many experts raised concerns, since this location had the highest biodiversity in Croatia and was one of the richest underground biodiversity sites in the world. Nevertheless, in 2011 the European Bank for Reconstruction and Development approved an EUR 123 million loan for the construction of HPP Ombla.

In order to protect Croatian biodiversity, Green Action—Friends of the Earth Croatia (a Croatian environmental association) filed formal complaints at the international level. The first set of complaints was addressed to the European Commission and the European Parliament.[54] The obstacle here was that Croatia was still not a member of the EU. Thus, any recommendations that the EU institutions gave to the Croatian institutions on this matter would not be legally binding. The second formal complaint was to the European Bank of Reconstruction and Development (EBRD). The complaint was based on the EBRD's Project Complaint Mechanism.[55] The Mechanism is open to individuals and groups directly located or having interest in the area of an EBRD-financed project, as well as to civil society organisations. The EBRD decided to suspend the loan disbursement until the launch of a new biodiversity study for Ombla. The study that came out in March 2013 showed that there would be damage to biodiversity. On 27 May 2013, HEP announced that they agreed with EBRD to cancel the loan.[56]

This case illustrates two main points. First, it was impossible for civil society organisations to challenge the EIA study of 1999, since it had become final 12 years

---

[54] CEE Bankwatch Network, Ombla hydropower project under fire in the European Parliament. http://bankwatch.org/bwmail/52/ombla-hydropower-project-under-fire-european-parliament. Accessed 30 June 2013.

[55] Zelena akcija/Friends of the Earth Croatia, Complaint to the EBRD's Project Complaint Mechanism regarding the Ombla hydropower project, Croatia. http://www.ebrd.com/downloads/integrity/Ombla_complaint_17.11.2011.pdf. Accessed 30 June 2013.

[56] EBRD's response to the civil society organisation letter. http://bankwatch.org/sites/default/files/response-EBRD-Ombla-04Jun2013.pdf. Accessed 30 June 2013.

previously and all the deadlines for submitting legal remedies had passed. Therefore, they did not have access to any adequate and effective remedies for initiating a review procedure of the legality of the construction of the Ombla hydropower plant. The only way of instituting some kind of control mechanism was at the international level. Second, the case demonstrates the positive impact of Croatian accession to the EU on decision-making in environmental matters. On the day of Croatia's EU accession, the location of Ombla entered into the Natura 2000 network. HEP has to prove that the final result of the project cannot be achieved by any other means without a harmful impact on nature. The conclusion is that such a new process means prolonging the procedure because of necessary changes to the project and obtaining new permits. This new procedure will have to be carried out in accordance with the relevant national and EU environmental legislation that was not applicable in 1999 when the first environmental impact assessment for this project was conducted.

A similar dispute regarding the construction of the *Boškov Most* hydropower plant in Macedonia was also initiated before the EBRD.[57] This project involves the construction of a 33 m high accumulation dam and hydropower plant with a total capacity of 68 MW. The total project cost is EUR 84 million, with the EBRD providing a loan of 65 million. The EBRD approved the project in November 2011 and signed the finance contract the same year.[58] One civil society organisation Eko-svest from Macedonia submitted a complaint to the Project Complaint Mechanism. The complaint stated that the Environmental and Social Impact Assessment study for the project was incomplete, and important biodiversity facts about the project area were unknown.[59] The complaint was found eligible and an eligibility report was published in May 2012. This and the Croatian case illustrate that civil society organisations are using all the available complaint mechanisms that could potentially lead to better decisions concerning projects that have a significant adverse effect on nature.

6 Conclusion

Members of the public in the countries of Southeast Europe have access to several mechanisms to ensure the effective and proper implementation of the Aarhus Convention. Indeed, the Convention prohibits discrimination, which means that members of the public from one country, as the public concerned, can exercise the

[57] Risteska and Miševa (2013).

[58] CEE Bankwatch Network, the Boskov Most hydropower plant (Macedonia) and the EBRD's Project Complaint Mechanism. http://bankwatch.org/sites/default/files/briefing-EBRD-BoskovMost-10May2013.pdf. Accessed 30 June 2013.

[59] Eko-svest, Complaint to the EBRD's Project Complaint Mechanism regarding the Boskov Most hydropower project, Macedonia. http://www.ebrd.com/downloads/integrity/Boskov_complaint_7.11.2011.pdf. Accessed 30 June 2013.

rights guaranteed by the Convention in another country that is also party to the Convention. Mechanisms that can be used include a review by the Constitutional Court on whether the provisions of domestic laws and regulations are in accordance with the Aarhus Convention. So far, there has been only one such case in Slovenia.

Civil society organisations sometimes use complaints mechanisms that are available at the international level (e.g. communications to the Aarhus Convention Compliance Committee and submission of complaints to the EBRD's Project Complaint Mechanism). Some examples from Albania, Croatia and Macedonia demonstrate that these mechanisms can lead to positive changes regarding public participation in decision-making in environmental matters.

Our survey showed that there have not been many examples of the direct application of the Aarhus Convention by the courts in SEE countries. In situations where the Aarhus Convention could be applied, the courts would rather apply the rules of domestic legislation that are relevant to the merits of the case, or the provisions of the EU directives that regulate access to information, public participation in decision-making and access to justice in environmental matters. In addition, in many environmental cases the Aarhus Convention will not be applicable, since it does not contain any substantive rules regarding the right to a healthy environment. However, this does not diminish its importance. The creators of the Aarhus Convention predicted the obstacles to access to justice in environmental cases at all stages of a procedure, and for each of these obstacles they tried to give an appropriate solution. Therefore, there is big task before the public concerned to take joint action to enhance the level of implementation of environmental law and the exercise of the right to a healthy environment. This requires greater professionalisation of environmental organisations and the use of advice of legal experts and attorneys who are sufficiently capable to represent in such cases before the courts. This also requires the introduction of high-quality environmental education of law students in legal studies, as well as of civil servants and judges in the framework of their professional training.

References

Andrusevych A, Alge T, Konrad C (eds) (2011) Case law of the Aarhus Convention Compliance Committee (2004–2011), 2nd edn. RACSE, Lviv

Betaille J (2009) The direct effect of the Aarhus Convention as seen by the French Conseil d'Etat. Environ Law Netw Int Rev 2:63–73

Černý P (2009) Practical application of Article 9 of the Aarhus Convention in some EU countries – comparative remarks. In: Environmental Law Service et al (eds) Selected problems of the Aarhus Convention application based on experience and court practice of NGOs in 7 EU countries. http://www.justiceandenvironment.org/_files/file/2009/09/access_to_justice_collection.pdf. Accessed 30 June 2013

Drenovak Ivanović M, Lukić M (2013) Questionnaire – judicial application of the Aarhus convention in Serbia

Jans JH, Marcory R, Moreno Molina A-M (eds) (2013) National courts and EU environmental law. Europa Law Publishing, Groningen

Jendrośka J (2011) Public participation in environmental decision-making. Interactions between the Convention and EU law and other key legal issues in its implementation in the light of the opinions of the Aarhus Convention Compliance Committee. In: Pallemaerts M (ed) The Aarhus Convention at ten: interactions and tensions between conventional international law and EU environmental law. Europa Law Publishing, Groningen, pp 91–147

Koester V (2007) The compliance committee of the Aarhus convention: an overview of procedures and jurisprudence. Environ Policy Law 37(2–3):83–96

Krämer L (2011) The application of the Aarhus Convention in the European Union. In: Radojčić D (ed) Enforcement of the Aarhus Convention in the Adriatic region countries. Zelena Istra, Pula, p 34

May J, Daly E (2009) Vindicating fundamental environmental rights: judicial acceptance of constitutionally entrenched environmental rights. Or Rev Int Law 11:365–439

Meškić Z, Samardžić D (2013) Questionnaire – judicial application of the Aarhus Convention in Bosnia and Herzegovina

Ofak L (2012) Public participation in decisions on specific activities in environmental matters in Croatia. Environ Law Netw Int Rev 1:16–17

Omejec J (2009) Legal framework and case-law of the Constitutional Court of Croatia in deciding on the conformity of laws with international treaties, pp 7–8

Pallemaerts M (2004) Proceduralizing environmental rights: the Aarhus Convention on Access to Information, public participation in decision-making and access to justice in environmental matters in a human rights context. In: Perrez FX et al (eds) Human rights and the environment: proceedings of a Geneva environment network roundtable, pp 14–21

Passer JM (2001) European perspectives on access to justice in environmental matters. In: Radojčić D (ed) Enforcement of the Aarhus Convention in the Adriatic region countries. Zelena Istra, Pula, pp 41–48

Pedersen OW (2008) European environmental human rights and environmental rights: a long time coming? Georgetown Int Environ Law Rev 21(1):73–111

Risteska M, Miševa K (2013) Questionnaire – judicial application of Aarhus Convention in Macedonia (answers to the questionnaire on file with the author)

United Nations Economic Commission for Europe (2013a) The Aarhus Convention: an implementation guide. http://www.unece.org/fileadmin/DAM/env/pp/ppdm/Aarhus_Implementation_Guide_second_edition_-_text_only.pdf. Accessed 30 June 2013

United Nations Economic Commission for Europe (2013b) Guidance document on the Aarhus Convention compliance mechanism. http://www.unece.org/fileadmin/DAM/env/pp/compliance/CC_GuidanceDocument.pdf. Accessed 30 June 2013

Wates J (2011) An introduction to the Aarhus Convention. In: Radojčić D (ed) Enforcement of the Aarhus Convention in the Adriatic region countries. Zelena Istra, Pula, p 14

Part III
National Reports on the Judicial Application of International Law

‘Europeanisation’ of the Judiciary in Southeast Europe

Sanja Bogojević

1 Introduction

With the creation of what today is the European Union (EU) began the practice of ‘Europeanisation’ of laws in Europe. This signifies the processes of endorsing EU law and European integration by, *inter alia*, implementing the corpus of laws stemming from European law making, as well as adapting and training domestic official bodies to cooperate with EU-based institutions.[1] This process was catalysed by the Court of Justice of the EU (CJEU), which proclaimed EU law a ‘new legal order’, distinct from both national and international law,[2] and having supremacy over national bodies of laws of the Member States.[3] In this chapter, what is examined are the ways in which the judiciary in Southeast Europe—covering Slovenia, Croatia, Bosnia and Herzegovina (BiH), Serbia, Kosovo*,[4] the Former Yugoslav Republic of Macedonia (FYR Macedonia), and Albania—has dealt with the process of Europeanisation in the light of EU membership and membership aspirations. The courts in Southeast Europe make a fascinating study for at least two reasons.

To start with, they are the legal cornerstones of countries that share a common political and legal history; or, in the recent past they were run according to communist ideology. The Communist Party seized control of Albania following

[1] Howell (2004), p. 20. For an overview of the Europeanisation of different areas of law in Europe, see Snyder (2000).

[2] Case 26/62 *Van Gend en Loos v. Nederlandse Administratie der Belastingen* [1963] ECR 1.

[3] Case 6/64 *Costa v. ENEL* [1964] ECR 585.

[4] This designation is without prejudice to positions on status, and is in line with UNSC 1244 and the ICJ Opinion on the Kosovo Declaration of Independence.

S. Bogojević (✉)
Lund University, 22100 Lund, Sweden
e-mail: Sanja.Bogojevic@jur.lu.se

S. Rodin, T. Perišin (eds.), *Judicial Application of International Law in Southeast Europe*, DOI 10.1007/978-3-662-46384-0_5

the Second World War, and officially it became the People's Republic in 1946.[5] In the same period, Slovenia, Croatia, BiH, Montenegro, Serbia, Kosovo and FYR Macedonia formed part of the Socialist Federal Republic of Yugoslavia (SFRY, 1945–1991).[6] This communality is significant because it implies that the judiciary in Southeast Europe has, due to its history, had similar attitudes towards law and the legal profession. Rodin explains that in a communist legal system:

> [j]udges were supposed to follow, not to interpret, the will of the legislature not only and not primarily because of the hierarchical structure of the legal system, but because of the authoritarian nature of the political system.[7]

This technocratic role of judges meant that law was understood as being objective, and the act of legal interpretation 'a process of deduction, void of any contextual considerations'.[8] Examining the application of international law, as well as the national courts' reasoning in this regard, allows us to analyse whether, and if so, how, the judiciary in Southeast Europe has moved away from its communist-oriented legal reasoning.

Moreover, countries in Southeast Europe share a common political and legal goal: to be part of the 'new legal order', or the EU. They, nevertheless, are at different stages of fulfilling this objective. Slovenia has formed part of the EU since 2004 and Croatia, joining on 1 July 2013, is the EU's newest member. BiH, Albania, Serbia, FYR Macedonia and Kosovo are at different stages of being granted or of negotiating their candidacy.[9] Examining whether the respective national courts have embraced these legal aspirations and applied international law is a useful exercise in analysing the extent to which both the idea and realisation of EU membership have impacted on the legal reasoning of the national courts.

There are a number of important caveats to bear in mind when analysing the application of international law by the domestic courts in Southeast Europe. To start with, this is not an exercise in simply spotting the formal rules and procedures allowing such application. Rather, the actual life given to international law, that is, the meaning and the legal implication that follow such interpretation, is the focal part of this investigation. Another important limitation is that such an enquiry does not seek to prescribe a particular judicial route for national judiciaries in new, or aspiring, EU Member States. Instead, this study has the objective of identifying *whether* national courts in the Southeast parts of Europe have taken international law into consideration and, if so, *how* this has been done.

---

[5] For an overview, see Oakes and Verrija (2002), p. 25.

[6] In line with the 1974 Constitution of SFRY, the Federation was constituted by Bosnia, Croatia, Macedonia, Montenegro, Serbia and Slovenia, as well as two 'socialist autonomous provinces'—Kosovo and Vojvodina.

[7] Rodin (2009). See also Kühn (2006), p. 19.

[8] Rodin (2009). p. 2.

[9] Serbia, FYR Macedonia and Albania are 'candidate countries' and Kosovo, BiH are 'potential candidate countries'. For an overview, see http://ec.europa.eu/enlargement/countries/check-current-status/index_en.htm.

The next part of this chapter goes on to explain why national courts matter in the process of the 'Europeanisation' of law. In the third section, the different judicial systems examined in this book are introduced: first, against their historical backgrounds, and then by outlining their judicial constructions. Here, discussion focuses on legal culture or the importance of going beyond the mere wording of the law in order to appreciate the implications of law. In the fourth section, the national reports are analysed in a comparative manner and, finally, fifth section evaluates these, together with the general findings of this chapter.

2 What Have National Courts Got to Do with It?

At the risk of stating the obvious, a necessary condition for effective judicial control is a rational judicial architecture.[10] It is crucial to consider national courts, as well as international courts, in any investigation of the exercise of law. Along similar lines but in a more general context, Ewing and Kysar describe the role of the judiciary as forming part of a system of 'prods and pleas'. This refers to the capacity of different authorities to push each other into action; in the case of judges, they are understood to perform their roles with a view to catalysing activity somewhere else in the system.[11] This means that the role of the court is ultimately to activate a series of actors, including governments or businesses, to take measures to make international law both effective and possible. Over and above these considerations, it is crucial to examine the judiciary in the process of the 'Europeanisation' of law for at least two reasons.

First, the EU is based on a system of cooperative federalism, meaning that all courts—national, as well as EU courts—are entitled and obliged to apply EU law to the disputes before them.[12] Following Article 4(3) TEU[13]—and more precisely, the principle of loyal cooperation—the national courts have a duty to apply EU law. Article 19(1) TEU, which states that Member States shall provide sufficient remedy to ensure effective legal protection in all fields of EU law, supports this duty. From this perspective, national courts are the 'guardians' of the EU legal order,[14] and, as such, the key players in making EU law effective. This means that the Europeanisation of laws in Southeast Europe depends, and will depend once all Southeast European states become EU members, on the national judiciaries.

Second, national courts are crucial actors in the process of shaping the EU legal system. It is primarily via preliminary rulings that a cross-judicial dialogue between domestic and EU courts is created, which tends to lead to this shaping process.

[10] Craig (2012), p. 261.

[11] Ewing and Kysar (2011), p. 350.

[12] Schütze (2012), p. 289.

[13] Consolidated Versions of the Treaty on European Union (TEU) [2008] OJ C115/13.

[14] Schütze (2012).

Indeed, as a result of manifold initiatives from the national courts demanding clarification of EU law, core doctrines of EU law have been established, including direct effect (in *Van Gend en Loos*), the principle of supremacy (*Costa v. ENEL*, *Simmenthal II*), state liability (*Francovich and Bonifaci*), horizontal direct effect (*Defrenne II*), direct effect of directives (*Van Duyn, Marshall*), as well as indirect effect (*Von Colson*).[15] It is mainly, although not exclusively, the lower national courts that have pushed for these references, meaning that in investigating the 'Europeanising' effects in Southeast Europe, the judiciary is a necessary case study—and one that needs to cover all instances.

In short, in the EU legal system, national courts are obliged to follow EU law and ensure its effective application. In doing so, Čapeta explains, the national judges

> were willing to challenge established legal rules...[t]hey challenged either domestic rules, relying on the new values imported by the new European legal order, or the newly-established rules of the European legal order, defending the values of the domestic legal order. They were creative judges who used all the possibilities of the two legal orders to try and improve legal rules.[16]

To what extent such creativity exists in the courts in Southeast Europe is the query investigated next.

3 Starting Point: Looking Back, Going Forward

With the exception of Albania, countries in Southeast Europe were, until recent history, part of a single jurisdiction: SFRY (1945–1991).[17] Like other socialist states, SFRY attempted to create a legal system based on Marxist principles.[18] This changed following the break with Stalin in 1948 when Yugoslavia started creating versions of its own socialist laws,[19] which, following Kühn's explanation, served 'solely the interest of the Party'.[20] This body of law was also uniformly applied through a centralised judiciary, which was created by the federal authorities, and the federal Supreme Court, whose aim was to ensure uniformity in judicial decisions.[21]

This legal system was largely decentralised once the constitution was revised in 1974; each federation received its own constitutional court, leaving the Federal Court with little power. With the proclamation of independence by Slovenia and

15 Čapeta (2005), pp. 23–53. For a more general overview of the procedure of preliminary references, see Tridimas (2003), p. 9.

16 Čapeta (2005), pp. 30–31.

17 See n 6.

18 Hayden (2002), pp. 1799, 1801. For an overview, see Collins (1982).

19 Hayden (2002). For an overview, see Chloros (1970).

20 Kühn (2011), p. 64. Note that Kühn discusses socialist laws more generally.

21 Hayden (2002), p. 1802.

Croatia on 24 June 1991, SFRY began its process of disintegration, and moved toward independent, liberal legal systems.[22] That same year, communism fell also in Albania, where the Communist Party had seized control in 1946.[23]

Today, different legal jurisdictions with distinct judicial structures exist in Southeast Europe. For the most part, judicial power is organised in a four- or three-tiered hierarchical structure with the Supreme Court on top, followed, for example, by courts of general jurisdiction, and administrative and commercial courts. In this type of legal structure, the constitutional court formally falls outside the judicial branch; its role is to rule on the conformity with the constitution of national, and, in certain regards, also international laws. This is the case, for instance, in Albania,[24] FYR Macedonia,[25] and Serbia.[26]

In Slovenia and Croatia,[27] EU law has precedence over national law, and it is the CJEU that is entrusted with the highest authority to rule on its validity. Similarly, the jurisdiction of the European Court of Human Rights is binding. The national courts are organised into courts of general and specialised jurisdiction, the highest court being the Supreme Court. Any questions concerning the constitutionality of laws, however, are—similarly to the jurisdictions mentioned previously—referred to the constitutional court.[28]

Kosovo and BiH share similar judicial structures to the extent that international judges were installed in the national court systems following the Kosovo conflict and the Bosnian War respectively. In accordance with the Dayton Accord that marked the end of the Bosnian War, BiH is composed of two separate entities: a joint Muslim-Croat Federation of Bosnia and Herzegovina (the Federation), and the Serbian Republic of Bosnia and Herzegovina (Republic of Srpska, 'RS').[29] This division is reflected also in the country's judicial system, which has two separate three-tier judicial systems, that is, two different constitutional courts, supreme courts and district courts. BiH also has a national Constitutional Court which has binding legal authority across the entire country—including both the Federation and the RS. This court, which has nine members, is composed of four judges elected by the Federation's House of Representatives, two are appointed by the RS National Assembly and three are international judges named by the president of the

[22] Ibid.

[23] For an overview, see Oakes and Verrija (2002), p. 25.

[24] The High Court, the courts of appeal and the courts of first instance exercise judicial power in Albania. In addition, the Constitutional Court interprets the constitution and decides on the constitutionality of laws via judicial review. See *ibid*, 29–30.

[25] See Risteska and Miševa in this book.

[26] In Serbia, the judicial structure consists of courts of general and specialised jurisdiction. See Mirjana Drenovak Ivanović and Maja Lukić in this book.

[27] For an overview of the Croatian legal structure, see Uzelac (2002), pp. 389, 393. Note, however, that with Croatia joining the EU, the Court of Justice of the European Union has sole competence to interpret the compatibility of Croatian national law and EU law.

[28] Klemenčić (2002), p. 1465.

[29] Gould (2002), pp. 175, 176.

European Court of Human Rights.[30] The Constitutional Court has the sole jurisdiction to resolve any constitutional conflicts between the Federation and RS, as well as to review the laws of the two entities and their conformity with the Bosnian constitution, in addition to decisions made by any other courts in the country.[31] Similarly in Kosovo, international judges form part of the Kosovo judiciary both in the Constitutional Court and the courts of general jurisdiction. These exist within the framework of the European Union Rule of Law Mission in Kosovo (EULEX), which was created and instituted to help adjudicate, for example, crimes committed during the Kosovo conflict.[32]

What this shows is that following the break-up of communism in Southeast Europe in the early 1990s, distinct judicial structures took shape. For the most part, the judiciary in this region consists of a three- or four-tier court system with the Supreme Court entrusted with the highest judicial authority and the constitutional court with the interpretation of constitutional law matters. EU Member States—here, Slovenia and Croatia—follow a slightly different judicial architecture in that it is the CJEU that interprets EU law, which ultimately is also national law. In Kosovo and BiH, on the other hand, the judiciary construction is distinct from all others in Southeast Europe, with international judges forming an important part of the higher court structures. It is important to bear these distinct institutional features in mind in order to understand *how* the judiciary in Southeast Europe is built and how it ultimately functions. This, however, is only part of the story. To appreciate the meaning given to law by these different courts, the legal culture in which these exist and from which they derive must first be examined.

3.1 Beyond Words: The Importance of Legal Culture

'Legal culture' is a ubiquitous concept.[33] It reflects a fusion of social, political, and economic forces that impacts on a law's development, significance and process of implementation, and also expresses the institutional and historical traditions through the legal language in a particular jurisdiction.[34] Each rule or legal framework has a particular meaning tied to a particular place and time,[35] and each legal concept and line of legal argument operates in predetermined traditional contexts that spring from different cultural traditions, or according to a so-called *mentalité*.[36] As such, a rule or regime cannot be examined only as a black-letter text; rather, it

[30] Ibid, p. 178.

[31] Ibid.

[32] See Istrefi and Morina in this book.

[33] Gibson and Caldeira (1996), p. 55. See also Cotterrell (1997), p. 14.

[34] Bogojević (2013), ch. 3.

[35] Legrand (2001), pp. 57–58.

[36] Ibid, p. 65.

must be scrutinised through a culture-specific lens, taking into consideration its legal culture.[37] Such a study may be carried out in various ways: for instance, by focusing on legal culture as a series of 'internal' factors—including judicial decisions, scholarly comments, the architecture of legal institutions—and/or 'external' elements—comprising social behaviour, attitudes to judicial decisions and the informal organisation of behaviour within a community.[38] In this collection of papers, legal culture is explored by examining judicial decisions and how the courts have given effect to international law in Southeast Europe.

Here, it is important to highlight the historical commonality of the countries of Southeast Europe examined, as this explains how the judiciary has traditionally viewed (international) law, as well as the judicial profession. It has already been noted that the judiciaries of Southeast Europe come from authoritarian and totalitarian traditions: its members were trained under a centrally planned economy, receiving a legal education different from that in Western Europe at the time.[39] In Kühn's description, following World War II, continental legal culture underwent a gradual transformation—distinct from that of Southeast Europe. Having strictly adhered to the letter of laws under the Nazi era—leading to some grossly unjust and horrific verdicts—meant that, once the war came to an end, the law and its implications were thoroughly reconsidered.[40] For instance, during this period judicial review of constitutional laws was increasingly practised. This, together with the expansion of state powers and the building of welfare and regulatory social structures, contributed to the transformation of the concept of law. As a result, in 1990—when Southeast European states emerged from their five decades of intellectual isolation from modern Western thought—Western legal culture was very different from what it had been before World War II.[41]

During the same period, in the post-communist countries, the emphasis of the legal profession was placed on the written law with no role, or only a minor one, for interpretation.[42] Rodin explains that, for over 50 years, the development of law in the Southeast Europe was facilitated by:

> an understanding of law as an autonomous science, and an understanding of the task of jurists, both practitioners and legal theorists, as finding the 'right answers' for all legal questions exclusively within the legal system, regardless of social reality.[43]

This static understanding of law had a huge impact on how the judicial profession in the Southeast parts of Europe at the time was viewed. More precisely, legislative sovereignty was put on a pedestal, and law 'operated with the notion of

---

[37] Ibid.

[38] See Friedman (1997), p. 33.

[39] Kühn (2004), p. 531. Note that reference to 'Western' connotes countries that where on the non-communist side of the Iron Curtain, see also Komàrek (2014a).

[40] Kühn (2004), p. 535.

[41] Ibid.

[42] Ibid, p. 540.

[43] Rodin (2005), pp. 1, 6.

unity of state power, not the separation of powers'.[44] Indeed, in the Communist legal systems, 'judges had no discretion at all, even within the bounds of the law',[45] and so both the legal texts, and the judiciary applying these, were understood to operate void of their social context.

In Kühn's view, judicial discourses in the post-communist European states still adopt formalist understandings of the law, although these are 'often clothed in a new legal vocabulary'.[46] Indeed, the national reports that form part of this collection of essays similarly illustrate that the judiciary in Southeast Europe conducts a formalistic reading of the law, even if hints of change are noticeable. This, Kühn explains, is because the effects of Marxism–Leninism run deep into the layers of legal culture, generating 'a significant time lag in the intellectual development of Central and Eastern Europe which could not be overcome within the first post-Communist decade.'[47] Komàrek, however, offers a more nuanced explanation as to why the legal consciousness emerging in post-communist Europe is different from that of its Western counterpart, arguing that:

> 1989 revolutions were somehow taken away from the people of post-communist Europe who never got control over their lives. Liberal democracy coupled with market economy was presented to them as the only alternative...More critical accounts of the post-1989 period thus show how the collapse of communism helped to cement the dominant political-economic order of the last twenty years, which now goes under the name of neoliberalism – and has become contested in the last few years.[48]

What Komàrek vividly points out is that although history is crucial in understanding how a particular legal culture views law, this exercise is rarely straightforward or easy. Clearly, what is needed is a more open engagement with the past. Although this falls outside of the scope of this book, an important first step, as part of such an exercise, is to analyse how the national courts apply (international) law, and whether this has changed, in this case, through the process of the Europeanisation of laws.

4 State of Affairs According to the National Reports

The countries discussed in this book created new constitutions and legal frameworks in the years following the transition from communist to capitalist legal systems. The national reports, examining the institutional capacity to identify and apply international law and international law standards, show that although ratified international law is given preference to national law by the courts examined, the

[44] Bobek (2011), pp. 1, 4.

[45] Ibid.

[46] Kühn (2004), p. 550.

[47] Kühn (2011), p. 160.

[48] Komàrek (2014b).

judiciary remains largely reluctant to apply non-domestic law. It seems, as will be discussed later, that education is a key factor in turning this trend around.

4.1 Constitutional Status of International Law

Ratified international treaties and law are widely incorporated in the constitutional bases of the countries in Southeast Europe—indeed, many of these constitutions are founded on international law. In BiH, for example, the constitution is based on the Dayton Peace Agreement, signed in 1995. Similarly, in FYR Macedonia, the constitution was developed in a 'laboratory' fashion, founded on an extensive list of international treaties,[49] protecting, for example, human rights, largely corresponding to the ECHR, as well as the International Convention on Civil and Political Rights and the International Convention on the Elimination of All Forms of Racial Discrimination.[50] A similar bill of rights exists in the Albanian constitution, as well as in the remaining Southeast European countries, where explicit reference to the ECHR exists.[51] In Croatia, one of the highest constitutional values is the concepts of civil, social and human rights, sometimes directly borrowing the language of the ECHR.[52] The Slovenian constitution also contains a number of elaborated human and social rights and civil liberties based on the ECHR,[53] as does Kosovo's, which was set up following a 'strong regime of domestic incorporation of international law'.[54]

In many of these jurisdictions, a continuous 'Europeanisation' of the national constitutions is taking place. As explained by Meškić and Samardžić, in BiH, international law is incorporated in the domestic legal system in a cooperative, as opposed to hierarchical, fashion.[55] This approach reflects the so-called Solange approach in determining the relationship between different legal orders.[56] In the remaining legal systems in the region, the constitution is traditionally the supreme normative source of law, meaning that all legislation—including applicable international law—must be in conformity with it.[57] Here, international law is normally given effect through ratification, primacy and domestication, or through the incorporation and reproduction of international law and jurisprudence.[58]

[49] Risteska and Miševa in this book.

[50] Krug (2002), pp. 931, 933. For a general overview, see for instance Brashear (1997), p. 18.

[51] Oakes and Verrija (2002), p. 28.

[52] Uzelac (2002), p. 392.

[53] Klemenčić (2002), pp. 1460, 1462.

[54] Istrefi and Morina in this book.

[55] Meškić and Samardžić in this book.

[56] Ibid.

[57] See for instance FYR Macedonia, Krug (2002).

[58] See for instance Kosovo, Istrefi and Morina in this book.

In Slovenia and Croatia, independence in 1991 brought new constitutions that allow for the application of international law, or, more precisely, they provide that laws and regulations must be in compliance with the international agreements that bind them. Moreover, ratified and proclaimed international treaties are directly applicable and have legal force above that of regulatory statutory law. In the initial format, however, supremacy was reserved for the constitution—as tends to be the case in civil law countries. Once Slovenia joined the EU in 2004, and Croatia in 2013, constitutional amendments were required to secure the supremacy of EU law.[59]

Ultimately, what this overview shows is that the jurisdictions in Southeast Europe, as examined in this book, are open to and accepting of international law. To understand to what extent the judiciaries in actual fact apply international law, court practice in this regard needs to be examined. It is to this exercise that we now turn.

4.2 The Application of International Law by National Courts

The national reports show that, on a general level, courts in Southeast Europe practise the application of international law. These are primarily higher courts that focus on rights codified in the ECHR, as exemplified by the report on Kosovo, as well as FYR Macedonia and BiH[60]—at least in relying on international law directly. The remaining court instances refer to international law more frequently once it is transposed in national law. Thus, international law is applied to different degrees depending on which court deals with the particular case.

The most frequently applied source of international law, according to all national reports, is the ECHR. In Kosovo, 90 % of the case law concerning international law in a domestic context is related to rights derived from the ECHR. Similarly, in Slovenia, BiH and FYR Macedonia, the ECHR and its case law are the main international source of law referred to. In Serbia, the judiciary is under an obligation to take international law and its practice into consideration. There, international law has been used to interpret Serbian law, and although it may not have any legal binding force, it is deemed to carry 'moral and political value'.[61] This includes referring to ECHR case law (mainly in specific cases concerning damages for defamation, family disputes, and property disputes), if only to justify the court's

---

[59] See Klemenčić (2002), p. 1462; Uzelac (2002), p. 392.

[60] The *Kalinic* case is particularly interesting in this regard where the Constitutional Court of Bosnia and Herzegovina concluded that BiH had violated Article 13 of the ECHR also when international territorial administrations were responsible for the breach, see Schaap (2011). Available at: http://www.academia.edu/4076996/The_strained_relationship_between_international_administrators_and_local_institutions_Judicial_activism_in_BiH_and_the_demand_for_access_to_justice.

[61] Mirjana Drenovak Ivanović and Maja Lukić in this book.

decision.[62] Along similar lines, the Albanian judiciary has in almost all human rights-related cases pointed to the ECHR.

When it comes to EU law, Slovenia and recently also Croatia, as EU Member States, are under a legal obligation to apply EU law. Slovenia, however, reports little EU-law activity before the national courts; the few cases that deal with this body of law concern mainly asylum and taxation. The Slovenian judiciary has, nonetheless, included references to the Italian, German and North American constitutional courts in interpreting its own constitution. Interestingly, the Albanian judiciary has made direct references to EU law, as has the Supreme Court in Serbia, raising issues relating to the Charter.

In the non-EU states, focus is on the application of SAA, as opposed to the direct application of EU law. These agreements tend to be granted direct effect, which is at least the case in BiH and FYR Macedonia. In the case of the latter, since 2004, when the SAA was signed, a series of new institutions have been created and the WTO, ICTY and the Århus Convention ratified. However, the impact of these institutional changes has been limited, as the judiciary rarely makes reference to any of these international bodies of law (apart from the ECHR).[63] In Albania, on the other hand, the SAA has been in force since 2009 but not all the necessary institutional reforms have been carried out. In Serbia, the SAA is not yet in force. At the time of writing, accession talks are set to open in January 2014 but the Interim Agreement of 2010 is enforced.[64]

Several Southeast European states have also established special institutions and judicial pathways to facilitate the application of international law. In Serbia, a special institution—the Commission for Information of Public Importance and Personal Data Protection—has been set up to help litigators make the necessary international law reference. Additionally, in BiH, litigants have the right to appeal to the provincial Human Rights Commission after they have exhausted all access to the domestic judiciary. This system is understood to help ensure that judicial decisions are in line with European and international principles of human rights.[65] Similarly, the lower courts may refer to constitutional court issues concerning the ECHR or matters of public international law.[66]

Thus, the following national reports on the Europeanisation of laws by the judiciary in Southeast Europe show that institutional structures have been established in such a way so as to facilitate the court's consideration of ratified international law. Although the reports illustrate that such consideration is steadily increasing in number, it is a trend mainly referring to the application of the ECHR, as opposed to international law more generally. The question that emerges, and

[62] *Ibid.*

[63] See Risteska and Miševa in this book.

[64] Mirjana Drenovak Ivanović and Maja Lukić in this book.

[65] Gould (2002), p. 179.

[66] Ibid, p. 178.

which is dealt with in the following and final part of this chapter, is the way in which, if at all, such a trend could be turned around.

5 Reflections

The Southeast European countries examined in this book share a similar recent legal history, but also a future goal: accessing the EU. Indeed, and as illustrated by the national reports, Kosovo, BiH, FYR Macedonia, Serbia, and Albania are all oriented toward signing and joining the EU. In the case of Croatia and Slovenia, this goal has already been reached, but the obligation remains for them to respect their legal commitments. From this perspective, a general political will exists to abide by international law, which, moreover, is clearly expressed in the respective constitutions, allowing supremacy, or at least direct applicability, of ratified international agreements. Still, as the national reports show, national courts are generally reluctant to apply international law directly—unless it is expressly incorporated into national law.[67] This indicates that it is not sufficient to look at the formal rules allowing international law to be part of national jurisprudence when examining the Europeanisation of the judiciary, or when furthering this particular legal development.

Instead, and as argued by Bobek, the focus should be directed at the extent to which the judiciary engages in independent thinking. In other words, what is important is not the creation of institutional frameworks *per se*, but the degree to which the judiciary is able to critically assess and apply various, sometimes conflicting laws.[68] According to the Chief Justice of the Czech Supreme Court, the understanding of the law 'is a matter of legal culture',[69] which can be transformed or/and developed through education that indeed endorses critical thinking. Thus, robust education is the fundamental pillar in creating, and later maintaining, a progressive judicial system.

The national reports similarly point to the importance of education in considering international law within domestic legal systems. However, they paint a pretty dire picture of the extent to which international and EU law is taught at the various universities, and of the stability of these studying possibilities. In Kosovo, for instance, no legal education was available between 1990 and 1999, which is understood to have left the legal profession lagging behind international legal developments. Similarly in BiH, EU law has been taught only in the last 3 years, and in FYR Macedonia only a small percentage of the accredited universities in the country teach EU and international law. Along similar lines, the report from

[67] Uzelac (2002), p. 392. Observation made at least with regard to Croatia.

[68] Bobek (2008), p. 99.

[69] As quoted in Kühn (2004), p. 564. Here, the Chief Justice refers to the Czech judiciary more specifically.

Albania refers to the lack of in-depth training in international law as a possible explanation of why no case has to date dealt with any potential clashes between Albanian constitutional law and international law.

When it comes to educating judges in international and EU law, many Southeast European states provide such training at special institutions, such as the Judicial Academy in Serbia. These often teach EU law, international law, as well as ECHR and ECtHR jurisprudence, with the aim of educating the members of the judiciary in the most recent international law developments. Such training, however, is often dependent on external funding, meaning that it is an unsustainable or at least unreliable educatory system for judges in the region.

Here, Slovenia could be thought of as an exception. International law has been taught since 1992 both at undergraduate and graduate level and judges regularly receive training in both EU law and international law. However, also in this case, little awareness of international law is reported from the Slovenian courtrooms. Obviously, just because EU law is taught in domestic law schools does not mean that the domestic courts will necessarily apply EU law. The fact that the national courts within the EU use preliminary reference in a dramatically uneven number is evidence thereof.[70]

What is crucial, therefore, is not so much the mere *existence* but the *content* of EU law and international law courses, and legal education more generally. Indeed, and as argued by Malleson, robust education can be beneficial to a judicial system if it focuses on the *methods* by which judges arrive at their decisions, rather than simply studying the decisions themselves, or the black-letter law in isolation.[71] In other words, legal education ought to foster and encourage creative and critical thinking, as opposed to simply teaching future lawyers how to mimic the law. Ultimately, the extent to which the future of the Europeanisation of law by the judiciary in Southeast Europe is viable is a question that depends on the type of legal education provided in the region.

References

Bobek M (2008) The fortress of judicial independence and the mental transitions of the central European judiciaries. Public Eur Law 14

Bobek M (2011) Judicial transformations in post-communist societies: a study in institutions, administration and interpretation. CAS Sofia working paper series no. 4, p 1

Bogojević S (2013) Emissions trading schemes: markets, states and law. Hart, Oxford

---

[70] Hornuf and Voigt (2011).

[71] Malleson (1997), pp. 655, 667.

Brashear L (1997) A year in the Balkans: Macedonia and the rule of law. Hum Rights 24
Čapeta T (2005) Courts, legal culture and EU enlargement. Croatian Yearb Eur Law Policy 1
Chloros A (1970) Yugoslav civil law: history, family, property. Oxford University Press, Oxford
Collins H (1982) Marxism and law. Oxford University Press, Oxford
Cotterrell R (1997) The concept of legal culture. In: Nelken D (ed) Comparing legal cultures. Dartmouth, Aldershot
Craig P (2012) EU administrative law, 2nd edn. Oxford University Press, Oxford
Ewing B, Kysar D (2011) Prods and pleas: limited government in an era of unlimited harm. Yale Law J 121
Friedman L (1997) The concept of legal culture: a reply. In: Nelken D (ed) Comparing legal cultures. Dartmouth, Aldershot
Gibson J, Caldeira G (1996) The legal cultures of Europe. Law Soc Rev 30
Gould J (2002) Bosnia and Herzegovina. In: Kritzer H (ed) Legal systems of the world: A political, social, and cultural encyclopedia. ABC-Clio, Santa Barbara
Hayden R (2002) Yugoslavia: kingdom of and socialist republic. In: Kritzer H (ed) Legal systems of the world: A political, social, and cultural encyclopedia. ABC-Clio, Santa Barbara
Hornuf L, Voigt S (2011) Preliminary references – analyzing the determinants that made the ECJ the powerful court it is. Berkeley program in law and economics working paper series
Howell K (2004) Developing conceptualisations of Europeanisation. Politics 24
Klemenčić G (2002) Slovenia. In: Kritzer H (ed) Legal systems of the world: A political, social, and cultural encyclopedia. ABC-Clio, Santa Barbara
Komàrek J (2014a) Waiting for the existential revolution in Europe. 12 International Journal of Constitutional Law 190
Komàrek J (2014b) The Struggle for legal reform after communism: A review of Zdenek Kuhn 'The judiciary in central and eastern Europe: mechanical jurisprudence in transformation?' LSE Law, Society and Economy Working Papers 10/2014
Krug P (2002) Macedonia. In: Kritzer H (ed) Legal systems of the world: A political, social, and cultural encyclopedia. ABC-Clio, Santa Barbara
Kühn Z (2004) Worlds apart: western and central European judicial culture at the onset of the European enlargement. Am J Comp Law 52
Kühn Z (2006) The authoritarian legal culture at work: the passivity of parties and the interpretational statements of supreme courts. Croatian Yearb Eur Law Policy 2
Kühn Z (2011) The judiciary in central and eastern Europe: mechanical jurisprudence in transformation. Martinus Nijhoff, Leiden
Legrand P (2001) What 'legal transplants'? In: Nelken D, Feest J (eds) Adapting legal cultures. Hart, Oxford
Malleson K (1997) Judicial training and performance appraisal: the problem of judicial independence. Mod Law Rev 60
Oakes R and Verrija A (2002) Albania. In: Kritzer H.M. (ed) Legal systems of the world: A political, social, and cultural encyclopedia. ABC Clio, Santa Barbara
Rodin S (2005) Discourse and authority in Europe and post-communist legal culture. Croatian Yearb Eur Law Policy 1
Rodin S (2009) Functions of judicial opinion - a view from a post-communist European state. In: Huls N, Adams M and Bomhoff J (eds) The legitimacy of highest courts' rulings: judicial deliberations and beyond. T.M.C Asser Press, The Hague, pp 369–388
Schaap M (2011) The strained relationship between international administrators and local institutions: judicial activism in BiH and the demand for access to justice. http://www.academia.edu/4076996/The_strained_relationship_between_international_administrators_and_local_institutions_Judicial_activism_in_BiH_and_the_demand_for_access_to_justice
Schütze R (2012) European constitutional law. Cambridge University Press, Cambridge
Snyder F (ed) (2000) The Europeanisation of law: the legal effects of European integration. Hart, Oxford

Tridimas T (2003) Knocking on heaven's door: fragmentation, efficiency and defiance in the preliminary reference procedure. Common Mark Law Rev 40

Uzelac A (2002) Croatia. In: Kritzer H (ed) Legal systems of the world: A political, social, and cultural encyclopedia. ABC-Clio, Santa Barbara

The Place and Application of International Law in the Albanian Legal System

Gentian Zyberi and Semir Sali

1 Introduction

This chapter aims to explore and analyse the place of international law in the Albanian legal system and its application by Albanian courts. First, the chapter addresses the status of international law under the 1998 Albanian Constitution and its interaction with other sources of law within the Albanian legal system. Subsequently, a number of important domestic cases are analysed so as to illustrate the approach taken by Albanian courts towards international law. The chapter focuses on issues concerning the place and application of human rights, European law, and international criminal law and related mechanisms in the Albanian legal system.

2 The Place of International Law in the Albanian Legal System

The place of international law in the Albanian legal system is regulated in some detail by the Albanian Constitution,[1] the supreme law of the land.[2] Article 5 of the Constitution stipulates that 'the Republic of Albania applies international law that is

[1] Constitution of the Republic of Albania (The Constitution), Law No. 8417, 21 October 1998, as modified by Law No. 9675, 13 January 2007 and by Law No. 9904, 21 April 2008.

[2] Article 4 of the Constitution.

G. Zyberi (✉)
Norwegian Centre for Human Rights, University of Oslo, PO Box 6706, St. Olavs plass, 0130 Oslo, Norway
e-mail: gentian.zyberi@gmail.com

S. Sali
Legal Officer, Supreme Court of Albania, Rruga "Ibrahim Rugova", Tirana, Albania
e-mail: semir.sali@gmail.com

S. Rodin, T. Perišin (eds.), *Judicial Application of International Law in Southeast Europe*, DOI 10.1007/978-3-662-46384-0_6

binding upon it'.[3] Albanian scholars have debated the exact scope of the term 'international law'. Some of them have opted for a narrow interpretation of the provision, claiming that it should be read in conjunction with other provisions regulating the incorporation of treaties in internal legislation. Others have opposed this view. They state correctly that the term 'international law' does not refer only to such treaties that may be in force between Albania and other subjects of international law, but must also include other sources of international law such as customary international law and general principles of law.[4] While at first sight, Article 5 appears to have only declaratory effects, it in fact functions as a singular and necessary link between two legal systems: international law (and Albania as a subject of it) on the one hand, and Albania's internal legislation (and international law when it becomes an integral part of it) on the other. Based on the *pacta sunt servanda* principle, this provision is the basis upon which international law enjoys a special status in Albania's internal legislation.

Part seven of the Constitution deals specifically with normative acts and international agreements. Under Article 116(1), ratified international agreements are listed immediately after the Constitution and below laws.[5] Although not explicitly mentioned in the text of the Constitution, scholars have always maintained that such an order of precedence constitutes a formal hierarchy of the sources of law in Albanian legislation for two main reasons.[6] First, Article 4 establishes the undisputed position of the Constitution as the supreme law of the land. Secondly, according to Article 122(2) 'an international agreement that has been ratified by law has superiority over laws of the country that are not compatible with it'.

It must be noted, however, that Article 116 mentions only 'ratified international agreements', whereas Article 122(2) grants hierarchical status only to those international agreements 'ratified by law'. This may raise doubts as to whether the framers of the Constitution intentionally added the qualifier 'by law' in Article 122 (2) or whether the omission in Article 116 was simply a drafting error. Such doubts are further reinforced by the Law on the Conclusion of Treaties and International Agreements, which in Article 2(b) stipulates that ratification means the 'act by which the Parliament *or* the President of the Republic gives the final approval to a

[3] Article 5 of the Constitution.

[4] See, Omari and Anastasi (2010), pp. 55–56 (quoting Zaganjori 2004, pp. 26–34).

[5] Article 16(1) stipulates: the normative acts that are effective in the territory of the Republic of Albania are:

a) the Constitution;
b) ratified international agreements;
c) the laws;
d) normative acts of the Council of Ministers (these are acts having the force of law, and are issued by the Government only during emergencies or times of crises. The Parliament, which should be convened within five days if it is not in session, must be promptly notified of such normative acts. Normative acts become void and lose effect retroactively if the Parliament fails to approve them within 45 days of their date of issuance).

[6] Omari and Anastasi (2010), p. 47.

treaty signed on behalf of the Republic of Albania'.[7] The article indicates two institutions authorised to ratify international agreements, by way of law or decree respectively. The answer to this doubt lies not in the framers' intention but is, in fact, simply technical.

Although still in force, the Law on the Conclusion of Treaties and International Agreements is not based on the current Constitution, but on the previous temporary constitutional arrangement under the Law on the Main Constitutional Provisions.[8] Article 28(10) of these previous constitutional provisions provided that the President of the Republic could also, in addition to the Parliament, ratify or denounce international treaties; the power being limited to only those which did not fall under the competence of the Parliament. However, such a prerogative has now been removed from the President's competences. Under the current Constitution, the President may only 'conclude' international agreements.[9] Therefore, it may be implied that, for the purposes of Albanian domestic legislation, 'ratification of an international agreement' means the act by which *only* the Parliament gives the final approval to a treaty signed on behalf of the Republic of Albania.[10]

In line with other European Constitutions,[11] the Albanian Constitution provides that ratification is mandatory for political treaties, such as those involving territory, peace, alliances, the military, freedoms and liberties, participation in international organisations or those involving the financial contribution of the state.[12] However, the list is not exhaustive, since the Parliament still retains discretionary power to ratify other international agreements which do not involve the abovementioned topics, but are still considered important enough to require decision-making by the Parliament.[13]

The process of ratification by the Parliament is done by law, and serves a double purpose. First, it vests the treaty with the force and solemnity of an act approved by the representatives of the people. Second, it directly incorporates it into internal legislation. A ratified international agreement becomes part of the domestic legal system after its publication in the Official Gazette.[14] It is implemented directly,

[7] Law No. 8371, 9 July 1998.

[8] Law No. 7491, 29 April 1991.

[9] Article 92(h) of the Constitution.

[10] This is not to be confused with the meaning of 'ratification' as an international act, which is usually done by the President through the signing of the instruments of ratification.

[11] Italian Constitution, Article 80; French Constitution, Article 53. Spanish Constitution, Section 93.

[12] Article 121(1).

[13] Article 121(2). As for international agreements of lesser importance or those having a technical nature (such as visa exemptions or the equivalence of driving licenses) which are not subject to ratification, Article 17 of Law No. 8371 of 9 July 1998 on the Conclusion of Treaties and International Agreements provides that they must only be 'approved' by the Council of Ministers. In any case, the Prime Minister has the duty to notify the Parliament whenever the Council of Ministers signs an international agreement that is not ratified by law.

[14] Article 122(1).

except for cases when it is not self-executing and its implementation requires passing new legislation.[15] As mentioned earlier, ratified international agreements are—owing to the *pacta sunt servanda* principle basis of Article 5 of the Constitution—hierarchically superior to other internal legislation and take precedence in the case of conflict.[16]

A further question raised and which is considered problematic is the status of other sources of international law, such as customary international law *vis-à-vis* conflicting internal legislation. Would Article 122(2) of the Constitution be applicable *mutatis mutandis* to also include customary international law obligations? This issue is not merely theoretical, as there are huge practical implications with regard to the application of customary international law rules by domestic Albanian courts.[17] Admittedly, a strictly textual interpretation of Article 122(2) does not support an assertion that customary international law or general principles of law are not only part of the Albanian legal system, but also prevail over domestic law. Moreover, the unique property of customary international law as a set of non-codified rules could hardly be reconciled with the requirement of formal 'publication in the Official Gazette'. Nevertheless, such a narrow interpretation of Article 122(2) would be ill-construed and ill-advised. It would place Albania in an awkward position, considering that 'all national legal systems ... accept customary international law as an integral part of national law'.[18] Likewise, Albania's international legal responsibility for violations of customary international law and general principles of international law can and actually has been engaged.[19] Finally, such a restrictive interpretation would also run against the wording and scope of Article 5 of the Constitution, which clearly provides for the application of international law (and not only conventional obligations) that is binding upon Albania. Unless there are exceptional grounds for arguing the applicability of the persistent objector doctrine, and only with regard to specific rules of customary international law, there is no justifiable reason why Article 5 of the Constitution should not also include customary international law and general principles of law.

---

[15] Ibid.

[16] Article 122(2).

[17] Let us simply recall that a majority of topics of public international law, such as state immunity or the law of armed conflict, are largely governed by long standing rules having the status of customary international law.

[18] Denza (2010), pp. 411–441 at p. 424. See also, International Court of Justice, *Corfu Channel (United Kingdom of Great Britain and Northern Ireland v. Albania)*, ICJ Reports 1949, especially p. 22.

[19] International Law Commission, Articles on State Responsibility, annex to General Assembly Resolution 56/83 of 12 December 2001, and corrected by document A/56/49(Vol. I)/Corr.4 (2001), Article 4: 'The conduct of any State organ shall be considered an act of that State under international law, whether the organ exercises legislative, executive, *judicial* or any other functions, whatever position it holds in the organization of the State, and whatever its character as an organ of the central Government or of a territorial unit of the State' (emphasis added).

3 The Application of International Law in the Albanian Legal System

The Albanian Constitutional Court (ACC or Constitutional Court) and the Albanian High Court, the highest courts in Albania, have dealt with cases involving the application of international law in Albanian domestic law. By analysing a number of relevant cases, we shall illustrate the relationship and interaction between Albanian domestic law and international legal obligations undertaken by Albania over the last 22 years, since the fall of the communist regime in 1991. Although the Albanian Constitutional Court is not formally part of the Albanian judiciary, under the Constitution it has been invested with a leading role in determining the compatibility of Albanian laws with international legal agreements to which Albania is a party. Thus, according to Article 131, the Constitutional Court has jurisdiction to decide, among other matters, on questions relating to: (1) the compatibility of laws with the Constitution or with ratified international agreements[20]; (2) the compatibility of international agreements with the Constitution, prior to their ratification[21]; and (3) complaints from individuals regarding the violation of their constitutional rights to due process of law, after all legal means for the protection of those rights have been exhausted.[22]

3.1 *The Compatibility of Albanian Laws with Ratified International Agreements*

No cases have been filed thus far seizing the Constitutional Court with questions relating to (potential) conflicts between national laws and ratified international agreements. Taking into consideration the lack of any objective data or statistics, one may only speculate as to the reasons behind the lack of case law on this issue. This situation may well relate to the limited place given to the study of international law in the training of national judges and prosecutors[23]; the paucity of publications

[20] Article 131(a).

[21] Article 131(b).

[22] Article 131(i).

[23] The School of Magistrates only last year included international law as a subject of the preliminary phase for admission to the school (excluding it, however, from the core topics in the second phase). However, there is an ongoing trend of raising awareness of international law, at least during the continuing education of judges, especially through short-term training events and seminars conducted by international organisations. The National Bar Association does not include questions of international law in the bar exam. While general international law is given limited attention, law schools offer extensive training and education with regard to the European Convention of Human Rights and the jurisprudence of its court.

featuring important international agreements ratified by Albania in the Albanian language[24]; or simply no serious conflict has been identified so far in legal practice.

Some Albanian constitutional scholars have gone as far as to question the authority of the Constitutional Court to pronounce on potential conflicts between laws and ratified international treaties. They argue that in the case that national judges encounter any such conflict, they should simply apply the superior norm, i.e. the international treaty, since the issue pertains to normal judicial interpretation, and not to the ambit of the Constitutional Court's jurisdiction.[25] They further claim that only if the national law conflicts with the European Convention of Human Rights (ECHR), should the judge instead refer the case to the Constitutional Court. They justify this difference of treatment with the 'constitutional status' that the ECHR enjoys on the basis of Article 17 of the Constitution. Dealing with impermissible limitations of rights and freedoms accorded by the Constitution, paragraph 2 of Article 17 provides that:

> These limitations may not infringe the essence of the rights and freedoms and in no case may exceed the limitations provided for in the European Convention on Human Rights.

What Article 17(2) provides is the actual 'reference' but not 'incorporation' of parts of the ECHR into the Albanian Constitution. Its purpose is to impose an absolute prohibition so that certain fundamental rights cannot, even in situations of war or public emergency, be derogated from. In this sense, the provision of Article 17(2) mentioning the 'limitations provided for in the ECHR' is a *renvoi* to Article 15(2) of the ECHR which reads:

> No derogation from article 2 [*right to life*], except in respect of deaths resulting from lawful acts of war, or from articles 3 [*prohibition of torture*], 4 (paragraph 1) [*prohibition of slavery*] and 7 [*no punishment without law*] shall be made under this provision (emphasis added).

Thus, Article 17(2) of the Constitution in effect provides a second layer of protection from torture, slavery, punishment without law, or arbitrary deprivation of life. The result of this reference is that, for the purpose of Albanian legislation, these parts of the ECHR also *become* an integral part of the Constitution. Therefore, when the Constitutional Court is asked to pronounce with regard to challenges to a law which allegedly exceeds the limitations imposed by Article 15(2) of the ECHR, the Court will act on the basis of its jurisdiction to decide on the 'compatibility of the law with the Albanian Constitution'. On the contrary, if the law conflicts with other parts of the ECHR, it may still be brought before the Constitutional Court, but this time on the basis of the Court's jurisdiction to decide on the 'compatibility of

[24] The issue is particularly striking concerning the prior practice of the Centre for the Publication of Official Acts to only publish the text of the ratification of an international treaty, but not the text of the treaty in Albanian. This has prompted the Office of the Ombudsman to recommend to the Parliament that the text of the treaty be attached to the ratification law, and has urged the competent authorities to translate and publish the remaining 'stock' of unpublished treaties. See http://www.avokatipopullit.gov.al/Raporte/RV12008.pdf. Accessed 16 August 2013.

[25] Omari and Anastasi (2010), p. 60.

laws with international agreements'.[26] The wording of Article 131 of the Constitution is clear in providing that the Constitutional Court may decide on the compatibility of the laws not only with the Constitution, but *also* with 'international agreements, as provided in Article 122'.

3.2 Compatibility of International Agreements with the Constitution

Article 131(b) of the Constitution provides that the Constitutional Court is competent to decide 'on the compatibility of international agreements with the Constitution before their ratification'. The choice to allow this constitutional review of international treaties is beneficial from both a theoretical and practical perspective. Theoretically, this upholds the hierarchy of the sources of law under Article 116 of the Constitution. The state is thus free to conclude any international agreement and to undertake any kind of international law obligations, as long as they do not come into conflict with the Constitution. This does not necessarily mean that the Constitution is considered as standing above international law. The wording of Article 5 of the Constitution which affirms that 'the Republic of Albania applies international law that is binding upon it' displays a fairly deferential stance towards international law. Through this provision Albania recognises its international legal obligations *vis-à-vis* the international community of states, while at the same time reaffirming its sovereignty in deciding *how* it incorporates such obligations within its own domestic legal system. The practical aspect of this approach involves avoiding a situation of conflict between the Constitution and an international obligation which could result in violation of the *pacta sunt servanda* principle.

The Constitutional Court has been asked twice to pronounce with regard to the compatibility of international agreements with the Constitution prior to their ratification. The first case was heard in 2002, when the Council of Ministers asked the Court whether the Statute of the International Criminal Court (ICC) was compatible with the Constitution.[27] While on that occasion the Court found no obstacle in clearing the way for the ratification of the ICC Statute by the Albanian Parliament, in the second case the issue was more complex. The Constitutional Court had to decide on the constitutionality of an agreement between Albania and Greece concerning the delimitation of their respective continental shelf areas and other maritime zones to which they are entitled under international law (Maritime Delimitation Agreement).[28] In its judgment, the Constitutional Court found that

[26] In practice this might not be necessary, as most of the rights and liberties provided in the ECHR are already explicitly included into the Albanian Constitution. As a consequence, any violation of a Constitutional fundamental right or liberty may potentially also be a violation of the ECHR.

[27] Constitutional Court, Judgment No. 186, 23 September 2002.

[28] Constitutional Court, Judgment No. 15, 15 April 2010.

the agreement: (1) was negotiated without the conferral of full powers by the President of the Republic; (2) that, contrary to its title, the agreement in fact delimited internal and territorial waters; (3) that it disregarded basic rules of international law on maritime delimitation in order to reach a fair and equitable result; and that (4) it failed to recognise certain islands as constituting *special circumstances* for the purpose of maritime delimitation. As a result, the Court struck down the agreement as unconstitutional. Although the decision of the Constitutional Court might have been controversial from a political perspective, it did not entail any breach of international obligations by the Albanian state, since such an agreement would need to be ratified by the Albanian Parliament so as to enter into force.

4 The Impact of the European Court of Human Rights in the Albanian Legal System

It is almost impossible to find any judgment of the Constitutional Court where the case law of the European Court of Human Rights (ECtHR) has not been cited at least once. Indeed, all Albanian courts, and the Constitutional Court in particular, have in the past decade given considerable attention to the ECtHR's case law. An attentive observer would note that even the structure of some of the Constitutional Court's judgments follows that of the ECtHR, with long citations of applicable law first, followed by the parties' submissions, and finally with the Court's assessment. Most of the time, the proceedings before the Constitutional Court have served as an effective filter before lodging an application with the ECtHR.

4.1 The Right to a Fair Trial: Xheraj v. Albania

The re-examination or reopening of criminal proceedings following a judgment of the ECtHR finding that the ECHR has been violated is certainly not a novel issue among member states of the Council of Europe.[29] Since 2000, the Council of Ministers of the Council of Europe has issued a recommendation to member states urging them:

> to ensure that there exist at national level adequate possibilities to achieve, as far as possible, *restitutio in integrum* … in particular, to examine their national legal systems

[29] See examples of requests for the reopening of proceedings in order to give effect to decisions by the European Court of Human Rights and the Committee of Ministers, Ref. H(99)10 rev, available at www.coe.int/t/dghl/monitoring/execution/Documents//Reopening_en.asp. Accessed 16 August 2013.

with a view to ensuring that there exist adequate possibilities of re-examination of the case.[30]

By 2006, a majority of 34 member states provided for the possibility of reopening criminal proceedings.[31] In seven states, reopening was still considered as impossible or unclear.[32] Albania was one of them. In 2008, Albania introduced new legislation to allow for the reopening of civil cases following a judgment of the ECtHR.[33] The reopening of criminal cases remains impossible, at least according to the Code of Criminal Procedure. While the Albanian government has been working on a draft amendment to the Code of Criminal Procedure for this purpose,[34] the Albanian Constitutional Court and the High Court seem to have already accepted this possibility. After the *Barberá, Messegué and Jarabo* case,[35] the *Xheraj* case officially became the second time[36] a Constitutional Court had ever directed other courts to reopen criminal proceedings following a judgment of the ECtHR, despite the absence of such a provision in the Code of Criminal Procedure.[37]

The facts of the case can be summarised as follows: accused of murder, Mr. Xheraj was found guilty by the Durrës District Court in 1996 and sentenced to life imprisonment. On appeal, Xheraj's sentence was reduced to 20 years of imprisonment. In 1997, his conviction became *res judicata* after the High Court confirmed the Appeals Court's judgment. A year later, on 14 December 1998, the Durrës District Court accepted a request from Xheraj to reopen proceedings. In the light of new evidence, the District Court then dropped all charges and acquitted Xheraj. As the prosecution failed to lodge any appeal within the proscribed limit of

[30] Recommendation No. R (2000) 2 of the Committee of Ministers to member states on the re-examination or reopening of certain cases at domestic level following judgments of the European Court of Human Rights, 19 January 2000.

[31] Steering Committee for Human Rights, Follow-up sheets on the implementation of the five recommendations, CDDH(2006)008 Addendum I, 7 April 2006, p. 4.

[32] Ibid, p. 5.

[33] Article 494(2)(ë) Code of Civil Procedure, added to by Law No. 10052, dated 29.12.2008.

[34] Communication from Albania concerning the case of Xheraj against Albania (Application No. 37959/02), DH-DH-DD(2013)700E, 19 June 2013, available at https://wcd.coe.int/ViewDoc.jsp?Ref=DH-DD%282013%29700&Language=lanEnglish&Site=CM. Accessed 16 August 2013.

[35] Spanish Constitutional Court (1991) Case No. 254/91, Boletín de Jurisprudencia Constitutional 129, p. 86.

[36] With the exception of the *Van Mechelen* case (*Van Mechelen and Others v. The Netherlands*, 55/1996/674/861-864, 23 April 1997), whereby in view of the impossibility of reopening criminal proceedings under Dutch law, it was the Minister of Justice who first ordered the applicants' provisional release and subsequently waived the remainder of their sentences.

[37] However, the Spanish Constitutional Court did not base its decision on the direct applicability of the ECtHR judgment, but rather on a derived violation of the Spanish Constitution. See Hartwig (2005), pp. 869–894 at p. 882.

10 days, the judgment of acquittal became *res judicata* on 24 December 1998. On 9 October 1999, the prosecution filed and obtained a request for leave to appeal out of time. Following the new proceedings in the District and Appeals Court, the judgment of acquittal was again confirmed. The prosecution thus appealed to the High Court, which in turn sent the case back to the Appeals Court for retrial. On 18 December 2000, the Appeals Court re-confirmed its judgment of acquittal. The prosecution lodged another appeal with the High Court. On 20 June 2001, the High Court accepted the prosecution's appeal and quashed the judgment of acquittal, therefore confirming the previous guilty verdict of 20 years of imprisonment. As this judgment was final, Xheraj lodged an application with the Constitutional Court claiming violation of his constitutional right to a fair trial. After the ACC rejected his claim, he subsequently lodged an application with the ECtHR which, in turn, found an infringement of the principle of legal certainty, and consequently a violation of Article 6(1) of the Convention.[38] While the ECtHR did not order any non-pecuniary remedies in its *dispositif*, it still considered:

> that the most appropriate form of redress for this continuing situation would be for the applicant's final acquittal of 14 December 1998 to be confirmed by the authorities and his conviction in breach of the Convention to be erased with effect from that date.[39]

Based on this passage, Xheraj seized the ACC again, seeking the annulment of the High Court's judgment of 20 June 2001 and the enforcement of the ECtHR's judgment. In his application, he claimed the existence of a legal vacuum in Albanian legislation, since Albanian courts did not consider the ECtHR's judgments as directly enforceable. In its decision of 9 March 2010, while rejecting Xheraj's application, the Constitutional Court noted that as Article 46 ECHR obliges states to abide by the ECtHR's final judgments, they [the states] were under an obligation to take all necessary measures to ensure the effective implementation of such judgments. The ACC stressed the importance of reopening criminal proceedings in implementing the ECtHR's judgments as a possible tool towards achieving an effective *restitutio in integrum* of the infringed right protected by the Convention.[40] It deplored the fact that the legislature had not yet amended the Code of Criminal Procedure with a provision similar to Article 494(2)(ë) of the Code of Civil Procedure, but added that the High Court, as the authority responsible for the breach of the Convention, must find a solution to the issue; even by way of analogy to the Code of Civil Procedure if it so deemed necessary.[41]

Xheraj then turned to the High Court, which on 9 July 2010 rejected his request to reopen proceedings, arguing that Article 450 of the Code of Criminal Procedure did not foresee final judgments of the ECtHR *per se* as grounds for reopening

---

[38] *Case of Xheraj v. Albania*, Application No. 37959/02, Judgment, 1 December 2008, para 61.

[39] Ibid, para 82.

[40] Constitutional Court, Decision of Inadmissibility No. 22/10, 9 March 2010, p. 6, para 4.

[41] Ibid, p. 5.

proceedings.[42] While paragraph 1(a) of Article 450 provided that reopening of proceedings may be accepted when the facts on the merits are contradicted by another final judgment, this was—according to the High Court—not the case here, since the ECtHR's judgment could only serve as circumstantial evidence for constitutional proceedings, but not as a basis for reopening criminal proceedings. Xheraj did not agree and reverted back to the Constitutional Court. On this occasion, the ACC made plain its disagreement with the High Court. The Constitutional Court first stated that:

> With regard to fundamental human rights, the ECtHR enjoys, in our legal system, an exclusive competence. This competence has been accepted by our internal legal system by virtue of Articles 17(2)[43] and 122 of the Constitution, which mandate that the ECtHR's judgments be directly implemented ... The Parliament is under an obligation to take such measures as to ensure compliance with the ECHR's dispositions. If it fails to do so, domestic courts must remedy this legal vacuum, and directly apply the ECtHR's judgments in accordance with Articles 122 of the Constitution and Articles 19 and 46 of the ECHR.[44]

Indeed, Article 122 of the Constitution provides for the direct application of the ECHR in the Albanian legal system. In addition, according to Article 46(1) of the ECHR, member states 'undertake to abide by the final judgment of the Court in any case to which they are parties'. It should be noted, however, that the remedies of the ECtHR are binding only when they are phrased in a mandatory manner and included in the *dispositif*.[45] In *Xheraj*, the ECtHR *ordered* the payment of pecuniary damages, but only *recommended* that confirming the judgment of acquittal would be 'the most appropriate form of redress'.[46] This is because states enjoy a certain margin of appreciation as to how to enforce the obligation present in Article 46 of the Convention.[47] The ECtHR itself has already noted that 'the Convention does not give it jurisdiction to direct a state to open a new trial or to quash a conviction' and

---

[42] Article 450 of the Code of Criminal Procedure envisions only four cases when reopening of proceedings is possible, namely when:

a) the facts on the merits conflict with those of another judgment which is final;
b) the judgment was based in a civil proceedings judgment, which has later been quashed;
c) new evidence has arisen, which if considered separately or in conjunction with any other previously tendered evidence, indicates that the judgment was wrongly decided upon.
d) it has been proved that the judgment was tainted by falsified evidence or any other facts constituting a crime.

[43] As mentioned above, it is doubtful whether Article 17(2) of the Constitution is actually relevant in this discussion. Moreover, the right of legal certainty under Article 6 of the ECHR is certainly not included in the list of absolute rights protected by Article 17(2) of the Constitution and Article 15(2) of the ECHR.

[44] Constitutional Court, Judgment No. 20/11, 1 June 2011, pp. 6–7.

[45] Helfer (2008), pp. 125–159 at p. 147, footnote 131.

[46] *Case of Xheraj v. Albania*, Application No. 37959/02, Judgment, 1 December 2008, para 61.

[47] Explanatory Memorandum on the Committee of Ministers' Recommendation No. R(2000)2 on the re-examination or reopening of certain cases at domestic level following judgments of the European Court of Human Rights, para 1.

that 'it cannot find a state to be in breach of the Convention on account of its failure to take either of these courses of action when faced with the execution of one of its judgments'.[48] Thus, contrary to the Constitutional Court's assertion, domestic courts are not obliged to act, and are not to be blamed if no legal remedy is available in their legal system to enforce the ECtHR's judgments.[49]

It should be noted that the ACC has only annulment powers.[50] The court can only strike down a law as unconstitutional, but it cannot declare it unconstitutional because it does not include a right or a liberty protected by the Constitution. For that reason, the ACC could not act like the Italian Constitutional Court, which only 2 months before had struck down Article 630 of the Italian Code of Criminal Procedure in the part where it did not provide other grounds for reopening criminal proceedings, 'when that is necessary ... to conform to a final judgment of the ECtHR'.[51] This is probably why the ACC decided to interpret Article 450(1)(a) of the Code of Criminal Procedure as widely as possible, so as to include the ECtHR's judgments. This was done by relying on Article 122 of the Constitution and Article 10 of the Code of Criminal Procedure (which deals with relationships with foreign authorities) in rejecting the High Court's interpretation that the ECtHR's judgments could not be equivalent to those of Albanian courts. Thus, according to the Constitutional Court's interpretation, the 'final judgments' referred to by Article 450(1)(a) do not only include judgments from Albanian courts, but also foreign ones (and thus those of the ECtHR). Finally, the Constitutional Court warned the High Court that:

> If the [Constitutional] Court has established that certain Constitutional rights have been infringed, as it did in its judgment No. 22, dated 09.03.2010, this fact cannot be further reviewed by anyone, especially the High Court, which is obliged to guarantee the correct application of the substantial and procedural criminal law from all courts, in accordance with the Constitution and the judgments of the Constitutional Court. Accordingly, in case of a conflict between two different judgments of the Constitutional and the High Court, there is only one solution, which is the quashing of the High Court's judgment by the Constitutional Court.[52]

However, the Constitutional Court did not deal with a crucial element of Article 450(1)(a) of the Code of Criminal Procedure, which clearly provides that a reopening of proceedings may by granted only when '*the facts* on the merits conflict with *those* of another judgment which is final'. Even accepting that an ECtHR judgment may be considered 'another judgment which has become final' for the purposes of Article 450(1)(a), it is still hard to accept that an ECtHR judgment is

---

[48] *Lyons et al. v. The United Kingdom*, Application No. 15227/03, Decision on Admissibility, 8 July 2003, p. 9.

[49] Hartwig (2005), pp. 869–894 at p. 886.

[50] Article 132(1) of the Constitution.

[51] Italian Constitutional Court, Judgment No. 113, 4 April 2001, available at www.cortecostituzionale.it/actionSchedaPronuncia.do?anno=2011&numero=113. Accessed 16 August 2013.

[52] Constitutional Court, Judgment No. 20/11, 1 June 2011, p. 11.

decided on other 'facts' which contradict a previous judgment. The ECtHR is certainly not a trier of *new* facts and does not decide on the guilt or innocence of a defendant, but only reviews the judgments of domestic courts *vis-à-vis* the rights and liberties guaranteed by the Convention. This approach is further confirmed by the well-established jurisprudence of Italian courts, which have always agreed that Article 630 of the Italian Code of Criminal Procedure—a *verbatim* of Article 450 of the Albanian Code of Criminal Procedure—is not applicable to ECtHR judgments.[53] It appears that the High Court was correct when it first denied the applicability of Article 450(1)(a) of the Code of Criminal Procedure to final judgments of the ECtHR.[54] Finally though, it had to succumb to the decision of the Constitutional Court.[55]

The eagerness of Albanian courts to follow the ECtHR's jurisprudence and their commitment to human rights issues is understandable. However, this cannot be achieved at the expense of sacrificing other important constitutional principles, namely the rule of law and the separation of powers. True, after the ECtHR's judgment in the Xheraj case, Albania might have been in a continuing breach of the Convention, but it is not for the judiciary to remedy to this legal vacuum by implicitly assuming competences which the Constitution attributes exclusively to the legislative branch.

5 Jurisdictional Immunities for International Organisations: The *Chemonics* Case

This case concerned an employment dispute between an individual and a company claiming immunity before Albanian courts.[56] The defendant, *Chemonics International Inc.*, was the Albanian branch of *Chemonics International Inc.*, an homonymous company based in Delaware, USA, which had won a contract with USAID, a US government agency, regarding the implementation of a project concerning the reform of the public administration in Albania. The plaintiff, a former employee of *Chemonics*, brought a civil suit before the Tirana District Court seeking compensation for unlawful dismissal. *Chemonics* challenged the jurisdiction of the Tirana District Court, claiming that on the basis of an international agreement between the

[53] Italian Constitutional Court, Judgment No. 113, 4 April 2001 (agreeing with the Bologna Court of Appeals which had denied the interpretation that an ECtHR judgment could be used as valid grounds for the applicability of one of the cases envisioned in Article 630 of the Code of Criminal Procedure).

[54] Although it should have probably followed another reasoning, i.e. the 'contradictory facts' requirement of Article 450(1)(a).

[55] Supreme Court, Judgment No. 52102-01226-00-2011, 7 March 2012.

[56] Albanian Supreme Court, Judgment No. 8 (United Chambers), 10 June 2011 (*Chemonics* Judgment).

Albanian and US Governments, it enjoyed immunity from civil liability before Albanian courts.

In 1992, the Albanian and the US Governments had entered into a bilateral economic agreement concerning US economic, technical and related assistance to Albania.[57] The agreement purported to set forth a

> framework concerning economic, technical and related assistance which, based on a request by the Government of the Republic of Albania, may be provided by the Government of the United States of America, subject to the applicable laws and regulations of the United States of America.[58]

It consisted of four articles, two of which provided for extensive privileges and immunities for different categories of US employees and contractors. *Chemonics* relied on paragraph 3(d) of the agreement, which provided that:

> In order to assure the maximum benefits to the people of the Republic of Albania from the assistance to be furnished hereunder and except as may be agreed by the two governments: . . .
>
> (d) Individuals, *public or private organizations*, and employees of public or private organizations, *under contract with or financed* by the Government of the United States of America, who are present in the Republic of Albania to perform work in connection with this agreement, shall be *immune from all civil liability directly related to the performance of such work* (emphasis added).

Ratione personae, the provision accorded immunity to virtually everyone,[59] as long as one was (1) present on Albanian territory and (2) had a contract with or was financed by the US Government to perform work in connection with the agreement. And since the agreement did not define what kind of *work*, it could well include any kind of 'economic, technical and related assistance' to the Albanian Government. *Ratione materiae*, it limited the immunity to all civil liability, but only if the activity was directly related to the performance of work connected to the agreement.

In its decision on jurisdiction, the Tirana District Court accepted that the defendant was included in the category of subjects listed in paragraph 3(d). However, it held that disputes arising from an employment dispute between *Chemonics* and one of its employees did not fall into the category of activities directly related to the performance of work connected to the agreement. Moreover, the District Court observed that in the employment contract itself the parties had specifically provided for the Tirana District Court's jurisdiction in case of disputes which could not be settled amicably.

---

[57] Economic Bilateral Agreement Between the Government of the Republic of Albania and the Government of the United States of America, 10 June 1992, Treaties and Other International Acts Series 12456.

[58] Ibid, p. 3.

[59] The agreement included both juridical persons (public or private organisations) and individuals (individuals and employees of public or private organisations).

Chemonics appealed the decision before the High Court. Considering the complexity of the issue, the Civil Law Chamber of the High Court referred the case to the United Chambers (the full court), asking the following questions:

- Do Albanian courts retain jurisdiction with regard to disputes between Albanian citizens and other subjects which enjoy immunity from Albanian jurisdiction (by virtue of the UN Convention on the Privileges and Immunities of Specialised Agencies or bilateral agreements between Albania and foreign states) if such disputes are employment related?
- If an employment contract between the abovementioned subjects provides for the jurisdiction of Albanian courts, would this be considered a voluntary waiver in accordance with Article 39(a) of the Code of Civil Procedure?[60]

With regard to the first question, the Court refused to set a general precedent on upholding or setting aside jurisdictional immunities in employment issues. Instead, it decided to be cautious and to limit its answer only with regard to employment issues arising in the application of the US–Albanian agreement. On the merits, the Court noted that the defendant was in charge of implementing the Millennium Challenge Corporation II programme, a project financed entirely by USAID. It thus concluded that, as a contractor of USAID in Albania, *Chemonics* was, according to Article 3(d) of the agreement, immune from all civil liability directly related to the performance of that project.[61]

The Court then turned to the question of whether the granting of immunity would infringe the fundamental right of access to court under Article 42(2) of the Constitution and Article 6(1) ECHR. Applying the *Ashingdane test*,[62] the Court quickly found that:

> On the basis of the scope of the agreement and its legitimate aim, [we] find no unreasonable relation of proportionality between this limitation and the aim sought. Accordingly . . . the Albanian state did not overstep the margin of appreciation in limiting the right of access to court. [63]

The Court stated that the conclusion was also consistent with the ECtHR's jurisprudence which had previously held that:

[60] Article 39 of the Code of Civil Procedure stipulates that:

Members of Consular and Diplomatic Missions accredited in the Republic of Albania shall not be subject to Albanian courts, except when:

a) they voluntarily accept (such jurisdiction)
b) there exist the cases and conditions provided by the Vienna Convention on Diplomatic Relations.

[61] Ibid, paras 12.1–12.2.

[62] *Case of Ashingdane v United Kingdom*, Application No. 8225/78, Judgment, 28 May 1985.

[63] *Chemonics* Judgment, paras 13–14.

> some restrictions on access must likewise be regarded as inherent, an example being those limitations generally accepted by the community of nations as part of the doctrine of State immunity.[64]

Accordingly, the Court upheld *Chemonics*' absolute immunity in civil cases, even employment related ones.[65]

With regard to the second question, the Court noted that, according to Article 32 (2) of the Vienna Convention on Diplomatic Relations, subjects who enjoy immunity from jurisdiction may waive their immunity. Although the US–Albanian agreement had not provided for such a possibility, this did not mean that a waiver was not possible. Indeed, the parties had waived their immunity by expressly mentioning the jurisdiction of Albanian courts in the employment contract. The Court also dismissed the claim that the 'waiver' was invalid because in view of Article 7(3) of the Labour Code, all 'Arrangements on jurisdiction are valid only if they are concluded after the dispute has arisen'. According to the Court, such a provision was inapplicable in this case, as it related to a waiver of jurisdiction and not an agreement on changing it.[66] Thus, the waiver had been valid.

The Court's opinion was split. While the judges who appended a dissenting opinion agreed with the majority on the first question but dissented on the second one (which was decisive for the case),[67] the judges who appended a concurring opinion agreed with the second question (and therefore the outcome) but strongly dissented on the first question.[68] An important aspect which deserves more scrutiny

[64] Ibid, para 14(1), (quoting *Case of McElhinney v. Ireland*, Application No. 31253/96, Judgment, 21 November 2001, para 37; *Case of Manoilescu and Dobrescu v. Romania and Russia*, Application No. 60861/00, Judgment, 3 March 2005, para 80; *Case of Treska v. Albania and Italy*, Application No. 26937/04, Judgment, 26 June 2006; *Case of Vrioni et al., v. Albania and Italy*, Application Nos. 35720/04 and 42832/06, Judgment, para 46).

[65] Ibid, para 16.

[66] Ibid, paras 18–25.

[67] The judges who appended a dissenting opinion maintained that the waiver should have been explicit and that Article 7(3) of the Labour Code was plain in prohibiting agreements on jurisdictions concluded before the arising of a dispute (pp. 10–12). They maintained that the whole purpose of Article 7(3) was to protect subjects who enjoy immunity from forgoing their rights before a dispute had arisen.

[68] The judges appending the concurring opinion noted that paragraph 3(e) of the agreement, which concerned the category of employees of the US Government, envisioned an absolute type of immunity, both civil and criminal, comparable to that of diplomatic agents. By contrast, the type of immunity which paragraph 3(d) envisioned was limited to civil liability, and only if such liability was *directly* related to the project covered by the agreement. Because of its nature, the employment contract did not fall into the category of those activities protected by paragraph 3(d) of the agreement. Any different interpretation would, therefore, render the term 'directly connected' moot and transform that provision into a *de facto* absolute immunity for all civil liabilities, irrespective of the nature of the activity. Secondly, the concurring opinion claimed that absolute immunity for employment disputes would also violate Article 6(1) ECHR, considering that such a limitation to the right of access to court would not be proportional to the aim sought. It then referred to the (then) most recent judgments of the ECtHR, which in the cases *Cudak v. Lithuania* (Application No. 15869/02, Judgment, 23 March 2010) and *Vilho Eskelinen et al. v. Finland*

is defining the type of immunity under discussion, whether it is treaty-based or customary-law based. The unique facts of the *Chemonics* case would, at a minimum, cast some doubt on whether state immunity is applicable. After all, *Chemonics* was not an integral part of the US government or part of its property.[69] Moreover, when dealing with state immunity, it is generally the state concerned which invokes its sovereign immunity. In this case, neither the US Government nor the US diplomatic mission in Albania, which according to paragraph 1 of the US–Albanian agreement was the competent authority to carry out and discharge the responsibilities arising under it, invoked immunity on behalf of *Chemonics*.

Although formally relying on the *Ashingdane* test, the Court failed to explain the reason why the granting of immunity for employment disputes to a private contractor would serve a legitimate aim? And if so, how was it proportionate to the absolute limitation of the right of access to court? Admittedly, the ECtHR has in the past accepted the doctrine of state immunity as sufficient, in principle, to counterbalance the limitation of the right of access to court.[70] However, this is valid only with regard to cases relating to tort claims against states, for acts considered *acta iure imperii*. The ECtHR has found that states cannot invoke immunity concerning employment disputes, except for cases listed in paragraph 2 of Article 11 of the UN Convention on Jurisdictional Immunities of the State.[71] Although not yet in force, on several occasions the ECtHR has emphasised that Article 11 of the UN Convention on the Immunities of the State has achieved the status of customary international law.[72] As Albania has not formally objected to the rule, it may be asserted that Article 11 of this convention also applies to Albania as a matter of

(Application No. 63235/00, Judgment, 19 April 2007) had excluded employment disputes from the doctrine of state immunity, therefore showing that 'absolute immunity does not exist anymore, that it should be assessed on a case by case basis and that the right of access to court should be given priority'.

[69] See for example, United Nations Convention on Jurisdictional Immunities of States and Their Property (Adopted by the General Assembly of the United Nations on 2 December 2004. Not yet in force), A/59/49, Article 1: 'The present Convention applies to the immunity of a State and its property from the jurisdiction of the courts of another State'.

[70] See for example, in addition to the case law cited in note 64 above, *Case of Al-Adsani v. UK*, Application No. 35763/97, Judgment, 21 November 2001, para 56: 'It follows that measures taken by a High Contracting Party which reflect generally recognised rules of public international law on State immunity cannot in principle be regarded as imposing a disproportionate restriction on the right of access to a court as embodied in Article 6 § 1'.

[71] See *Case of Wallishauser v. Austria*, Application No. 156/04, Judgment, 19 November 2012; *Case of Sabeh El Leil v. France*, Application No. 34869/05, 29 June 2011; *Case of Cudak v. Lithuania* Application No. 15869/02, Judgment, 23 March 2010.

[72] *Case of Wallishauser v. Austria, supra* at note 71, para 60; *Sabeh El Leil v. France*, *supra* at note 71, para 54.

customary international law. In other words, even the US Government itself could not have successfully invoked state immunity if, for example, the case had concerned a contractual employment dispute between a local employee and the US embassy in Tirana.

Likewise, if one were to consider *Chemonics*' immunity as detached from state immunity and based on treaty law, in analogy to that of international organisations, such broadly-construed immunity would still fail to pass the proportionality criterion of the *Ashingdane* test. In the landmark cases *Waite and Kennedy v. Germany*[73] and *Beer and Reagan v. Germany*,[74] the ECtHR was asked to pronounce with regard to the compatibility of jurisdictional immunities of international organisations *vis-à-vis* the rights protected under the Convention. Although both cases were decided in the affirmative, the Court warned that 'a *material factor* ... is whether the applicants had available to them reasonable alternative means to protect effectively their rights under the Convention'.[75] This passage sparked a debate amongst authors as to whether *a material factor* implied a pre-condition to the granting of immunity or whether it was simply one element to take into consideration.[76] Recently, the Court had the opportunity to clarify this dilemma, holding that the absence of alternative remedies could not be considered '*ipso facto* constitutive of a violation of the rights of access to court'.[77] Yet, the facts of the *Chemonics* case were substantively different. *Chemonics* was certainly not an international organisation. It was simply a private organisation that was eligible to functional immunity with regard to the performance of its contract with USAID. While the granting of such functional immunity may certainly serve a legitimate aim, it still remains highly disproportionate to a complete restriction of the right to access to court for employment disputes.[78]

The concurring opinion in the *Chemonics* case seems to be more correct and faithful to the ECtHR's case law. Although the majority opinion ultimately accepted the waiver doctrine, it was clear that upholding such immunity was tantamount to a complete infringement of the essence of the right of access to court.

[73] Application No. 26083/94, Judgment, 18 February 1999.

[74] Application No. 28934/95, Judgment, 18 February 1999.

[75] *Waite and Kennedy*, para 68.

[76] Brabandere (2010), pp. 79–119 at pp. 94–95; see also, Ryngaert (2010), pp. 121–148 at pp. 134–135 (accepting that the Court did not make it a 'strict prerequisite').

[77] *Stichting Mothers of Srebrenica and Others v. The Netherlands*, Application no. 65542/12, Decision, 11 June 2013, para 164.

[78] Moreover, is it highly doubtful whether employment disputes can be correctly categorised as 'civil liabilities directly related to the performance of its work'.

6 The Stabilisation and Association Agreement (SAA) and the Application of EU Law in Albania

Albania aspires to become a member of the European Union (EU).[79] The Stabilisation and Association Agreement (SAA) between Albania and the EU was signed on 12 June 2006 and entered into force on 1 April 2009.[80] This international agreement is directly applicable under Article 122(1) of the Constitution.[81] Public support for EU accession in Albania is probably the highest among the Western Balkan countries which are in the process of joining the EU.[82] The integration process has been a protracted one, as with most of the Western Balkan countries.[83] A number of legal reforms have been undertaken in the meantime in order to harmonise Albanian laws with EU law and to implement the EU *acquis*, as agreed under Title VI of the SAA, entitled Approximation of Laws, Law Enforcement and Competition Rules. As part of these efforts Albania has established the Albanian Competition Authority.[84] Albania submitted its application for EU membership on 28 April 2009, but progress since then has been quite slow.

The EU has set a number of key priorities which concern the following areas: the proper functioning of the Parliament; adopting reinforced majority laws; appointment procedures and appointments for key institutions; electoral reform; the conduct of elections; public administration reform; the rule of law and judicial reform; fighting corruption; fighting organised crime; addressing property issues; reinforcing human rights and implementing anti-discrimination policies; improving the treatment of detainees and applying recommendations of the Ombudsman.[85] The October 2012 EU Commission Report examines Albania's ability to take on the obligations of membership, i.e. the *acquis*, as expressed in the Treaties, secondary legislation and policies of the Union, including Albania's administrative

---

[79] For more information, visit http://ec.europa.eu/enlargement/potential-candidate-countries/albania/eu_albania_relations_en.htm. Accessed 16 August 2013.

[80] For the full text of the SAA, visit http://ec.europa.eu/enlargement/pdf/albania/st08164.06_en.pdf. Accessed 16 August 2013.

[81] See *inter alia* Zaganjori et al. (2011), p. 66.

[82] Namely, Bosnia and Herzegovina, Kosovo, Macedonia (FYROM), Montenegro and Serbia. Slovenia joined the EU on 1 May 2004 and Croatia joined on 1 July 2013.

[83] See *inter alia* Bogdani (2007); Zahariadis (2007).

[84] See Law No. 9121, On Competition Protection, 28 July 2003. The mission of the Competition Authority is the protection of free and effective competition in the market through the implementation of legislation on competition. For more information, visit http://www.caa.gov.al. Accessed 16 August 2013.

[85] See Albania 2012 Progress Report, COM (2012) 600 final, 10 October 2012, available at http://ec.europa.eu/enlargement/pdf/key_documents/2012/package/al_rapport_2012_en.pdf. Accessed 16 August 2013. For the full text of the key priorities, see Commission Opinion on Albania's application for membership of the European Union, COM (2010) 680, available at http://eur-lex.europa.eu/LexUriServ/LexUriServ.do?uri=COM:2010:0680:FIN:EN:PDF. Accessed 16 August 2013.

capacity to implement the *acquis*. The analysis contained in the report is structured according to the list of the 33 *acquis* chapters. The EU Commission's assessment covers the progress achieved during the reporting period, and summarises Albania's overall level of preparedness. On the whole, while Albania has made considerable progress in several areas, a lot still remains to be done.

Obviously, joining the EU raises a number of issues concerning the sharing of sovereignty, the application of the SAA and related mutual legal obligations, and solving potential conflicts of law.[86] A number of problematic legal issues have already been encountered in the practice of other states and the relevant solutions are reflected in the Albanian Constitution of 1998. Under Article 123 of the Constitution, Albania may delegate to international organisations state powers for specific issues on the basis of international agreements. Such agreements need to be ratified by a majority of all the members of the Parliament, or if the Parliament so decides, through a referendum. Thus, the delegation of certain powers by Albania to EU institutions could occur through such an agreement. With regard to the place of EU law in the Albanian domestic legal system, reference needs to be made to Article 122(3) of the Constitution, which provides that norms issued by an international organisation have priority, in case of conflict, over the law of the country when the direct application of the norms issued by the organisation is expressly contemplated in the agreement ratified by Albania for participation therein. This position is generally in line with the Treaty on the Functioning of the European Union (TFEU), which empowers EU institutions to adopt regulations, directives, decisions, recommendations and opinions aimed at the progressive integration of Member States' economic and political systems and the establishment of a single market based on the free movement of goods, people, money and services.[87] This also complies with the case law of the European Court of Justice.[88] On the basis of Article 288 of the TFEU, EU regulations would be directly applicable in Albania, whereas EU directives would eventually need to be transposed into the Albanian legal system by means of specific laws.[89] EU regulations, directives and decisions would take precedence over national law and would be legally binding on national authorities, whereas EU recommendations and opinions would have no such binding force.

---

[86] See *inter alia* Zaganjori et al. (2011), pp. 59–64, 66–71.

[87] Article 288, Treaty on the Functioning of the European Union, OJ C 326, 26.10.2012, also available at http://eur-lex.europa.eu/en/treaties/new-2-47.htm. Accessed 16 August 2013. According to this article, a regulation shall have general application and shall be binding in its entirety and directly applicable in all Member States.

[88] See *inter alia* Case 26/62 *Van Gend en Loos v Nederlandse Belastingen* [1963]; Case 6/64 *Costa v ENEL* [1964] ECR 585; Case 11/70 *Internationale Handelsgesellschaft mbH v Einfuhr- und Vorratsstelle für Getreide und Futtermittel* [1970] ECR 1125; Case 106/77 *Amministrazione delle Finanze v Simmenthal SpA* [1978] ECR 629; *Macarthys v Smith* [1979] 3 All ER 325; Case C-213/89 *R (Factortame Ltd) v SS for Transport* [1990] ECR I-2433.

[89] For a detailed discussion of EU laws, see Craig and de Búrca (2011). Also visit http://ec.europa.eu/eu_law/introduction/treaty_en.htm. Accessed 16 August 2013.

After the entry into force of the SAA in April 2009, the Constitutional Court has made direct reference to EU laws. In a case before the Constitutional Court, the complainant claimed among others that a decision by the Albanian Council of Ministers had to be annulled as it was incompatible with the Constitution and international agreements, referring specifically to the SAA.[90] According to the complainant, the decision favoured a private enterprise with a dominant position in the market for products which had similar use and created similar problems concerning environmental pollution. The Constitutional Court found that on the basis of the SAA, the right of the state to intervene in the regulation of exercise of economic freedom was restricted by Article 33(2) of the SAA, which provides that:

> From the date of entry into force of this Agreement no new quantitative restriction on imports or exports or measure having equivalent effect shall be introduced, nor shall those existing be made more restrictive, in trade between the Community and Albania.

Given the fact that the decision by the Council of Ministers allowed only the selling of diesel product D2 produced in Albania, as well as the selling of diesel product D1 produced in Albania under more favourable conditions than that imported from abroad, the Constitutional Court decided that this decision was in violation of Articles 33(2) and 42 of the SAA.[91]

Another relevant case was decided on by the Constitutional Court in March 2010. The complainant, namely the Professional Association of Economists, claimed that the law on legal auditing and the organisation of the profession of registered auditors and chartered accountants was in violation of EU law, since it created a monopoly situation through the Institute of Authorised Auditors (*Instituti i Ekspertëve Kontabël të Autorizuar*), interfered with independence in the exercise of the profession of auditors, and discriminated against foreign auditors.[92] For these reasons, this law had to be struck down as unconstitutional.[93] The Constitutional Court pointed out that under EU law the profession of auditing was regulated under Directive 2006/43/EC, which had to be implemented by EU countries by 2008.[94] The Constitutional Court emphasised that there was no case of monopoly, since Law No. 10091 did not impede any person from obtaining the licence of an auditor, but simply regulated the manner in which such a licence could be gained and its ongoing supervision. In addition, in the Court's view, the Institute of Authorised Auditors was a professional, non-profit organisation, entrusted by the state with duties of supervision over the profession of legal auditing, in order for the latter to

[90] Decision No. 24, 24 July 2009, available at http://www.gjk.gov.al. Accessed 16 August 2013.

[91] Article 42 of the SAA prohibits prohibitions or restrictions which constitute a means of arbitrary discrimination or a disguised restriction on trade between the Parties.

[92] Law No. 10091, Për auditimin ligjor, organizimin e profesionit të ekspertëve kontabël të regjistruar dhe të kontabilistit të miratuar, 5 March 2009.

[93] Decision No. 3, 5 February 2010, available at http://www.gjk.gov.al. Accessed 16 August 2013.

[94] Directive 2006/43/EC of the European Parliament, and of the Council of 17 May 2006 on statutory audits of annual accounts and consolidated accounts, amending Council Directives 78/660/EEC and 83/349/EEC and repealing Council Directive 84/253/EEC.

provide quality services to the public. Referring to Article 32 of Directive 2006/43/EC, the Constitutional Court held that this law did not violate the principle of independence from state interference in the exercise of the profession, since the participation of public authorities in checking the activity of auditors served the public interest and could not be seen as interference in the free exercise of economic activity. Finally, in addressing the claim of discrimination against foreign auditors, the Constitutional Court stated that establishing certain criteria for foreign citizens who wanted to exercise this function in Albania did not necessarily entail discrimination. According to the Court, they had to demonstrate a sufficient knowledge concerning domestic commercial or fiscal legislation in order to provide a good service to the public in general and their clients in particular. The Court concluded that this single legal requirement concerning the exercise of the profession of auditor not only did not impede foreign citizens from working as auditors, but, on the contrary, could be considered as one of the most liberal legal systems because of the minimum criteria established by the lawmaker for this purpose.

7 International Criminal Law and Mechanisms in the Albanian Legal System

This section deals with the incorporation of international criminal law in the Albanian legal system and Albania's legal obligations in this field of international law.

7.1 The Applicable Legal Framework

Albania has signed and ratified a number of international instruments in the field of international criminal law and was among the original signatories to the Statute of the International Criminal Court (ICC), which it finally ratified on 31 January 2003.[95] On 2 August 2006, Albania acceded to the Agreement on the Privileges and Immunities (APIC) of the ICC. While Albania has not yet signed an agreement on the enforcement of sentences with the ICC, it has already done so with regard to the International Criminal Tribunal for the former Yugoslavia (ICTY). The agreement of 19 September 2008 allows for persons convicted by the ICTY to serve their

[95] In its Resolution 1300 (2002), the Parliamentary Assembly of the Council of Europe called on Albania (and a number of other member states of the Council of Europe) to ratify the ICC Statute (para 14(i)(b)). Moreover, in the same resolution the Parliamentary Assembly called on all member and observer states of the Council of Europe not to enter into any bilateral exemption agreements which would compromise or limit in any manner their co-operation with the court in the investigation and prosecution of crimes within its jurisdiction (para 14(iii)(c)).

sentences in Albanian prisons.[96] To this date no ICTY convicts have been transferred to Albania, despite its proximity to these persons' home countries. In deciding about the state where a convicted person will be transferred to serve his sentence, particular attention is given by the Tribunal to the proximity of the proposed state to the convicted person's relatives.[97] Mr. Haradin Bala, a Kosovar Albanian convicted by the ICTY, was transferred to France to serve his sentence in May 2008. At the time when the Presidency and the Registry of the ICTY made that decision, there was no agreement between Albania and the Tribunal. It is of course hard to say whether Mr. Bala would have been transferred to Albania if the agreement had been adopted beforehand.

Some changes were made to Albanian substantive and procedural criminal law in order to bring it into conformity with the ICTY and ICC Statutes. Thus, Articles 73,[98] 74[99] and 75[100] of the Albanian Criminal Code now criminalise respectively: genocide, crimes against humanity and war crimes. The definitions of these crimes follow to some extent those contained in the ICTY Statute. However, the definitions of these crimes under the Albanian Criminal Code are far from the detailed provisions of the ICC Statute.

At the EU Foreign Ministers' meeting of 30 September 2002, the Council of the European Community adopted Conclusions on the International Criminal Court, which introduced the 'EU Guiding Principles concerning Arrangements between a State Party to the Rome Statute of the International Criminal Court and the United

---

[96] Agreement between the United Nations and the Republic of Albania on the Enforcement of Sentences of the International Criminal Tribunal for the former Yugoslavia, 19 September 2008. Available at http://www.icty.org/x/file/Legal%20Library/Member_States_Cooperation/enforcement_agreement_albania_19_09_08_en.pdf. Accessed 16 August 2013.

[97] Practice Direction on the Procedure for the International Tribunal's Designation of the State in Which a Convicted Person is to Serve His/Her Sentence of Imprisonment, 1 September 2009 (IT/137/Rev. 1), par. 5. The relevant part reads: 'Particular consideration shall be given to the proximity [of the State] to the convicted person's relations.' Available at http://www.icty.org/sections/LegalLibrary/PracticeDirections. Accessed 16 August 2013.

[98] Article 73 provides: 'The execution of a premeditated plan aiming at the total or partial destruction of a national, ethnic, racial or religious group or directed towards its members, and combined with the following acts: intentionally killing a group's members, serious physical and psychological harm, placement in difficult living conditions which cause physical destruction, applying birth-preventing measures, as well as the obligatory transfer of children from one group to another, is sentenced with no less than 10 years of imprisonment, or with life imprisonment.'

[99] Article 74 provides: 'Homicide, extermination, use as slaves, deportation and exile, or any kind of torture or other human violence that is committed with a pre-meditated concrete plan against a civilian population group for political, ideological, racial, ethnic or religious motives are all punishable by no less than 15 years in jail or by life imprisonment.'

[100] Article 75 provides: 'Acts committed by different people in war time such as murder, maltreatment or deportation for slave labour, as well as any other inhuman exploitation to the detriment of the civilian population in an occupied territory, the killing or maltreatment of war prisoners, the killing of hostages, the destruction of private or public property, and the destruction of towns, commons or villages, which are not ordained by military necessity, are sentenced with no less than 15 years of imprisonment, or life imprisonment.'

States Regarding the Conditions to Surrender of Persons to the Court'. Albania has entered into an agreement with the US about the non-surrender by Albania of US citizens to the ICC.[101] This agreement could unnecessarily complicate Albania's efforts to integrate into the EU. By entering into this agreement, it appears that Albania has assumed competing legal obligations under the ICC Statute and this agreement. The EU Commission has called on Albania to align its position with the EU's.[102]

In terms of procedure and state co-operation, the Law on Jurisdictional Relations with Foreign Authorities in Criminal Matters,[103] provides for supplemental procedures when dealing with incoming and outgoing requests of inter-judicial co-operation. Article 3 states that its provisions also cover cases of proceedings that fall under the jurisdiction of international criminal courts whose jurisdiction Albania has accepted. This law provides for various forms of co-operation including extradition, transmission of letters rogatory, transfer of criminal proceedings, transfer of sentenced persons, and recognition and execution of foreign court decisions. The Ministry of Justice is designated as the central authority in terms of ensuring necessary co-operation with international criminal courts and tribunals.

7.2 The Compatibility of the Rome Statute with the Albanian Constitution

Before the ratification of the Rome Statute, the Albanian Constitutional Court was asked by the Albanian Council of Ministers for an opinion about the compatibility of the ICC Statute with the Albanian Constitution. The decision of the ACC of 23 September 2002 discusses a number of important issues, including the application of the principle of complementarity and the legal regime applicable in Albania regarding international immunities for persons accused of crimes set out in the ICC Statute.[104] The Constitutional Court noted that the activity of the ICC is complementary with national criminal jurisdictions in exercising the prosecution of natural persons responsible for grave crimes that are an affront to the whole international community and that can endanger the peace, security, and well-being of humankind. Further, in considering the issue of ICC jurisdiction *vis-à-vis* the constitutional concepts of sovereignty the ACC clarified that the complementary function of the ICC towards domestic judicial criminal jurisdiction, or *even the incorporation of the provisions of the Statute in the domestic legal order are not in contradiction with the Constitution or more concretely with Article 135, where the organs*

[101] Law No. 9081 of 19 June 2003.

[102] See Albania 2012 Progress Report, COM (2012) 600 final, 10 October 2012, p. 23.

[103] Law No. 10193, dated 3.12.2009.

[104] See Decision No. 186 of the Albanian Constitutional Court (ACC) of 23 September 2002, available at www.gjk.gov.al. Accessed 16 August 2013.

of judicial power in Albania created by law are strictly defined (emphasis added), and where the establishment of extraordinary courts is categorically prohibited. The ACC held that, from the content of the Statute itself, it becomes clear that here we are not speaking about a national organ or an extraordinary court. According to the ACC, the ICC in its nature is a legal judicial institution, created with the free will of the sovereign state parties to the Statute, the provisions of which are based on the principle of respecting human rights and freedoms.

While the ICC Statute is annexed to Law No. 8984 of 23 December 2002, which ratifies Albania's participation in the ICC Statute, the issue of the effect within Albanian law of the Elements of Crimes could be subject to different legal interpretations. Some guidance in this regard can be provided by Article 122 of the Albanian Constitution.[105]

Hence, by reading jointly all three paragraphs of Article 122, it can be concluded that the Elements of Crimes would also be applicable within the Albanian legal system. According to Decision No. 186 of the ACC, Law No. 8984 of 23 December 2002 ratifying the Statute, and the Albanian Constitution, Article 122, paragraphs 1, 2 and 3, it does not appear necessary to undertake any legislative reform, as the respective articles of the ICC Statute would be directly applicable within the Albanian legal system.[106]

Both the principle of *nullum crimen sine lege* (no crime without law) and that of *nulla poena sine lege* (no punishment without law), as components of the principle of legality, are applicable under Albanian criminal law, enshrined under Articles 2 and 3 of the Albanian Criminal Code respectively. In its Decision No. 186, the ACC stated:

> In particular, the Constitutional Court notices that the basic principles for the protection of fundamental human rights and freedoms also sanctioned and guaranteed by the Constitution of the Republic of Albania, such as: presumption of innocence; *nullum crimen sine lege* and *nullum poena sine lege*; the prohibition of retroactive power [of criminal law]; the right to be defended by legal counsel; the independence of the judges; appearance before the court before arrest or the right to appeal a decision, are also guaranteed by the Statute.

---

[105] Article 122 reads:

1. Any international agreement that has been ratified constitutes part of the internal juridical system after it is published in the Official Gazette of the Republic of Albania. It is implemented directly, except for cases when it is not self-executing and its implementation requires issuance of a law. The amendment, supplementing and repeal of laws approved by the majority of all members of the Assembly, for the effect of ratifying an international agreement, are done with the same majority.
2. An international agreement that has been ratified by law has superiority over laws of the country that are not compatible with it.
3. The norms issued by an international organisation have superiority, in case of conflict, over the laws of the country if the agreement ratified by the Republic of Albania for its participation in the organisation expressly contemplates their direct applicability.

[106] This is also the view expressed by Albania during the Review Conference of the Rome Statute in 2010. See document RC/ST/CP/M.2, 1 June 2010.

On the issue of universal jurisdiction for internationally recognised crimes, it must be said that Article 7(a) of the Albanian Criminal Code extends the jurisdiction of Albanian courts for crimes against humanity, war crimes, genocide, torture and terrorism committed outside Albanian territory, also to foreign citizens who are present on Albanian territory and whose extradition has not been sought.

The issue of the legal regime applicable in Albania regarding international immunities for persons accused of the crimes set out in the ICC Statute was addressed by the ACC in Decision No. 186, Part II, entitled 'Immunity in the Criminal Process'. The ACC stated that:

> The [ICC] Statute does not contradict or sidestep constitutional provisions relating to the immunity of a head of state and a number of other subjects regarding the immunity of these subjects belonging to national jurisdiction. This cannot impede an international organ such as the ICC in exercising its jurisdiction over persons of this category who have committed the crimes foreseen under the Rome Statute.

Criminalisation of the crime of aggression under Albanian criminal law, although this term is not explicitly employed, can be found in the Albanian Criminal Code under Chapter V, entitled 'Crimes against the Independence and Constitutional Order', Section I, entitled 'Crimes against Independence and Integrity', Articles 211 and 212. Article 211, entitled 'Provocation of War', reads: 'The carrying out of actions aimed at provoking war or putting the Republic of Albania at risk of intervention from foreign powers is punishable by not less than 15 years' imprisonment.' Article 212, entitled 'Conspiracy of an Armed Attack', reads: 'Conspiracy with powers or foreign states to cause an armed attack against the territory of the Republic of Albania is punishable by imprisonment from 10 to 15 years.' Further, Articles 217 and 218 of the Albanian Criminal Code criminalise respectively the receiving of rewards for crimes foreseen under Section I of Chapter V, and placement in the service of foreign states for committing acts against the independence or integrity of the Republic of Albania.

8 Concluding Remarks

The Albanian Constitution of 1998 regulates in quite some detail the interaction between international law and other sources of law, as well as the hierarchy among them within the Albanian legal system. Moreover, it also ensures that decisions adopted by international organisations to which Albania is a party are given direct effect in the Albanian legal order, in accordance with the relevant international agreements entered into between Albania and such international organisations. In providing that Albania applies international law that is binding upon it, Article 5 of the Constitution includes not only international treaties, but also customary international law and general principles of international law. Such an understanding follows Article 38 of the Statute of the International Court of Justice, which is regarded as providing a general list of sources of international law.

The case law of the Constitutional Court and the High Court have shed light on the applicability of international law in the Albanian legal system and have helped resolve certain conflicts of laws. Through a limited number of cases, these courts have shown that by and large they are capable of interpreting correctly the application of Albania's international legal obligations in the domestic legal system. Occasionally, this has entailed going as far as practically legislating in order to fill the gaps and to ensure that Albania complies with its international legal obligations, especially those enshrined under the ECHR, which also have a constitutional status in Albania. Notably, with regard to the issue of jurisdictional immunities, the High Court seems to have erroneously upheld, in principle, a foreign company's absolute immunity in civil cases, even in employment related disputes.

European law has a special place in the Albanian legal system in view of the SAA and Albania's aim of joining the EU in the near future. Since the entry into force of the SAA in April 2009, Albanian courts have started referring to EU laws directly, although strictly speaking they are not directly applicable until Albania joins the EU. The Albanian domestic legal framework provides a sufficient basis, albeit not entirely up-to-date, for the investigation and prosecution of the serious crimes criminalised under the ICC Statute and customary international law. For that reason, in terms of the principle of complementarity, it would be unlikely that the ICC could find Albania unable to genuinely investigate and prosecute crimes within the Court's jurisdiction. With regard to a bilateral agreement between the ICC and Albania concerning the enforcement of sentences rendered by the ICC, it remains to be seen whether Albania will eventually negotiate such an agreement with the ICC in the future.

References

Bogdani M (2007) Albania and the European Union: the tumultuous journey towards integration and accession. IBTauris, London

Brabandere E (2010) Immunity of international organizations in post-conflict administrations. Int Organ Law Rev 7(1):79–119

Craig P, de Búrca G (2011) EU law: text, cases, and materials, 5th edn. Oxford University Press, Oxford

Denza E (2010) The relationship between international law and national law. In: Evans M (ed) International law, 3rd edn. OUP, Oxford, pp 411–441

Hartwig M (2005) Much ado about human rights: the Federal Constitutional Court confronts the European Court of Human Rights. Ger Law J 06(05):869–894

Helfer RL (2008) Redesigning the European Court of Human Rights: embeddedness as a deep structural principle of the European human rights regime. Eur J Int Law 19(1):125–159

Omari L, Anastasi A (2010) E Drejta Kushtetuese. ABC, Tiranë

Ryngaert C (2010) The immunity of international organizations before domestic courts: recent trends. Int Organ Law Rev 7:121–148

Zaganjori X (2004) Vendi i së Drejtës Ndërkombëtare në Kushtetutën e Republikës së Shqipërisë. Jeta Juridike 2:26–34

Zaganjori X, Anastasi A, Çani (Methasani) E (2011) Shteti i së Drejtës në Kushtetutën e Republikës së Shqipërisë (The rule of law in the Constitution of the Republic of Albania). Adelprint, Tirana

Zahariadis Y (2007) The effects of the Albania–EU Stabilization and Association Agreement: economic impact and social implications. ESAU working paper 17, February 2007. www.odi.org.uk/sites/odi.org.uk/files/odi-assets/publications-opinion-files/2527.pdf. Accessed 16 Aug 2013

The Application of International and EU Law in Bosnia and Herzegovina

Zlatan Meškić and Darko Samardžić

1 Introduction

The application of international law in national legal systems is a well-established question in legal literature.[1] Both the globalisation and internationalisation of legal systems have given rise to questions that need to be answered legally, by laws and jurisprudence, and in legal literature.[2] The question of the enforcement of inter- or supranational obligations is directly linked to this application.[3] The goal of Bosnia and Herzegovina (BiH) to become a member of the EU has raised the question of the application of supranational law (EU law) in BiH, both in terms of preparing for membership and the country's status after entering the EU.[4] The Europeanisation of the national constitutions is already taking place.[5] For BiH, this is evident in the signing of the SAA and confirmed by the jurisprudence and literature oriented towards EU law. Formally, the EU is not a state and the treaties are not a constitution.[6] Nevertheless, the European treaties deal with constitutional questions and provide answers in a legally binding way.[7] At the same time, international law

[1] Denza (2006), p. 423; Keller (2003); Menzel (2011); Amrhein-Hofman (2003), p. 146; Pfeffer (2009).

[2] Emmerich-Fritsche (2007), pp. 41–50, 62–89; Payandeh (2010).

[3] Frowein (1987a), pp. 54–68; Meron (2008), pp. 247–301; Geiger (2010), Art. 4 EUV recital 37–48; Kaczorowska (2011), pp. 385–421, 924–960.

[4] Chalmers et al. (2010), p. 184; Menzel (2011), p. 352.

[5] Frowein (1987b), pp. 469–485.

[6] Kaczorowska (2011), pp. 198–234; Ullerich (2011), pp. 52, 69, 173; Streinz (2007), p. 395.

[7] Frowein (1987c), pp. 451–468; Bieber (1991), pp. 393–414; Pernice (2000), pp. 205–232.

Z. Meškić (✉) • D. Samardžić
Faculty of Law, University of Zenica, Fakultetska 3, 72000 Zenica, Bosnia and Herzegovina
e-mail: zmeskic@hotmail.com; darko.samardzic@conti.de

S. Rodin, T. Perišin (eds.), *Judicial Application of International Law in Southeast Europe*, DOI 10.1007/978-3-662-46384-0_7

has taken on the characteristics of constitutional law.[8] Hence, we have to clarify the relationships between international, supranational and constitutional competences, particularly the competences of the courts, the ECtHR (European Court of Human Rights), the ECJ (European Court of Justice) and national constitutional courts.[9] The need for such clarification is also based on the principle of the effectiveness of legal protection as an integral part of the principle of the rule of law.[10] The complexity of jurisdiction at the multi-system level can be described as 'conflicts among courts of different levels in networking legal systems'.[11] Other Member States of the EU and their constitutional courts likewise struggle with the hierarchy of norms and clarification of competences, both in terms of EU law[12] and international law.[13] It is remarkable that the *Solange* decision[14] of the German Constitutional Court of 1974–1986 is used as a model both in jurisprudence and legislation.[15] The key idea here is the 'model of co-operation' (*Kooperationsverhältnis*) instead of extremely divided competences creating a strict hierarchy among different legal systems.[16] Articles 52 and 53 of the Charter of Fundamental Rights of the EU guarantee a minimum standard of protection and acknowledge the guarantees provided by the ECHR.[17] The Charter of Fundamental Rights of the EU aims to achieve coherence in the protection of human rights at the different national, supra- and international levels.[18] To this end, the ECJ and ECtHR respect each other's decisions to ensure the greatest possible coherence of human rights standards by respecting other courts that are responsible for the protection of human rights.[19]

The application of international law is of particular interest for BiH, as the Constitution itself is part of an international agreement: Annex IV of the General Framework Agreement for Peace in Bosnia and Herzegovina (The Dayton Peace Agreement or DPA).[20] The Constitution entered into force in December 1995 with

[8] Kleinlein (2011); Klabbers et al. (2009); Geiger (2010), Art. 6 EUV recital 19–22.

[9] Ekardt and Lessmann (2006), pp. 381 f.; Nunner (2009); Sauer (2008), in particular pp. 261–344; Stender (2004).

[10] Munding (2010).

[11] Sauer (2008).

[12] Kaczorowska (2011), pp. 296–364; Geiger (2010), Art. 4 EUV recital 29–35.

[13] Frowein (1987d), pp. 407–431.

[14] Bleckmann (2011), pp. 149–219; Geiger (2010), Art. 4 EUV recital 29, 34, 35.

[15] Geiger (2010), Art. 4 EUV recital 29, 34, 35; Nunner (2009), pp. 159–164.

[16] Nunner (2009), pp. 50–408.

[17] Borowsky (2011), pp. 628–641, 667–715; Jarras (2010), Art. 52 recital 23–25, 34, 60–65, Art. 53; Stender (2004), pp. 82–85.

[18] Schneiders (2009), pp. 145–265; Brummund (2010).

[19] Stender (2004), pp. 69–85; Jarras (2010), Art. 52 recital 65; Nunner (2009), pp. 227–242, 249–258; Borowsky (2011), pp. 667–704.

[20] The General Framework Agreement for Peace in Bosnia and Herzegovina was signed between the Republic of Bosnia and Herzegovina, the Republic of Croatia and the Federal Republic of Yugoslavia on 14 December 1995.

the signing of the DPA, which was never ratified by the Parliament of BiH. The Constitution was written in English without an official translation into the official languages of BiH (Bosnian, Croatian and Serbian). Therefore, only unofficial translations are in use, which leads to different understandings of certain provisions or terms.[21] BiH is characterised by a complex state structure, as defined in the Constitution, with two entities (the Federation of BiH and Republika Srpska) and the District of Brčko. Republika Srpska is more centralised while the Federation of BiH is more decentralised and consists of ten cantons. Hence, altogether 13 constitutions exist within BiH: one for each entity and each canton in addition to the constitution at the state level. Due to this complex state structure, it is not easy to provide a comprehensive overview of the application of international legal sources in BiH.

The work in this book raises various crucial questions yet to be solved, such as the incorporation of international legal sources into the national legal system, the question of their direct effect, the position of international agreements within the national hierarchy of laws, which level of authority is competent for adopting legislative measures on the basis of the Stabilisation and Association Agreement (SAA), the need for a supreme court at the state level to become a member of the EU, etc. All these questions are classical issues of international and EU law. The additional complexity is caused by the constitutional structure of BiH itself. Nevertheless, the Constitution of BiH is open to development, and the goal of becoming a full member of the EU has advanced the application of international legal sources in BiH. The Constitutional Court of BiH (CC) does not always provide consistent conclusions or argumentation patterns, but it deals with crucial questions concerning the application of international law in the national legal systems. At the very least, the jurisprudence of the CC and the ECtHR has encouraged legal literature to become involved in these discussions.

2 Monistic and Dualistic Approaches in the Legal System of BiH

The incorporation of international law in national law is characterised by the two classical theories of monism and dualism.[22] In the theory of monism, only a single legal system of international and national law exists, with international law at the top of the hierarchy.[23] A transformation into the national legal system is not required and international law has precedence. From the dualistic perspective, international and national law represent two separate levels. Hence, an act

[21] Trnka (2006), p. 41.

[22] Amrhein-Hofman (2003); Emmerich-Fritsche (2007), pp. 90–103.

[23] Pfeffer (2009), pp. 85, 90; Amrhein-Hofman (2003), pp. 146–295.

transforming international law into the national legal system is needed.[24] The practical impact of these theories can be put aside, in that moderate dualistic and monistic approaches give rise to the same results.[25] From both perspectives, the effect within the national legal system has to be clarified. The Constitution of BiH does not explicitly provide for a monistic or dualistic approach towards international law. The non-ratification of the DPA formally speaks in favour of a monistic method.[26] However, ratification is only one indicator. With regard to other international legal sources, the conclusion depends on the interpretation of several provisions of the Constitution.

The Constitution of BiH explicitly qualifies the incorporation of international legal sources within the national legal system in Article III/3(b) with regard to general principles: 'general legal principles are an integral part of the legal system of Bosnia and Herzegovina and its entities'. Besides general principles, the Constitution explicitly mentions international agreements only with reference to human rights. All other international agreements need to be interpreted. According to Article II/2 of the Constitution of BiH, the rights and freedoms foreseen in the ECHR and its protocols have to be applied directly. These legal sources overrule other laws. Pursuant to Article II/4 of the Constitution of BiH, the rights and freedoms foreseen in the international agreements in Annex I of the Constitution are guaranteed to all people in BiH without discrimination. The title of Annex I is Additional Human Rights Agreements to be applied in Bosnia and Herzegovina. Articles II and III seem to follow a monistic approach of a unified legal system consisting of international and national law which apply directly within the national legal system.[27]

The question is whether the Constitution of BiH allows a general decision in favour of the monistic theory or if *argumentum e contrario* it is reasonable that the legislator has limited this understanding to the legal sources explicitly named. Thus, all other provisions are dedicated to the dualistic theory. An analogous application to all other legal sources could be explained by Article VI/3(c) of the Constitution of BiH. This provision enables the CC of BiH to judge if a 'law which is the basis for a decision is in line with the constitution, the ECHR and its protocols or with the laws of Bosnia and Herzegovina or with a general rule of public international law crucial for the decision of the court.'

The question arises as to whether the general rules of public international law, Article VI/3(c), and the general principles of international law, Article III/3(b), can be treated equally. On the one hand, the question is whether international law and public international law both comprise only public law, and on the other hand, whether the rules and principles are comparable in terms of their nature.

---

[24] Amrhein-Hofman (2003), pp. 80–144; Pfeffer (2009), p. 82.

[25] Denza (2006), p. 429; Ademović et al. (2012), p. 37; Stein et al. (2012), p. 58.

[26] Ademović et al. (2012), p. 39.

[27] Pobrić (2000), p. 20.

The dualistic system is dealt with in Article IV/4(d) of the Constitution of BiH, which requires ratification by the Parliamentary Assembly, whereupon the Presidency of Bosnia and Herzegovina, upon obtaining the formal consent of the BiH Parliamentary Assembly, decides on the ratification of an international treaty (Article V/3(d)). Once a decision is made, it is signed by the Presidency of BiH and published in the Official Gazette of BiH (the section on international treaties). This understanding is supported by Article 17 of the Procedure for the Conclusion and Execution of International Treaties Act.[28] According to this, the Presidency needs the ratification of the Parliamentary Assembly before acting.[29] Pursuant to Article 22 of the aforementioned law, an agreement comes into full force and effect if it complies with the provisions of the agreement, the law and the ratification.

Jointly and severally, the Constitution of BiH is based on a combination of monistic and dualistic approaches. The monistic approach relates to legal sources of international law with direct effect specified in the Constitution, while other legal sources of international law are covered by a moderate dualistic understanding.[30]

3 International Law in the Hierarchy of Laws in BiH

3.1 The ECHR and Its Protocols as Part of the DPA

A remarkable internationalisation of human rights has taken place and has given rise to questions such as direct effect and supremacy in a world of multilevel legal systems.[31] The protection of human rights has been implemented and intensified by legislation and jurisprudence at all these levels, with the consequence of an overlapping of legal protection. Meanwhile, we can speak about universal rights[32] and the individual being partly acknowledged as a subject of international law.[33] Without any doubt this triple dimension of protection (national, supra- and international) is positive, although we have to clarify the questions that arise. The application of the ECHR and its protocols in national legal systems is not answered in the ECHR itself, which gives rise to the need for interpretation.[34] The Member States of the EU and their constitutional courts try to give answers to this question.[35] One of the guides here is the German Constitutional Court with its

[28] Official Gazette BiH, No. 29/2000.

[29] The decision on the giving of consent by the Parliamentary Assembly for the signing of the SAA is published in OG BiH, No. 11/08, international agreements supplement.

[30] Degan (2000), p. 15.

[31] Schilling (2010), pp. 2–15; Steiner et al. (2007), pp. 3–456; Addo (2010), pp. 83–152.

[32] Kälin and Künzli (2005), pp. 22–35; Schilling (2010), p. 16.

[33] Steiner et al. (2007), pp. 475–668; Kälin and Künzli (2005), pp. 17–22.

[34] Pfeffer (2009), p. 147; Steiner (2006), p. 753; Addo (2010), in particular pp. 287–342.

[35] Borowsky (2011), pp. 628–641, 667–715; Frowein (1987d), pp. 407–431.

well-known *Solange* decision and implementation of the co-operation model (*Kooperationsverhältnis*). Such innovative decisions have supported the development of human rights protection and guarantees. Legislators have now acknowledged this with multilevel guarantees, as provided for in Article 6 TEU.[36]

The Constitution of BiH explicitly gives direct effect to the ECHR and its protocols. Article VI/3(c) enables the CC to examine if a law is in line with the general rules of international law, which indicates the primacy of the general rules of international law over national law. This leads to the conclusion of the precedence of international law, given the Constitution declares the direct effect of international law. According to Article II/2 of the Constitution of BiH: 'The rights and freedoms set forth in the European Convention for the Protection of Human Rights and Fundamental Freedoms and its Protocols shall apply directly in Bosnia and Herzegovina . . . and have priority over all other law.' International conventions listed in Annex I to the Constitution of BiH that provide protection to human rights are considered to be at constitutional level due to their formal inclusion in the Constitution.[37] However, the wording of Article II/2, 'whereby the rights and freedoms set forth in the ECHR shall have priority over all other law', does not clarify if the ECHR has priority over the Constitution itself. Some authors argue in favour of the supremacy of the ECHR over the Constitution.[38]

This question was the issue in Case No. U 5/04 before the CC of BiH. The Court had to decide if it was competent to judge on the compatibility of the Constitution with the ECHR. According to Article II/2 of the Constitution of BiH, the ECHR is directly applicable.[39] However, the Court restricted its competence to the interpretation of the Constitution and not an examination of the ECHR itself. In an *obiter dictum*, it concluded that the ECHR cannot have priority over the Constitution of BiH, because it entered into force by means of the Constitution itself. This *obiter dictum* creates a formal hierarchy limiting the power of the Parliament. The Parliament has the legitimacy to change the Constitution to declare an integration of international law in national legislation.

The question of the relationship between the ECHR and the Constitution is of great importance for BiH, especially in the light of the recent *Sejdić and Finci* judgment of the ECtHR.[40] The conclusion of this decision is that the provisions of the Constitution of BiH violate Article 14 ECHR together with Article 3 Protocol No. 1, as well as Article 1 Protocol No. 12, because of the ineligibility of the applicants to stand for election to the House of Peoples and the Presidency of BiH due to their Roma and Jewish origins. The compliance of electoral rights with this

---

[36] Schneiders (2009); Geiger (2010), Art. 6 EUV; Kaczorowska (2011), pp. 235–255; Munding (2010).

[37] Ademović et al. (2012), p. 38.

[38] Steiner and Ademović (2010), p. 154, with further references.

[39] Dougan (2007), p. 934.

[40] European Court of Human Rights, 22.12.2009, Applications Nos. 27996/06 and 34836/06 (Sejdić and Finci); Kulenović et al. (2010), p. 18.

decision is a *condition sine qua non* required by the EU for the SAA[41] with BiH to enter into full force and effect. This precondition set by the EU requires amendments to the Constitution which are difficult to achieve in legislation. The CC could have supported the legislative process by declaring the supremacy of the ECHR. Therefore, the supremacy of the ECHR over the Constitution combined with the direct effect expressly provided for in Article II/2 of the Constitution of BiH would eliminate such discrimination in a more effective way. In addition, the CC has to recognise the supremacy of EU law as the result of its direct effect at the latest when BiH becomes a full member of the EU.[42] The protection of human rights on the basis of the ECHR was recognised as a general principle of EU law and as part of the rule of law by the ECJ as far back as the 1960s and subsequently in countless decisions.[43]

3.2 Other International Agreements in the Annexes of the DPA

For other sources of international law in the legal system of BiH, there is no explicit provision regulating the hierarchy of laws. Since the Constitution of BiH is contained in an international agreement (the DPA), the question has arisen whether other Annexes of the DPA are at the same legal level as the Constitution itself. In decisions U 7/97,[44] U 7/98[45] and U 40/00,[46] the CC decided the Annexes of the DPA supplement each other and cannot be examined in terms of their inconsistency with the Constitution, confirming the other Annexes of the DPA and general legal principles of international law to be at a constitutional level.[47] This opinion is supported by the Constitution in Article III/3(b), acknowledging general principles of international law to be an integral part of the law of BiH and its entities.

[41] SAA signed on 16.6.2008; *OJ of Bosnia and Herzegovina* No. 5/08, international agreements.

[42] Dougan (2007), p. 934.

[43] The development of the practice of the ECJ slowly began with the decision of 12 November 1969, 29/69 - *Stauder* [1969] ECR 419, para 7; now provided for under Art. 6(3) TEU; Samardžić and Meškić (2012), pp. 11–35.

[44] CC, U 7/97 of 22.12.1997.

[45] CC, U 7/98 of 26.2.1999.

[46] CC, U 40/00, of 2.2.2001.

[47] CC, U 5/09 of 25.9.2009, 30.

3.3 Other International Agreements Not Contained in the DPA

For other international agreements, besides those listed in Annex I of the Constitution of BiH, the CC decided (Decision U 5/09):

> there is no constitutional provision regulating the introduction of international treaties in domestic law as condition for their applicability; in particular, the constitution does not prescribe to 'transform' international rules in domestic law through a law. If consequently international treaties on human rights have a quasi-constitutional rank, there is no indication of a simply ordinary legislative rank for the other treaties in the constitution.

Thereby the CC excluded the *argumentum a contrario* that international treaties on human rights explicitly enjoy constitutional rank and therefore all other treaties are at the level of regular laws. It seems that the court presumes international agreements to be below constitutional rank but above regular laws, although there is no deeper argumentation or any legislative basis provided to support this view.[48]

3.4 The SAA for BiH

The SAA for BiH does not give rise to any doubt as to its direct effect. The Parliament approved this agreement in accordance with the internal provisions of BiH. Hence, it can immediately enter into full force and effect. Individual provisions of this agreement as well as the Interim Agreement have already entered into force and effect with the signing of the SAA.[49] The EU usually ratifies 'mixed agreements' directly after the Member States have done so, so that there is no partial application of the agreement on the territory of the EU.[50] France was the last Member State to ratify the SAA with BiH on 10 February 2011.[51] However, the EU will not ratify the SAA until BiH implements the ECtHR *Sejdić-Finci* decision, because without its implementation BiH violates Article 1 of the Interim Agreement.

The position of the SAA within the hierarchy of laws is not regulated. Thus, it has to be determined by interpretation. The first indicator is the direct effect of the SAA as acknowledged by the Parliament. Secondly, Article 28 of the Procedure for the Conclusion and Execution of International Treaties Act provides that 'international agreements which establish direct obligations for Bosnia and Herzegovina are executed by the competent institutions of the state administration whose

---

[48] Ibid; Ademović et al. (2012), p. 38.

[49] The Interim Agreement was published in the OG BiH international agreements supplement, No. 5/08 and entered into force on 30 June 2008.

[50] Vöneky (2009), para. 27.

[51] Http://www.consilium.europa.eu/App/accords/Default.aspx?command=details&id=297&lang=EN&aid=2008023&doclang=EN. Accessed 1 March 2011.

competence covers areas regulated by those agreements'. According to the subsequent Article: 'International agreements which are concluded by Bosnia and Herzegovina, and which establish obligations for domestic legal persons, are directly executed by those legal persons'. It is clear that the legal system of BiH recognises the direct effect of international agreements outside of the system of protection of human rights and general principles of international law that establish obligations which nationals of BiH may directly refer to domestic institutions. However, neither the Constitution nor other provisions in the legal system of BiH explicitly solve the problem of which law is applicable in the case of a conflict between national law and the provisions of international treaties which do not regulate human rights. Generally, the direct effect of an international treaty would be annulled in the event of a conflict of its provisions with national law, and the latter would be applicable. This argument may be supported by Article 32 of the Procedure for the Conclusion and Execution of International Treaties Act, according to which an 'international treaty will temporarily or permanently cease in its application in accordance with its provisions or the general rules of the international law of treaties'. However, a conflicting national law cannot eliminate the application of international agreements. Finally, the Constitution of BiH consistently gives the provisions of international agreements which are directly applicable the power of supremacy over national laws. Therefore, there is no reason for international agreements which gain direct effect through the internal procedure of ratification to have the same legal power as regular laws, as then they could be derogated by the latter.

Secondary association law, according to the jurisprudence of the ECJ established in *Sevince*,[52] is an integral part of EU law and can have direct effect under the same conditions as the provisions of the SAA. The ECJ has explained that the decisions of the Association Council (in the case of BiH, the Stabilisation and Association Council) are based on the Agreement, as the Association Council is an authority established by it with the responsibility for its implementation.[53] The decisions of the institutions established by the SAA fulfil the goal of the Agreement,[54] and consequently do not require any implementing act in order to have effect.[55] In addition, the direct effect of secondary association law cannot be denied either because the provisions of the SAA do not have direct effect[56] or because the decision of the Association Council was not published.[57] In legal science, such a view of the ECJ is justified by the fact that the decisions of the institutions which adopted secondary association law are part of the international agreement by their

[52] Case C-192/89 *S. Z. Sevince v. Staatssecretaris van Justitie* [1990] I-3461, 9.

[53] Ibid.

[54] Case C-277/94 *Z. Taflan-Met v. Bestuur van de Sociale Verzekeringsbank* [1996] I-4085, 18.

[55] Case 30/88 *Greece v. Commission* [1989] I-3711, 16.

[56] Schmalenbach (2007).

[57] Case C-192/89 *S. Z. Sevince v. Staatssecretaris van Justitie* [1990] I-3461, 24.

nature, and therefore they have the same direct effect as primary association law.[58] Consequently, secondary association law in the hierarchy of law within EU law is below primary association law, but at the same level as the SAA in relation to the national law of BiH.

The specific content, nature and purpose of the SAA, together with its direct effect and supremacy, give rise to complex legal questions with regard to its application and execution. As an example, Article 71(2) of the SAA provides that:

> Any practices contrary to this Article shall be assessed on the basis of criteria arising from the application of the competition rules applicable in the Community, in particular from Articles 81, 82, 86 and 87 of the EC Treaty and interpretative instruments adopted by the Community institutions.

The direct effect of Article 72(2) would mean that BiH, when applying national competition law (which is harmonised with EU law), needs to apply the decisions of the Commission and ECJ adopted on the basis of its provisions. This does not only cause practical problems, bearing in mind that there is no official translation of these decisions in any of the three official languages in BiH and nor are people who finished law school more than 3 years ago educated in any EU Law, but this obligation also requires a transition of legislative powers to the EU, stating that BiH is obliged to directly apply all competition rules, not only from primary but also from secondary EU law, as well as future provisions and interpretations adopted by the Commission and the ECJ. Such a conclusion is based on the wording 'in particular', which shows that a whole set of competition rules from EU law is meant by Article 71(2) SAA, comprising those becoming applicable on the basis of the SAA at the moment of ratification, as well as those which are going to be adopted by the EU legislature in the future.[59]

The confirmation of such an interpretation can also be found in the 'harmonisation clause' in Article 70 of the SAA, which obliges BiH to 'ensure that its existing laws and future legislation will be gradually made compatible with the Community *acquis*. Bosnia and Herzegovina shall ensure that existing and future legislation will be properly implemented and enforced'. When speaking about the *acquis*, it is clear that it also includes provisions at the EU level which are adopted after the ratification of the SAA, as in the contrary case, BiH would by the time it became a full member of the EU (which could take several years) have the legal status it had in 2008. An additional confirmation may be found in Article 43 of the Competition Act of BiH,[60] which provides that 'For the purpose of the assessment of a specific case, the Council of Competition may use the case law of the European Court of Justice and decisions of the European Commission'. While this provision proves that national institutions are going to harmonise the domestic legal order with current and future EU law, it is noticeable that the formulation of Article 43 of the Competition Act leads to the conclusion that the Council of

---

[58] Vöneky (2009); K. Schmalenbach, u Ch. Calliess/M. Ruffert, Art. 310, para 34.

[59] Vukadinović (2010).

[60] OG BiH, No. 48/05; amendments OG BiH Nos. 76/07 and 80/09.

Competition may, but does not have to, take into consideration the jurisprudence of the ECJ and the Commission. Such a solution is reminiscent of the practice of the CC of Hungary when it was a candidate country and ratified an Association Agreement with the Member States and the EU. At that time, the CC decided that Article 62(2) of the Association Agreement signed between Hungary and the EU, which in its formulation corresponds to Article 71(2) of the SAA signed between BiH and the EU, represented an 'unconstitutional transfer of legislative powers as a part of state sovereignty to another sovereign body', and therefore the criteria listed in the Article could not be applied directly, but might be 'taken into consideration'.[61] One solution for the relationship of the Constitution of BiH to the SAA can be found in the *Kupferberg*[62] decision, where the ECJ pointed out that according to international law the parties needed to execute the agreement *bona fide*. Therefore, every party may choose the legal means which are appropriate to fulfil the commitments made, unless through interpretation of the agreement in terms of its nature or purpose it arises that measures listed in the agreement need to be conducted. The obligation specified in the harmonisation clause of Article 70 SAA demand harmonisation at two levels for BiH:

1. harmonisation of entity provisions in order to create the preconditions for the full freedom of movement of goods, persons, services and capital according to Article I/4 of the Constitution of BiH;
2. harmonisation of entity legislation with EU law with the goal of entry into the new market.[63]

As the example from competition law shows, certain provisions of the SAA have direct effect in the legal system of BiH, but the whole national law when implemented and applied also needs to be interpreted in line with EU law.[64] It needs to be remembered that the harmonisation clause became obligatory with the signing of the SAA, regardless of the entry into force of the complete SAA.

4 Direct Application of International Agreements Listed in Annex I of the Constitution

A further interesting question the CC has had to clarify is whether the international agreements listed in Annex I of the Constitution of BiH are applicable independently or only in combination with the prohibition of discrimination contained in Article II/4 of the Constitution of BiH. Article II does not expressly give an answer to this question. According to Article II/1 'the highest level of internationally

[61] Vukadinović (2010).

[62] Case 104/81 *Hauptzollamt Mainz v. C.A. Kupferberg & Cie KG a.A* [1982] 3641, 4.

[63] Popović (2010).

[64] Rodin (2003).

recognized human rights and fundamental freedoms' shall be ensured, while according to Article II/7, 'BiH shall remain or become party to the international agreements listed in Annex I to this Constitution'. Consequently, Article II/4 on 'Non-discrimination' is the only paragraph expressly regulating the applicability of the international agreements listed in Annex I: 'the enjoyment of the rights and freedoms provided for in this Article or in the international agreements listed in Annex I to this Constitution shall be secured to all persons in Bosnia and Herzegovina without discrimination'.

The CC in its most recent decisions denies the independent application of the international agreements listed in Annex I.[65] In the view of the Court, the international agreements, unlike the ECHR, which is directly applicable under Article II/2, are only applicable if the applicant claims that he has been discriminated against in the enjoyment of the rights and freedoms guaranteed in the international agreements. Steiner and Ademović give some convincing arguments against this view. Firstly, Article II/2 on 'Non-discrimination' does not exclusively refer to Annex I, but to Article II as a whole. It is unclear why the right of refugees to freely return to their home guaranteed by Article II/5 applies independently of the prohibition of discrimination, and the rights and freedoms contained in the international agreements do not.[66] In addition, the application of certain rights and freedoms only in combination with the prohibition of discrimination makes no sense. For example, bearing in mind Article 2 of the Optional Protocol No. 2 to the International Covenant on Civil and Political Rights, which in principle prohibits the imposition of the death penalty in a time of peace, we could come to the absurd conclusion that the violation of this right might be established only if the death penalty was imposed on individuals in a selective and discriminatory manner.[67]

5 The Application of ECJ and ECHR Judgments by the Constitutional Court: The Example of the Adoption of Private Law

Constitutional rights are deemed as a guarantee ensured by the state authorities, and human rights are no longer only the protection of rights against breaches by state authorities. In addition, the direct and horizontal effects of international law on national and private law are increasing. This is evident in private law relations, bearing in mind that the state needs to ensure constitutional rights but is not competent in the adoption of private law. The Constitution of BiH in Article III/1 lists exclusive competences and in Article III/5 provides certain additional

[65] CC, 20.03.2007., AP-379/07, MPA "Posavina promet" d.o.o, para 17; CC, 9.5.2007, AP-813/06, Rahman Selimović, para 17.

[66] Steiner and Ademović (2010), p. 165.

[67] Ibid, p. 163; See also Marković (2011), p. 344.

competences of the authorities. All state competences not expressly assigned to the state level are the responsibility of the entities in accordance with Article III/3(a). Thus, BiH has four Labour Acts (three established by the entities and the District of Brčko, and one at the state level)[68] and also three company acts (one for each entity).[69] In addition, private law acts assumed in the basis of succession from Yugoslavia are considered to be entity acts, such as the acts on obligations.[70]

Altogether the division of competences between the state and entity levels in Article III is not clear and has to be interpreted.[71] Interpretation is also needed for competences established outside of Article III. A further question is which level is responsible for the enforcement of international obligations established by the Constitution at the state level. The focus here is on the guarantee of human rights and fundamental freedoms in accordance with Article II, as well as market freedoms in accordance with Article I/4.

According to Article I/4, neither the state nor the entities shall impede the full freedom of the movement of persons, goods, services, and capital throughout BiH. This provision on the one hand requires the creation of a 'free area' in the territory of BiH (negative integration), and on the other hand the adoption of all necessary measures in order to establish market freedoms throughout BiH (positive integration). The CC has not specified the requirements of Article I/4. Thus, it considers that an interpretation in line with EU law and jurisprudence is needed.[72]

To handle constitutional competences, the CC uses the theory of 'implied powers'.[73] The implied powers theory does not allow intervention in the existing division of powers, but supplements the execution of explicitly listed competences.[74] There is a weakness in the theory of implied powers if there is no common understanding, which was made clear by the CC in its statement:

[68] OG BiH, Nos. 26/04, 7/05, 48/05 and 60/10; OG FBiH, Nos. 43/99, 32/00 and 29/03; OG RS, Nos. 38/00, 40/00, 47/02, 38/03, 66/03, 66/03 and 20/07; OG DB, Nos. 19/06, 19/07 and 25/08.

[69] OG FBiH, Nos. 23/99, 45/00, 2/02, 6/02, 29/03, 68/05, 91/07, 84/08, 88/08, 7/09 i 63/10; OG RS, Nos. 127/08, 58/09, 100/11; OG DB, Nos. 11/01, 10/02, 14/02, 1/03, 8/03, 4/04, 19/07, 34/07.

[70] Since the break-up of Yugoslavia, this Act (Official Journal of the Socialist Federal Republic of Yugoslavia, Nos. 29/78, 39/85, 46/85, 45/89, 57/89) by virtue of succession has remained applicable in two slightly different versions in each entity of Bosnia and Herzegovina: the Obligations Act of Republika Srpska (OJ of Republika Srpska, Nos. 17/93, 57/98, 39/03, 74/04) and the Obligations Act of the Federation of Bosnia and Herzegovina (OJ of the Republic of Bosnia and Herzegovina, Nos. 2/29, 13/93, 13/94 and Official Journal of the Federation of Bosnia and Herzegovina, No. 29/03).

[71] See in more detail, Steiner and Ademović (2010), p. 577; Meškić (2011a), p. 355; Trnka (2006), p. 274; Begić (1997), p. 300.

[72] CC BiH, 25.06.2004, U 68/02, para 41.

[73] The theory of 'implied powers' seeks to make the restrictive interpretation of listed competences more flexible. For the EU, this theory means that institutions have the necessary powers to execute the powers listed in the Treaties; Joint cases 281, 283, 285 and 287/85 *Germany v. Commission* [1987] I-3203.

[74] Case 165/87 *Commission v. Council* [1988] I-5545; Nettesheim (2003), pp. 389–441.

> Bosnia and Herzegovina, functioning as a democratic state, was authorised to establish, in the areas under its responsibility, other mechanisms, besides those provided in the constitution of Bosnia and Herzegovina, and additional institutions that were necessary for the exercise of its responsibilities.[75]

The question is whether common responsibility means shared competence for the regulation of the matter. The more recent practice of the CC supports the model having joint obligations.[76] Previously, the Human Rights Commission of the CC expressly established shared competences.[77] The Constitution does not contain an exhaustive list of shared competences, as is the case with exclusive competences. The Constitution provides shared competences for co-operation between the entities and the state, e.g. Article III/2(b) or Article III/2(d). With shared competences, more flexible and dynamic solutions between the state and entities can be achieved.[78] Therefore, the transformation of common responsibilities into shared competences has been accepted in jurisprudence and the literature.[79] The criteria of the necessity of adopting acts in order to fulfil constitutional obligations has been introduced and examined on the basis of the principles of subsidiarity and proportionality.[80]

The CC points out in Decision U 68/02 that the general clause on the internal market in BiH needs to be interpreted in line with EU law and the ECJ.[81] Here, the Court relies on the ECJ *Schul*[82] judgment, stating that the substantive notion of a 'single market' implies that the internal market of Bosnia and Herzegovina 'should be created by repealing all technical, administrative and other measures'. By means of a grammatical interpretation of Article I/4, the Court firstly concludes:

> entities are obliged not to prevent the accomplishment of this principle (second sentence, Article I/4), and that this does not prevent the State from acting positively so as to fulfil its goal (first sentence, Article I/4), and thus confirms the principles of negative and positive integration with regards to Article I/4.

Secondly, in the same decision, the Court established a connection between Articles I/4 and II/4 on the prohibition of discrimination. The notion of prohibition

---

[75] CC BiH, 18.2.2000, U 5/98-II, para 29; CC BiH, 28.09.2001, U-26/01, para 26; CC BiH, 10.5.2002, U 18/00, paras 47 and 51; CC BiH, 28.5.2010, U 12/09, para 31.

[76] CC BiH, 28.5.2010, U 12/09, para 31: 'the State and the Entities have the joint obligation not only to ensure the highest level of protection of human rights but also to guarantee an equal implementation of these rights.'

[77] Human Rights Commission within the CC, 13.06.2006, CH/02/12468 *et al.*, para 152.

[78] This is suggested by the title of the chapter 'Concurrent competences' in Steiner and Ademović (2010), p. 585.

[79] E.g. Steiner and Ademović (2010), p. 580; Begić (1997), p. 300; Kurtćehajić and Ibrahimagić (2007), p. 274. For an opposite opinion, see Pobrić (2000), p. 344. With regard to certain responsibilities, authors argue in favour of the exclusive competence of the state, e.g. macroeconomic stability in BiH. See European Commission Delegation to BiH (2003), p. 42.

[80] Meškić (2011b), p. 54.

[81] CC BiH, 25.06.2004, U 68/02, para 41.

[82] Case 15/81 *Schul* [1982] I-1409, para 33.

of discrimination includes not only technical measures but also positive legislation and a positive obligation of the state to guarantee the institutional protection of prohibition of discrimination.[83] With regard to the single market, the state is obliged to institutionally guarantee the prohibition of discrimination on the grounds of residence or entity citizenship.[84] Thirdly, the Court deems it possible to ensure the principles of the common market although the competences are split:

> Although the constitutional distribution of competences under Article III of the Constitution of Bosnia and Herzegovina allocated certain competences to the Entities that may influence the creation of a single market as the State's obligation, the autonomous status of the Entities is conditioned by the hierarchically superior competences of the State, which includes protection of the Constitution of Bosnia and Herzegovina and its principles ... In this regard, the supremacy of the State over the Entities and the District of Brčko, which follows from Article III (3) (b) of the Constitution, allows it to take appropriate measures to secure the enjoyment of constitutional rights to all persons.

It is noticeable that the lack of state competence in adopting private law has shifted the question of positive integration under Article I/4 into the focus of the CC. By interpreting the state obligation to guarantee rights under Articles I/4 and II in a non-discriminatory way, the Court has the tendency to give competences to the state to adopt private law where it finds it 'necessary', but it does not expressly state in which form this is to be conducted.

This is clearly expressed in Decision U 5/98-II[85]:

> The different legal systems of the Entities, with different types of property or regulations of property law, may indeed form an obstacle to the freedom of movement of goods and capital as provided for in Article I/4 of the Constitution of BiH. Moreover, the constitutionally guaranteed right to privately owned property, as an institutional safeguard throughout Bosnia and Herzegovina, requires framework legislation by the State of Bosnia and Herzegovina in order to specify the standards necessary to fulfil the positive obligations of the Constitution elaborated above. Hence, such framework legislation should determine, at least, the various forms of property, the holders of these rights, and the general principles for the exercise of property rights in property law that usually constitute an element of civil law codes in democratic societies.

Negative integration in the spirit of Article I/4 has not been the subject of private law cases before the CC. However, bearing in mind the practice of the Court, Article I/4 should be interpreted in the light of the ECJ demanding the consideration of horizontal effect (*Drittwirkung*)[86] as a link between public and private law. An example is Case U 12/09,[87] where the CC analysed the maternity pay of public servants at state institutions. Since issues connected with the principle of the welfare state fall within the competence of the entities, the challenged provision

[83] CC BiH, 5.10.2002, U 18/00 No. 30/02.

[84] CC BiH, 28.5.2010, U 12/09, para 30.

[85] CC BiH, 18.2.2000, U 5/98-II, para 29.

[86] Case C-281/98 *Roman Angonese v. Cassa di Risparmio di Bolzano* [2000] I-4139, para 34; Meškić and Samardžić (2012), p. 297.

[87] CC BiH, 28.5.2010, U 12/09, para 30.

of Article 35 of the Salaries and Remunerations in the Institutions of BiH Act[88] with regard to the calculation and payment of maternity leave benefits only referred to 'the regulations governing this field according to the place of payment of the contributions per each employee'. In practice, this provision had the effect that employees resident in Republika Srpska are guaranteed to receive their whole salary, while in the Federation of BiH this issue is ruled by the Federation authorities as well as by the cantons or even the municipalities, which results in important differences, with some cantons not paying any benefits at all.

The CC firstly stated that female employees in state institutions had been treated differently in comparable situations. As a justification for such discrimination, the division of competences between the state and the entities was taken into consideration. The Court pointed out that in this area responsibilities are granted by the Constitution to the state. These responsibilities are partly of an international and partly of a national character, and arise with regard to the creation of working conditions without discrimination under Article II/4 of the Constitution of BiH together with Article 1 Protocol No. 12 ECHR, and under Article I/4 on the establishment of the single market in BiH. The Court emphasised its previous practice, according to which Article I/4 needs to be interpreted in the light of ECJ jurisprudence, which is why:

> social benefits like maternity leave for employees of state institutions should not depend on the residence of the person in question, given that the idea of a single market implies that the state makes an employment opportunity equally attractive to all citizens of BiH, notwithstanding entity boundaries, entity citizenship, or place of residence.

The Court pointed out that EU Regulation No. 1408/71 on the application of social security schemes to employed persons and to members of their families moving within the Community[89] needs to be respected, as well as further international conventions.[90] Finally, the Court concluded: 'the competence of the entities to regulate social policy is not appropriate to the aim sought to be achieved with regard to social protection and equal remuneration', and 'thus, the state and the entities have the joint obligation not only to ensure the highest level of protection of human rights but also to guarantee an equal implementation of these rights'.

[88] OG No. 50/08 and 35/09.

[89] OJ EU 1997, L 28, p. 1.

[90] These are the Convention on the Elimination of All Forms of Discrimination against Women (1979), International Covenant on Civil and Political Rights and the 1966 and 1989 Optional Protocols thereto (1966).

6 Application of SAA and ECJ Jurisprudence: The Example of Competition Law

Another example is the Competition Act of BiH.[91] Pursuant to Article 71(2) SAA, any practice shall be assessed on the basis of criteria arising from the application of the competition rules applicable in the Community, in particular from (ex) Articles 81, 82, 86 and 87 of the EC Treaty and interpretative instruments adopted by Community institutions. Although the Competition Act was adopted 3 years before the ratification of the SAA, Article 43 states that the Competition Council, as the competent institution for the protection of fair competition in the first instance, 'may for the purpose of the examination of a concrete case, take into account the judicial practice of the ECJ and the decisions of the European Commission'. In a recent judgment, the Court established that the exclusive importer of Volkswagen cars for BiH, ASA Auto, violated the Competition Act, because it abused its dominant position on the market by discriminating against a contracting party.[92] ASA Auto signed a letter of intent with MRM., a potential distributor of Volkswagen cars, but the terms of the letter of intent were less favourable than those signed with previous traders. When MRM. violated the less favourable clauses of the letter of intent, ASA Auto decided not to conclude the licence agreement.

In general, every party, even those with a dominant market position, is free to choose its contracting partners.[93] However, the Court clarified that ASA Auto, by means of the letter of intent had already established a business relationship with MRM. Namely, it is easier to establish the abuse of the dominant market position when an already existing relationship is cancelled, since it changes the present situation on the market, than in the case of denial of entry into a new contractual relationship.[94] The cancellation of an existing business relationship by a party in a dominant market position represents an abuse if it is not justified and does not fulfil the requirements of proportionality.[95] ASA Auto used the violation of the clauses of the letter of intent as justification. The Court took into consideration that the violated clauses were not included in the letters of intent signed with other traders, and therefore declared the justification discriminatory and the cancellation of the business relationship unjustified. The Court concluded all licensed traders are treated unequally and discriminatorily by the application of different conditions for the same business with different parties/distributors.

Additionally, the Court examined the obligation of ASA Auto to conclude a contract with MRM. It based its argumentation on the abovementioned Article

[91] OG BiH, No. 48/05, 76/07 and 80/09.

[92] Court of BiH, decision No. S1 3 U 005412 10 Uvl, 15.3.2012., M.R.M. Ljubuški/ASA Auto d.o.o. Sarajevo (*ASA Auto*); See Meškić (2012).

[93] Case 27/76 *United Brands* [1978] I-207, para 184.

[94] Jung (2009), para 153.

[95] Brinker (2009), para 36.

43 of the Competition Act and relied on the practice of the ECJ. The Court listed four requirements for the obligation to conclude a contract:

1. a licence is necessary for the other party in order to access and stay on the relevant market;
2. the risk of exclusion of efficient competition if the licence is not given;
3. a future negative influence on technical developments in the field to the detriment of consumers;
4. there is no objective justification for the denial of a licence.

The Court did not expressly refer to a particular decision of the ECJ, but the conditions named may be found in the *IMS Health* decision.[96]

7 The Judicial System in BiH and the Lack of a Supreme Court at the State Level

The judicial system of BiH currently consists of:

- three constitutional courts (the Constitutional Court of BiH, the Constitutional Court of the Federation of BiH and the Constitutional Court of Republika Srpska)
- the Court of BiH (with competences related to criminal and administrative acts adopted at the state level, not at the entity level)
- two Supreme Courts of the entities
- sixteen cantonal courts and district courts (ten in the Federation of BiH, five in Republika Srpska and one in the District of Brčko)
- forty-eight municipal and elementary courts (28 in the Federation of BiH, 19 in Republika Srpska and one in the District of Brčko)
- five district commercial courts in Republika Srpska and a higher commercial court in Banja Luka.

One particularity of the judicial system of BiH is the presence of judges who are not nationals of BiH, so-called 'international judges'. Three out of nine judges in the CC are international judges. Nevertheless, the court rarely refers to the practice of foreign constitutional courts. When establishing the principle of the equality of the constituent peoples in BiH, the Court relies on the binding effect of the wording in the preamble of the Constitution, and therefore bases its argumentation on the judgment of the Canadian Supreme Court in the case *Reference re Secession of Quebec*.[97] Even the dissenting opinions of international judgments show no signs of additional reference to comparative constitutional law. However, the CC

[96] Case C-418/01 *IMS Health* [2004] I-5039, para 52; See also the decision of the Commission, 24.3.2004, COMP/C-3/37.792 (Microsoft), para 428; Henning and Stephanie (2005), p. 112.

[97] The Supreme Court of Canada (1998), 2.S.C.R; See Alijević (2012).

continuously and regularly refers to the ECtHR to an extent that the ECtHR has a fundamental influence on the jurisprudence of the CC, which means that its jurisprudence may be regarded as being at least partially influenced by international judges.[98] On the other hand, the regular reference to the jurisprudence of the ECtHR may also be seen as a result of the very important position of the ECHR within the Constitution of BiH with its direct effect on the legal system of BiH.

The lack of a supreme court at the state level is deemed by several authors as a weakness in ensuring common legal standards, equality and a free economic area.[99] While the Supreme Courts of the Federation of BiH (FBiH) and Republika Srpska (RS) assume this role at the level of the entities, and the Appellate Court of the District of Brčko in the territory of the District of Brčko, but only regarding questions contained in the Constitution of BiH 'arising out of a judgment of any other court in Bosnia and Herzegovina' in accordance with Article VI/3(b) of the Constitution, the appellate jurisdiction of the CC in Article VI/3(b) of the Constitution of BiH is the only legal area where a judicial hierarchy all the way to the state level is established. Therefore, the judges of the CC regard this jurisdiction as partial compensation for the lack of existence of a supreme court at the state level.[100] The Commission stated in its BiH Progress Report for the year 2007, which is adopted on the basis of the criteria listed in Article 49 TEU,[101] that the CC due to the lack of a supreme court is acting more and more as an appellate court.[102] Such a development makes it difficult for the CC to fulfil its basic function of protecting constitutional rights.

The EU Commission mentioned the lack of a supreme court at the state level in its annual reports on BiH 2007–2010.[103] In this analysis, it is not intended to provide answers to the question of whether it would be good for BiH to have a supreme court, given that every other EU state has already provided the answer. The intention is rather to analyse, by taking into consideration the constitutional structure of BiH and the difficulty of the political elements agreeing on any institution at the state level, whether a supreme court at the state level is really

[98] Dicosola (2010).

[99] Trnka (2006), p. 346; Dauster (2010), p. 11; Steiner and Ademović (2010), p. 99; Alijević (2010), p. 209; Dobrača (2005), p. 60; Sadiković (2003), p. 13, available at: http://www.soros.org.ba/index.php?option=com_content&view=article&id=64%3Austav-bih-ka-novim-rjeenjima&catid=49&Itemid=89&lang=ba. Accessed 15.4.2011.

[100] Miljko (2001), p. 39; Trnka (2006), p. 349; Simović (2003), p. 22, available at: http://www.soros.org.ba/index.php?option=com_content&view=article&id=64%3Austav-bih-ka-novim-rjeenjima&catid=49&Itemid=89&lang=ba. Accessed 15 April 2011.

[101] OJ EU 2010, C 83, 1–388.

[102] Commission, 6.11.2007, Bosnia and Herzegovina Progress Report for the year 2007, COM (2007) 663, p. 13.

[103] Commission, 6.11.2007, Bosnia and Herzegovina Progress Report for the year 2007, COM (2007) 663, p. 13; Commission, 5.11.2008, Bosnia and Herzegovina Progress Report for the year 2008, COM (2008) 674, p. 13; Commission, 14.10.2009, Bosnia and Herzegovina Progress Report for the year 2009, COM (2009) 533, p. 12; Commission, 9.11.2010, Bosnia and Herzegovina Progress Report for the year 2010, COM (2010) 660, p. 12.

necessary or if it could possibly be a condition for membership of the EU. Analysing this question from the perspective of the preliminary reference in Article 267 III TFEU, there is a requirement for 'a court or tribunal of a Member State against whose decisions there is no judicial remedy under national law' to bring relevant questions of EU law before the ECJ. In legal science, the abstract theory, which interprets the formulation 'a court against whose decisions there is no judicial remedy' as the highest court in the constitutional order of the Member State, is in conflict with the concrete theory, which speaks in favour of any court against whose decision no legal remedy is possible in that particular matter. In favour of the abstract theory, there is the formulation 'against whose *decisions*' in the plural, while the concrete theory provides wider possibilities for individual legal protection.[104] The ECJ stated in the *Lyckeskog* decision that Article 267 III TFEU does not necessarily demand the existence of a supreme court. The material function can be exercised by another court with the power of making a final decision, which in legal science leads to the conclusion of the application of the concrete theory.[105] The purpose of Article 267 III TFEU is to hinder the establishment of jurisprudence in a Member State which would not be in line with EU law.[106] The goal is that one court with the highest power or the final decision at the national level is obliged to assign issues to the ECJ in accordance with Article 267 III TFEU.[107]

From the perspective of legal protection, in the part of the Report of the Commission where the judicial system is analysed, there is a direct criticism of the lack of a judicial organ which could harmonise the application of laws between the four internal judicial competences: the state level, the Federation of BiH, Republika Srpska and the District of Brčko. In this way, the fragmentation of the legal frameworks endangers effectiveness, a criterion that is not mentioned in the conclusions of the European Council[108] but which is an integral part of the whole analysis of the report on the progress of BiH towards the EU. The question arises as to whether, from the principle of effectiveness together with the obligation to transpose the *acquis* throughout the whole territory of BiH, an obligation can be concluded to establish a supreme court at the level of BiH which would ensure that legislation which is uniformly transposed in national law is actually uniformly applied throughout the whole territory. Without the establishment of a state institution which would have the competence of a supreme court, there would be no institution which would, after the legislator has done its part of the assignment by

[104] Hartley (2003), p. 283.

[105] Case C-99/00 *Criminal proceedings against Kenny Roland Lyckeskog* [2002] I-4839, para 14. On the basis of this judgment, the concrete theory is supported by eg. Karpenstein (2009), para 52; Stanivuković (2009), p. 106; Oppermann et al. (2009), p. 272; Haratsch et al. (2010), p. 247; Supporters of the abstract theory include Hartley (2003), p. 284; Wegener (2007), para 24.

[106] Case 107/76 *Hoffmann-La Roche AG v. Centrafarm Vertriebsgesellschaft Pharmazeutischer Erzeugnisse mbH* [1977] 957, para 5.

[107] Stanivuković (2009), p. 106.

[108] Priebe (2008), p. 314.

transposing the *acquis*, ensure the effective and uniform application of such legislation throughout the whole territory of BiH.[109] From the EU perspective, the power of the state authorities is not divided. All authorities are accountable when it comes to ensuring the effectiveness of EU law at the national level. The ECJ confirmed in the *Köbler* decision that all state authorities, including the court with the highest power or right of final decision, can be liable for breach of EU law.[110]

The reason for the absence of a supreme court at the state level can be seen in the division of competences among the state and the entities. Article III of the Constitution of BiH established competences for the entities in criminal and civil matters. The Venice Commission performed an analysis of the need for a supreme court in BiH in 1998.[111] The Commission deemed it necessary for there to be a common court for electoral and administrative matters. Based on this conclusion, a common court was established in BiH in 2000 with competence in state law.[112]

The Venice Commission did not examine if Article III of the Constitution of BiH contained all the competences divided between the state and the entities. Namely, the previous analysis of the division of competences between the state and the entities is confirmed in the legislative practice of BiH, where different private laws with the goal of harmonisation with EU law are adopted at the state level regardless of the lack of an explicit competence based on Article III/1 of the Constitution. This is true in the field of intellectual property law, including the Copyright and Related Rights Act,[113] the Trademark Act, the Patent Act, and the Industrial Designs Act,[114] as well as in the field of consumer law, which mostly regulates civil obligations,[115] and the Competition Act.[116]

Now the question needs to be asked as to which court in BiH will ensure the uniform application of laws at the state level adopted with the purpose of establishing a common market, based on the provision in Article I/4 of the Constitution, as well as the obligation of the state to harmonise its legal order with EU law. On the basis of the laws mentioned above, state institutions have been established such as the Competition Council, the Council for Authors' Rights and the Ombudsman for the Protection of Consumer Rights (with competences in criminal and administrative proceedings, excluding property claims in civil litigation). The CC in these areas has appellate jurisdiction, which is mostly connected to the protection

---

[109] Meškić (2011b).

[110] Case C-224/01 *Gerhard Köbler v. Austria* [2003] I-10239, para 31.

[111] Venice Commission, Opinion on the need for a judicial institution at the level of the state of Bosnia and Herzegovina, CDL-INF (98) 17, Strasbourg 1998, available at: http://www.venice.coe.int/docs/1998/CDL-INF%281998%29017-e.asp. Accessed 10 April 2011.

[112] BiH Court Act, OG BiH Nos. 29/00, 15/02, 16/02, 24/02, 03/03, 37/03, 42/03, 04/04, 09/04, 35/04, 61/04, 32/07 and 97/09; Consolidated version published in OG BiH No. 49/09.

[113] OG BiH No. 63/10.

[114] OG BiH No. 53/10.

[115] Consumer Protection Act, OG BiH No. 25/06.

[116] Competition Act, OG BiH Nos. 48/05 and 76/07; Act on Amendments to the Competition Act, OG BiH No. 80/09.

of human rights. The Court of BiH has competences in criminal and administrative matters, electoral rights, and property litigation between the state, the entities and the District of Brčko, and also in cases of a conflict of competences involving the District of Brčko and the Court of BiH. The competences in these areas are restricted to the meaning and application of state laws,[117] Thus, the Court of BiH represents a judicial and legal area at the state level as a separate legal order which exists alongside the entity areas. Therefore, it is correct to conclude that the Court of BiH, as a special court, stands outside the hierarchy of the entities, and whose current competences in the worst case could lead to additional diversification of law in BiH.[118]

8 Conclusion

The application of international legal sources in national law is theoretically determined by two classical theories with different specific features. For the application of international legal sources, the Constitution of BiH provides arguments for both monistic and dualistic theories. This theoretical question does not need a unilateral decision in favour of one approach or the other, because the practical impact is not significant in the moderate approaches of dualism and monism.

International law is distinguished in the Constitution of BiH in different ways by means of the Constitution being part of the DPA. As the general principles and ECHR and its protocols have direct effect, they are deemed to have primacy over national law. For all other international agreements, the *argumentum e contrario* has not been used appropriately by the CC. These agreements although not explicitly mentioned in the Constitution are of a constitutional rank, but do not have precedence over the Constitution. The SAA, as an agreement concluded with the EU as a supranational organisation, has a specific ranking within the national legal system.

The wording of Article II/4 of the Constitution of BiH has raised questions because human rights are mentioned in connection with the prohibition of discrimination. This inauspicious wording has to be clarified by the classical methods of interpretation, in particular by systematic and teleological interpretation.

[117] One exception exists, according to Art. 7(2) of the Court Act of BiH, which is constituted by jurisdiction over criminal acts established by the criminal laws of the entities and the District of Brčko, but again with very narrow conditions, namely when such criminal offences endanger the sovereignty, territorial integrity, political independence, national security or international personality of Bosnia and Herzegovina; may have serious repercussions or detrimental consequences to the economy of Bosnia and Herzegovina; may have other detrimental consequences to Bosnia and Herzegovina or may cause serious economic damage or other detrimental consequences beyond the territory of an entity or the District of Brčko of Bosnia and Herzegovina.

[118] Dauster (2010), p. 12.

In international law, this is expressed in Article 31(1) of the Vienna Convention: '[the] treaty shall be interpreted in good faith in accordance with the ordinary meaning to be given to the terms of the treaty in their context and in the light of its object and purpose.'[119] Human rights enjoy direct application parallel to the existing principle of prohibition of discrimination. The dogma of fundamental rights has acknowledged that the rights of freedom and equality are two different categories of human rights, and are not dependent on each other.

The division of competences with regard to private law has led to a quantity of parallel laws at the different state levels in BiH. Fundamental questions of harmonisation have to be solved by the legislator or jurisprudence. Co-operation between the courts and legal literature could be more effective than new definitions of competences, particularly if there is no majority for constitutional changes.

The SAA for BiH has been ratified by BiH but not by the EU. Thus, it cannot enter into full force and effect, although single provisions have already been applied, and jurisprudence and legal literature already refer to the content of the SAA. The EU has declared that it will not ratify the SAA until BiH implements the ECtHR *Sejdić-Finci* decision, because without its implementation BiH violates Article 1 of the Interim Agreement. Overall, the direct effect of the SAA is acknowledged. The question of the hierarchy of laws as usual has to be interpreted. Due to the nature and purpose of the SAA, it can be deemed as having precedence over national laws but being subordinate to constitutional provisions. Jointly and severally, the SAA with its direct effect and supremacy causes complex legal and practical questions in a country which currently lacks sufficient skills for the application and enforcement of EU law.

An organisational question in BiH is the infrastructure of the judiciary. The creation of a supreme court is a reasonable requirement. This can be seen as a political question, but irrespective of the creation of a supreme court, the courts could enhance voluntary co-operation in order to establish a unified system in terms of the principles of transparency, legal certainty and equality in guaranteeing the rule of law and human rights.

References

Addo MK (2010) The legal nature of international human rights. Martinus Nijhoff, Leiden

Ademović N, Marko J, Marković G (2012) Ustavno pravo. Konrad Adenauer Stiftung, Sarajevo

Alijević M (2010) Uloga sudske vlasti u BiH. Anali Pravnog fakulteta Univerziteta u Zenici 3

Alijević M (2012) Tekst preambule kao pomoćna metoda tumačenja Ustava. Anali Pravnog fakulteta Univerziteta u Zenici 5

Amrhein-Hofman C (2003) Monismus und Dualismus in den Völkerrechtslehren. Duncker & Humblot, Berlin

[119] Meron (2008), pp. 193–201.

Begić K (1997) Bosna i Hercegovina od Vanceove misije do Daytonskog sporazuma. Bosanska Knjiga, Sarajevo
Bieber R (1991) Verfassungsentwicklung und Verfassungsgebung in der Europäischen Gemeinschaft. In: Wildenmann R (ed) Staatswerdung Europas? Nomos, Baden-Baden
Bleckmann M (2011) Nationale Grundrechte im Anwendungsbereich des Recths der Europäischen Union. Mohr Siebeck, Tübingen
Borowsky M (2011) Titel VII Allgemeine Bestimmungen über die Auslegung und Anwendung der Charta. In: Meyer J (ed) Charta der Grundrechte der Europäischen Union. Nomos, Baden-Baden
Brinker I (2009) Art. 82 EGV. In: Schwarze J (ed) EU-Kommentar. Nomos, Baden-Baden
Brummund F (2010) Kohärenter Grundrechtsschutz im Raum der Freiheit, der Sicherheit und des Rechts. Nomos, Baden-Baden
Chalmers D, Davies G, Monti G (2010) European Union law. Cambridge University Press, Cambridge
Dauster M (2010) Ustav Bosne i Hercegovine: Nesavršena država-diskurs. Sveske za javno pravo 1
Degan VĐ (2000) Međunarodno pravo. Pravni fakultet Sveučilišta u Rijeci, Rijeka
Denza E (2006) The relationship between international and national law. In: Evans MD (ed) International law, 2nd edn. OUP, Oxford
Dicosola M (2010) Constitutional courts and globalisation of law: the international judges. The cases of Bosnia and Herzegovina and Kosovo. www.juridicas.unam.mx/wccl/ponencias/12/199.pdf. Accessed 1 Apr 2013
Dobrača N (2005) Nezavisno pravosuđe s posebnim osvrtom na reformu pravosudnog sistema u Bosni i Hercegovini. Pravni fakultet Univerziteta u Sarajevu, master's thesis, p 60
Dougan M (2007) When worlds collide! Competing visions of the relationship between direct effect and supremacy. Common Mark Law Rev 44
Ekardt F, Lessmann V (2006) EuGH, EGMR und BVerfG: Die dritte Gewalt im transnationalen Mehrebenensystem. Kritische Justiz
Emmerich-Fritsche A (2007) Vom Völkerrecht zum Weltrecht. Duncker & Humblot, Berlin
European Commission Delegation to BiH (2003) Study on potential revenue sources for the institutions of Bosnia and Herzegovina. Sarajevo, p 42
Frowein JA (1987a) Collective enforcement of international obligations. In: Hartwig M, Nolte G, Oeter S, Walter C (eds) Völkerrecht – Menschenrechte – Verfassungsfragen Deutschlands und Europas. Springer, Heidelberg
Frowein JA (1987b) Die Europäisiserung des Verfassungsrechts. In: Hartwig M, Nolte G, Oeter S, Walter C (eds) Völkerrecht – Menschenrechte – Verfassungsfragen Deutschlands und Europas. Springer, Heidelberg
Frowein JA (1987c) Wesentliche Elemente einer Verfassung. In: Hartwig M, Nolte G, Oeter S, Walter C (eds) Völkerrecht – Menschenrechte – Verfassungsfragen Deutschlands und Europas. Springer, Heidelberg
Frowein JA (1987d) Das Bundesverfassungsgericht und die Europäische Menschenrechtskonvention. In: Hartwig M, Nolte G, Oeter S, Walter C (eds) Völkerrecht – Menschenrechte – Verfassungsfragen Deutschlands und Europas. Springer, Heidelberg
Geiger R (2010) In: Geiger R, Khan D-E, Kotzur M (eds) EUV/AEUV Kommentar. C. H. Beck, München
Haratsch A, Koenig C, Pechstein M (2010) Europarecht. Mohr Siebeck, Tübingen
Hartley TC (2003) The foundations of European community law. Oxford University Press, Oxford
Henning L, Stephanie P (2005) IMS Health vs. Microsoft – Befindet sich die Kommission bei kartellrechtlichen Zwangslizenzen (erneut) auf Konfrontationskurs mit dem EuGH? Europäisches Wirtschafts- & Steuerrecht 16
Jarras HD (2010) Charta der Grundrechte der Europäischen Union. C. H. Beck, München
Jung C (2009) Art. 82 EGV. In: Grabitz E, Hilf M (eds) Das Recht der Europäischen Union-Kommentar. Beck, München

Kaczorowska A (2011) European Union law. Routledge, London

Kälin W, Künzli J (2005) Universeller Menschenrechtsschutz. Helbing Lichtenhahn Verlag, Basel

Karpenstein U (2009) Art. 234 EGV. In: Grabitz E, Hilf M (eds) Das Recht der Europäischen Union-Kommentar. Beck, München

Keller H (2003) Rezeption des Völkerrechts. Springer, Heidelberg

Klabbers J, Peters A, Ulfstein G (2009) The constitutionalization of international law. Oxford University Press, New York

Kleinlein T (2011) Konstitutionalisierung im Völkerrecht. Springer, Heidelberg

Kulenović N et al (2010) Presuda Sejdić i Finci protiv Bosne i Hercegovine: Konkretne posljedice-prvi pregled. Sveske za javno pravo-Blätter für Öffentliches Recht 1

Kurtćehajić S, Ibrahimagić O (2007) Politički sistem Bosne i Hercegovine. Magistrat, Sarajevo

Marković G (2011) Ustavnopravni osnov za ostvarivanja ekonomskih prava u BiH. In: Pravni fakultet u Istočnom Sarajevu (ed) Zbornik radova, Aktuelnosti i značaj ljudskih prava i sloboda, Istočno Sarajevo

Menzel J (2011) Internationales Öffentliches Recht. Mohr Siebeck, Tübingen

Meron T (2008) The humanization of international law. Martinus Nijhoff, Leiden

Meškić Z (2011a) Četiri osnovne slobode kao ustavni osnov za harmonizaciju entiteskih privatnopravnih propisa. In: Pravni fakultet Univerziteta u Tuzli (ed) Ustavnopravni razvoj Bosne i Hercegovine (1910–2010), Zbornik radova Pravnog fakulteta Univerziteta u Tuzli, Tuzla

Meškić Z (2011b) Osnivanje Vrhovnog suda Bosne i Hercegovine kao uslov za članstvo u Evropskoj uniji. Sveske za javno pravo-Blätter für Öffentliches Recht 2

Meškić Z (2012) Jurisdikcija Suda EU u praksi Suda BiH-Povodom odluke Suda BiH br. S1 3 U 005412 10 Uvl, 15.3.2012, M.R.M. Ljubuški/ASA Auto d.o.o. Sarajevo (*ASA Auto*). Sveske za javno pravo-Blätter für öffentliches Recht 3

Meškić Z, Samardžić D (2012) Pravo Evropske unije I. GIZ, Sarajevo

Miljko Z (2001) Apelaciona jurisdikcija Ustavnog suda Bosne i Hercegovine. In: Okrugli stolovi Ustavnog suda BiH, Ustavni sud BiH i druge sudske instance, Sarajevo

Munding C-D (2010) Das Grundrecht auf effektiven Rechtsschutz im Rechtssystem der Europäischen Union. Duncker & Humblot, Berlin

Nettesheim M (2003) Kompetenzen. In: Von Bogdandy A (ed) Europäisches Verfassungsrecht – theoretische und dogmatische Grundzüge. Springer, Berlin

Nunner M (2009) Kooperation internationaler Gerichte. Mohr Siebeck, Tübingen

Oppermann T, Classen D, Nettesheim M (2009) Europarecht. Beck, München

Payandeh M (2010) Internationales Gemeinschaftsrecht. Springer, Heidelberg

Pernice I (2000) Der Europäische Verfassungsverbund auf dem Weg der Konsolidierung. Jahrbuch für das Öffentliche Recht 48

Pfeffer R (2009) Das Verhältnis von Völkerrecht und Landesrecht. Mohr Siebeck, Tübingen

Pobrić N (2000) Ustavno pravo. Slovo, Mostar

Popović P (2010) Neki aspekti harmonizacije prava Republike Srpske sa Sporazumom o stabilizaciji i pridruživanju. Pravni život

Priebe R (2008) Beitrittsperspektive und Verfassungsreformen in den Ländern des Westlichen Balkans. Zeitschrift Europarecht 43

Rodin S (2003) Sporazum o stabilizaciji i pridruživanju u pravnom poretku Evropske zajednice i Republike Hrvatske. Zbornik radova Pravnog fakulteta u Zagrebu 53

Sadiković Ć (2003) Za državu novog stoljeća-Bosna i Hercegovina kao savremena demokratska država. Fond otvoreno društvo Bosna i Hercegovina, Sarajevo

Samardžić D, Meškić Z (2012) The principle of the 'rule of law' or '*Rechtsstaatlichkeit*' as the basis for human rights protection in European Union law. Summer academy, The rule of law, human rights and the European Union, Skoplje

Sauer H (2008) Jurisdiktionskonflikte im Mehrebenensystem. Springer, Heidelberg

Schilling T (2010) Internationaler Menschenrechtschutz. Mohr Siebeck, Tübingen

Schmalenbach K (2007) Art. 310. In: Calliess C, Ruffert M (eds) Das Verfassungsrecht der Europäischen Union mit Europäischer Grundrechtecharta, Kommentar. Beck, München
Schneiders B (2009) Die Grundrechte der EU und die EMRK. Nomos, Baden-Baden, pp 145–265
Simović M (2003) Ustavnopravni osnov vladavine prava u Bosni i Hercegovini kroz funkcionisanje ustavnih institucija. Fond otvoreno društvo Bosna i Hercegovina, Sarajevo
Stanivuković M (2009) Pojedinac pred sudom Evropskih zajednica. Službeni glasnik, Beograd
Stein T, Von Buttlar C, Seidel-Hohenveldern I (2012) Völkerrecht. Heymanns, München
Steiner HJ (2006) International protection of human rights. In: Malcolm DE (ed) International law, 2nd edn. OUP, Oxford
Steiner C, Ademović N (2010) Ustav Bosne i Hercegovine-Komentar. Konrad Adenauer Stiftung, Sarajevo
Steiner HJ, Alston P, Goodman R (2007) International human rights in context. Oxford University Press, New York
Stender H (2004) Überschneidungen im internationalen Menschenrechtsschutz. Berliner Wissenschaftsverlag, Berlin
Streinz R (2007) Die Europäische Union als Rechtsgemeinschaft. In: Kirchhof P, Papier H-J, Schäffer H (eds) Festschrift für Detlef Merten. C. F. Müller, Heidelberg
Trnka K (2006) Ustavno pravo. Fakultet za javnu upravu, Sarajevo
Ullerich R (2011) Rechtsstaat udn Rechtsgemeinschaft im Europarecht. Nomos, Baden-Baden
Vöneky S (2009) Art. 310 EGV. In: Grabitz E, Hilf M (eds) Das Recht der Europäischen Union-Kommentar. Beck, München
Vukadinović R (2010) Neposredna primjena Sporazuma o stabilizaciji i pridruživanju-Usklađivanje domaćeg prava sa pravnim tekovinama Evropske unije. Pravni život 59
Wegener B (2007) Art. 234. In: Calliess C, Ruffert M (eds) Das Verfassungsrecht der Europäischen Union mit Europäischer Grundrechtecharta, Kommentar. Beck, München

Judicial Application of International and EU Law in Croatia

Ivana Božac and Melita Carević

1 Introduction

After years of development, various instruments of international and EU law have built strong guarantees for the protection of individual rights, ranging from fundamental human rights to fundamental market freedoms. However, the best law can at the same time be the worst if it is not applied in practice. Therefore, the aim of this chapter is to look at how international and EU law are actually applied in the European Union's newest Member State, the Republic of Croatia.

This chapter follows the structure of other national reports. It first analyses the constitutional framework for the application of international law in the Republic of Croatia. It then looks into the case law of the Constitutional Court on the review of conformity of national laws with international treaties, as well as on the review of constitutionality of international treaties. Subsequently, the focus of the research shifts towards the cases in which Croatian courts have applied and cited international law. Since most of those cases consider the European Convention on the Protection of Human Rights and Fundamental Freedoms, a special part of the text will deal with the Convention.

The Constitutional status and the application of EU law is analysed separately from international law, due to its specific nature and the important role it has in the

The opinions expressed in this work are those of the author and do not represent the views of the Court of Justice of the European Union.

I. Božac (✉)
Court of Justice of the European Union, Kirchberg, Luxembourg
e-mail: ivanabozac@gmail.com

M. Carević
University of Zagreb Law School, Zagreb, Croatia
e-mail: melita.carevic@gmail.com

S. Rodin, T. Perišin (eds.), *Judicial Application of International Law in Southeast Europe*, DOI 10.1007/978-3-662-46384-0_8

Croatian legal system. The authors attempt to identify some of the main challenges judges might face when applying EU law.

The last part of this chapter is dedicated to the organisation of the judicial system in Croatia and to the education of legal practitioners in areas of EU and international law. Since Croatia has only recently joined the European Union, special attention is paid to workshops and training organised for judges which should serve as a catalyst for the application of EU law.

2 Constitutional Status of International Law in the Republic of Croatia

2.1 International Treaties

The constitutional status of international law in the legal order of the Republic of Croatia is defined, on one hand, by constitutional provisions and other relevant legislation[1] and, on the other, by the case law of the Constitutional Court.[2]

The most important legal source for determining the constitutional status of international law in Croatia is Article 141 of the Constitution[3] which stipulates that:

---

[1] Notably, the Act on the Conclusion and Implementation of International Agreements (Zakon o sklapanju i izvršavanju međunarodnih ugovora) (Official Gazette 28/96) and the Courts Act (Zakon o sudovima) (Official Gazette 150/05, 16/07, 113/08, 153/09, 116/10, 122/10, 27/11, 57/11, 130/11, 28/13).

[2] The Constitutional Court of the Republic Croatia is composed of 13 judges appointed by the Parliament for a term of 8 years. Its president is elected by his or her peers for a term of 4 years. The Constitutional Court decides on the conformity of laws with the Constitution and the legality of administrative acts and regulations. It ensures respect for the autonomy of local authorities and respect of the division of powers between the legislative, executive and judicial branches; it protects citizens' fundamental rights and freedoms, rules on the responsibility of the Head of State, controls the programmes of political parties and may, if appropriate, prohibit their activity. It also oversees the constitutionality of elections and referendums and validates the results. The fundamental provisions concerning the jurisdiction of the Constitutional Court of the Republic of Croatia are contained in the Constitution of the Republic of Croatia. The jurisdiction of the Constitutional Court, as stipulated by the Constitution, is elaborated in the Constitutional Act on the Constitutional Court of the Republic of Croatia (Ustavni zakon o Ustavnom sudu Republike Hrvatske) (Official Gazette 99/99, 29/02, 49/02), which was enacted in accordance with the procedure determined for amending the Constitution.

[3] The Croatian Constitution was adopted on 22 December 1990 (Official Gazette 56/1990) and has so far been amended five times—by a constitutional law in 1997 (Official Gazette 135/1997), by parliamentary decisions in 2000 (Official Gazette 113/2000), 2001 (Official Gazette 28/2001) and 2010 (Official Gazette 76/2010), and by a referendum in 2013. The last official version of the consolidated text of the Constitution was published in 2010 (Official Gazette 85/2010). The status of international treaties was originally regulated by Article 134 of the Constitution, which was slightly changed in 1997. It subsequently became Article 140, and is currently Article 141 in the 2010 consolidated text (the numeration of which shall be used for the purposes of this chapter). At present, there is no official version of the Constitution in the English language or in any other

> International treaties which were signed and ratified in accordance with the Constitution, made public and are in force, are part of the internal legal order of the Republic of Croatia and are above law in terms of legal effects. Their provisions may be changed or repealed only under the conditions and in the way specified by the international treaties themselves, or in accordance with the general rules of international law.

It follows that international treaties in force in the Republic of Croatia enjoy, from a formal perspective, a supra-legislative status, but in relation to the national Constitution they retain a sub-constitutional status.[4]

Furthermore, Article 118(3) of the Constitution specifies that 'the Courts shall administer justice according to the Constitution, laws, international agreements and other valid sources of law'. Before the 2010 Constitutional changes, the aforementioned article used to read 'The courts shall administer justice on the basis of the Constitution and laws'.[5] The 2010 Constitutional changes have made it clear that on the basis of this constitutional provision, Croatian courts are obliged to apply the relevant rules of international treaties, just as they are obliged to apply Croatian internal rules. The same obligation is also contained in Article 5 of the Courts Act, which, by mimicking the wording of Article 118(3) of the Constitution, prescribes that 'the courts shall administer justice on the basis of the Constitution, laws, international treaties and other valid sources of law'. However, the wording of Article 5 of the Courts Act used to be a bit more generous when it comes to the application of international law and used to read: 'The courts shall administer justice on the basis of international treaties which are a part of the legal order of the Republic of Croatia' and 'The courts shall apply other rules which have been enacted in accordance with the Constitution, international treaty or a law of the Republic of Croatia'. In other words, the 2005 version of the Courts Act expressly obliged Croatian courts to apply international agreements as well as legal rules which have been enacted in accordance with them. The current wording of the Courts Act of 2013, identical to the wording of Article 118(3) of the Constitution, could mislead the reader into concluding that in the hierarchy of legal rules Croatian laws have primacy over international treaties which are in force in the Republic of Croatia. Such a conclusion is expressly dismantled by Article 141 of the Constitution, which prescribes that signed, ratified and published international treaties which are in force are above laws in terms of legal effects.

From its wording, it can be concluded that the Croatian Constitution adopts a monist concept of the relationship between Croatian internal law and international law,[6] that Article 141 of the Constitution creates a hierarchy of legal rules which the

foreign language published in the Official Gazette. However, an unofficial translation of the Constitution is available on the Parliament's website at: http://www.sabor.hr/Default.aspx?art=2405. Accessed 20 November 2013. The quality of the translation was severely criticised by the Constitutional Court in its Report U-X-5076/2013 of 15 October 2013.

[4] Omejec (2009a), p. 11. http://www.venice.coe.int/webforms/documents/?pdf=CDL-JU(2009)035-e. Accessed 20 September 2013. The author is currently serving as President of the Constitutional Court of the Republic of Croatia.

[5] Article 115 of the Constitution of the Republic of Croatia (Ustav Republike Hrvatske) (Official Gazette 8/1998).

[6] Omejec (2009a), p. 9. http://www.venice.coe.int/webforms/documents/?pdf=CDL-JU(2009)035-e. Accessed 20 September 2013; Smerdel and Sokol (2009), p. 101.

courts are obliged to respect,[7] and that national courts should directly apply ratified and published international treaties which are in force. In other words, such international treaties—as part of the internal legal order—may create individual rights that the courts are obliged to protect.[8] Therefore, after their ratification and publication, self-executing international treaties may be directly applied in Croatia. As pointed out by Omejec, this conclusion is corroborated by the fact that the Act on the Conclusion and Implementation of International Agreements requires no regulatory action in order for a ratified and published international agreement to be directly applicable.[9]

As mentioned above, the legal status of international treaties in the Republic of Croatia is also defined by the Constitutional Court's case law. For the purpose of clarifying the legal status of international treaties in the Republic of Croatia, the Constitutional Court's case law may be grouped in four types of cases: firstly, cases where the international treaties were used as benchmarks for monitoring national laws in the abstract-review procedures; secondly, constitutional complaint procedures in which international treaties were applied as a standard of review; thirdly, cases regarding the review of constitutionality of international treaties; and, fourthly, cases regarding the review of constitutionality of national laws ratifying international treaties.

2.1.1 Cases Where International Treaties Were Applied in the Abstract-Review Procedures of National Laws

The Constitutional Court has developed the practice of using international treaties as benchmarks for monitoring domestic law, recognising in this way the *de facto quasi-constitutional* status of international treaties, as pointed out by Omejec.[10]

A milestone decision for the recognition of the *quasi-constitutional* status of international treaties in the Croatian legal system was the Constitutional Court's decision in Case U-I-745/1999, which concerned an abstract review of the compatibility of the Croatian Expropriation Act with the Constitution.[11] In this decision,

[7] Rodin (1995), p. 785.

[8] Omejec (2009a), p. 10. http://www.venice.coe.int/webforms/documents/?pdf=CDL-JU(2009)035-e. Accessed 20 September 2013.

[9] Omejec (2009a), p. 9. http://www.venice.coe.int/webforms/documents/?pdf=CDL-JU(2009)035-e. Accessed 20 September 2013; Zakon o sklapanju i izvršavanjau međunarodnih ugovora (Official Gazette 28/96).

[10] Omejec (2009a), p. 11. http://www.venice.coe.int/webforms/documents/?pdf=CDL-JU(2009)035-e. Accessed 20 September 2013.

[11] Decision No. U-I-745/1999 of 8 November 2000 (Official Gazette 112/2000). It should be noted that the Constitutional Court decided for the first time on the incompatibility of national legislation with an international treaty in 1998, although not explicitly, and without an explanation on the basis on which it established its competence to decide on the matter. This was in the case of the assessment of the constitutionality of certain provisions of the Croatian Railways Act with Article

the Constitutional Court for the first time explicitly adopted the view that any non-compliance of national legislation with the European Convention for the Protection of Human Rights and Fundamental Freedoms (hereinafter: ECHR) represented the non-compliance of national laws with the principle of the rule of law laid down in Article 3[12] of the Constitution, the principles of constitutionality and legality enshrined in Article 5 of the Constitution, and the principle of legal monism of national and international law stipulated in Article 141 of the Constitution. Consequently, the Constitutional Court abolished parts of the Expropriation Act while exercising its power of abstract constitutional review.

As stated above, the Constitutional Court applied the reasoning that since parts of the Act were contrary to the ECHR, they were at the same time contrary to the Constitution. However, in order to reach this decision, the Constitutional Court first had to establish its jurisdiction to review the compatibility of national law with an international treaty, since the Constitution itself does not explicitly empower the Constitutional Court to do so. The Constitutional Court took Article 129 of the Constitution as the basis for establishing its jurisdiction. It prescribes that the Constitutional Court 'decides upon the conformity of laws with the Constitution' and 'upon the conformity of other regulations with the Constitution and laws'. In paragraph 7 of its decision, the Constitutional Court stated that Article 129, together with Article 5 of the Constitution which requires that 'all laws must be in conformity with the Constitution, and all other regulations in conformity with the Constitution and laws', entitle and oblige the Constitutional Court to supervise the conformity of legal norms of different legal force within the Croatian legal order. Since the hierarchy of legal norms in Croatia consists of the Constitution, ratified and published international treaties, laws and other regulations, the Constitutional Court concluded that it is entitled to review the compatibility of laws with superior legal norms, that is, international treaties. The Constitutional Court considered this conclusion as the only logical consequence of Article 141 of the Constitution, which prescribes that ratified and published international treaties which are in force are above laws in terms of legal effects.[13] This view has been confirmed by

8 of the International Covenant on Economic, Social and Cultural Rights of the United Nations. In its Decision U-I-920/1995, U-I-950/1996, U-I-262/1998, U-I-322/1998 (Official Gazette 98/98), the Constitutional Court found that 'the non-compliance of Article 23 Section 4 Paragraph 1 of the Croatian Railways Act with the mentioned provisions of international law represented a violation of the principle of rule of law from Article 3 of the Constitution, as a fundamental value of the constitutional order of the Republic of Croatia'. For more details, see Omejec (2009a), p. 15. http://www.venice.coe.int/webforms/documents/?pdf=CDL-JU(2009)035-e. Accessed 20 September 2013.

[12] Article 3 of the Constitution specifies the fundamental values ('the highest values') of the Croatian Constitutional order, notably freedom, equal rights, national and gender equality, peace-making, social justice, respect for human rights, inviolability of ownership, conservation of nature and the environment, the rule of law and a democratic multiparty system.

[13] Paragraph 7 of the Decision. Translation of the Decision into English can be found at: http://sljeme.usud.hr/usud/prakswen.nsf/Venecijan/C1256A25004A262AC12569930035474E?OpenDocument. Accessed 12 January 2014.

the subsequent case law of the Constitutional Court, most recently in case U-III-3304/2011.

2.1.2 Constitutional Complaint Procedures in Which International Treaties Were Applied as a Standard of Review

Another set of cases decided by the Constitutional Court which are worth mentioning in the context of the constitutional status of international law in the Croatian legal system are those involving a violation of an individual's constitutional right by a court's judgment delivered in breach of international commitments.

The same approach described above, adopted in the procedure of the abstract review of the constitutionality of national laws, was applied in cases brought before the Constitutional Court through the constitutional complaints of individuals. Thus, the Constitutional Court applied international treaties as a standard of review in the constitutional complaint procedure.[14]

In its case law, the Constitutional Court of the Republic of Croatia has held on several occasions that human rights and fundamental freedoms of individuals, guaranteed by the Constitution of the Republic of Croatia, may be violated in the case where the adjudicating court in its judgment does not comply with the international obligations which the Republic of Croatia assumed through the ratification of an international treaty. For example, in its decision U-III-1801/2006 of 20 May 2009, the Constitutional Court quashed the judgments of competent national courts on the grounds that they had violated the provisions of the Hague Convention on the Civil Aspects of International Child Abduction. The Constitutional Court ruled that the courts, by having denied the applicant the right she enjoyed on the basis of the Hague Convention, had violated their constitutional obligation to protect that individual right. It established that the lower-instance judgments had violated the right of access to courts under Article 29 of the Constitution, as well as Article 35, and Article 62, which offers special protection to maternity and children, and at the same time interpreted Article 62 very broadly, so that it also encompasses the rights under the Hague Convention. When establishing whether Article 35 of the Constitution regarding the right to family life had been breached, the Constitutional Court followed the case law of the ECtHR which states that the Hague Convention must be taken into account when determining whether Article 8 of the ECHR has been breached. In other words, the

[14] According to subparagraph 4 of Article 129 of the Croatian Constitution, the Constitutional Court decides on constitutional complaints against individual decisions taken by governmental agencies, bodies of local and regional self-government and legal persons vested with public authority where such decisions violate human rights and fundamental freedoms, as well as the right to local and regional self-government guaranteed by the Constitution of the Republic of Croatia. This jurisdiction of the Constitutional Court is further elaborated in the Constitutional Act on the Constitutional Court.

Constitutional Court considers a breach of an international treaty which is in force in the Republic of Croatia at the same time as a breach of the Constitution.

Similarly, in its decision U-III-4182/2008 of 17 March 2009, the Constitutional quashed the judgments of the competent national courts on the grounds that they had violated the provisions of the Constitution and the ECHR.

2.1.3 Cases Regarding the Review of Constitutionality of International Treaties

Another important element for clarifying the legal status of international treaties in the Republic of Croatia is the case law of the Constitutional Court regarding the question of review of international treaties as to their compatibility with the Croatian Constitution. It should first be noted that the Croatian legal system does not contain prior review of the constitutionality of international treaties. Furthermore, the Croatian Constitution and the Constitutional Act on the Constitutional Court do not contain any explicit provisions regarding the possibility of ex post judicial review of international treaties as to their constitutionality. Although there have been several theoretical possibilities that could have justified the constitutional review of international treaties,[15] the Constitutional Court has held on various occasions that it was not competent to assess the compliance of international treaties with the Constitution. In its decision U-I-825/2001,[16] the Constitutional Court rejected the proposal to institute proceedings to review the constitutionality of several Treaties between the Republic of Croatia and the Holy See. Shortly afterwards, it confirmed the same reasoning in decision U-I-672/2001 of 25 February 2004 and rejected the proposal to institute proceedings to review the constitutionality of the Agreement on Social Security between Croatia and Bosnia and Herzegovina (concluded on 4 October 2000). In both decisions, the Constitutional Court used identical wording and held that 'the Constitutional Court of the Republic of Croatia is not competent to assess the compliance of international treaties with the Constitution'. The only explanation given by the Constitutional Court was that Article 129 of the Constitution, which lists the powers of the Constitutional Court, does not expressly give it such authority. The same view was confirmed in a number of subsequent decisions (e.g. U-I-350/2004 of 17 June 2009, U-I-4043/2003 of 7 July 2009 and U-I-3246/2004 of 22 December 2009).

[15] See e.g. Rodin (1995), p. 791.

[16] Decision U-I-825/2001 of 14 January 2004 in which the Constitutional Court rejected a proposal to institute proceedings to review the constitutionality of the Treaty between the Holy See and the Republic of Croatia on Legal Matters (19 December 1996), the Treaty between the Holy See and the Republic of Croatia on Cooperation in the Field of Education and Culture (19 December 1996), the Treaty between the Holy See and the Republic of Croatia on Spiritual Counselling of Catholics Members of the Armed Forces and Police of the Republic of Croatia (19 December 1996) and the Treaty between the Holy See and the Republic of Croatia on Economic Issues (9 October 1998).

As we have previously seen, the Constitutional Court did not stop at the mere wording of the Constitution when establishing its jurisdiction to decide on the conformity of national laws with ratified agreements which are in force in the Republic of Croatia. It is therefore a pity that the Constitutional Court did not elaborate its conclusion of this vital constitutional issue. By giving well-supported arguments for its decisions, the Constitutional Court should set an example to all courts in the judicial structure to do the same, and thereby contribute to legal certainty and the legitimacy of judicial decisions.[17] The problem of the judicial review of the constitutionality of international treaties which have already been signed and ratified lies in their very nature as instruments of international law. As stated in Article 141 of the Constitution, 'their provisions may be changed or repealed only under the conditions and in the way specified by the international treaties themselves, or in accordance with the general rules of international law'. It can be concluded, therefore, that neither the Croatian Constitution nor the case law of the Croatian Constitutional Court allows a review of the constitutionality of international treaties.

2.1.4 Cases Regarding the Review of Constitutionality of National Laws Ratifying International Treaties

In its case law, the Constitutional Court of the Republic of Croatia has also addressed the problem of the review of constitutionality of national laws ratifying international treaties. The Constitutional Court held that it had jurisdiction to review the constitutionality of Croatian laws which ratify international treaties only from the formal aspect (i.e. the assessment of whether a law was passed by the competent authority and following the procedure prescribed by the Constitution) and that it was not competent to assess the compliance of domestic laws ratifying treaties with the Constitution from a substantive aspect.[18] In its Decision U-I-1583/2000 and U-I-559/2001 of 24 March 2010, the Constitutional Court held in paragraph 6 that:

> From the jurisdiction of the Constitutional Court established in Article 129 of the Constitution and the conditions under which international agreements can be amended or repealed, laid down in Article 141 of the Constitution, it stems that the Constitutional Court, in reviewing the constitutionality of a law, has the competence to review the constitutionality of a law on ratification of an international treaty, but not the constitutionality of international treaties themselves. In other words, in relation to the laws on ratification of international treaties, the competence of the Constitutional Court is limited, because it does not include the review of the constitutionality of the substantive content of an international treaty, which is an integral part of the law. This is so because, according to Article 141 of the Constitution, the provisions of the ratified and published international treaties may be amended or repealed only under conditions and in the manner specified in themselves, or in accordance with the general rules of international law.

[17] Rodin (2009), pp. 317–245, 325.

[18] For an analysis of the possibility to review the substance of act of ratification, see the opinion of Professor Vukas in Omejec (2009a), p. 14. http://www.venice.coe.int/webforms/documents/?pdf=CDL-JU(2009)035-e. Accessed 20 September 2013.

The Constitutional Court therefore declined its jurisdiction to rule on the matter. For the same reasons, in its decision U-I-64462/2009 of 7 July 2010, the Constitutional Court rejected the proposal to institute proceedings to review the constitutionality of the Act on the Ratification of the Arbitration Agreement between the Government of the Republic of Croatia and the Government of the Republic of Slovenia, while in decision U-I-2057/2009 of 30 March 2011, the Constitutional Court rejected a proposal to institute proceedings to review the constitutionality of the Act on the Ratification of the North Atlantic Treaty.

2.1.5 Short Conclusion

Summarising the presented case law, we can conclude that the Constitutional Court checks the respect of international treaties, both in the procedure of the abstract review of conformity of national laws with international treaties, and in cases brought before it by constitutional complaints against final decisions in individual cases, but that it declines competence to review the compatibility of international treaties with the Constitution. Certain academics have therefore suggested that prior review of the constitutionality of international treaties should be added to the Croatian legal system, in order to improve it.[19] Under the current solution, responsibility to check the conformity of an international treaty with the Croatian Constitution lies with the executive branch, which negotiates it, and primarily with the legislative branch, which ratifies it.

2.2 *Customary International Law*

There are no constitutional provisions on the application of customary international law in the Croatian legal order, and the Constitutional Court has not yet ruled on the issue. Accordingly, it may be concluded that the Croatian Constitution *tacite* distinguishes international treaties and other sources of international law, granting supra-legislative legal force only to international treaties which have been explicitly accepted. This view has been endorsed by a number of Croatian academics.[20] On the other hand, some authors consider that, even though the Constitution does not expressly provide for the application of customary international law, it can be concluded from the Constitution as a whole that the Constitution intended to allow its application.[21] However, Omejec points out that the fact that customary international law is applicable in Croatia does not mean that it enjoys the same supremacy

---

[19] Smerdel and Sokol (2009) p. 172, 185; Omejec (2009b), p. 138.

[20] Andrassy et al. (1998), p. 6; Omejec (2009a), p. 9. http://www.venice.coe.int/webforms/documents/?pdf=CDL-JU(2009)035-e. Accessed 20 September 2013.

[21] Rodin (2003), pp. 591–613, 14; Omejec (2009b), p. 137, citing Bačić (2006).

over national law as ratified and published international treaties do under Article 141 of the Constitution.[22]

3 Application of International Law

Generally speaking, international law is relatively seldom applied by Croatian courts. This conclusion has been reached by means of search engines on the case-law databases of the Supreme and Constitutional Courts, the SupraNova database and the IUS INFO private case-law database. As will be explained in the chapter on the availability of national case law, this conclusion can be overturned by the fact that there are certain flaws in the search engines of the databases and that the case law of lower courts is hardly accessible. However, the performed research of the most representative databases can be considered a good indication of what is happening in the system, and this indication has been confirmed in informal conversations by the authors with the judges of various court instances.

3.1 European Convention on the Protection of Human Rights and Fundamental Freedoms (ECHR)

By far the most often applied source of international law is the ECHR. However, since the application of the ECHR is not the focus of this chapter and since there is already an abundance of literature on the subject,[23] the authors will just point out the main characteristics of its application. The Republic of Croatia became a party to the Convention in 1997.[24] So far, there have been several Constitutional and legislative changes due to the Convention.[25] According to the information from the HUDOC database, by February 2014 a total of 325 cases against Croatia had been decided on the merits before the ECtHR, of which a violation of the Convention was found in 269 cases.[26] On the other hand, as pointed out by Omejec, the case law of the Croatian courts is far less voluminous and the Convention is not sufficiently applied.[27] So far, most of the ECHR related case law comes from the Constitutional

[22] Omejec (2009b), p. 137.

[23] Omejec (2013); Omejec (2007), pp. 1–9 and 1–15; Vajić (2002). https://www.pravo.unizg.hr/_download/repository/godisnjaci/1-godisnjak.pdf. Accessed November 2013.

[24] Zakon o potvrđivanju Konvencije za zaštitu ljudskih prava i temeljnih sloboda i Protokola br. 1, 4, 6, 7 i 11 uz Konvenciju za zaštitu ljudskih prava i temeljnih sloboda (Official Gazette—International Treaties 18/97).

[25] Rodin (2012), pp. 135–162, 139–145; Omejec (2007), pp. 1–15, 5–6.

[26] An overview of the most important judgments against Croatia is available at http://www.echr.coe.int/Documents/CP_Croatia_ENG.pdf. Accessed November 2013.

[27] http://www.poslovni.hr/hrvatska/omejec-sudovi-nedovoljno-primjenjuju-konvenciju-o-zastiti-ljudskih-prava-251495. Accessed 17 December 2013. Omejec (2007), pp. 1–15, 7.

Court,[28] which can be explained by an overlap of the Constitutional protection of fundamental rights with that guaranteed by the Convention. Furthermore, the vast majority of cases concern the right to trial within a reasonable time, protected by Article 6 of the Convention. In a smaller number of cases a breach of the Convention was found, including breaches of Article 6 (Decision U-III-3304/2011), Article 5(1) (Decisions U-III-3797/2008, U-III-4286/2007), etc.

In 2011, Rodin characterised the Constitutional Court as a 'sophisticated interpreter of fundamental rights and a national leader in the application of the ECHR', but also expressed concerns that its reactions were of a 'troubleshooting nature and not systematic, and that, substantively, [they] did not genuinely contribute to the strengthening of fundamental rights guarantees'.[29] These concerns were based on the Constitutional Court's application of the principles of proportionality (Decision U-III-4584/2005), indirect indiscrimination (Decision U-III-3138/2002) and the selective reading of the ECtHR's case law (for example, Decision U-III-41640/2009). While the case law of the ECtHR or the ECHR itself are often quoted, at least by the Constitutional (for example, Decision U-III-1067/2009) and the Supreme Court (Kž 37/2009-6), its direct application is much less frequent.

3.2 *Other Sources of International Law*

Regarding the application of other sources of international law in Croatia, one of the good and very rare examples of the direct application of an international treaty can be found in the Constitutional Court's Decision U-III-1337/2008. The case concerned the registration of a subsidiary of a foreign law office, for the provision of consulting services regarding the national law of the foreign service provider and foreign and international law. The Croatian Bar Association complained against the approval of the registration and claimed before the Constitutional Court that

[28] According to a search made in the private database IUS-INFO in February 2014, a total of 386 decisions of the Constitutional Court mention the words 'europska konvencija'. When the same search is performed regarding the decisions of the Supreme Court, there are 364 matches. Six matches occur for all the county courts and six for the High Administrative Court. These results must be considered as just an indicator of how often the Convention is cited, since the database does not contain all the judgments of the aforementioned courts. However, it should be said that the Convention is actually applied in a significantly lower number of cases. A search of the Constitutional Court's database at www.usud.hr reveals 20 hits when "Europska konvencija za zaštitu ljudskih prava i temeljnih sloboda" is selected as the search term in the Venice Glossary. However, this search is not very reliable since some of the decisions shown in the results do not even mention the ECHR (U-I-3084/2008). According to the research done by Preložnjak in 2012, a search of the Supreme Court's database revealed only seven judgments in which the ECHR had been applied. Preložnjak (2012), pp. 109–152, 113.

[29] Rodin (2011a), p. 2. http://excellence.com.hr/Opatija/w/wp-content/themes/ec/working_papers/WP%20Opatija%202_2011.pdf. Accessed 17 December 2013.

Articles 14[30] and 27[31] of the Constitution had been breached. The Constitutional Court ruled that:

> The basis for the registration of the subsidiary of a foreign law firm in question is not a Croatian law, but the Marrakesh Agreement[32] as an international agreement with all the consequences which this fact produces in the internal legal order. Therefore, in the case at hand, no special approval or permit is required for the registration of the subsidiary because the basis for the registration is an international agreement which explicitly states that a foreign founder can found a subsidiary for the provision of certain services on the territory of the Republic of Croatia.

The constitutional complaint of the Bar Association was therefore rejected.

Other cases on the application of international treaties include the United Nations Convention on the International Sales of Goods[33] applied directly in several judgments of the High Commercial Court (Pž-5827/06, Pž-907/06, Pž-5580/03), the Convention on the Contract for the International Carriage of Goods by Road (CMR) Convention, applied in the High Commercial Court's rulings Pž-2573/07, Pž-7956/04-3, Pž-5446/04-3, and the Supreme Court's ruling Rev 1631/89 concerning the Convention for the Protection of Cultural Property in the Event of Armed Conflict. The High Commercial Court also applied the Hague Convention on Civil Procedure[34] in case Pž-1219/07-3.

On several occasions, such as in the Constitutional Court's Decision U-III-388/2012, arguments based on international law seem to be raised by the Court itself. In paragraph 5 of this Decision, the Constitutional Court raised the issue of whether the Convention on the Rights of the Child[35] had been breached, but did not engage in a thorough analysis and did not base its decision on this Convention. In the same decision, the case law of the ECtHR was also analysed in a similar manner.

The case law of foreign courts is occasionally cited, but mostly by the Constitutional Court. For example, in Decision U-I-295/2006 and U-I-4526/2007 which concerned the constitutionality of the Public Assembly Act, the case law of the constitutional courts of some members of the Council of Europe was listed, albeit in an annex to the Decision. It was stated in the annex that the legislation and case law of other members of the Council of Europe are taken into account when the level of

---

[30] 'All shall be equal before the law.'

[31] 'The Bar, as an autonomous and independent service, shall provide everyone with legal aid, in conformity with law.'

[32] The General Agreement on the Trade of Services (hereinafter GATS) and the Schedule of specific commitments of the Republic of Croatia, as attached to the GATS which has been confirmed by the Act on confirmation of the Protocol of accession of the Republic of Croatia to the Marrakesh agreement establishing the World Trade Organisation signed in Geneva on 17 July 2000.

[33] Konvencija Ujedinjenih naroda o ugovorima o međunarodnoj prodaji robe—Sl. list SFRJ-dodatak Međunarodni ugovori broj 10/84, 15/98.

[34] Haška konvencija o građanskom postupku od 1. ožujka 1954. godine (Official Gazette—International Agreements 4/94).

[35] The Convention on the Rights of the Child has also been applied by the courts of lower instance, such as the Municipal Court in Varaždin in Case 6P-54/10-35.

consensus among its member states has to be determined, because the agreed 'common grounds' between the member states can limit the legislator when regulating certain areas. In the Decision itself, the Constitutional Court only determined in paragraph 22 that so far 'common ground' between the member states had not been reached regarding the issue at hand. The same Decision also extensively listed the case law of the ECtHR and the Convention itself, along with the International Covenant on Civil and Political Rights and the Universal Declaration on Human Rights. Another example of quoting judgments of foreign jurisdictions can be found in the Constitutional Court's Decision U-III-3304/2011, which concerned a failure of Croatian courts to execute a judgment of the ECtHR, where a decision of the German Budesverfassungsgericht was quoted. From the above-mentioned decisions of the Constitutional Court, it can be seen that foreign case law is quoted in order to increase the legitimacy of the decision, but without an explanation of to what extent the decision was influenced by the practice of the foreign courts.

4 EU Law

The Republic of Croatia became a Member State of the European Union on 1 July 2013. The process of harmonisation of the Croatian legal order with the *acquis communautaire* began with the signing of the Stabilisation and Association Agreement in 2003, which entered into force on 1 February 2005. Article 69 of the Stabilisation and Association Agreement played an important role as a general basis for harmonisation: 'Croatia shall endeavour to ensure that its existing laws and future legislation will be gradually made compatible with the Community *acquis*.' A relatively small but important body of case law was developed in relation to the Agreement, mainly by the Constitutional and Supreme Courts. Since this practice of Croatian courts will be analysed in a separate chapter dealing with the application of the stabilisation and association agreements, it will not be a part of the present analysis.

4.1 Constitutional Changes in Relation to EU Law

The accession of the Republic of Croatia to the European Union brought changes throughout the Croatian legal system. The 2010 Constitutional changes introduced a separate chapter on the EU into the Constitution, which formed the legal basis for Croatia's membership in the Union.[36] The status of the European Union law is described in Article 145 of the 2010 consolidated text[37]:

[36] Decision Promulgating the Changes to the Constitution of the Republic of Croatia (Odluka o proglašenju promjena Ustava Republike Hrvatske) (Official Gazette 76/2010). According to the 2010 consolidated text of the Constitution (Official Gazette 85/2010), Chapter VIII of the Constitution.

[37] Paragraph numbering added by the authors.

(1) Realisation of rights stemming from the acquis communautaire shall be deemed equal to the realisation of rights guaranteed under the Croatian legal order.
(2) Legal acts and decisions accepted by the Republic of Croatia in the institutions of the European Union shall apply in the Republic of Croatia in accordance with the acquis communautaire.
(3) Croatian courts shall protect individual rights based on the acquis communautaire.
(4) State bodies, bodies of local and regional self-government and legal persons vested with public authorities shall apply the acquis communautaire directly.

As can be seen from the text of Article 145, the Croatian Constitution does not explicitly address the principle of primacy of EU law, as established by the judgment of the Court of Justice of the European Union in *Costa v. ENEL*.[38] However, Article 145 should not be read in a strictly technical way. Since Croatia willingly joined the Union's legal order, it also willingly undertook the obligation to play by its rules. Consequently, Article 145(2) should not be read in a way which would exclude the application of legal acts and decisions which have been adopted in the EU institutions, but without the explicit consent of the Republic of Croatia (for example, by being outvoted in the Council). Furthermore, certain EU institutions, such as the Commission and the Court of Justice, are not even foreseen to represent national interests, so, strictly speaking, Croatia as a Member State cannot even express its approval of the acts which are adopted within them. However, since Croatia is a party to the Treaty of Lisbon and forms part of the European integration process, any systematic non-application of EU institutions' decisions, such as the judgments of the Court of Justice of the EU, would be in severe breach of the *bona fide* fulfilment of its obligations as a Member State. In other words, membership in the Union is inseparable from the application of the entire *acquis*. This *acquis* is, by its very nature, to be applied in line with the principles of direct and interpretative effect and primacy over national law, which have been developed by the case law of the Court of Justice. Precisely because of the principle of supremacy of EU law, its status does not depend on the provisions of national law. Even though Article 145(2) of the Constitution should be read to include the application of the principles of the supremacy of EU law and direct effect, as of 1 July 2013 those principles would still apply in the Croatian legal order, regardless of whether such application is foreseen by the Croatian Constitution. The same view has been expressed by Rodin, who considers Article 145 to be 'a constitutional declaration of the legal principles on which the law of the EU is founded'.[39] In conclusion, despite the fact that the principle of the supremacy of EU law is not mentioned in the Constitution, that principle nevertheless applies in the Croatian legal order.[40]

Article 145 makes it clear that Croatian courts are obliged to protect individual rights based on EU law. As explained above, those rights must be protected in line with the *acquis*, meaning that the Croatian courts must apply the standards

---

[38] Case 6 /1964 *Flamino Costa v. ENEL*, ECR 585.

[39] Rodin (2011b), pp. 87–118, 89.

[40] For a detailed analysis of Article 145 of the Constitution, see Rodin (2011b), pp. 87–118.

developed by EU law, and especially by the case law of the Court of Justice, when protecting them. In other words, Croatian courts are obliged to make every effort to secure efficient protection of individual rights based on EU law, and, if necessary, to apply EU law directly, or interpret national law in line with EU law.

As of September 2014, a search of the Constitutional Court's database reveals no case law regarding Article 145 of the Constitution.

4.2 *Application of EU Law by Croatian Courts*

Generally speaking, after 1 year of EU membership, Croatian courts have started applying EU law, but mainly, or even exclusively, by applying Croatian legislation which has been harmonised with EU law. This approach can produce satisfactory results only if a national law encompasses all the standards for the correct application of EU law (which can hardly be the case), and as long as those standards of EU law do not change.

So far, some of the most interesting cases which offer some insight into the courts' notion of EU law have arisen in the context of discussions on whether a preliminary reference should be addressed to Luxembourg. By September 2014, one request for a preliminary ruling under Article 267 of the Treaty on the Functioning of the EU had been submitted by a Croatian court. That reference is analysed more closely under Sect. 4.3 of this chapter. However, apart from that reference, a search of the IUS-INFO database reveals that parties have requested preliminary references from the Administrative Court in Rijeka in Case 2 UsI-1472/12-59, but the Administrative Court rejected the request with the explanation that the interpretation of EU law would not be useful for the resolution of the dispute in hand, since the facts of the case took place before 1 July 2013, that is, before the directives the plaintiff was invoking came into force in the Republic of Croatia.[41] By doing so, the Administrative Court showed good knowledge of the basic principles of EU law, such as direct and indirect effect and the scope of application of EU law. A preliminary reference was also requested by the parties in Case Kv–eun- 2/14 concerning the Croatian Act on Judicial Cooperation in Criminal Matters with EU Member States,[42] which was decided by the County Court in Zagreb on 8 January 2014. The County Court decided not to send a preliminary reference to Luxembourg, with the following explanation:

> ... a strict division exists between the Court of Justice and national courts, which is normatively prescribed in Article 220 of the Treaty on the European Community, based on which the European Court of Justice has jurisdiction over the interpretation of law of the Community and Union, and *a contrario*, the highest national courts have jurisdiction over

[41] Judgment of the Administrative Court in Rijeka of 18 October 2013 in Case 2 UsI-1472/12-59.

[42] *Zakon o pravosudnoj suradnji u kaznenim stvarima s državama članicama Europske unije* (Official Gazette 91/10, 81/13, 124/13).

the interpretation of national law, that is, in the present case, the Act on Judicial Cooperation in Criminal Matters with EU Member States.

In the same case, the County Court analysed and dismissed the arguments of the defendant based on the case law of the Court of Justice. The case later reached the Supreme Court, which, in its Decision of 17 January 2014 Kž-eun-2/14-5, approved the explanation of the County Court for not sending a preliminary reference. Interestingly, due to a lodged constitutional complaint, the Constitutional Court had the chance to rule on the same case. According to point 7.4 of the Constitutional Court's Decision U-III-351/2014 of 24 January 2014, the complainant cited the Court's case law and the judicial practice of other Member States in support of his substantive arguments, and according to point 7.8 of the Decision, he suggested that the Constitutional Court refer two questions on the interpretation of EU law and even suggested the wording of those questions. The Constitutional Court dismissed the constitutional complaint because it did not have the jurisdiction to rule on the legality of the decisions of ordinary courts, but only to assess whether the constitutional rights of the complainant had been violated. However, the Constitutional Court used the opportunity to explain the legal context in which the European arrest warrant operates and cited the Court's judgment in Case C-105/03 *Pupino* and extensively in Case C-396/11 *Radu*, the official translation of which was at the time not available in Croatian. The Constitutional Court even briefly addressed the Opinion of Advocate General Sharpston in the latter case. This shows that the Constitutional Court researches and pays regard to the case law of the Court of Justice, even when official translations are not available in Croatian. However, it must be noted that so far the case law of the Court has not been applied as a source of law, but is merely quoted as part of the explanation of the legal background of the case, but not relevant for the outcome of the case.[43] Finally, the Constitutional Court also addressed the suggestion of the complainant to refer two preliminary questions on the interpretation of EU law to the Court. In point 19 of the Decision, it stated that the same suggestions had been directed towards the courts which had decided in the first and second instances, and that both courts had explained that they considered that Croatian courts had exclusive jurisdiction to interpret the Act on Judicial Cooperation in Criminal Matters with EU Member States, which implements the framework decision. No further explanation on this matter was given.

Furthermore, the authors are not aware of any decision of Croatian courts in which EU law has been directly applied. However, it must be stated that it is not surprising that there are yet no such decisions by the highest courts, because of the relatively recent EU membership and the length of the proceedings, that is, the time it takes parties to reach the highest judicial instances. A promising example in this direction can be found in the Supreme Court's Decision Kž-eun-11/2013-4 of 20 September 2013, concerning the European Arrest Warrant, where a lower-

[43] A similar example of citation of the case law of the Court of Justice can be found in point 5 of the Constitutional Court's Decision U-I-2403/2009 of 25 February 2014.

instance judgment was quashed because it contravened the Act on Judicial Cooperation in Criminal Matters with EU Member States. The Supreme Court stated that:

> . . .the Act on Judicial Cooperation in Criminal Matters with EU Member States is based on the EU acquis, and should be interpreted and applied in line with the acquis and the case law of the Court of Justice of the EU.

Another encouraging example is the Supreme Court's Decision in Kž-eun-5/14-4 and Kž-eun-14/14-4, where it stated that:

> . . . during the application of national law, it must, as far as possible, be interpreted in light of the wording and purpose of relevant framework decisions and directives, in order for the result which those framework decision and directives aim for, to be achieved. . ..

Regarding the case law of the Constitutional Court, in its Decision U-I-3861/2013 of 16 July 2013, the Constitutional Court also expressed its intention to analyse the case law of the ECtHR and the Court of Justice of the EU and Directive 2006/112/EC in order to assess the constitutionality of a part of the Act on Value Added Tax, and to determine whether the Charter of Fundamental Rights was applicable to the case it was deciding.[44] However, the Act had been amended before the Constitutional Court ruled on the issue of its constitutionality, so the aforementioned analysis did not take place.[45] Had the Constitutional Court engaged in the planned analysis, it would have represented an important step towards the application of the case law of the Court of Justice as a source of law directly relevant for the resolution of the Constitutional Court's case.

When it comes to pre-accession cases citing the case law of the Court of Justice, there have been several occasions of such citation, mainly in competition law cases, which will be analysed under a separate chapter of this book. Another example can be found in the Constitutional Court's Decision U-III/2340/2008 of 17 February 2011. The Constitutional Court rejected the constitutional complaint against the Decision of the High Commercial Court, which rejected the request for the registration of a subsidiary of a foreign firm. The plaintiffs, among others, made the claim that the High Commercial Court's decision breached the *Centros*[46] judgment of the Court of Justice. The Constitutional Court briefly dismissed the argument by stating that a host Member State is allowed to apply measures for the prevention of fraud. The Constitutional Court neither performed a detailed analysis of the case law of the Court of Justice, nor made sure that the fact regarding whether the plaintiff had acted in fraud was established. It furthermore refused to perform a

[44] Point 6 of the Decision.

[45] The procedure before the Constitutional Court was terminated by Decision U-I-3861/2013 of 12 December 2013.

[46] Case C-212/1997, *Centros Ltd v. Erhvervs- og Selskabsstyrelsen* ECR 1999. It should be mentioned that in none of the Croatian courts cases that the authors have analysed has the case law of the Court of Justice been properly cited by using the case number, the name of the case and the paragraph which is being referred to.

proportionality analysis, because under the current case law of the Constitutional Court, it only performs such analysis in the abstract review of constitutionality, and not within individual complaint procedures.

4.3 Croatian Courts and the Preliminary Reference Procedure Under Article 267 TFEU

Let us start by briefly analysing the national legislative framework on the preliminary reference procedure. It should firstly be noted that Croatia does not regulate the preliminary reference procedure within a single act, but that several procedural acts contain provisions determining the issue. For example, Article 213 of the Civil Procedure Act[47] prescribes that the court shall stay the proceedings when it wishes to refer a question on the interpretation or validity of EU law to the Court of Justice. A similar legislative solution can be found in Article 18 of the Criminal Procedure Act.[48] However, so far other procedural acts do not contain similar provisions, which could allow the wrong conclusion to be drawn that it is not possible to make preliminary references in, for example, administrative procedures. It would therefore be advisable to either regulate the preliminary reference within a single act, which would be applicable to all types of judicial procedures, or to amend existing procedural acts which do not contain provisions on communication with the Court of Justice.[49] Furthermore, both current legislative solutions in the Civil and Criminal Procedure Acts require thorough knowledge of EU law on the preliminary reference procedure in order to be applied in line with Article 267 of the Treaty on the Functioning of the European Union.

Turning to the application of the above-mentioned Croatian legislative framework, it should be noted that, as of September 2014, the Court of Justice of the EU has received one preliminary reference from Croatian courts. The first Croatian preliminary reference was submitted, after only 10 months of EU membership, by the Municipal Court in Velika Gorica (Općinski sud u Velikoj Gorici) and concerned consumer protection in the area of water charges.[50] It was received by the Court on 26 May 2014 and will be decided as case C-254/14 *VG Vodoopskrba d.o.o. za vodoopskrbu i odvodnju v Đuro Vladika*.[51]

[47] *Zakon o parničnom postupku* (Official Gazette 53/91, 91/92, 58/93, 112/99, 88/01, 117/03, 88/05, 02/07, 84/08, 123/08, 57/11, 148/11, 25/13).

[48] *Zakon o kaznenom postupku* (Official Gazette 152/08, 76/09, 80/11, 121/11, 91/12, 143/12, 56/13, 145/13).

[49] Croatian academics have argued in favour of regulating the preliminary reference procedure in one act. Ćapeta and Petrašević (2011), p. 5.

[50] http://eur-lex.europa.eu/legal-content/EN/TXT/?uri=CELEX:62014CN0254&qid=1410859779106. Accessed 16 September 2014.

[51] At the time of writing, the case was still being handled by the Court of Justice of the European Union.

Even though under Article 267 TFEU, Croatian courts enjoy direct authority to send preliminary references to the Court of Justice, there are currently two concerns in the Croatian legal order that deserve attention in relation to the preliminary reference procedure.

The first concern is raised by Article 37 of the Constitutional Act on the Constitutional Court of the Republic of Croatia[52] which prescribes that:

> if during the proceedings the court determines that a law, or its provision, which should be applied to the case at hand, is not in accordance with the Constitution, it shall stay the proceedings and submit a request for the review of constitutionality of that law, or its provision, to the Constitutional Court.

The problem with the aforementioned Article 37 is that the Constitutional Court has developed consistent case law according to which it considers the question of conformity of a law with an international treaty to be a question of constitutionality, over which it has jurisdiction.[53] Therefore, since both the Constitution and the Constitutional Act on the Constitutional Court do not contain special provisions on EU law regarding this issue, it could be concluded that, according to the existing practice of the Constitutional Court, a court which considers that a law, which it has to apply in a case it is deciding upon, is contrary to EU law, would first have to submit a request for a review of constitutionality of that law to the Constitutional Court. Such an obligation of ordinary courts is liable to significantly hinder their access to the Court of Justice and impede its assistance in applying EU law. The Court of Justice addressed this issue in *Simmenthal II* where it stated the following:

> ... a national court which is called upon, within the limits of its jurisdiction, to apply provisions of Community law is under a duty to give full effect to those provisions, if necessary refusing of its own motion to apply any conflicting provision of national legislation, even if adopted subsequently, and it is not necessary for the court to request or await the prior setting aside of such provision by legislative or other constitutional means.[54]

According to EU law, which has primacy over Croatian law, a Croatian court which considers a national law to be contrary to EU law has the power not to apply such a law to the case it is deciding, without the prior approval of the Constitutional Court. Even though, as suggested by Ćapeta,[55] there are ways of interpreting Article 37 of the Constitutional Act on the Constitutional Court in conformity with this

---

[52] *Ustavni zakon o Ustavnom sudu* (Official Gazette 99/1999, 29/2002). The consolidated text was published in Official Gazette 49/2002.

[53] For a detailed analysis of the Constitutional Court's case law on this matter, see Sect. 2.1.1 of this chapter.

[54] Case 106/77 *Amministrazione delle Finanze dello Stato v. Simmenthal SpA* (1978) ECR 643, para 24.

[55] Ćapeta (2009), pp. 63–96, 90. The paper is also available at http://hrcak.srce.hr/index.php?show=clanak&id_clanak_jezik=52084. Accessed 15 January 2014. Both Rodin (2011b), pp. 87–118, 118, and Ćapeta (2009), pp. 88–90 have warned against this impediment to the *Simmenthal mandate* of ordinary courts. For a detailed analysis of the *Simmenthal* duty, see the same text from Rodin (2011b).

Simmenthal mandate of ordinary courts, it would have been useful if the Act were amended, to ensure that all judges are fully aware which course of action EU law requires in such a situation.

The second concern regarding the authority of ordinary courts to seek interpretation or a decision on the validity of EU law from the Court of Justice has recently been raised by the Constitutional Court's Decision U-I/4175/2013 of 27 August 2013. In its Decision, the Constitutional Court rejected the request for a review of the constitutionality of the Act on Financial Dealings and Pre-bankruptcy Settlement submitted by a judge of the Commercial Court in Zagreb under Article 37 of the Constitutional Act on the Constitutional Court. What makes the Decision controversial from the point of view of EU law is that the request for a review of constitutionality was rejected because it was signed by the judge of the Commercial Court who was deciding the case, and not by the Commercial Court as an institution (even though the request bore the stamp of the Court). Such a restrictive interpretation of the notion of 'court' which is entitled to submit a request for a review of constitutionality is very formalistic and detrimental to communication between judges, who are ultimately responsible for deciding cases, and the Constitutional Court. If the same logic is to be applied to the preliminary reference procedure, a judge who wishes to seek guidance regarding the application of EU law from the Court of Justice would first have to ask for the approval of the president of his/her court to do so. Such a restriction is contrary to the very purpose of the preliminary reference procedure, which has been developed precisely to enable every judge in every Member State to communicate freely and uninterruptedly with the Court of Justice. The aforementioned recent Decision of the Constitutional Court is therefore surprising when taking into account Croatia's recent accession to the Union. When deciding this case, the Constitutional Court was aware that it was setting a rule for future cases, since, as stated in paragraph 4 of the Decision, Croatian courts have very rarely used Article 37 to request a review of constitutionality.[56] The argumentation of the Constitutional Court is very unconvincing because, as the starting point for its analysis, it used the old text from the 1991 Act, which had been even more restricting regarding the request for a review of constitutionality submitted by the court deciding a case, but which has subsequently been changed (as quoted above). The Constitutional Court furthermore stated that, despite its ruling, judges are still entitled to request a review of constitutionality under Article 38 of the Constitutional Act on the Constitutional Court, just like any other individual. However, the difference between Articles 37 and 38 is that the latter serves as the basis for the abstract review of constitutionality, meaning that a judge deciding a case would not be entitled to stay the proceedings and wait for the Constitutional Court's decision on the constitutionality of a law, but would have to apply the law he/she considers unconstitutional and decide the case. In other words, the Constitutional Court's decision on constitutionality would not necessarily have an impact on the case a judge has to decide. It is incomprehensible why the Constitutional Court did not

[56] Several earlier cases regarding the same issue are cited in point 9.3 of the Decision.

want to encourage judges to request reviews of constitutionality and make them, and not the courts as institutions, the ones entitled to start the procedure, especially because so far there have been so few requests under Article 37. In any case, the same logic will not be applicable to EU law because it entitles every judge to start the preliminary reference procedure on his/her own motion.

5 Organisation of the Judicial System in Croatia

In order to paint a complete picture of how the judicial system, which serves as the ultimate safeguard of the application of international and EU law, works in practice, the following part of the text will briefly present its structure, the procedural rules it follows, and the availability of its decisions for the general public.

According to the Constitution, in the Republic of Croatia the government is organised on the principle of separation of powers into the legislative, executive and judicial branches.[57] Judicial power[58] is exercised by the courts, which administer justice according to the Constitution, laws, international treaties, and other valid sources of law. This provision applies to all courts in the national system.[59] In Croatia, judicial power is vested in ordinary and specialised courts. Ordinary courts (i.e. courts of general jurisdiction) are municipal courts, county courts and the Supreme Court of the Republic of Croatia. Specialised courts are misdemeanours courts, commercial courts, administrative courts, the High Misdemeanour Court of the Republic of Croatia, the High Commercial Court of the Republic of Croatia, and the High Administrative Court of the Republic of Croatia. There are in total 158 courts in Croatia (of which 82 are ordinary courts)[60] and the Constitutional

[57] Article 4 of the Constitution.

[58] Articles 115–121 of the Constitution.

[59] The same provision is repeated in the Courts Act (see reference above), which regulates the organisation, competence and jurisdiction of courts, their internal organisation, the rights and responsibilities of judges, the internal organisation of the Supreme Court of the Republic of Croatia and other provisions regarding the appointment of jurors, official court interpreters, expert witnesses and appraisers, as well as judicial administration. The conditions for the appointment, promotion, transfer and removal of judges, the procedure for the determination of their disciplinary responsibility, and the procedures for the appointment and dismissal of presidents of the courts are regulated by the State Judicial Council Act (Zakon o državnom sudbenom vijeću) (Official Gazette 116/10, 57/11, 130/11, 13/13, 28/13).

[60] According to the Statistical Report of the Ministry of Justice for the year 2012 (the Report was released in May 2013), on 31 December 2012 in the Republic of Croatia there were in total 67 municipal courts, 15 county courts, seven commercial courts, four administrative courts, 61 misdemeanours courts, the High Commercial Court of the Republic of Croatia, the High Administrative Court of the Republic of Croatia, the High Misdemeanours Court of the Republic of Croatia and the Supreme Court of Croatia. The Ministry of Justice has suggested a reform of the judicial system which would significantly reduce the number of courts, and which might be implemented in 2015.

Court of the Republic Croatia as a separate body. The misdemeanour courts, municipal courts and commercial courts are courts of first instance, while the High Commercial Court, the High Administrative Court as well as the county courts are courts of second instance.[61] The Supreme Court of the Republic of Croatia is the highest judicial instance and its constitutional duty is to ensure the uniform application of law and the equality of citizens before the law.

As stated above, according to the Constitution and the Courts Act, the courts in Croatia have the obligation to apply international treaties. Given that the Croatian Constitution accepts the system of incorporation and legal monism for international treaties signed and ratified in accordance with the Constitution and published, the courts have legal authority to apply them directly. Neither the Croatian Constitution nor any other national sources of law contain an explicit general norm regulating the application of the general rules of international law in the national legal order.

There are no specific procedural rules for the application of international law by the national courts. Therefore, it seems that in cases where international treaties are applicable, national courts are bound by the same principles as in cases concerning the application of national law. Generally in Croatia, the application of law by the courts depends on three main elements: first, the type of proceedings (civil, criminal, administrative proceedings—the type of proceedings determining the powers of the court); second, whether it is a question of substantive or procedural law (in relation to questions of substantive law, the *iura novit curia* principle applies and the courts are not bound by the legal basis raised by the parties and are obliged to evaluate the issues independently); and third, at what instance the case is adjudicated (in the Croatian system, there is no *beneficio novorum* at the appeal stage, while the Supreme Court decides only on the points of law raised in the appeal).

Since ratified and published international agreements which are in force form part of the Croatian legal order, and since, by joining the Union, EU law became applicable in Croatia, it can be concluded that the *iura novit curia* principle applies to these sources of law as well. Therefore, in cases where international treaties and EU law are applicable, Croatian courts are obliged to apply international treaties and EU law *ex officio*.

In cases where the national court finds that a provision of a law does not conform to the Constitution, it must stay the proceedings and refer a request for the control of the constitutionality of the law in question to the Constitutional Court. This means that the national courts do not have the legal authority to set aside a provision of

[61] County courts decide on appeals lodged against the first-instance decisions of municipal courts, but they also have first-instance jurisdiction to adjudicate crimes which may be punished by imprisonment of more than 10 years, and carry out any other activities which are provided for by law (e.g. conduct investigations, decide on appeals against the decision of an investigating judge, and make decisions about his/her proposals, conduct proceedings for the extradition of indicted or convicted persons unless the law specifies the jurisdiction of the Supreme Court of the Republic of Croatia). In civil matters, county courts have first-instance jurisdiction in cases concerning joint anti-discrimination actions and in cases of bans on strikes and lockouts.

national law which does not conform to the Constitution. Consequently, since there are no national provisions regulating the matter (except those that provide a sub-constitutional and supra-legal status for international treaties), it appears that the national courts are also obliged to follow the same procedure described above if they assess that a national law does not conform to an international treaty. This conclusion is corroborated by the described practice of the Constitutional Court of using international treaties as benchmarks for the abstract control of constitutionality of national laws—granting international treaties *a quasi-constitutional* status. Until now, only a very small number of cases of this type have arisen.[62]

The majority of Croatian courts are technically well equipped and judges have internet access which makes it possible to search foreign sources of law. A court case management system, the ICMS—Integrated Case Management System—has gradually been introduced into Croatian courts[63] since 2007. It provides an immediate insight into cases at all stages of the judicial procedure, enables a faster exchange of data between courts, and optimises costs.

So far, only the Supreme Court regularly publishes all its decision on its website. The decisions are anonymised and may be browsed using the search engine of the database '*SuPra*'.[64] The database provides access to case law published in bulletins of the Croatian Supreme Court called '*Izbor odluka*',[65] but also to previously unreleased full texts of decisions of the Supreme Court since 1993 to date. The database also provides access to a selection of important decisions of other courts in Croatia. A new and improved information system, '*SupraNova*', should soon replace the existing one. A test-version is at present accessible to members of the judiciary and it allows users to browse the decisions of other courts using the same system.[66]

The case law of other courts in Croatia is still not easily available. Some courts publish a selection of the most important decisions (e.g. the High Commercial Court, the High Administrative Court, Varaždin County Court) on their websites or as hard-copy bulletins. Some private commercial providers, such as IUS-INFO and

[62] According to the information received from the Constitutional Court's Records and Documentation Centre on 27 February 2013, to date the Constitutional Court has decided on the merits seven requests for the control of the constitutionality of laws and/or for the control of the legality of administrative acts and regulations referred to it by national courts (six of which on the legality of administrative acts and regulations and only one on the conformity of a law with the Constitution).

[63] On 31 December 2012 the ICMS was introduced into all county courts and commercial courts, in 33 municipal courts and partially into the High Commercial Court and the Supreme Court (information provided by the Supreme Court's IT Department on 28 March 2013).

[64] http://sudskapraksa.vsrh.hr/supra/. Accessed February 2013.

[65] The bulletin '*Izbor odluka*' contains a selection of the most important legal decisions with the text of the legal standpoints/sentences of the Supreme Court.

[66] In 2012, 42 courts recorded their decisions in the '*SupraNova*' database (information provided by the Supreme Court's IT Department on 29 March 2013).

Sudačka mreža,[67] offer the possibility of browsing the case law of Croatian courts, often in a more efficient manner than the official websites of the institutions concerned.

The Constitutional Court publishes selected case law on its website and in the Official Gazette of the Republic of Croatia, '*Narodne novine*'. The case law published on the website may be consulted using a search engine.[68]

To date, the decisions (with very few exceptions) of the Croatian courts are available only in Croatian. The Constitutional Court offers the possibility of searching the case law in English and publishes legal summaries of selected decisions in English on its website, but the integral texts are available only in Croatian.

During our research we detected a systemic problem with the availability of the ECtHR and pre-accession CJEU case law in the Croatian language. The ECtHR case law is available in Croatian only concerning cases involving the Republic of Croatia as a party in the proceedings,[69] while the 'historic', pre-accession CJEU case law is still being translated into Croatian.[70] In contrast to the CJEU case law, the pre-accession primary and secondary legislation in force has been translated into Croatian and has been gradually published in the Special Edition of the Official Journal of the European Union.[71] Therefore, the described situation poses a serious question about the possibility of Croatian jurists to prepare themselves adequately for the application of ECHR and EU law.

Hence, although Croatian judges (and more generally Croatian jurists) have internet access which makes it possible to search foreign sources of law and the ECtHR and CJEU case law, effective access to these sources is clearly in doubt because of the language barrier.

---

[67] http://www.iusinfo.hr/ and http://www.sudacka-mreza.hr/. Accessed February 2013.

[68] http://www.usud.hr/default.aspx?Show=kako_pretrazivati_bazu_ustavnosudske_prakse&m1=2&m2=68&Lang=hr. Accessed February 2013.

[69] Offering in this way an incomplete overview of the ECtHR's case law.

[70] The historic case law selected for the accession of Croatia consists of 1,143 judgments, opinions and orders of the Court of Justice and the General Court (1956 – June 2013). The documents have been sent to the Croatian Translation Centre of the Ministry of Foreign and European Affairs. The 57 historic decisions translated by the Court's Croatian translation Unit are available at: http://curia.europa.eu/jcms/jcms/P_119447/. Accessed 13 March 2014. Before the accession of Croatia to the EU, there was a total of about 100 decisions which were partially translated for educational purposes by the academic staff of the Croatian law schools and most of them may be found on several websites, such as http://www.sudacka-mreza.hr/euodluke.aspx?Lng=hr (accessed 10 February 2013), while the remaining decisions may be consulted only as hard-copy commercial editions. From the date of the accession of Croatia to the European Union (1 July 2013), the CJEU case law is undergoing translation into Croatian by the CJEU translation services.

[71] The texts in Croatian are available online at http://eur-lex.europa.eu/RECH_DDProv.do?ihmlang=hr&dd_lng=HR. Accessed 10 February 2013.

6 Legal Education on International and EU Law

Finally, let us examine briefly the scope of education of legal professionals in the areas of international and EU law in Croatia. As the Republic of Croatia entered the European Union, education in EU and international law, whose scope also broadened with EU membership, became an inevitable component of legal education. Since an adequate background in international and EU law is a precondition for the successful work of the entire legal profession, including the administration, the judiciary, in-house lawyers and attorneys, an analysis of the current state and the potential for the application of international and EU law would be incomplete without this component.

There are four law schools in Croatia, all of which teach mandatory courses in international and EU law in their undergraduate programmes. Therefore, during their undergraduate studies, all students are required to obtain basic and general knowledge of international law, EU law and the ECHR. Optional advanced courses in different areas of EU law (such as Fundamental Rights in the EU, EU Internal Market Law, EU Migration Law and Policy, etc.), international law (International Human Rights Protection, International Criminal Law, International Law of the Seas, etc.) and the ECHR are also offered, but are usually chosen by a smaller number of students. Several law schools have Jean Monnet Chairs or Modules which are financed by the European Commission. Special postgraduate studies in EU and international law are also offered.

The bar exam in Croatia[72] is required for the performance of the duty of judge, attorney-at-law and notary public. It does not include an examination in international law, except for the European Convention on Human Rights and Fundamental Freedoms, while a textbook on the basis of EU law became part of the compulsive sources for the preparation of the bar exam in 2008. Both are examined as part of the examination on constitutional and institutional issues.[73]

Concerning the education and appointment of judges, Croatia has set a new legislative framework for the system of recruitment, training, appointment and promotion of judicial officials. Since 1 January 2013, Croatia has switched to a process of selection of judges which is not based on experience, but on a specific public examination and a period of initial training in a judicial studies school.[74]

[72] According to the Judicial Trainees and Bar Examination Act (Official Gazette 84/08, 75/09) and the Rules on the Bar Examination, the written part consists of the drafting of two judicial decisions and one essay, while the oral part of the bar examination consists of five groups of subjects: Civil and Commercial Law; Civil Procedural and Family Law; Criminal Law and Criminal Procedure; Labour Law and Administrative Law; the Constitutional System, the Basis of the System of the European Union and the Organisation of the Judiciary. Candidates are eligible to sit the bar exam if they have a graduate law diploma and the required professional experience.

[73] The required literature is available at http://www.mprh.hr/Default.aspx?sec=325. Accessed 22 February 2014.

[74] The law bringing the reform of the system of judicial appointments was passed in 2009, establishing a State School for Judicial Officials as a separate unit of the Judicial Academy, the

During the period of initial training in the National School for the Judiciary, future judges follow basic courses in EU law and on the ECHR.[75]

When it comes to judges who have already been appointed, the situation changes. The Judicial Academy organises workshops on the application of EU law and of the ECHR for judges, but participation is voluntary and is not systematic.[76] At the end of 2013, the Judicial Academy developed an e-learning course in EU law, which targets primarily judicial advisors and is planned to be offered in the Academy's programme in 2014. A series of lectures on EU law has also been organised by certain courts, such as the Commercial Court in Zagreb and the Civil Municipal Court in Zagreb, with voluntary attendance.

Based on the results of our research, we can conclude that there are very few forms of legal training dedicated to the application of international law. The situation is slightly better when it comes to EU law, but the system lacks a systematic and comprehensive education for judges.

7 Conclusion

Having analysed the Constitutional and legal framework for the application of international and EU law in the Republic of Croatia, we can conclude that it sets a good basis for their direct application. When it comes to international treaties, their status is clearly defined—the Constitution states that they are above the law in terms of legal effect, but it remains silent regarding the general rules of international law. The status of EU law has been addressed in a newly added Constitutional chapter on EU law. While it clearly prescribes the duty of Croatian courts to protect individual rights based on EU law respecting the principle of equivalence and the duty of state bodies to directly apply the *acquis communautaire*, the wording is a little ambiguous regarding the scope of the acts and decisions of EU institutions that

national institution in charge of the professional training of judges and prosecutors. Before 2009, judges were appointed by the State Council of the Judiciary on the basis of their experience and CVs and the opinion of the Judicial Council for the relevant court. Between 2009 and 2013, a transitional system of appointment was established. Judges were appointed after passing the judicial examination, consisting of the examination of a judicial file and the drafting of an integral judicial decision and a structured interview with the members of the State Judicial Council. The first generation of future judges and prosecutors started their initial training at the National School for Judicial Officials in 2011, and their final exam was held in 2013; the second generation began initial training in 2012, while the selection procedures for the third generation are still underway.

[75] According to the Programme of the second generation of the National School for the Judiciary, which started the initial training in 2012, approximately 20 % of the courses are dedicated to EU law and the Convention.

[76] The Programme of Professional Training for 2014 of the Judicial Academy shows that judges, prosecutors and their legal advisors had the possibility to participate in three types of workshops dedicated to 'European and International Law', a significant part of which is dedicated to the ECHR. http://pak.hr/cke/pdf%20hr/Program%20cjeloziv%20usavrsavanja%20%20PA_2014%20web%20konacno.pdf. Accessed 27 February 2014.

are to be applied in line with the *acquis*. However, one vital part of the *acquis* that the Constitution does not expressly mention is the principle of supremacy of EU law. Nevertheless, despite the constitutional silence on the matter, its application is not questionable, primarily because it depends on EU law itself.

A study of the case law of Croatian courts paints a somewhat different picture of unused potential.[77] The same conclusion has been reached in several earlier studies by Croatian academics.[78] It should be said, though, that due to the unavailability of a significant body of national case law in the databases, the conclusions of this chapter are limited mainly to the practice of the Constitutional and Supreme Court. However, due to their role, they can be considered as indicators of judicial practice throughout the legal system. Most of the case law of Croatian courts on international law concerns only one international treaty—the ECHR. Perhaps this can be explained by the fact that the Constitutional protection of human rights overlaps with the Convention, that an international court supervises its application, and that the parties to the Convention are financially liable if they violate it. Although Croatian courts have cited the Convention and the case law of the ECtHR on numerous occasions, the citations are still significantly more frequent than direct application. So far, the Constitutional Court has played a vital role in addressing and applying the ECHR, but from time to time its citing of the ECtHR case law remains selective.

Through its case law, the Constitutional Court has established its jurisdiction to review the conformity of national laws with international treaties, but has declined it when it comes to the review of constitutionality of the treaties themselves. The Constitutional Court considers a violation of an international treaty to be at the same time a violation of the Constitution. This could prove to be problematic from the point of view of the *Simmenthal mandate*, should the Constitutional Court consider ordinary courts to be obliged to request the review of constitutionality every time they consider a national law to be contrary to EU law.

Finally, even though courses on international and EU law are part of the mandatory curriculum of all four law schools in Croatia, there is a need for the systematic education of practising legal professionals, such as attorneys, state attorneys and judges in those areas, especially in EU law which has only recently been added as a part of mandatory undergraduate legal education. A study conducted in 2011 among Croatian judges on the knowledge and understanding of international and EU law has shown that judges considered their knowledge on EU law to be mediocre.[79] The study was undertaken among judges who, at the time,

---

[77] According to the information obtained in a phone conversation with the Ministry of Foreign and European Affairs, in February 2014 the Republic of Croatia was a party to over 3,000 instruments of international law (such as bilateral agreements and acts and multilateral agreements and acts). It must be taken into account that most of those instruments are by their nature not such as to create individual rights. Nevertheless, according to our research, just a dozen international treaties have been discussed, and even a smaller number of them applied by Croatian courts.

[78] Ćapeta (2005), pp. 23–54, 35; Rodin (2003), pp. 591–613, 14.

[79] They gave it an average mark of 3 on a scale of 1 to 5. Preložnjak (2012), p. 127.

had just finished attending courses on EU and international law, which they chose on a voluntary basis. Surprisingly, only 69 % of the judges who took the survey answered correctly what the interpretative effect of EU law required them to do.[80] Results were better regarding knowledge of EU institutions and the effects of international law. When reflecting on the results of the survey, it must be emphasised that only a minority of judges attended the training on EU and international law, and that it would be reasonable to expect that the results would have been lower if the survey had been conducted among 'average' judges who had not taken the courses. In the meantime, many more judges have taken some form of training on EU and international law, but, undoubtedly, a systematic and comprehensive education in those areas would significantly contribute to the more frequent and more efficient application of EU and international law in the Republic of Croatia.

References

Andrassy J, Bakotić B, Vukas B (1998) Međunarodno pravo, vol 1. Školska knjiga, Zagreb

Bačić A (2006) Ustavno pravo Republike Hrvatske

Ćapeta T (2005) Courts, legal culture and enlargement of the EU. Croatian Yearb Eur Law Policy 1

Ćapeta T (2009) Nacionalni Ustav i nadređenost prava EU u eri pravnog pluralizma. Zbornik Pravnog Fakulteta u Zagrebu 59(1)

Ćapeta T, Petrašević T (2011) Kako će hrvatski suci surađivati s Europskim sudom. Informator, Zagreb

Omejec J (2007) Primjena Konvencije za zaštitu ljudskih prava i temeljnih sloboda u radu domaćih sudova. Hrvatska pravna revija 7(7–8)

Omejec J (2009a) Legal framework and case-law of the Constitutional Court of Croatia in deciding on the conformity of laws with international treaties. Report for the Venice Commission, CDL-JU (2009)035, November 2009

Omejec J (2009b) O potrebim promjenama u strukturi hrvatskog ustavnog sudovanja. In: Barbić J (ed) Hrvatsko ustavno sudovanje – de lege lata i de lege ferenda. HAZU, Zagreb

Omejec J (2013) Konvencija za zaštitu ljudskih prava i temeljnih sloboda u praksi Europskog suda za ljudska prava. Novi Informator, Zagreb

Preložnjak B (2012) Poznavanje, razumijevanje i stavovi hrvatskih sudaca o europskom i međunarodnom pravu. In: Šimonović I (ed) Poznavanje i vrijednosno prihvaćanje Europskog i međunarodnog prava u Republici Hvatskoj. Sveučilište u Zagrebu, Pravni fakultet, Zagreb

Rodin S (1995) The Constitutional Court of the Republic of Croatia and international law. Zeitschrift für ausländisches öffentliches Recht und Völkerrecht (ZaöRV) 55(3)

Rodin S (2003) Sporazum o stabilizaciji i pridruživanju u pravnom poretku Europske zajednice i Republike Hrvatske. Zbornik Pravnog fakulteta u Zagrebu 53(3–4)

Rodin S (2009) Ustavni sud i članstvo Republike Hrvatske u Europskoj uniji. In: Kačer H, Momčinović H, Žuvela M (eds) Liber amicorum in honorem Jadranko Crnić (1928.-2008.). Novi informator, Zagreb

Rodin S (2011a) Croatia: developing judicial culture of fundamental rights. Opatija Inter-University Centre of Excellence, working paper WP E2/2011

[80] Preložnjak (2012), p. 134.

Rodin S (2011b) Pravo Europske unije i pravni poredak Republike Hrvatske nakon 20 godina hrvatskog Ustava. In: Bačić A (ed) Dvadeseta obljetnica Ustava Republike Hrvatske: okrugli stol održan 16. prosinca 2010. u palači HAZU u Zagrebu

Rodin S (2012) Croatia. In: Hammer L, Emert F (eds) The European convention on human rights and fundamental freedoms in Central and Eastern Europe. Eleven International Publishing

Smerdel B, Sokol S (2009) Ustavno pravo. Narodne Novine, Zagreb

Vajić N (2002) Djelovanje Europskog suda za ljudska prava s osvrtom na presude protiv Republike Hrvatske. Bilten Kluba pravnika od 17. lipnja 2002 8, Pravni fakultet Sveučilišta u Zagrebu, Zagreb

Judicial Application of International Law in Kosovo

Kushtrim Istrefi and Visar Morina

1 Introduction

The Constitution of the Republic of Kosovo (hereinafter the 'Constitution' or the 'Kosovo Constitution') follows a 'strong regime of domestic incorporation' of international law.[1] Certain international human rights conventions are domesticated through the Constitution, and all ratified international agreements and legally binding norms of international law are granted supremacy over Kosovo laws.[2] The constitutional provisions related, *inter alia*, to the status of international law in the Kosovo legal order and the protection of minorities reflect largely verbatim the Comprehensive Proposal for the Status Settlement of Kosovo (the Ahtisaari Status Proposal), a framework document prepared by United Nations Special Envoy Mr. Martti Ahtisaari for the determination of the final political status of Kosovo.[3]

---

[1] Posner (2009), p. 111. For a categorisation of constitutions that permit the incorporation of international law, see particularly Cassese (1985), p. 394. The text of the Constitution and its amendments is available in the Official Gazette of the Republic of Kosovo at http://gazetazyrtare.rks-gov.net. Accessed 20 April 2013.

[2] On the process of constitution drafting, see Weller (2009), pp. 240–259; Tunheim (2009), p. 18.

[3] On the Ahtisaari Status Proposal, see http://www.unosek.org/unosek/en/statusproposal.html. Accessed 15 May 2013. For more on the Ahtisaari Status Proposal, see Weller (2009), pp. 244–249.

K. Istrefi (✉)
Graduate Institute of International and Development Studies, Geneva, Switzerland

University of Graz, Graz, Austria
e-mail: kushtrim.istrefi@gmail.com

V. Morina
Faculty of Law, Department for Constitutional and Administrative Law, University of Prishtina, Prishtina, Kosovo
e-mail: v_morina@yahoo.com

S. Rodin, T. Perišin (eds.), *Judicial Application of International Law in Southeast Europe*, DOI 10.1007/978-3-662-46384-0_9

While Kosovo is not yet a member of the United Nations (UN) or the Council of Europe, it has accorded constitutional rank to the provisions of eight international human rights instruments, including the Universal Declaration of Human Rights (UDHR) and the Council of Europe Framework Convention for the Protection of National Minorities (Framework Convention on Minorities). Furthermore, Article 53 of the Kosovo Constitution requires that all human rights be interpreted consistently with the case-law of the European Court of Human Rights (ECtHR). These peculiar features of the reception of international law in the Kosovo Constitution are scrutinised in the second part of this contribution.

The paper develops by examining the judicial application of international law by domestic and international judges embedded in Kosovo courts. The Kosovo Constitutional Court[4] has rendered some landmark decisions concerning the place of international law in the Kosovo legal order.[5] In its rather embryonic phase, domestic and international judges of the Constitutional Court have been challenged with cases that prompted the statehood of Kosovo and the mandate of the Assembly of Kosovo to adopt laws that invalidate international legal obligations, namely Regulations of the United Nations Interim Administration Mission in Kosovo (UNMIK).[6] In addition, the application of international human rights instruments and the ECtHR case-law is indispensable in the Constitutional Court's jurisprudence. These interactions with the UN and ECHR law, coupled with initial remarks on the Constitutional Court's mandate to deal with international law, are covered in the third section.

International judges have also been embedded in courts of general jurisdiction within the framework of the European Union Rule of Law Mission in Kosovo (EULEX), and whose decisions constitute part of the Kosovo domestic jurisprudence.[7] In inspecting the war crimes jurisprudence of EULEX international judges, fourth section analyses the challenges in adjudication of crimes emanating from the internal armed conflict and the challenges in utilising customary international law in the Kosovo legal order. The same section observes the judicial application of international agreements concerning state succession and the degree of application of the ECtHR case-law in the jurisprudence of EULEX international judges.[8]

---

[4] Article 112 of the Kosovo Constitution. For more on the Kosovo Constitutional Court, see Morina (2010), pp. 129–158; Hill and Linden-Retek (2010), p. 26; Hasani et al. (2012), pp. 49–69.

[5] All decisions of the Kosovo Constitutional Court are published in three languages: Albanian, Serbian and English and are available on the Constitutional Court's official web site http://www.gjk-ks.org. Accessed 11 May 2013.

[6] The Kosovo Constitutional Court is composed of six domestic and three international judges.

[7] On the establishment and the mandate of EULEX, see the European Union Council Joint Action 2008/124/CFSP of 4 February 2008 on the European Union Rule of Law Mission in Kosovo, EULEX Kosovo, OJ 2008 L 42. For the jurisdiction of EULEX international judges as provided in Kosovo law, see the Law on the Jurisdiction, Case Selection and Case Allocation of EULEX international judges and Prosecutors in Kosovo; Law on the Special Prosecution Office of the Republic of Kosovo.

[8] The vast majority of the decisions of EULEX international judges are published in English and at least one of the official languages in Kosovo, namely Albanian or Serbian. Decisions of EULEX

The fifth section examines the judicial application of international law by local judges of courts of general jurisdiction.[9] In elucidating the scarce application of ECtHR case-law, this part shows the challenges associated with resources and education of judges and suggests tools to strengthen the application of international law.[10]

Finally, the discussion is wrapped up with highlights and concluding remarks.

2 Reception of International Law in the Kosovo Constitution

As to the manner in which international law is incorporated in the Kosovo legal order, at least three models can be identified in the Kosovo Constitution.

Firstly, by means of *ratification* of international agreements by Kosovo institutions, international treaties become 'part of the internal legal system … [and] are directly applied except for cases when they are not self-applicable and the application requires the promulgation of a law'.[11] In the process of accession to international agreements, the Kosovo institutions with ratifying powers may make reservations or withdraw from the international agreements.[12] The Constitution emphasises in Articles 16 and 19 that Kosovo shall respect international law and that ratified international agreements have supremacy over Kosovo laws.

Secondly, international law reaches the Kosovo legal system through Article 19 (2) of the Constitution, which accords priority over Kosovo laws to the legally

international judges (including mixed panels) are available on the EULEX official website http://www.eulex-kosovo.eu/en/judgments/. Accessed 11 May 2013.

[9] Upon the adoption of Law No. 03/L-199, as of January 2013, the Kosovo court system disbanded from the old Yugoslav court structure and significantly transformed the organisation of the courts. The Law on Courts provides that all first-instance cases are adjudicated in specialised Departments of the Basic Courts, and appealed second-instance cases are adjudicated in one single Court of Appeals located in Prishtina. In the first and second instance, the Kosovo Courts operate with the Department for Serious Crimes, General Department, Department for Administrative Matters, Department for Commercial Matters, and Department for Minors. The Supreme Court deals with third-instance cases, extraordinary legal remedies and renders opinions related to the uniformity of court practices in Kosovo. The Supreme Court also includes the Appeals Panel of the Kosovo Property Agency and the Special Chamber of the Supreme Court, the judges of which are part of the Supreme Court.

[10] The judgments of the Supreme Court of Kosovo are largely accessible on the official website of the Supreme Court of Kosovo, while the decisions of other Kosovo courts of general jurisdiction are hardly accessible.

[11] Article 19(1) of the Constitution. On the instrument of ratification by the Kosovo institutions, see Article 18 of the Constitution.

[12] Article 18(4) of the Constitution. See also Articles 19, 54 and 62 of the Vienna Convention on the Law of Treaties (VCLT).

'binding norms of international law'. Yet, the Constitution does not clarify this concept. Furthermore, since the *travaux préparatoires* on the constitution drafting are inaccessible, the scope of 'legally binding norms of international law' remains open for interpretation. One may view that the 'legally binding norms of international law' encompass norms of *jus cogens*, other recognised norms of customary international law, and potentially the obligations emanating from the Security Council resolutions adopted under Chapter VII of the UN Charter. A wider interpretation would allow considerations that all sources of international law listed in Article 38 of the Statute of the International Court of Justice (ICJ) could be covered by the 'legally binding norms of international law'.[13] These pending questions yet remain to be answered by the Constitutional Court. So far, the judicial practice of Kosovo courts reveals that at least norms of customary international law are applicable in the Kosovo domestic legal order.[14] In light of Kosovo's endeavours to join the European Union (EU), Article 19(2) of the Constitution presents a potential question if EU law, too, would be accommodated. Where the EU Member States used their constitutional provisions on international law in integrating EU law, one could argue that similarly Article 19(2) of the Constitution opens the door for EU law.[15]

The third model is peculiar to the Kosovo legal order in that it *reproduces* certain international instruments and jurisprudence. In particular, Article 22 of the Constitution provides that

> [h]uman rights and fundamental freedoms guaranteed by the following international agreements and instruments are guaranteed by this Constitution, are directly applicable in the Republic of Kosovo and, in the case of conflict, have priority over provisions of laws and other acts of public institutions:
>
> (1) Universal Declaration of Human Rights;
> (2) European Convention for the Protection of Human Rights and Fundamental Freedoms and its Protocols;
> (3) International Covenant on Civil and Political Rights and its Protocols;
> (4) Council of Europe Framework Convention for the Protection of National Minorities;
> (5) Convention on the Elimination of All Forms of Racial Discrimination;
> (6) Convention on the Elimination of All Forms of Discrimination Against Women;
> (7) Convention on the Rights of the Child;

[13] See, e.g., Joost Pauwelyn who employs the term 'legally binding norms' as a synonym for all sources of international law 'as they may be invoked before an international court or tribunal'. Pauwelyn (2006), pp. 7, 89–91.

[14] See, e.g., SC Case No 386/10, Decision of the mixed panel of EULEX international judges, Supreme Court of Kosovo, 7 September 2010, at p. 6.

[15] See, e.g., the Italian Constitution of 22 December 1947 as a classical model. In the application of EU law and international law, Italy applies Article 11 of the Constitution which provides that Italy agrees to limitations of sovereignty where they are necessary to allow for a legal system of peace and justice between nations, provided the principle of reciprocity is guaranteed; it promotes and encourages international organisations furthering such ends. This provision is inspired by the UN system and by the obligations emanating from the UN Charter. However, Italy continued to utilise Article 11 of the Constitution to allow for the supremacy and direct effect of EU law.

(8) Convention against Torture and Other Cruel, Inhumane or Degrading Treatment or Punishment.

Further, Article 53 requires that '[h]uman rights and fundamental freedoms guaranteed by this Constitution shall be interpreted consistently with the court decisions of the European Court of Human Rights' (ECtHR). Article 22 of the Constitution, which domesticates international human rights instruments, is a verbatim rendering of the Ahtisaari Status Proposal.[16] This model particularly reveals the role of international actors in defining the place of international law in the Kosovo domestic legal order.[17] As the ECtHR Judge Lech Garlicki observes from experiences in constitution drafting in emerging democracies:

> [s]hort of military intervention and/or economic pressure, the most civilised way of imposing certain standards upon national processes of constitution drafting is to 'universalise' these standards by expressing them in the norms of international law. Such norms, if vested with sufficient binding authority, can pre-define the content of national constitutions leaving to the framers of a particular constitution no alternative but to reproduce them in the text of the constitution.[18]

A concern with regard to pure constitutional domestication of international law is the viability of its application. Notwithstanding the significance of Articles 22 and 53 of the Constitution, as Marc Weller remarks, some of the international conventions and instruments listed in these constitutional provisions 'may not in fact be suited to operating as self-executing provisions' in the Kosovo legal order.[19] While the Kosovo Constitution makes directly applicable the UDHR and the Framework Convention on Minorities, the former is a non-binding UN General Assembly resolution, and the latter was deliberately drafted as a 'framework' convention, as it was assumed that its provisions would not be directly enforceable.[20] Furthermore, since Kosovo has not yet joined the United Nations or the Council of Europe, citizens as well as other interested parties cannot benefit from the political or judicial mechanisms of the respective international organisations in terms of supervising or enforcing international human rights by Kosovo institutions.

As to the supremacy and direct effect of the UDHR, it would be interesting to observe what the response of the Kosovo courts and other institutions would be if, with Kosovo's economy as it is, claims were filed based on the right to social security as guaranteed under Article 22 of the UDHR, or the right to food, clothing, housing and medical care foreseen under Article 25 of the UDHR.

---

[16] Article 2, Annex I of the Comprehensive Proposal for the Kosovo Status Settlement.

[17] The Constitution did not incorporate social, economic and cultural rights (save for the provisions of the UDHR). For an overview see, e.g., Istrefi (2013), pp. 271–272.

[18] Garlicki (2005), p. 263.

[19] Weller (2009), p. 257.

[20] Ibid, p. 245.

3 Judicial Application of International Law by the Constitutional Court

3.1 Preliminary Remarks: Institutional Competencies to Provide Judicial Review on Issues Involving International Law

In 5 years of operation of the Kosovo Constitutional Court, significant jurisprudence has been developed with regard to the place of *domesticated* international instruments and the ECtHR in the Kosovo legal order. However, international instruments and the ECtHR case-law have been applied not as part of foreign (international) law but as a matter of domestic constitutional law. Furthermore, due to the lack of membership in the Council of Europe, the decisions of the Kosovo Constitutional Court are not subject to the jurisdiction of the ECtHR.

Once Kosovo accedes to more international agreements, it may be anticipated that the Constitutional Court will contribute to shaping the relationship between international and domestic law. In addition, since many provisions of the Constitution are not lucid with regard to the competences of the Constitutional Court, it will equally have to interpret domestic provisions concerning its jurisdiction to engage in legal matters related to international law. In this vein, although the Constitution is silent as to whether courts can review legislation for compatibility with international law, the Constitutional Court has not been reluctant to challenge the legality of the Statute of the Municipality of Prizren for its non-compliance with the Constitution and the Framework Convention on Minorities. In the *Kurtishi* case, the Constitutional Court highlighted that the review of the contested municipal statute must be carried out not only against the Constitution but also the Framework Convention, which enjoys supremacy over law.[21] This approach provides that at least as far as Article 22 of the Constitution is concerned, the Constitutional Court can review the compliance of laws and other legal acts with those domesticated international instruments.

Regarding the review of compatibility of the ratified international agreements with the Constitution, no explicit provision could be found in the Constitution. However, since international agreements are ratified by the Assembly of Kosovo in the form of an *enactment of a law*,[22] or are ratified by the President of the Republic in the form of a presidential *decree*, in both cases the deputies of the Assembly are

[21] CC, 18.03.2010, Case No. KO 01/09, *Qemailj Kurtisi v. Municipal Assembly of Prizren*. Judgment of the Constitutional Court of the Republic of Kosovo, para 42. The decision is available at the http://www.gjk-ks.org/. Accessed 12 April 2013.

[22] Article 10(2) of the Law on International Agreements (Law No. 2004/14) provides that International Agreements shall be ratified by a law by a two-thirds (2/3) vote of all deputies of the Assembly of the Republic of Kosovo. The Law is available in the Official Gazette at http://gazetazyrtare.rks-gov.net. Accessed 12 April 2013.

entitled to file a referral to the Constitutional Court to review the respective law or presidential decree before it enters into force.[23]

With regard to a review of the consistency of the constitutional amendments with international law, the Constitution in clear terms enables the Constitutional Court to review the 'compatibility of a proposed constitutional amendment with binding international agreements ratified under this Constitution'.[24]

3.2 The Application of UN Law

As far as the law of the UN Charter is concerned, the Constitutional Court in case No. KI 25/10 addressed not just a legal, but also a political question, that of Kosovo's statehood and the ability of State institutions to exercise their constitutional public authority after the adoption of the Kosovo Declaration of Independence of 17 February 2008 (Declaration of Independence). The case was brought before the Constitutional Court after EULEX international judges of the Special Chamber of the Supreme Court of Kosovo (Special Chamber) refused to accept the validity of laws adopted by the Assembly of Kosovo insofar as they repealed the UNMIK Regulations.

The approach of the EULEX international judges of the Special Chamber raised two relevant issues. Firstly, whether in the case of inconsistency, the UNMIK Regulations adopted by the UNMIK Special Representative of the Secretary-General ('SRSG') pursuant to the SC Resolution 1244 prevailed over the Kosovo Constitution and the laws adopted by the Assembly of Kosovo after the Declaration of Independence. Secondly, whether the Assembly of Kosovo, by adopting national legislation after the Declaration of Independence, could *repeal* the UNMIK regulations adopted on the authority deriving from the UN Charter and thus possessing an international law character.

3.2.1 Relevant Facts and Previous Stages Before EULEX International Judges

Prior to the adoption of the Declaration of Independence, laws adopted by the Assembly of Kosovo could be promulgated only upon the final approval of the SRSG.[25] UNMIK Regulations and Administrative Instructions were adopted and

[23] Regarding the procedure for the possibility to file referrals by the deputies of the Assembly of Kosovo, see Article 113 of the Constitution.

[24] Articles 113(3) and 113(4) of the Constitution.

[25] Resolution 1244, UN Doc S/RES/1244; 54 UN SCOR, UN Security Council, 10 June 1999; UNMIK Regulation No. 1999/24 on the Law Applicable in Kosovo (12 December 1999) as amended by the UNMIK Regulation No. 2000/59 (27 October 2000) ('UNMIK Regulation 1999/24 as amended') and the UNMIK Regulation No. 2001/9 on a Constitutional Framework

promulgated exclusively by the SRSG. Since the adoption of the Declaration of Independence, the Assembly of Kosovo promulgated the Constitution and laws without requesting the consent of the SRSG as to their compatibility with UN SC Resolution 1244 or UNMIK Regulations.

Three months after Kosovo declared its independence, the Assembly of Kosovo passed the Law on the Privatisation Agency of Kosovo (Law on PAK).[26] The Law on PAK established the Privatisation Agency of Kosovo (PAK) as an 'independent public body [and as] the successor of the Kosovo Trust Agency' (KTA) previously regulated under UNMIK Regulation No. 2002/12 as amended.[27] Article 31(1) and Article 31(2) of the Law on PAK provides that this Law 'shall supersede any provisions in the Applicable Law which are inconsistent herewith [and that the] UNMIK Regulation 2002/12 as amended will cease to have legal effect after the Law on PAK enters into force'.

In the case concerning PAK's activities in the privatisation process in Kosovo, the Special Chamber of the Supreme Court of Kosovo (Special Chamber), composed of EULEX international judges, in the first and second instance refused to recognise the Law on PAK as applicable law. As a consequence, it did not recognise the PAK as a successor of the KTA, but instead considered UNMIK Regulation 2002/12 as amended to be still in force, and the Law on PAK as a non-law.[28]

On 23 April 2010, PAK filed a referral to the Constitutional Court of the Republic of Kosovo, asking the Court to review the constitutionality of Decision No. ASC-09-089 of the Special Chamber.

3.2.2 The Constitutional Court's Assessment

From a domestic constitutional perspective and in view of the Constitutional Court's jurisdiction, the Court had to elucidate whether the Assembly of Kosovo duly adopted the Law on PAK and whether, according to the Constitution, the Assembly had a mandate to repeal UNMIK Regulation No. 2002/12 as amended on the establishment of the KTA. On this matter, the Court referred to pertinent constitutional provisions and reasoned:

> [i]n accordance with Article 145 [of the Constitution,] ... [UNMIK] Regulations and Administrative Instructions as well as other legislation will only continue to apply to

for Provisional Self-Government in Kosovo (15 May 2001) ('UNMIK Constitutional Framework').

[26] Law No. 03/L-067 on the Privatisation Agency of Kosovo (21 May 2008), entered into force 15 June 2008.

[27] Article 5 of Law No. 03/L-067 on the Privatisation Agency of Kosovo (21 May 2008), entered into force 15 June 2008.

[28] SC, 16.10.2009, Decision No. SCEL-09-0003, Special Chamber of the Supreme Court of Kosovo, cited in Decision No. ASC-09-089 of the Appellate Panel of the Special Chamber of Supreme Court of Kosovo, 4 February 2010 Decision No. ASC-09-089 of the Appellate Panel of the Special Chamber of Supreme Court of Kosovo, 4 February 2010, p. 1.

> the extent they are in conformity with the Constitution until repealed, superseded or amended in accordance with the Constitution.
> Therefore, relevant UNMIK Regulations and Administrative Instructions only continue to be applicable as long as they are in conformity with Law [on PAK].
> In these circumstances, ... the Special Chamber of the Supreme Court, in its Decision ASC-09-089, clearly did not 'ensure the uniform application of the law', as envisaged by the [Ahtisaari Status] Proposal, nor did it act in conformity with its duties under .... Article 102 [3] of the Constitution [which reads that courts shall adjudicate based on the Constitution and the law], since it did not apply Law [on PAK] ... as a Law, duly adopted by the Assembly of Kosovo, but as valid and binding internal rules of organization for PAK.[29]

In the Court's view, this *problematique* emanated because the 'Special Chamber does not apply the laws lawfully adopted by the Assembly [and] simply continues to ignore the existence of Kosovo as an independent State and its legislation emanating from its Assembly'.[30]

The Court reminded EULEX international judges of their paradoxical approach with regard to the applicable law in Kosovo and viewed that:

> [it is] inconceivable that EULEX international judges – integrated in the Special Chamber of the Supreme Court of Kosovo in accordance with Law on [the Jurisdiction, Case Selection and Case allocation of EULEX international judges and Prosecutors in Kosovo], duly adopted by the Assembly of [the Republic of] Kosovo – refuse to apply laws duly adopted by the Assembly of the Republic of Kosovo.[31]

The Court also referred to the ICJ Advisory Opinion in the *Kosovo* case and held

> the establishment of the Republic of Kosovo as an independent and sovereign state, based on the declaration of independence and whose statehood was recognized, so far, by ... countries, is, therefore, not contrary to Security Council Resolution 1244(1999) as well as international law.[32]

One might view that the discussion on the compatibility of the Declaration of Independence with SC Resolution 1244 is an attempt to establish judicial comity between the Constitutional Court and EULEX international judges. In its deductive reasoning, the Constitutional Court seems to have instructed EULEX international judges that because the Declaration of Independence is not contrary to SC Resolution 1244, the laws adopted by the Assembly of Kosovo are *also* compatible with SC Resolution 1244, even when they *repeal* UNMIK Regulations.

---

[29] Article 102(3) stipulates: Courts shall adjudicate based on the Constitution and the law.

[30] Constitutional Review of the Decision of the Special Chamber of the Supreme Court of Kosovo ASC-09-089, Case No. KI 25/10, Judgment of the Kosovo Constitutional Court, ILDC 1606 (KO 2011), 31 March 2011, para 53.

[31] Constitutional Review of the Decision of the Special Chamber of the Supreme Court of Kosovo ASC-09-089, Case No. KI 25/10, Judgment of the Kosovo Constitutional Court, ILDC 1606 (KO 2011), 31 March 2011, para 61.

[32] Accordance with international law of the unilateral declaration of independence in respect of Kosovo, Advisory Opinion, ICJ Reports 2010, p. 403, 10 July 2010, para 54.

Based on the foregoing constitutional considerations, the Court invalidated decision No. ASC-09-089 of the EULEX international judges of the Special Chamber and remanded it to comply with the decision of the Constitution Court.

Following that decision of the Constitutional Court a mixed panel of EULEX international judges of the Special Chamber in the decision SCA-09-0042 of 29 November 2012 recognised that the reasoning of the Constitutional Court was binding only with respect to interpretation of the Kosovo Constitution but not of the UN law.[33] The Special Chamber further held

> [Declaration of Independence of Kosovo] did not have any influence on the validity and applicability of UN law [including UNMIK regulations] as the latter did not depend on the acceptance of the addressee. [34]

Accordingly, from the perspective of UN law, UNMIK regulations could not be affected or repealed by Kosovo law. However, in the view of the Special Chamber UNMIK Regulation No 2002/12 as amended was not anymore applicable because the interim administration had in fact ended.[35] The Special Chamber concluded

> [i]n view of the inability of the Security Council to resolve the status of Kosovo and the omission of UNMIK to administer Kosovo (which would require more than expressing concern and protesting) the acts of Kosovo legislature were valid even if they conflicted with UN regulations issued by UNMIK.[36]

The outcome reached by the mixed panel of EULEX international judges and by the Constitutional Court was the same. Both judicial bodies opined that the law applicable to privatisation matters was the Law on PAK and not UNMIK Regulation 2002/12. However, the paths of legal arguments employed in arriving at that conclusion, particularly as concerns UN law, differed greatly.

This tensed judicial dialogue showed not only a different understanding by the Constitutional Court and by EULEX international judges of the place of UN Charter in the Kosovo legal order, it also revealed political and legal challenges of the Constitutional Court in guarding the *primum verum*—the first truth of the newly established State Parliament's mandate to legislate. In doing so the Constitutional Court also guided EULEX international judges and other international authorities in Kosovo—who remained *neutral* on Kosovo's political status—in the enforcement of legal framework adopted by the Assembly of Kosovo subsequent to the Declaration of Independence.

---

[33] Decision of the Special Chamber of the Supreme Court of Kosovo on Privatization Agency of Kosovo Related Matters SCA-09-0042, SOE XX, XX v. A.A., XX, 29 November 2012, at 4.

[34] Ibid.

[35] Ibid.

[36] Ibid, p. 5.

3.3 The Application of the ECHR and the ECtHR's Case-Law

The Constitutional Court's 2012 annual report indicates that more than 90 % of the constitutional referrals originated from individuals on matters involving human rights.[37] In scrutinising the Constitutional Court's case-law, it is evident that ECtHR jurisprudence has been indispensable in the Court's adjudication.

In the case concerning the deprivation of life of Ms. D.K., the parents of the deceased submitted a referral to the Constitutional Court against the Municipal Court of Prishtina for the failure of the latter to issue an emergency protection order to prevent continuous threats from the perpetrator.[38] The applicants argued that the Municipal Court of Prishtina, by its inaction to deal with the request for the emergency protection order, had violated, *inter alia*, the right to life of D.K., guaranteed under Article 25 of the Kosovo Constitution and Article 2 of the ECHR. It is noteworthy that the applicants requested that the Constitutional Court address this issue with the aim of preventing similar tragic cases in the future, as well as to increase public awareness of the functionality of the regular courts.

The Constitutional Court recalled that, 'in accordance with Article 53 of the Constitution, it is its constitutional obligation to conduct an interpretation of human rights and fundamental freedoms in accordance with the case-law of ECtHR'.[39] By referring to the ECtHR cases *L.C.B. v. the United Kingdom* and *Osman v. the United Kingdom,* the Constitutional Court held:

> it is the duty of the state authorities not only to refrain from the intentional and unlawful taking of life, but also to take appropriate steps to safeguard the lives of those within its jurisdiction... This involves in appropriate circumstances positive obligations on the authorities to take preventive operational measures to protect an individual whose life is at risk from the criminal acts of another individual.[40]

Relying on ECtHR case-law, the Constitutional Court held that the inaction of the Municipal Court of Prishtina represented a violation of Article 25 of the Constitution and Article 2 of the ECHR.[41]

The 'constitutional obligation' to conduct an interpretation in accordance with the case-law of the ECtHR is reflected in other cases pertaining to human rights and fundamental freedoms. In a case concerning labour rights,[42] the applicant requested an assessment of the constitutionality of the judgment of the Supreme Court,

---

[37] 2012 Annual Report of the Kosovo Constitutional Court, pp. 29–30, available at http://gjk-ks.org/repository/docs/RAPORTI%20VJETOR%202012.pdf. Accessed 12 May 2013.

[38] CC, 26.02.2013, Case KI 41/12, *Gëzim dhe Makfire Kastrati v. Municipal Court in Prishtina and Kosovo Judicial Council*, Judgment of the Constitutional Court of the Republic of Kosovo.

[39] Ibid, para 58.

[40] Ibid, para 59.

[41] Ibid, para 63.

[42] SC, 5.12.2011, Case KI 108-2010, *Fadil Selmanaj v. Judgment A.* No. 170/2009 of the Supreme Court, Judgment of the Constitutional Court of the Republic of Kosovo.

because of an alleged 'lack of official communication between the Supreme Court and the respondent'.[43] The applicant argued that he was an interested party in the case lodged by his employer at the Kosovo Supreme Court and therefore, by not being informed of the ongoing case against him, this 'provided room for suspicions that we are dealing here with manipulations and that as a consequences of this, he as an interested party, has been materially and morally damaged'.[44]

The applicant considered that his right to a fair trial had been infringed 'because neither the employer nor the Supreme Court notified him of the appeal or its disposition'.[45]

Declaring invalid the decision of the Supreme Court, the Constitutional Court held that a failure of the Kosovo Supreme Court to duly inform the applicant of the judicial process and to enable the submission of evidence and facts in the judicial proceedings constituted a breach of Article 31 of the Constitution and Article 6 (1) of the ECHR.[46] The Constitutional Court went on to say that although the right to take part in a hearing was not expressly mentioned in Article 6(1) of the ECHR, the case-law of the ECtHR revealed that:

> the object and purpose of the Article taken as a whole show that a person charged with a criminal offence is entitled to take part in the hearing.... This right is implicit in the very notion of an adversarial procedure ... [and] applies to both civil and criminal proceedings.[47]

In a case concerning the participation of the public in an environmental decision-making process, the reference to ECtHR jurisprudence was pivotal in interpreting the scope of constitutional rights. In the case *Hoxha et al v. Municipal Assembly of Prizren,* the applicant claimed that the constitutional right to public participation was infringed when the Municipal Assembly of Prizren amended the Detailed Urban Plan (DUP), allowing the construction of high tower blocks.[48] The applicant argued that the DUP decision taken in the absence of public review and public participation violated Article 52(2) of the Constitution, which provides:

> everyone should be provided an opportunity to be heard by public participation and have their opinions considered on issues that impact the environment in which they live.

The Constitutional Court viewed that the adoption of the DUP decision by the Municipality of Prizren without any public consultation or any other type of participation had violated the applicant's rights guaranteed under Article 52(2) of

---

[43] Ibid, para 3.

[44] Ibid, para 3.

[45] Bulletin of Case-law No. 2 (2011) Publication of the Constitutional Court of Kosovo, p. 579.

[46] CC, 5.12.2011, Case KI 108-2010, Fadil Selmanaj v. Judgment A. no. 170/2009 of the Supreme Court, Judgment of the Constitutional Court of the Republic of Kosovo, para. 75.

[47] Ibid, paras 58–59.

[48] CC, 22.12.2010, Case No. KI 56/09, *Fadil Hoxha and 59 Others v. Municipal Assembly of Prizren*, Judgment of the Constitutional Court of the Republic of Kosovo, paras 27–30.

the Constitution.[49] Furthermore, the Constitutional Court viewed that the ECtHR 'has given clear guidance that both Article 2 (the right to life) and Article 8 (the right to respect for the home, private and family life) include environmental protection'.[50] On this argument, the Constitutional Court referred to the ECtHR cases *Hatton and Others v. the United Kingdom*, *Guerra and Others v. Italy* and *McGinley and Egan v. the United Kingdom* and indicated:

> [w]here a State must determine complex issues of environmental and economic policy, the decision-making process must firstly involve appropriate investigations and studies in order to allow them to predict and evaluate in advance the effects of those activities which might damage the environment and infringe individuals' rights and to enable them to strike a fair balance between the various conflicting interests... The importance of public access to the conclusions of such studies and to information which would enable members of the public to assess the danger to which they are exposed is beyond question.[51]

The case reveals that the Constitutional Court not only advanced the standards of the participation processes in the environment-related decision-making process in line with the interpretation of the right to a healthy environment,[52] but also made an invaluable impact on shaping pertinent State policies.

The Constitutional Court has also relied on the principles of proportionality and continued violation, as developed by the Strasbourg Court.

In *Bislimi v. Ministry of Internal Affairs*, also known as the *Passport* case, the Constitutional Court followed the proportionality principle in order to assess whether measures undertaken by the Ministry of Interior, amounting to a restriction on the freedom of movement as provided by Article 35 of the Constitution in conjunction with Article 2(2) of Protocol No. 4 to the Convention, were proportionate. The Constitutional Court declared that depriving a person of a passport where he or she did not present a 'certificate that they are not under criminal investigation' violated the freedom of movement and concluded that 'the authorities have failed in their obligation under Article 2 of Protocol No. 4 to the [ECHR] to ensure that any interference with an individual's right to leave his or her country is, from the outset and throughout its duration, justified and proportionate in the light of the circumstances'.[53] In the case of *Ibrahimi and others v. Kosovo Supreme Court*, the applicants argued that a failure of their former employer, the Kosovo

[49] Ibid, paras 66 and 71.

[50] Ibid, para 65.

[51] Ibid.

[52] Ibid, paras 62–64. The Constitutional Court further took note of the right to a healthy environment by inserting pertinent provisions of the Aarhus Convention, the Rio Declaration on Environment and Development and Recommendation 1614 (2003) of the Parliamentary Assembly of the Council of Europe.

[53] CC, 30.10.2010, Case No. KI 06/10 *Valon Bislimi v. Ministry of Internal Affairs, Kosovo Judicial Council and Ministry of Justice*. Judgment of the Constitutional Court of the Republic of Kosovo, para 78.

Energy Corporation (KEK), to pay the agreed pension packages constituted a violation of the constitutional right to property.[54] The subject matter was initially dealt with by the Municipal Court, which approved the applicants' claims and ordered monetary compensation. Deciding on the appeal, the District Court in Prishtina rejected the appeals of KEK and found their submissions ungrounded. However, the Supreme Court accepted the revisions of KEK, and quashed the judgment of the District Court of Prishtina and rejected the applicants' claims as unfounded. The parties filed a complaint with the Constitutional Court, seeking relief for the alleged constitutional violation of the right to property and a fair trial. In assessing the admissibility requirements, the Constitutional Court was confronted with the question as to whether the complaint was admissible *ratione temporis* as provided by the Law on the Constitutional Court:

> [t]he referral should be submitted within a period of four (4) months. The deadline shall be counted from the day upon which the claimant has been served with a court decision. In all other cases, the deadline shall be counted from the day when the decision or act is publicly announced.

The Constitutional Court noted that the 4-month period for the submission of the referral was not observed by the applicants, but argued that

> the time limit as prescribed by the European Convention of Human Rights does not start to run if the Convention complaint stems from a continuing situation ... According to the case-law, where the alleged violation is a continuing situation, the time limit starts to run only from the end of continuing situation.[55]

In declaring the complaint as admissible and constitutionally grounded, the Court recalled the doctrine of continuous violation, and argued that

> [i]n the present case the Applicants still suffer from the unilateral annulment of their Agreements signed by KEK. They argue that it is well established that the Pension and Invalidity Insurance Fund has not been established to date. Therefore, there is a continuing situation. As the circumstance of which the Applicants complain continued, the four months period as prescribed in Article 49 of the Law is inapplicable to these cases.[56]

In another case concerning continued violation, the Constitutional Court utilised the said principle but without referring to the ECtHR case-law.[57] In the *President Sejdiu* case,[58] 32 deputies of the Kosovo Assembly filed a referral to the Constitutional Court arguing that Mr. Sejdiu had violated Article 88 of the Constitution by holding simultaneously the position of President of the Republic of Kosovo and that

[54] CC, 23.06.2010, Case No. KI 40/09 *Imer Ibrahimi and 48 Other Former Employees of the Kosovo Energy Corporation v. 49 Individual Judgments of the Supreme Court of the Republic of Kosovo*, Judgment of the Constitutional Court of the Republic of Kosovo, paras 5–6.

[55] Ibid.

[56] Ibid, para 41.

[57] For a critical approach to the application of the principle of continued violation in the *President Sejdiu* case, see Istrefi (2013), pp. 275–277.

[58] CC, 28.09.2010, Case No. KI 47/10, *Naim Rrustemi and 31 other Deputies of the Assembly of the Republic of Kosovo v. His Excellency, Fatmir Sejdiu, President of the Republic of Kosovo*, Judgment of the Constitutional Court of the Republic of Kosovo.

of President of his political party, the Kosovo Democratic League (LDK).[59] It was considered that Mr. Sejdiu held the position of President of the LDK for more than 3 years from the date of the filing of the referral with the Constitutional Court. Therefore, the Constitutional Court had, *inter alia*, to assess whether the referral was lodged within the time limit as required by Article 45 of the Law on the Constitutional Court of the Republic of Kosovo, which provides that:

> the referral should be filed within a period of thirty (30) days starting from the day the alleged violation of the Constitution by the President has been made public.

In addressing the time limit for filing a claim before the Constitutional Court, the majority of the judges asserted:

> 32. [i]n the case of President Sejdiu it is necessary to look at the factual situation to see whether the holding of the office of President/Chairman of the LDK, 'but freezing that position', was a single event that occurred at one time or whether it amounts to a continuing day by day situation .... The President admits that he has continued to be the Chairman of LDK and President of Kosovo at all times since his election to the office of President in 2006.
> 33. If this is the case, the consequences of the freezing of the position continue and therefore there is a day by day ongoing situation. To conclude otherwise could result in a situation whereby the President of Kosovo could be barred from holding the Office of the President because of a constitutional violation, but be allowed to continue in office simply because a referral was not made to the Constitutional Court in a timely manner. Nowhere in the Constitution is there any authority for such an irrational result. Nor does Article 45 of the Law on the Constitutional Court envision such an irrational result.[60]

The Constitutional Court found that the violation in question was continuous and the time foreseen in Article 45 of the Law on the Constitutional Court could not apply to a serious violation that continued.[61] While the Constitutional Court applied the principle of a continued violation, it is to be expected that the reference to the ECtHR would have made the Constitutional Court's judgment in the *Sejdiu* case not only logical, but also persuasive in view of the principles of the ECtHR.[62]

In view of the foregoing, the degree of adherence to the ECHR by the Constitutional Court in the protection of constitutional rights and fundamental freedoms has at least two significant impacts. The first is an explicit manifestation of the direct application of the ECHR and the ECtHR jurisprudence by virtue of Articles 22 and 53 of the Constitution. In this vein, the Constitutional Court seized the momentum to influence the courts of general jurisdiction and encouraged them to

[59] Article 88 of the Kosovo Constitution provides: 1. The President shall not exercise any other public function. 2. After election, the President cannot exercise any political party functions.

[60] CC, 28.09.2010, Case No. KI 47/10, *Naim Rrustemi and 31 other Deputies of the Assembly of the Republic of Kosovo v. His Excellency, Fatmir Sejdiu*, President of the Republic of Kosovo, Judgment of the Constitutional Court of the Republic of Kosovo, paras 32–33.

[61] Ibid, para 34.

[62] In support of its view, the Constitutional Court could have made reference to *Papamichalopoulos and Others v. Greece*, ECHR, Judgment of the Court (Chamber) of 24 June 1993, at paras 40 and 46; *Agrotexim and Others v. Greece*, ECHR, Judgment of the Court (Chamber) of 26 September 1995, at paras 56–58; *Loizidou v. Turkey*, ECHR, Judgment of the Court (Chamber) of 18 December 1996, at paras 26–64.

follow the practice of the direct application of the ECHR and its Court's case-law. The second important dimension relies on the fact that the Constitutional Court's reception of the ECHR has gradually increased the awareness of individuals and others about the ECHR and its requirements. In light of Kosovo's endeavours to join the Council of Europe, the educational role of the Constitutional Court is of invaluable pertinence in preparing litigants to utilise the ECHR system.

4 Judicial Application of International Law by Mixed Panels of EULEX International Judges

4.1 The Application of International Criminal Law

In international criminal adjudication, the challenges often rest in the applicable law. In responding to questions of retroactivity, elements of crimes, standards that apply to internal and international armed conflicts, judges of international criminal tribunals in their judicial creativity utilise customary international law 'with an immense flexible technique ... to mould and develop the law'.[63] However, international judges in Kosovo, being fully integrated in the domestic judicial system, do not have that privilege of making use of their own statutory sources of law in the process of adjudication. Instead, they may generally resort to those sources of international law which have been made applicable in the domestic legal order. With regard to war crimes in the 1998–1999 Kosovo conflict, the point of consideration is the international law part of the national legal order at that time.[64] With that task not being easy, controversies may be revealed when unwrapping the war crimes jurisprudence of EULEX international judges, and further in comparison with the jurisprudence of their predecessors, UNMIK international judges.

Before further discussion on jurisprudence, it is first appropriate to outline the legal provisions governing the law applicable in Kosovo. In particular, the UNMIK Regulation provides that the law applicable in Kosovo shall include the UNMIK Regulations and

> ... [t]he law in force in Kosovo on 22 March 1989...

---

[63] Schabas (2009), p. 78. See also Case No. IT-01-47-PT, *Prosecutor v. Hadžihasanović, Alagić and Kubura*, Trial Chamber, Decision on Joint Challenge to Jurisdiction, 12 November 2002; Case No. IT-01-47-AR72, *Prosecutor v. Hadžihasanović, Alagić and Kubura*, Appeals Chamber, Decision on Interlocutory Appeal Challenging Jurisdiction in Relation to Command Responsibility, 16 July 2003, paras 22, 26–29 and 31; Mettraux (2009), pp. 96–97.

[64] Both the EU and Kosovo law on the mandate of EULEX international judges provide for obligations to apply Kosovo law. See Council Joint Action 2008/124/CFSP of 4 February 2008 on the European Union Rule of Law Mission in Kosovo, EULEX Kosovo, OJ 2008 L 42, Article 3 (d); the Law on the Jurisdiction, Case Selection and Case Allocation of EULEX International Judges and Prosecutors in Kosovo, Article 3; the Law on the Special Prosecution Office of the Republic of Kosovo, Article 16.

> 1.2 If a court of competent jurisdiction or a body or person required to implement a provision of the law, determines that a subject matter or situation is not covered by the laws set out in section 1.1 of the present regulation but is covered by another law in force in Kosovo after 22 March 1989 which is not discriminatory and which complies with section 1.3 of the present regulation, the court, body or person shall, as an exception, apply that law.[65]

The aforementioned provision has proved to be of fundamental importance in the discussion on the relevant legal framework, particularly in the process of identifying the applicable constitution between the Constitution of the Federal Republic of Yugoslavia of 27 April 1992 (1992 FRY Constitution) and the Constitution of the Socialist Federal Republic of Yugoslavia of 21 February 1974 (1974 SFRY Constitution). The consequence of that decision has a significant impact upon the adjudication of war crimes in that the former permits the application of customary international law and the latter does not.

On this question, an important response came in 2003 from the District Court of Prishtina in the panel composed of UNMIK international judges. In the war crimes case known as *Gashi and others*, the trial panel applied the 1992 FRY Constitution in order to employ customary international law with respect to charges of war crimes in the 1998–1999 Kosovo conflict.[66] In that manner, the trial panel resorted to norms of customary international law with regard, *inter alia*, to unlawful internment and command responsibility.[67] This decision, however, was reversed upon appeal. In 2005, the Supreme Court of Kosovo, in a panel composed of UNMIK international judges, held that according to the UNMIK Regulation 1999/24 it was not the 1992 FRY Constitution but the 1974 Constitution that applied in Kosovo.[68] The appeals panel found that Articles 181 and 210 of the 1974 SFRY Constitution did not make customary international law applicable and thus the trial panel had erred in law in its findings on unlawful internment and command responsibility in the Kosovo internal armed conflict.[69] The appeals panel ruled that through the 1974 Constitution only the four ratified Geneva Conventions and the Additional Protocols I and II were applicable at the material time.[70] As a result, the appeals panel ordered the re-trial of *Gashi and others*.

[65] UNMIK Regulation No. 1999/24 as amended by the UNMIK Regulation No. 2000/59 on the Law Applicable in Kosovo.

[66] DC, 16.07.2003, Case No. 425/2001 *Latif Gashi and others*, Decision of the District Court of Prishtina, pp. 22–26.

[67] Ibid, pp. 20–26; See also McCormack and McDonald (2003), pp. 594–601. For considerations related to the District Court of Prishtina's progressive approach to customary international law, see Baker (2010), pp. 201–203.

[68] SC, 21.07.2005, AP-KZ No. 139/2004 *Latif Gashi and others*, Decision of the Supreme Court, panel of UNMIK judges, p. 6.

[69] Ibid, pp. 6, 8.

[70] Ibid, p. 6.

EULEX international judges continued from where UNMIK international judges had left off, including the *Gashi and others* case.[71] Yet, a different approach from that of their predecessors surfaced. While in 2005 the appeals panel of UNMIK international judges had firmly rejected the application of customary international law, EULEX international judges considered otherwise. Namely, the Supreme Court of Kosovo, in a mixed panel of EULEX international judges, in the further proceedings in *Gashi and others* appeared to read the aforementioned pronouncement of the appeals panel of UNMIK international judges rendered in 2005 in a somewhat varied manner:

> . . . the question of command responsibility in internal armed conflicts and the applicability of customary international law in Kosovo has been elaborated in detail in the judgment of the District Court of Prishtine/Pristina dated 16 July 2003 (P 425/2001) and that this part of the decision was confirmed by the Supreme Court in its decision Ap.-KZ. 139/2004, which the first instance re-trial court has referred to . . .[72]

It may be observed that the foregoing observation runs counter to the language of the 2005 decision of the appeals panel of UNMIK international judges in that it ruled out the application of customary international law. While UNMIK international judges in *Gashi and others* endeavoured to untangle the complexities of the law applicable in the course of the 1998–1999 Kosovo conflict from the perspective of the domestic legal order, panels of EULEX international judges on the other hand make direct recourse to customary international law, also as spelled out in the ICTY jurisprudence, without clarifying the legal basis for such application and deviation from the 2005 decision in *Gashi and others*. By way of example, in the *Kleçka* case, the mixed panel of EULEX international judges of the District Court of Prishtina considered that customary international law made the doctrine of command responsibility applicable also to a non-international armed conflict.[73] EULEX international judges constantly apply the criteria and definitions provided in the ICTY case-law when defining, *inter alia*, what constitutes an internal armed conflict,[74] the

[71] See chronologically the decisions of the mixed panel of EULEX international judges in *Gashi and others*:

- DC, 02.10.2009, Case P No 526/05, Decision of the District Court of Prishtina;
- SC, 26.01.2011, Case Ap-KZ No 89/2010 Decision of the Supreme Court of Kosovo.

  On 7 June 2013, a mixed panel of EULEX international judges of the Supreme Court of Kosovo took a new decision in *Gashi and others*. While the judgment is not yet available, an official press release and a video confirm that the panel of judges upheld the 2011 judgment of the Supreme Court of Kosovo. Available at http://www.eulex-kosovo.eu/en/pressreleases/0452.php. Accessed 4 September 2013.

[72] SC, 26.01.2011, Case Ap-KZ No 89/2010 Decision of the Supreme Court of Kosovo, para 111.

[73] DC, 02.05.2012, Case No 425/11, Decision of the District Court of Prishtina, paras 146–147.

[74] DC, 23.11.2011, Case P No. 371/10, Decision of the District Court of Prishtina, para 96.

existence and the timing of an internal armed conflict in Kosovo,[75] the definition of inhumane treatment,[76] what the essential criteria for crimes of torture are, etc.[77]

The remark in the direction of EULEX international judges on the lack of elaboration in their recourse to customary international law is not to say that it should not be incorporated. Instead, it would be paradoxical if EULEX international judges or Kosovo judges were not in a position to adjudicate a full range of war crimes allegedly committed in the 1998–1999 Kosovo conflict, while the ICTY judges are able to do so by use of customary international law. Further, having in mind the ICTY's significant contribution in spelling out the elements of crimes, the impossibility for the EULEX international judges to use that case-law would negatively reflect upon their adjudication capacity.

Yet the operation as part of domestic judiciary makes it appropriate to justify the application of customary international law in the national legal system. If EULEX international judges wished to depart from the 2005 UNMIK decision in *Gashi and others* and other similar jurisprudence with regard to the application of customary international law, an explanation to this effect should have been given.

In this regard, a different reading of the UNMIK Regulation 1999/24 as amended may be proposed. While the application of certain post-1989 laws has been barred due to their discriminatory nature, at the same time the UNMIK Regulation 1999/24 Section 1.2 permits the exceptional application of post-1989 law if a subject matter or situation is not covered by the laws that were in force before 1989.[78] In that manner, one indeed may observe that the 1992 FRY Constitution contained discriminatory provisions with regard to Kosovo's autonomy and its population. At the same time, it can also be argued that Article 16(3) of the 1992 FRY Constitution incorporating in the domestic legal order the 'generally accepted rules of international law' was not designed to target the Kosovo population. One might rightly argue that it was just for the opposite effect regarding the application of generally accepted rules of international law in Kosovo. On those grounds, its application would sit well with the UNMIK Regulation 1999/24 as amended. The authors are aware that this approach advocates selecting individual provisions of a legal act and thus may be perceived as further fragmenting the Kosovo legislative framework and adding to its uncertainty. Such difficulties on the other hand fall short of a legitimate reason to leave out the whole source of international law, preventing the prosecution and adjudication of a whole set of war crimes entrusted to international prosecutors and judges in Kosovo.

[75] DC, 23.11.2011, Case P No. 371/10, Decision of the District Court of Prishtina, para 99; DC, 9.11.2010, Case P No. 285/10, District Court of Peje, p. 13.

[76] DC, 29.07.2011, Case P No. 45/10, Decision of the District Court of Mitrovica, para 218.

[77] DC, 02.05.2012, Case No 425/11, Decision of the District Court of Prishtina, para 33.

[78] UNMIK Regulation No. 1999/24 as amended by UNMIK Regulation No. 2000/59 on the Law Applicable in Kosovo.

Further, to wipe out any possible concerns in the context of Article 7 ECHR, previously[79] and now[80] made directly applicable in the Kosovo legal order, it is relevant to observe the ECtHR's findings in *Šimšić v. Bosnia*. In this case, the applicant argued before the Strasbourg Court that he had been convicted of crimes which had not constituted criminal offences at the material time, and thus his punishment in the courts of Bosnia and Herzegovina had violated Article 7 ECHR, namely the principle of *nullum crimen, nulla poena sine lege*. The ECtHR rejected this argument and held:

> [w]hile the impugned acts had not constituted a crime against humanity under domestic law until the entry into force of the 2003 Criminal Code, it is evident from the documents cited in paragraph 8–13 above that the impugned acts constituted, at the time when they were committed, a crime against humanity under international law.[81]

It is relevant to observe that the ECtHR did not rule out the application of the 2003 Criminal Code with respect to the crimes allegedly committed during the 1990s. The Strasbourg Court rather deemed it essential that the acts in question had constituted crimes under international law at the material time. In this context, it may be noted that a mixed trial panel of EULEX international judges in the *Kleçka* case in utilising international criminal law deemed it appropriate to incorporate the ECtHR's finding in *Kononov v Latvia*. In particular:

> [i]n assessing the superior responsibility, the Trial Panel has considered the elements of the mode of responsibility as established in customary international law and discussed above. In this regard, the Trial Panel observes that it has been held by the European Court of Human Rights (ECtHR) in *Kononov v. Latvia*, that there is no violation of *nullum crimen, nulla poena sine lege* (Article 7(1) ECHR), when at the time of the charged acts, they constituted offences defined with sufficient accessibility and foreseeability by the laws and customs of war.[82]

This may be taken to signal that judges, mindful of their duty to ensure the ECHR standards in the course of adjudication, found it necessary to erase concerns for the application of customary international law even though they remained silent on how that source of law constituted part of the applicable law. At the same time, no similar reference could be found in other decisions rendered by mixed panels of EULEX international judges. Accordingly, their jurisprudence does not provide a sufficient basis to draw conclusions as to the grounds for departure from the previous jurisprudence that in clear language excluded customary international law from the scope of the applicable law.

---

[79] Ibid, Section 1.3.

[80] Articles 22 and 52 of the Kosovo Constitution.

[81] *Boban Šimšić v. Bosnia and Herzegovina*, ECHR, Judgment of the Court (Chamber) of 10 April 2012, at para 23.

[82] DC, 02.05.2012, Case No. 425/11, Decision of the District Court of Prishtina, para 162.

4.2 *The Application of International Agreements Concerning State Succession*

In a case related to terrorism, a mixed panel of EULEX international judges responded to a burning issue concerning Kosovo's succession to an international agreement that was signed by Serbia before Kosovo declared its independence.[83]

The case reached Kosovo courts, after the United States Secretary of State submitted a request to the Kosovo Ministry of Foreign Affairs for the arrest and extradition of B.A., a resident and citizen of Kosovo, to the United States. The request for extradition was based on the allegations of the US State Department that B.A., while in Kosovo, had committed the criminal offences foreseen by the US law of providing material support to terrorists and conspiracy to kill, kidnap, maim or injure persons or damage property in a foreign country.[84]

The US claimed that the legal basis for the extradition was made pursuant to the Extradition Treaty signed on 25 October 1901 between the US and the Kingdom of Serbia (hereinafter '1901 Extradition Treaty'), which continues to apply in Kosovo by means of state succession.

By exchange of diplomatic notes between the US and Kosovo, at the executive level, Kosovo implicitly recognised the validity and application of the 1901 Extradition Treaty by agreeing to undertake practical arrangements for the transfer of B.A. to the US.[85]

When Kosovo courts received the request for the extradition of B.A., a mixed panel of EULEX international judges in the first and second instance examined the following considerations.

Firstly, what is the Kosovo constitutional and legal framework with regard to extradition of its own citizens? *Secondly*, does the 1901 Extradition Treaty constitute an international agreement recognised by international law? *Thirdly*, is the treaty in question signed by Serbia valid and applicable in Kosovo by means of state succession to international agreements? *Finally*, since B.A. was accused of breaching US law while residing in Kosovo, does the scope of the 1901 Extradition Treaty permit the extradition of B.A. in connection to the alleged criminal acts for which his transfer to the US has been sought?

Concerning the applicable law regarding the extradition of own citizens, EULEX international judges recalled that according to Article 35(4) of the Kosovo Constitution, as well as Article 533 of the KCCP, 'citizens of the Republic of Kosovo shall not be extradited unless it has been foreseen differently by

[83] For another analysis of this case, see Zane Ratniece, PN KR No. 386/2010, ILDC 1964 (XK 2010). International Law in Domestic Courts Reports, Oxford University Press, 18 February 2013.

[84] SC, 7.09.2010, Case No 386/10, Decision of the Supreme Court of Kosovo, p. 1.

[85] Ibid, p. 2.

international law or agreement'.[86] Although the word *treaty* is not mentioned in the Kosovo law, EULEX international judges elucidated that 'the term international agreement must be understood as an agreement, more commonly known in the international plane as a treaty, concluded between States, or States and international organizations, which is and is intended to be legally binding under international law'.[87] Thus, in the view of EULEX international judges, the 1901 Extradition Treaty qualifies as a binding international agreement for the purpose of Article 35 (4) of the Constitution.

Since, in the exchange of diplomatic notes, Kosovo already expressed its willingness to extradite B.A., the panel of EULEX international judges observed that the exchange of diplomatic notes between the US and Kosovo 'does not constitute an international agreement as required by law ... [but it constitutes] an agreement on practical arrangements concerning the sought transfer of [B.A.]'.[88]

As a next step, it remained to be determined whether Kosovo had succeeded in respect of the 1901 Extradition Treaty. To respond to this legal and political question, the panel of EULEX international judges employed Article 24 of the Vienna Convention on Succession to Treaties of 1978 (VSCT) and considered that 'a legally binding succession to the 1901 Extradition Treaty may have taken place ... [*inter alia*] if it is established that the treaty was in force at the date of succession in respect of the territory of Kosovo'.[89] The Court was cognisant that Kosovo was not party to the VSCT, although its provisions were applicable in Kosovo as they constituted norms of customary international law.

The EULEX prosecutor argued that the treaty '[was] applicable to Kosovo as a former part of the SFRY and of the Federal Republic of Yugoslavia (Serbia and Montenegro)'.[90] While EULEX international judges viewed that Kosovo, by means of its expression in the Declaration of Independence, was bound by international obligations emanating from SFRY, they did not consider the allegation of the EULEX prosecutor that the 1901 Extradition Treaty applied in Kosovo as a former constituent part of the SFRY.

As SFRY remained the only *nexus* for succession the panel of EULEX international judges ruled that while the SFRY could be considered a successor to the 1901 Extradition Treaty, it had ceased to exist at the time Kosovo declared independence. Hence, for EULEX international judges, it was doubtful whether the 1901

[86] Ibid, p. 4. The English version of the Kosovo Constitution, in Article 35(4) reads 'Citizens of the Republic of Kosovo shall not be extradited from Kosovo against their will except for cases when otherwise required by international law and agreements'. The authors are referring to the language of Article 35(4) of the Constitution as formulated by the OSPK and confirmed by the Kosovo Supreme Court. The Supreme Court of Kosovo considered that the authentic Albanian version of the Kosovo Constitution provides for a different language and it must apply in the present case.

[87] SC, 7.09.2010, Case No 386/10, Decision of the Supreme Court of Kosovo, p. 5. See also SC, 30.01.2006, Case PN-KR 333/05, pp. 5–8 of the English version.

[88] SC, 7.09.2010, Case No. 386/10, Decision of the Supreme Court of Kosovo, p. 5.

[89] SC, 7.09.2010, Case No. 386/10, Decision of the Supreme Court of Kosovo, p. 6.

[90] Ibid.

Extradition Treaty could be considered applicable in Kosovo by means of state succession.[91] In this examination, EULEX international judges did not consider whether the 1974 SFRY Constitution was still in force by virtue of UNMIK Regulation 1999/24 as amended and give life to international agreements that were valid at a time. Nevertheless, by employing UNMIK Regulation 1999/24, the EULEX international judges would jeopardise the Kosovo Constitution by re-enforcing the UNMIK regulations and disregarding the newly established legal reality. Hence, the panel of EULEX international judges eloquently omitted a firm legal answer on the legal and political aspects of Kosovo's succession to international agreements. Instead, they left a pending answer on the validity of the treaty and emphasised that they would now move to consider the *scope* of the 1901 Extradition Treaty in order to see if pertinent Articles of the treaty itself permitted the extradition of B.A., *even if* the treaty were to be considered valid and currently in force in the relation between the United States and Kosovo.

As to the content of the 1901 Extradition Treaty, the panel of EULEX international judges ruled that since the alleged criminal acts for which B.A. is accused were committed in the territory of Kosovo, the case falls within the jurisdiction of the courts of Kosovo and outside the scope of the 1901 Extradition Treaty. The panel of EULEX international judges of the Supreme Court also confirmed that 'the 1901 Extradition Treaty applies exclusively to situations where the person, whose transfer has been sought, is found in a country other than the one where the suspected criminal offence was committed'.[92] The Supreme Court held that 'the purpose of the treaty is clearly to prevent persons from evading justice by remaining within a territory which does not have any interest or even the legal basis to conduct criminal proceedings against the sought person upon the suspected criminal offence'.[93]

In conclusion, a mixed panel of EULEX international judges rejected the request for the extradition of B.A. to the US, by considering that 'it has not been established that the 1901 Extradition Treaty would permit the extradition of B.A. in connection to the alleged criminal acts for which transfer to the US has been sought, even if the treaty were to be considered valid and currently in force in the relation between the US and Kosovo'.[94]

In the authors' view, the present case is significant for at least three legal and political considerations.

Firstly, from the legal point of view, the Supreme Court confirmed that customary international law is binding in the Kosovo legal order. In addressing the criteria for succession to treaties, the Supreme Court held that parts of the VCST that reflect customary international law are applicable in Kosovo. Yet, while taking this position, the mixed panel of EULEX international judges did not outline which

---

[91] Ibid, p. 7.

[92] Ibid, p. 8.

[93] Ibid.

[94] Ibid, p. 9.

constitutional prerogative provides for the application of customary international law. One might anticipate that the EULEX international judges implied that Article 19(2) of the Constitution permitting the application of legally binding norms of international law includes also customary international law.

Secondly, the Supreme Court, by clarifying on the one hand the equivalence between international agreements and treaties, as well as the status of diplomatic notes, clarified what constitutes a binding international agreement in the Kosovo legal order.

Thirdly, while the Kosovo Government in an exchange of diplomatic notes with the US had agreed to extradite B.A. to the US, the Kosovo Government's understanding of the validity of the Treaty in issue was challenged by EULEX international judges. That is particularly relevant as the issue of State succession in respect of international agreements is not decided in a judicial vacuum but often depend on political considerations of executive branch.[95] Whereas, in the present case the refusal of EULEX international judges to extradite B.A. to the US resulted in Kosovo's refusal to comply with the US Secretary of State's request to cooperate on issues of terrorism. Having in mind the US significant political contribution in Kosovo and the importance of the fight against terrorism, it may not be certain that a panel of local judges would have reached the same conclusion had the case been before them.

4.3 *The Application of the ECHR and the ECtHR's Case-Law*

In the decisions rendered by the mixed panels of the EULEX international judges, the ECHR and Strasbourg case-law are frequently observed when interpreting the provisions of domestic law. The ECHR and its case-law are particularly employed in response to some systematic challenges that the Kosovo judiciary is facing in criminal as well as civil adjudication. This includes human rights standards in cases of internments and other coercive measures to ensure the presence of defendants, the (in)admissibility of evidence of unchallenged out-of-court statements, the publicity of the court, access to judgments and long judicial proceedings.[96]

In the *Kleçka* case, the mixed panel of EULEX international judges of the (then) Prishtina District Court issued a ruling on admissibility of evidence, the circumstances of which, according to the panel, were 'highly unusual, exceptional and possibly even unique'.[97] The defence considered that the statements and diaries of

[95] See e.g. Slovenia in the chapter by Janja Hojnik, Judicial Application of International and EU Law in Slovenia

[96] Some of these concerns are addressed in the EULEX Manual on selected topics of criminal procedure. See EULEX International Judges Peeck et al. (2012). For the reference to the ECHR and ECtHR, see particularly pp. 101–105, 127–129 and 134–149.

[97] DC, 21.03.2012, Case P No. 425/11, case against Arben Krasniqi et al., Ruling on admissibility of Agim Zogaj's statements and diaries (also known as witness X), District Court of Prishtina, para 2.

witness X should not be taken into account, since the defence was unable to challenge the reliability and credibility of the testimony after witness X had committed suicide while the trial was uncompleted. In a situation where defence has *only partially* participated during the testimony of witness X, the panel of judges had to observe the requirements of the Kosovo Code of Criminal Procedure (KCCP) with regard to the admissibility of such evidence and the scope of the right of defence to challenge a witness in light of the ECHR.

The pertinent Article 156(2) of the KCCP states that:

> [a] statement of a witness given to the police or the public prosecutor **may** be admissible evidence in court only when the defendant or defence counsel has been given the opportunity to challenge it by questioning that witness during ***some stage of the criminal proceedings***.

Since the defence was given an opportunity to question witness X during *some stage of the criminal proceedings*,[98] and having in mind that Article 156(2) creates an ***exception*** that evidence taken out of court may be admissible,[99] the court had latitude to use its margin of appreciation in the present case. However, the EULEX panel considered that, pursuant to Article 22 and 53 of the Constitution, the scope of Article 156(2) of the KCCP on the right to challenge a witness should be interpreted consistently with Article 6(3)(d) of the ECHR and its case-law.[100] The Panel further viewed

> [although the ECtHR in *Doorson v. the Netherlands* and in *Al-Khawaja and Tahery v. the United Kingdom*] has reiterated that the admissibility of evidence is primarily governed by the rules of domestic law, and that, as a rule, it is for the national courts to assess the evidence before them, it has emphasized that the right of defence must be respected and the defendant must be given an ***adequate and proper*** opportunity to challenge and question a witness against him.[101]

Thus, according to ECtHR jurisprudence, the opportunity to challenge a witness as foreseen in Article 156(2) of the KCCP must be 'adequate and proper'.[102] While the Supreme Court agreed with the assessment of the District Court to the extent that the *opportunity to challenge* as used in Article 156(2) of the KCCP must be *adequate and proper* as required by the ECtHR, it nevertheless considered that the defence councils had the opportunity to examine witness X and thus no violation of Article 6 of the ECHR can be established here.[103] Consequently, the Supreme Court in the *Kleçka* case ruled that the statements and diaries of witness X were admissible and requested the lower court in a retrial to scrutinise only the reliability and

---

[98] Ibid, paras 31–33.

[99] Ibid, para 26.

[100] Ibid, para 27.

[101] Ibid, para 34.

[102] Ibid, para 35.

[103] SC, 20.11.2012, Case Ap.-Kz. No. 453/12, Ruling of the Supreme Court of Kosovo, paras 36–40; see also SC, 11.12.2012, Ap.-Kz. No. 527/12, Ruling of the Supreme Court of Kosovo, paras 31–50.

credibility of the evidence of witness X. While the oscillation of the EULEX international judges as to admissibility of evidence provides for diverging views on the interpretation of domestic law, the case is of invaluable importance for incorporating the ECHR and ECtHR case-law in interpreting the scope of domestic law in a serious war crimes case. In other cases, EULEX international judges have interpreted the scope of certain provisions of domestic law in light of ECtHR case-law.[104]

Another important contribution of the EULEX international judges in the utilisation of the ECHR system of human rights could be found in the case concerning the reasonable time guarantee principle.[105] The District Court of Prishtina, upon the intervention of the defence, found that the 'First Instance Court ... determined a material fact incorrectly, i.e., the date of the offense'.[106] While, according to Kosovo law, if there is an erroneous determination of the factual situation, the case, in principle, is returned for retrial, the EULEX international judges viewed that 'ordering a retrial to correct an obvious mistake would create a legal absurdity which must be avoided'.[107] The panel further referred to the ECtHR jurisprudence to underline the importance of rendering justice without delays and the importance of this principle for the interest of the person in question as well as of legal certainty.[108] Based on the argument of a reasonable time guarantee, the mixed panel of EULEX international judges of the District Court of Prishtina modified the mistake in the date of the crime without returning the case for retrial.[109] Hence, the thoughtfulness of the mixed panel of EULEX international judges on the reasonable time guarantee principles shows itself to be not only a coherent interpretation of domestic law with the ECHR and the ECtHR, but also a creative tool to successfully respond to concerns related to the backlog of cases faced by the Kosovo courts.

While the application of international human rights law and its jurisprudence is seen through a positive lens, EULEX case-law shows occasions of confusion with regard to the place of certain foreign legal standards in the Kosovo legal order. For instance, in a Supreme Court case PKL-KZZ-137/11, concerning the protection of legality, the prosecution challenged the decision of the first and second instance on rendering a decision on conviction without taking into account the standard *beyond any reasonable doubt*.[110] While the standard *beyond any reasonable doubt* is not indicated in Kosovo law, the prosecution relied on the ECHR and comparative law.

---

[104] See, e.g., supra note 15, at 3; Case KA No. 417/11, Blerim Devolli et al., Ruling upon appeals against a ruling on confirmation of indictment and admissibility of evidence, mixed panel of EULEX international judges of the District Court Prishtina, 22 March 2012, at paras. 9–10.

[105] DC, 3.12.2012, Case Ap.-Kz. No. 116/12, Judgment of the District Court of Prishtina.

[106] Ibid, para 30.

[107] Ibid, para 32.

[108] Ibid, para 33.

[109] Ibid, para 34.

[110] SC, 13.04.1012, Case PKL-KZZ-137/11, Judgment of the Supreme Court of Kosovo, p. 2.

The mixed panel of EULEX international judges viewed that while the standard *beyond any reasonable doubt* is present in the common law and some other legal systems, it is not a legal standard in Kosovo and that 'to state that the principle is implicit in the ECHR is not correct'.[111] In referencing the ECHR, ICCPR and the work of legal scholars, the Supreme Court viewed that 'as to the standard of proof, there is no clear statement that there is a requirement of proof of guilt beyond any reasonable doubt'.[112] The present case provides that a long list of international instruments and case-law contained in the Kosovo Constitution provides an opportunity for litigants to introduce confusing standards and principles. In these cases, if the panel of judges fails to understand the international jurisprudence, the consequences for accepting a standard that might not necessarily have legal support could occur. In the present case, the panel viewed that the prosecution was using a 'common legal expression that has become familiar in the legal jargon but not in the legal system of Kosovo'.[113]

5 (Non-) Application of International Law by Domestic Judges of the Courts of General Jurisdiction

Article 102(3) of the Kosovo Constitution stipulates that all '[c]ourts shall adjudicate based on the Constitution and the law'. Due to the integrated character of certain domesticated international human rights instruments and jurisprudence, it is expected that courts of general jurisdiction will comply with the requirements of Article 22 and 53 of the Constitution.

However, although the decisions of UNMIK international judges as of 2002 asserted that the ECHR 'constitute[s] an integral part of the Kosovo legal system',[114] the domestic judges of Kosovo courts of general jurisdiction before and after the entry into force of the Kosovo Constitution have occasionally failed to comply with requirements of the ECHR or other international conventions. This has particularly been observed in several reports of international organisations engaged in monitoring the judiciary in Kosovo.[115]

---

[111] Ibid, p. 3.

[112] Ibid.

[113] Ibid, p. 3.

[114] SC, 9.10.2002, Case AP—KZ No. 76/2002 against Ruzhdi Saramati, Decision of the panel of UNMIK judges of the Supreme Court of Kosovo, para 39. On the application of the ECHR and ECtHR case-law, see also Case AP No. 209/2002 against Xhavit Hasani, Verdict of the panel of UNMIK judges of the Supreme Court of Kosovo, 13 August 2002, p. 7; Case AP—KZ No. 263/2002 against Milorad Blagojevic, Decision of the panel of UNMIK judges of the Supreme Court of Kosovo, 2 April 2003, p. 6.

[115] With regard to the non-compliance of Kosovo courts of general jurisdiction with the ECHR, see, e.g., OSCE (2012) Report on execution of judgments. http://www.osce.org/kosovo/87004. Accessed 19 September 2012; OSCE Report on evidentiary procedure in civil cases in Kosovo

Significant efforts were put in place to identify decisions rendered by local judges which would contain reference to international law, or at least to international human rights instruments and case-law anchored in Articles 22 and 53 of the Constitution. Such reference has generally been absent, and only in a few decisions of local judges could the application of the ECtHR case-law be identified. In case PKR.N.14/13 of 29 January 2013, a panel of local judges of the Basic Court of Ferizaj, by referring to Article 53 of the Constitution, argued: 'human rights provisions shall be interpreted in harmony with decisions [of the ECtHR]'.[116] In case PKR.N.14/13, as well as in other cases of the Basic Court of Ferizaj, local judges in their progressive approach were keen to utilise interpretations of the ECtHR when construing concepts of reasonable suspicion, appropriate measures to ensure a defendant's presence, the principle *in dubio pro reo* and the presumption of innocence.[117] The application of the ECtHR's jurisprudence is made with invaluable relevance to substantiate their reasoning in interpreting domestic law.

While a few local judges are cognisant of the Constitutional obligation to observe the application of domestic law in compliance with international human rights, the vast majority of local judges do not share this concern.

In observing the reluctance to apply international conventions on the protection of human rights, the reasons lie in the maturity of the judiciary, including the place which human rights has in the minds of judges in the process of adjudication, expertise in work with international human rights instruments and case-law, as well as the accessibility of the sources in official languages. These challenges are not unique, particularly for Kosovo, but have been present to varying degrees in other legal orders at the beginning of the application of international law in national legal orders.

Stefan Oeter, in surveying the period of non-application of international human rights conventions in German courts, observed that '[i]f state authorities, the legislator or judicial organs violate international human rights, they usually do not do so with the conscience of disregarding international human rights. They are simply not accustomed to keeping international human rights foremost in mind'.[118]

(2011). http://www.osce.org/kosovo/83301. Accessed 19 September 2012, pp. 10–16; OSCE Report on confirmation of indictment concerns (2012) Issue 8. http://www.osce.org/kosovo/73711. Accessed 19 September 2012, pp. 1–4.

[116] Basic Court, 29.01.2013, Case PKR.N.14/13, Basic Court of Ferizaj—Serious Crimes Department, p. 12.

[117] Judge Bashkim Hyseni, President of Ferizaj Basic Court (former Ferizaj Municipal Court) has made references to ECtHR case-law in his court decisions. In cases KP no. 33/11 and KP no. 100/12, Judge Hyseni explains the ECtHR's interpretation of the concept of 'reasonable suspicion' by making reference to the case *Fox, Campbell and Hartley v. The United Kingdom*, ECHR, Judgment of the Court of 30 August 1990, at para 32. In the third case, P no. 355/12 related to measures to ensure a defendant's presence, Judge Hyseni made reference to the case *I.A v. France*, ECHR, Judgment of the Court of 23 September 1998. For references to the ECtHR case-law concerning the interpretation of measures to ensure a defendant's presence, the principle *in dubio pro reo* and presumption of innocence, see also the decisions of Judge Agim Maliqi from the Basic Court of Ferizaj, PKR N. 38/13; PKR N.9/2013-P94/12 PR1.

[118] Oeter (2001), pp. 871, 880.

In scrutinising the reasons for the rare application of international human rights in German courts, Judge Bruno Simma in 1997 wrote that the following practical reasons explained the reluctance of German judges:

1. International human rights norms are not part of the core curricula in the legal education and practical training of lawyers and judges.
2. Some courts may have difficulties in obtaining . . . translations.
3. Access to the texts of international norms sometimes proves to be difficult.[119]

From the foregoing observations, one can draw the conclusion that the non-application particularly of international human rights by domestic judges of the courts of general jurisdiction most likely has its roots in the education and training of judges, including knowledge of foreign languages, understanding of the law of treaties, international jurisprudence, and so forth. These concerns, coupled with recommendations, are addressed in the following section.

5.1 Legal Education of Judges

The legacies of the past have had a strong impact on the quality of legal education in Kosovo. Firstly, Kosovo, having been a constitutive part of the SFRY, has inherited a legal tradition that was not quite gracious towards the judicial application of international law. Secondly, and most importantly, after the abolishment of Kosovo's autonomy by the Serbian regime, from 1990 until 10 June 1999, the judicial and educational system in Kosovo was removed.[120]

Hence, for more than a decade, Kosovar Albanian judges did not have the opportunity to practise their profession, let alone to educate a new generation or to appoint new ones.

Thus, the current judicial system is to a large extent composed of a generation of senior judges who were appointed before 1990 and who were unfortunate to be expelled from the courts for 10 years. Just after the war, in an emerging situation of establishing the courts, new judges were trained and appointed in an accelerated procedure. The last generation of judges, appointed in the last few years, has been educated in the training offered mainly by senior judges and professors. The vicious circle of legal education has only recently found light at the end of the tunnel.

Notwithstanding the unique inherited problems, the UN administration after 1999 adopted a legislative framework that called upon judges to uphold internationally recognised human rights in the course of judicial proceedings.[121] Such

[119] Simma et al. (1997), p. 107.

[120] See generally Malcolm (1998).

[121] On the establishment of the UN Mission in Kosovo and its role in the construction of the post-conflict judiciary in Kosovo, see Chesterman (2001), pp. 143–158; Irmsher (2001), pp. 353–395; Stahn (2001), pp. 105–183.

development marked a new beginning in terms of investing in the judge's legal education in Kosovo after a decade of institutional discontinuity. The sanctioning of international human rights acts in the Kosovo legal system rendered it necessary for the international community to invest in the legal education of judges by focusing on the application of human rights treaties, with particular emphasis on the application of the ECHR and its case-law.[122] International organisations, as well as local institutions such as the Kosovo Judicial Institute (KJI) and the Kosovo Judicial Council (KJC), have undertaken a number of training sessions on the applicability of the ECHR in order to increase the awareness of judges of the relevance of adhering to ECHR standards.[123] In addition, international judges in UNMIK and recently EULEX who adjudicate in mixed panels with local judges have contributed to raising the awareness of domestic judges of the importance of observing international law in domestic adjudication.

Concerning legal education at the university level, law studies are organised in 4-year studies. International law, European law and human rights law are offered in the first 3 years of education, and in the last academic semester students have an opportunity to specialise in courses of international law. Masters programmes in international law are intended to provide thorough understanding of various branches of public and private international law.[124]

In judicial education, international law is also part of the bar exam in Kosovo, which is a professional legal exam developed under the aegis of the Ministry of Justice in order for law graduates to be able to provide certain types of legal services or engage in the litigation process.[125] The current legislation in Kosovo provides that candidates for the post of judges and prosecutors who are selected based on a public and open competition after having passed the preparatory exam for judges

[122] Many international organisations have offered assistance to support the reforms undertaken in the field of legal education in Kosovo by supporting initiatives for the revision of educational curricula, advancing legal skills, organising legal clinics, legal commentaries, etc., such as the USAID, European Commission, DFID, GIZ, etc.

[123] Interview with the Director of the Kosovo Judicial Institute, Mr Lavdim Kransiqi, January 2013. See also the OSCE second review of the criminal justice system (1 September 2000 to 28 February 2001) which recommended that the KJI should provide more comprehensive training on the application of international human rights law in the criminal justice context to both local and international judges and prosecutors. The report is available at http://www.osce.org/kosovo/13043. Accessed 12 May 2013.

[124] Interview on 18 April 2013 with Prof. Dr. Qerim Qerimi, Vice-Dean for Academic Affairs of the Law Faculty of the University of Prishtina.

[125] The Bar examination consists of a written and verbal part. In the written part of the examination, practical assignments are given from criminal and civil law. The oral part of the examination consists of these subjects: (a) Principles, constitutional structures and judiciary organisation; (b) Criminal law (material and procedural); (c) Civil law (material, procedural, family, hereditary and obligatory); (d) Trade law (economic); (e) Labor law; (f) Administrative law, and (g) International law and European Union law on human rights. See Law No. 02/L-40 on the Bar Exam.

and prosecutors are required to attend the Initial Legal Education Programme (ILEP).[126] This programme, organised by the KJI, also covers International Law, European Law and Human Rights Law.[127] Although the existing legislation does not provide for compulsory attendance of continuous legal education by judges, the Code of Ethics and Professional Conduct of Judges requires that judges maintain and improve the highest standards of professionalism and legal expertise and engage in the Continuous Legal Education Programme and training as provided by the Kosovo Judicial Council.[128] Given the constitutional requirements to observe the internationally recognised human rights conventions, it is viewed that the KJC and KJI, mandated to administer the judiciary and train judges and prosecutors, are under the obligation to develop strategies and provide intensive training in order to increase the degree of familiarity for the judicial application of international law.

In order to comply with these constitutional demands, the authors suggest that Kosovo authorities should consider taking immediate short-term actions and engaging in planning a sustainable judiciary that is competent to cope with international law. A short-term plan could include the establishment of legal research departments at higher courts of Kosovo, and organising regular training and providing materials for judges, at least on pertinent human rights issues. Depending on the court, the legal research departments should attract young lawyers with expertise in specialised areas of international law. In addition, the institutions mandated to provide training for judges should offer mandatory courses for current judges on the application of, *inter alia*, general international law, international human rights instruments and jurisprudence, as well as on areas of customary international law. The KJC should ensure that translations into official languages of the eight international instruments in Article 22 of the Constitution, and the most important practice of the ECtHR, are provided for Kosovo courts. While these actions could help judges become accustomed to international law (with an emphasis on international human rights), a sustainable plan must reflect on the education of future generations of lawyers. International law, with particular focus on human rights instruments and case-law, should be an indispensable component of the

[126] The Initial Legal Education Programme (ILEP) is a training programme dedicated to potential candidates for future judges and prosecutors. The ILEP programme consists of an intensive 15 month training programme with a number of training modules. Upon completion of this programme, candidates are professionally prepared and ready for the function of judge or prosecutor.

[127] Law on the Establishment of the Kosovo Judicial Institute, Law No. 02/L-25. The KJI is responsible for (a) the training of office holders and potential office holders in the judiciary (judges and prosecutors); (b) the assessment and organisation of the preparatory exam for judges and prosecutors; (c) special training courses for the promotion of judges and prosecutors; (d) basic training courses for lay judges; and (e) training courses for other professionals in the area of the judiciary as identified by the KJI. For more, see Art. 2.

[128] The Code of Ethics and Professional Conduct of Judges was adopted on 25 April 2006 and is available at the official site of the Kosovo Judicial Council: http://www.kgjk-ks.org/. Accessed: 27 May 2013. See Section 3 para. 3 of the Code.

programmes designed for future attorneys, judges, prosecutors, and those who apply the law generally.

The experience of the Supreme Administrative Court in the Czech Republic and other European countries could serve as a reference in identifying the tools that could be used in the transition from isolation to interaction with international law.[129] In addition, the practice of the Kosovo Constitutional Court and EULEX international judges could assist in understanding the relationship between domestic and international human rights.

6 Conclusions

The 'internationally oriented character' of the Kosovo Constitution allows for the direct application and supremacy of international law over Kosovo laws.[130] Furthermore, Articles 22 and 53 of the Constitution provide for an invaluable catalogue of international human rights instruments and case-law that constitute an integral part of the Kosovo legal order.

In observing the embryonic jurisprudence of the newly established Kosovo legal order, the judicial application of international law is not yet equally embraced at all levels of Kosovo courts, and the intensity of interaction with international human rights law and other branches of international law differs.

The jurisprudence of the Constitutional Court and the EULEX international judges reveals a rich and vivid interaction with the ECHR and ECtHR case-law. Firstly, this interaction manifests compliance with the constitutional requirement of adequate judicial protection of human rights and, secondly, it raises local awareness of the indispensability of ECtHR case-law in the Kosovo legal order. The latter influence is of significant importance in view of Kosovo's ambition to join the Council of Europe and accept the ECtHR's jurisdiction.

While the vast majority of the Constitutional Court's case-law is related to human rights, the role of the Court in shaping the relationship with international law is evident. The Constitutional Court's reasoning in the *PAK* case, provide for the challenges in safeguarding the Constitution *vis à vis* the international authorities which remain neutral towards the political status of Kosovo. The status of international law in the Kosovo legal order remains to be elucidated once the Constitutional Court defines the substance of 'legally binding norms of international law',

[129] After the accession of the Czech Republic to the European Union (EU), the Supreme Administrative Court in the Czech Republic established its Research and Documentation Unit composed of young legal researchers to assist judges on issues related to EU law, international law and comparative law. See http://www.nssoud.cz/The-Activities-of-the-Service/art/499?menu=191. Accessed 12 May 2013.

[130] For a categorisation of constitutions that permit the incorporation of international law, see Cassese (1985), p. 394.

the self-executing effect of the UDHR, and the place of customary international law, to name just a few issues.

In the adjudication of war crimes cases, the fashion in which EULEX international judges amalgamated customary international law in the Kosovo legal order does not align with an already established UNMIK jurisprudence and the orthodox understanding of law. While the authors recognise the difficulties of international criminal adjudication in domestic courts, this contribution echoes that international judges operating in hybrid courts should not shrink away from complex legal issues. Instead, by means of judicial creativity, EULEX international judges should aim to establish jurisprudence that builds principles and provides guidance for future adjudication for local judges and not to see its mission merely as temporary machinery for the adjudication of serious crimes.

Regarding the state succession to international agreements, EULEX international judges were reluctant to rule on the succession of Kosovo to international agreements signed by Serbia. In the *B.A.* case concerning succession to the 1901 Extradition Treaty signed between the US and Serbia, EULEX international judges contributed to defining what constitutes an international agreement and what place customary international law has in the Kosovo legal order. In addition, by rejecting the claim on the extradition of a suspected terrorist, EULEX international judges relied on a strict legal interpretation and did not hesitate to contradict the understanding of the Kosovo government and the US Secretary of State with regard to the application and scope of the 1901 Extradition Agreement. As indicated in the analysis, in view of the legal and political implications of the case, it is hardly conceivable that domestic judges would have taken the same approach in the present case.

In contrast to the jurisprudence of the Constitutional Court and EULEX international judges, the scarce application of international human rights by courts of general jurisdiction reflects a set of inherited problems and ineffective new policies related to the education of judges. Furthermore, if the Kosovo judiciary fails to promptly reduce the backlog of cases, it is hard to imagine that international norms will find a place in the routine work of local judges.

Considering the temporary nature of the presence of international EULEX and Constitutional Court judges, the fate of the judicial application of domesticated international agreements on human rights, and international law more generally, rests on the capacity and professionalism of local judges.

In view of Kosovo's aspirations to join the UN, the Council of Europe, the EU and other treaty regimes, the Kosovo judiciary must be able not only to comply with domesticated international instruments in Articles 22 and 53 of the Constitution, but also to honour new international agreements undertaken by means of ratification. Hence, Kosovo judges should be equipped to engage in the complexities of international agreements and case-law in the context of the national legal order. Understanding the conventional systems and international jurisprudence (e.g. ECtHR) is only the starting point for a competent local judiciary. The peculiarities of the relationship between national and international law require that judges in their *double function* engage not only in the mechanical application of international law, but also quest for techniques of legal interpretation and legal reasoning that lead to judicial comity when addressing different and sometimes conflicting legal obligations.

References

Baker R (2010) Customary international law in the 21st century: old challenges and new debates. Eur J Int Law 21(1)

Cassese A (1985) Modern constitutions and international law. Collected courses of the Hague Academy of International Law 192. Martinus Nijhoff, Dordrecht

Chesterman S (2001) Justice under international administration: Kosovo, East Timor and Afghanistan. Finn YB Int Law 12

Garlicki L (2005) Democracy and international influences. In: Nolte G (ed) European and US constitutionalism. Council of Europe Publishing, Strasbourg

Hasani E, Paczolay P, Riegner M (eds) (2012) Constitutional justice in Southeast Europe: constitutional courts in Kosovo, Serbia, Albania and Hungary between ordinary judiciaries and the European Court of Human Rights. Nomos, Baden-Baden

Hill S, Linden-Retek P (2010) Supervised independence and post-conflict sovereignty: the dynamics of hybridity in Kosovo's new Constitutional Court. Yale J Int Law

Irmsher T (2001) The legal framework for the activities of the United Nations Interim Administration Mission in Kosovo: the charter, human rights, and the law of occupation. Ger YB Int Law 44

Istrefi K (2013) Constitutional domestication of international human rights in the Kosovo legal order. Law Journal, Special Edition

Malcolm N (1998) Kosovo: a short history. Macmillan, London

McCormack TLH, McDonald A (eds) (2003) Yearb Int Humanit Law 6

Mettraux G (2009) The law of command responsibility. OUP, New York

Morina V (2010) The newly established Constitutional Court in post-status Kosovo. Rev Cent East Eur Law 35

Oeter S (2001) International human rights and national sovereignty in federal systems: the German experience. Wayne Law Rev 47

Pauwelyn J (2006) Conflict of norms in public international law: how WTO law relates to other rules of international law. CUP, Cambridge

EULEX International Judges Peeck et al (2012) In: Rojek C (ed) Manual: selected topics on criminal procedure. Kosovo Law Center, Prishtina

Posner E (2009) The perils of global legalism. University of Chicago Press, Chicago

Schabas W (2009) Customary law or judge-made law: Judicial creativity at the UN criminal tribunals. In: Doria J, Gasser H-P, Cherif Bassiouni M (eds) The legal regime of the International Criminal Court. Martinus Nijhoff. Leiden, Boston

Simma B et al (1997) The role of German courts in the enforcement of international human rights. In: Conforti B, Francioni F (eds) Enforcing international human rights in domestic courts. Martinus Nijhoff, The Hague

Stahn C (2001) The United Nations Transitional Administration in Kosovo and East Timor: a first analysis. Max Planck Yearb U N Law 5

Tunheim J (2009) Rule of law and the Kosovo constitution. Minn J Int Law 371

Weller M (2009) Contested statehood: Kosovo's struggle for independence. OUP, New York

The Application of International Law in Macedonia

Marija Risteska and Kristina Miševa

1 Introduction

The concept of an international society exists

> when a group of states, conscious of certain common values, form a society in the sense that they conceive themselves to be bound by a common set of rules in their relations with one another, and share in the working of common institutions. (Bull 1995, p. 13)

This concept emphasises the importance of principles of international order, such as state sovereignty and non-intervention, but also acknowledges the commitment of states in protecting values such as justice, free trade and human rights. The theory recognises that there is a conflict between the order provided by states and various aspirations for justice. However, scholars take two different positions on the issue of resolving this tension: the pluralist and the solidarist view.

Pluralists argue that order is always prior to justice, and that justice is only possible within the context of order, but never at the price of it. Solidarists, in contrast, look at the possibility of overcoming this conflict by recognising the mutual interdependence of the two concepts. Their main focus is on individuals as the principal holders of rights and duties in international relations and the realisation of individual justice.

The values that states commit themselves to acknowledging and promoting are enshrined in international legal documents, whereas the order states provide is regulated by domestic legal documents. This paper looks at the position of international law in the Macedonian legal system and the scope of its application by the

M. Risteska (✉)
Faculty of Political Science and Diplomacy, FON University, Skopje, Macedonia
e-mail: risteska@crpm.org.mk

K. Miševa
Faculty of Law, Goce Delchev University, Shtip, Macedonia
e-mail: kristina.miseva@ugd.edu.mk

S. Rodin, T. Perišin (eds.), *Judicial Application of International Law in Southeast Europe*, DOI 10.1007/978-3-662-46384-0_10

Macedonian judiciary. It identifies achievements and challenges, and provides an analysis and recommendations on how international values can be applied and achieved at home.

2 The Position of International Law in the Macedonian Legal System

In realising the values that states commit themselves to in international relations and which are evoked with the adoption of international legal documents, two preconditions are necessary. First of all, states need to be democratic and adopt a domestic legal framework that will provide the basis for the realisation of internationally agreed rights, freedoms and values, as 'without good written legal acts, moving in the right direction will be difficult to be achieved' (Blankenagel 1996, p. 57). Secondly, states need to build an effective mechanism for implementation of the legal framework (domestic and international) as 'even the most brilliant legal texts provide no guarantee for adequate implementation' (ibid).

Since its independence from federal Yugoslavia in 1991, the Republic of Macedonia has undergone serious constitutional reforms which have encompassed the adoption of a democratic political system and acceptance of the 'justice for all' concept (Kambovski 2008). This has been coupled with the signing and ratification of all international legal documents that envision the protection of human rights, but also other values such as free trade and environmental protection. The Constitution of the Republic of Macedonia has been developed in a 'laboratory' rather than by state institutions, which means the country has been privileged to learn from the best constitutional practice in democratic Western societies, and selectively copy modern constitutional models, terminology and concepts (Weruszewski 1992, p. 191). As such, it has adopted a liberal democratic approach towards human rights and freedoms.

In addition, the Constitution of Macedonia regulates the position of international law in the legal order of the country and thereby sets out an important basis for the application of international law in Macedonia. Article 118 of the Constitution stipulates that international agreements that are ratified and in accordance with the Constitution are an integral part of the domestic legal order and cannot be changed or derogated with laws. Given that ratification is needed for an international legal act to be transformed into the national legal system, one might conclude that in Macedonia there is a dualistic approach to the incorporation of international acts in national law. From the dualistic perspective, international and national law represent two separate levels. Hence, a transformation act into the national legal system is needed (Amrhein-Hofman 2003).

The Constitution also stipulates the hierarchy of domestic and international general legal acts. Emphasising the unity of the Macedonian legal system, Article 51 also regulates that the Constitution is the supreme legal act. To this effect, 'all laws and other general legal acts promulgated in the Republic of Macedonia must comply with the Constitution, and all other regulations must comply with the laws and the Constitution of the Republic of Macedonia'. In this respect, international treaties and other international legal acts that are transformed into the Macedonian legal system through a ratification act adopted by the Parliament have equal treatment as domestic legal acts, although the Constitution stands above them in the hierarchy.

The Constitution of the Republic of Macedonia explicitly specifies the incorporation of international legal sources within the national legal system. For example, Article 8 on the basic values of the constitutional order of the country regulates the fundamental human rights and freedoms recognised by international law and determined by the Constitution (paragraph 2), and respect for the generally accepted norms of international law (paragraph 12). Although it seems that the Constitution mirrors the European Convention for Human Rights (ECHR) in terms of guarantees for human rights and freedoms, it also regulates numerous (26 reservations) legal limitations of the same. Treneska-Deskovska (2008) categorises these limitations into two groups: (1) legal reservations that allow room for the human rights and freedoms determined by the Constitution to be further regulated in detail by other domestic legal acts, e.g. this is the case with the rights of foreigners (Articles 29 and 31); the right to marriage and family life (Article 40); the right to defend the country (Article 28); and the right to labour relations (Article 32); and (2) legal reservations that allow for an internationally recognised human right or freedom determined by the Constitution to be limited by a domestic law, e.g. this is the case with the right to freedom (Article 12); the right to movement and housing (Articles 26 and 27); the right to freely assemble (Article 28); the right to property (Article 30); the right to form a union and the right to strike (Articles 37 and 38).

The dualism in the legal order of the Republic of Macedonia is once again demonstrated in Article 98 of the Constitution, which regulates the application of domestic laws and international legal acts by the judiciary: 'the courts decide, on the basis of the Constitution, the laws of the country and international agreements that are ratified and in compliance with the Constitution of the Republic of Macedonia'. The only law in domestic jurisprudence that makes a reference to direct application of the rights stipulated in an international legal document, including the decisions of an international court, is the recently adopted Civil Liability for Defamation and Libel Act (Official Gazette (OG) No. 143/2012). Article 2 (paragraph 2) of this act stipulates that 'limitations on freedom of speech are regulated by this law in accordance with the European Convention for Human Rights and the practice of the European Court of Human Rights (ECtHR)'. Furthermore, it reaffirms the primacy of the ECHR over domestic laws in specific situations. Article 3 stipulates:

> if the court by applying the provisions of this law cannot resolve a certain issue that is related to responsibility for defamation or libel, or it determines that there is a legal loophole or conflict of this law with the ECHR, based on the principle of primacy, the

court will apply the provisions of the ECHR and the legal position of the ECtHR as expressed in its judgments.

The authorised Agent of the Republic of Macedonia in front of the ECtHR in an interview with the authors made it clear that this formulation was adopted 'on purpose to encourage Macedonian courts to apply the ECHR and the decisions of the ECtHR directly rather than to apply the mirror provisions of the same that have been integrated into domestic laws' (interview with Bogdanov 2013), the latter being the predominant strategy in the application of international law by the judiciary, as fourth chapter will demonstrate.

2.1 *The Position of International Agreements in the Macedonian Legal System*

On the basis of succession, the independent Macedonia inherited from the former federal Yugoslavia membership of certain international organisations (such as the IBRD, World Bank, IFC, IDA, and MIGA (OG 23/93)) and also assumed responsibilities from international agreements signed before independence. However, many important legal documents were signed after 1991.

In January 1998, the Signing, Ratification and Execution of International Agreements Act was passed (OG 5/98). This law regulates the procedure, ratification, manner of implementation and execution of international agreements (bilateral and multilateral) in accordance with the Constitution of the Republic of Macedonia and international law. This law replaced the Signing and Executing International Agreements Act of the Socialist Federal Republic of Yugoslavia (SFRY) (OG 55/78, 47/89).

2.1.1 The Stabilisation and Association Agreement (SAA)

In 1997, the Co-operation Agreement[1] between the European Community and the Former Yugoslav Republic of Macedonia was signed in Luxembourg, accompanied by a Financial Protocol and Transport Agreement.[2]

In 1999, the EU proposed a new Stabilisation and Association Process (SAP) for five countries in South-Eastern Europe. On 16 June 1999, negotiations with Macedonia were launched and a Stabilisation and Association Agreement was signed with the European Union on 9 April 2001, which entered into force on 1 April 2004. The SAA replaced the Co-operation Agreement of 1997. The SAA in its preamble calls for commitment to political, economic and institutional stabilisation through the development of civic society and democratisation, institution-building and

[1] Entered into force 1 January 1998.

[2] Entered into force 28 November 1997.

public administration reform, enhanced trade and economic co-operation, the strengthening of national and regional security, as well as increased co-operation in justice and home affairs (SAA FYR Macedonia OJ L 49/1). However, the agreement does not provide for any vehicles of democratisation, although it endorses the EU focus on output legitimacy, effectiveness and efficiency in enforcement of EU policies (Risteska 2013). In addition, it provides that:

> parties will attach particular importance to the reinforcement of institutions at all levels in the areas of administration in general and law enforcement and the machinery of justice in particular. This includes the consolidation of the rule of law . . . and the independence of the judiciary, the improvement of its effectiveness and training of the legal professions'. (Article 74)

The SAA includes chapters on political dialogue, regional co-operation, free movement of goods and people as well as trade co-operation. It regulates implementation of SAA provisions over a period of 10 years divided into two periods. The SAA was ratified by the Macedonian Parliament with the adoption of the Ratification of the SAA Act 5 days after its signing, and the Macedonian translation of the agreement was published in the Official Gazette. The SAA was applied through this the dualist approach.

For the implementation of the SAA, an institutional framework was established. This encompassed: the SAA Council, SAA Committee and seven SAA sub-committees. In accordance with Article 68 of the SAA, Macedonia started the gradual approximation of its existing and future laws (competition law, intellectual property law, etc.), and the Interim Agreement on Trade and Trade Related Matters was signed and entered into force on 1 June 2001 (OJ L124/3 of 4 May 2001).

The Interim Agreement between the EC and Macedonia regulates all issues related to trade between the EU and Macedonia through an improvement in the balance of trade. The Interim Agreement allows for the full liberalisation of trade between the EU and Macedonia, except for fish, wine and spirit products. The aim of the Interim Agreement was to increase trade, eliminate increases in tariffs and decrease trade barriers. An additional protocol to the Interim Agreement/SAA on wine entered into force in January 2002, covering reciprocal preferential trade concessions for certain wines, and reciprocal recognition, protection and control of wine names/designations for spirits and aromatised drinks.

As trade relations between Macedonia and the EU grew, the SAA went through several amendments. In 2005, Article 27 of the SAA was amended with a protocol on a tariff quota for imports of sugar and sugar products originating from Macedonia and exported into the EU. In 2008, the double-checking system for imports of steel products from Macedonia into the EU was abolished (Council Regulation No. 79/2008 repealing EC Regulation No. 152/2002 for Macedonia; OJ L25/3 of 30.01.2008). Finally, the SAA Council decided that Article 7 of Protocol 2 of the SAA and Annex 1 of the same Protocol would be repealed as of 1 January 2008 (OJ L 25/10 of 30.01.2008).

2.1.2 WTO

The SAA does not exclude WTO provisions and specifically refers to Article 24 of the GATT on customs unions, and Article 5 of the GATS on economic integration and market liberalisation between the signatory countries. This makes the two processes of accession to the European Union and WTO reform complementary. The high level of political commitment to the first process was reflected in WTO membership success. Macedonia was able to complete the overall accession process within a record period of 3 years (1999–2002) and become the 146th member of the WTO in April 2003. Consequently, Macedonia has signed bilateral free trade agreements with all neighbouring countries and territories. To facilitate the application of the WTO agreement, the Macedonian Parliament adopted the ratification of the accession package, which was also published in Macedonian in the Official Gazette of Macedonia, while the Government provided additional information about the WTO through the official websites of the Government and the Ministry of the Economy, national strategies, and several translated books and printed brochures. The WTO agreement, accepted and ratified by the Parliament of the Republic of Macedonia, has the status of national law, which is derived from the Constitution of the Republic of Macedonia. Since members of the WTO accept WTO agreements as a 'single undertaking', a different period of time is needed to apply its provisions. The TRIPS agreement is part of this package, so most of its provisions are implemented and harmonised as part of the domestic law of Macedonia that refers to intellectual property law, i.e. the Industrial Property Act (OG No. 21/09, No. 24/11), the Copyright and Related Rights Act (OG No. 115/10, No. 51/11), and the Protection of Competition Act (OG No. 145/10).

In 1991, Macedonia joined WIPO, with the result that most of the rules that refer to intellectual and industrial property rights were approximated with national law.

2.1.3 The ICTY

The International Criminal Tribunal for the Former Yugoslavia (ICTY) constitutes a judicial signed intervention, i.e. intervention by legal means, without the use of force (Birdsall 2007). The ICTY as a case of judicial intervention is a concrete expression of the conflict between order and justice. It constitutes external intervention by a number of states in the internal affairs of another sovereign state in order to enforce human rights laws and to protect principles of justice. This means that one state's sovereignty (as a fundamental principle of international order) is compromised to protect human rights (as a principle of individual justice). The ICTY is a means rather than an end in itself, making the enforcement of universal justice norms possible on an international basis (ibid).

Macedonia signed a co-operation agreement with the ICTY, which was transformed into the domestic legal system with the Co-operation with the ICTY Act, in which 'all state bodies committed themselves to joint co-operation, and exchange of information and documents that are within the competence and interest of the International Criminal Court' (OG 73/2007, Article 1). This law implements UNSC Resolution 827. The law allows for proceedings in front of the ICTY (for crimes regulated by the ICTY Statute) to have primacy over proceedings against the same person on the same criminal charge in front of the public prosecutor or a domestic court (Article 8, paragraph 1). In 2010, the International Co-operation in Criminal Matters Act was passed (OG 124/2010). By means of this law, Macedonia agreed to co-operate in all matters with the European Court of Justice (ECJ), European Court for Human Rights (ECtHR), International Criminal Court (ICC) and other international organisations that Macedonia is a member of or has signed international agreements with (Article 3).

2.1.4 The Aarhus Convention

The first steps towards providing a legal framework for access to environmental information were undertaken by the Republic of Macedonia in 1999 when the Parliament of the Republic of Macedonia ratified the Convention on Access to Information, Public Participation in Decision-making and Access to Justice in Environmental Matters, also known as the Ratification of the Convention on Access to Information, Public Participation in Decision-Making and Access to Justice in Environmental Matters (Aarhus Convention) Act (Official Gazette of the Republic of Macedonia No. 40/99).

Since Article 118 of the Constitution of the Republic of Macedonia states that 'international agreements ratified in accordance with the Constitution are part of the internal legal system and cannot be changed by law', and since Article 68 (Constitution of the Republic of Macedonia) declares that 'the Parliament of the Republic of Macedonia ... ratifies international agreements', the Aarhus Convention is considered to be of the same rank as national law. As such, and in accordance with Article 98 (Constitution of the Republic of Macedonia), 'the courts shall judge on the basis of the Constitution and the laws and international laws ratified in accordance with the Constitution'.

3 The Macedonian Judicial System

The judicial system in Macedonia is regulated by the Constitution of the Republic of Macedonia (Part III point 4, Articles 98–105 and Amendments XXV, XXVI, XXVII, XXVIII) and the Courts Act (OG Nos. 58/06, 35/08 and 150/10). According to the Macedonian Constitution (Article 98), judicial power is exercised by the courts, which are autonomous and independent. The court system has a single organisation. With the latest changes to the Courts Act (OG No. 150/10), proponents of the European continental model (Davitkovski and Pavlovska-Daneva 2006, p. 114; Hristov 1981, p. 449) in the field of administrative justice came out on top in the debate with the proponents of the Anglo-Saxon model (Gelevski 1997a, b, pp. 73–74; pp. 242, 252, 254), which resulted in the decision to introduce a specialised administrative court in the judicial system which seeks to address ongoing and unacceptable delays at the Supreme Court level in resolving administrative appeals and the consequent expense and inefficiencies (Davitkovski 2005, pp. 1–3). The new court system structure, however, still does not allow for the establishment of ad-hoc courts. To summarise, the Macedonian court system encompasses basic courts (27 in total), courts of appeal (4 in total), the Administrative Court, the Higher Administrative Court and the Supreme Court of the Republic of Macedonia (Courts Act, Article 22).

The post-Yugoslav phase in the development of the country's judiciary commenced in 1995 when the new Courts Act was adopted, introducing the election of judges by Parliament and life-long service. Under democracy, litigation increased, judicial proceedings took longer and efficiency and effectiveness decreased. With the process of accession of the country to the EU, external pressure for reform of the judiciary increased, mainly focusing on increasing efficiency in court proceedings. In 2005, a new Judicial Council was established (Amendment XXIX of the Constitution of the Republic of Macedonia) so that the election of judges, lay judges and court presidents is carried out by this Council, while members of the Judicial Council are elected by the Parliament of the Republic of Macedonia.

The Constitutional Court of Macedonia is not part of the regular court system of the country, but a special organ of the Republic established for the protection of the legal principles of constitutionality and legality. Constitutional Court competencies include: decisions on the conformity of laws with the Constitution and on the conformity of other regulations and collective agreements with the Constitution and laws; protection of the freedoms and rights of the individual and citizen relating to the freedom of personal conviction, conscience, thought, and public expression of thought, political association and activity, and prohibition of discrimination against citizens on the basis of sex, race, religion, or national, social or political affiliation; decisions on conflicts of competencies between holders of offices in the legislative, executive and judicial branches of state power; decisions on conflicts of competency between the organs of the central government and organs of the units of self-government; decisions on the accountability of the President; decisions on the constitutionality of the programmes and statutes of political parties and associations of citizens; and decisions on other issues as determined by the Constitution. The decisions of the Constitutional Court are final and binding.

3.1 The Authority to Apply International and EU Law

Amendment 15 of the Constitution of the Republic of Macedonia declares that judicial power is exercised by independent courts that function according to the Constitution and laws and also international agreements ratified pursuant to Constitutional authority. It defines the authority of all courts to perform their adjudication function on the basis of the Constitution, the laws and international agreements ratified in accordance with the Constitution (the Constitution of the Republic of Macedonia 1991, Amendment 15). The Supreme Court, on the other hand, ensures the uniform implementation of laws by all courts (Klimovski 2005, p. 505). In accordance with Amendment 10 of the Constitution, the Supreme Court of the Republic of Macedonia is the highest court in the country's judicial system.

In the Macedonian system, the decisions of the court are treated as sources of law only for the parties involved in the case (*res iudicata facit jus inter partes*). The decisions of upper courts are not formally binding on lower courts but it is necessary for them to respect them, especially in the area of intellectual property law (Dabovik-Anastasovska et al. 2011).

The Constitutional Court, in addition to deciding on the lawfulness and constitutionality of laws and other regulations, collective agreements, statutes, or the programme of a political party or association, also provides protection for 3 of the 24 basic human rights and freedoms (Article 110, Constitution of the Republic of Macedonia, 1991), and in this respect applies the international law that regulates these rights.

3.2 The Capacity to Apply International and EU Law

When it comes to the application of international and EU law, the capacity of the judicial institutions to employ provisions from international legal documents and agreements is pertinent. Capacity is built up through the education system and the training of legal professionals.

3.3 International Law Education

Legal training in Macedonian is provided by: (1) higher education institutions (faculties of law); (2) an academy for training judges and public prosecutors; (3) civil society and professional organisations.

In Macedonia, there are 24 accredited higher education institutions, of which 17 are private and 7 are publicly managed. In total, approximately 10,000 students graduate each year. The National Bureau of Statistics said that in 2011 9,802 students graduated from higher schools and faculties in Macedonia, which is 1.4 % fewer than in 2010. Analysis of the statistics also shows a decrease in enrolment on undergraduate courses and an increase in enrolment on post-graduate ones.

Of these, four public and five private universities offer undergraduate studies in law. The recent changes in the Higher Education Act (OG Nos. 35/08, 103/08, 26/09, 83/09, 99/09, 115/10, 17/11, 51/11, 123/12, 15/13 and 24/13) introduced doctoral studies. Of the higher education institutions currently operating in the

Table 1 International and EU law studies at Macedonian universities

University	International law	EU law
Saints Cyril and Methodius—Skopje	Yes	Yes
Kliment Ohridski—Bitola	Yes	No
Goce Delchev—Shtip	Yes	Yes
State University Tetovo	Yes	No
South East European University	Yes	No
First Private European University	Yes	No
FON University	Yes	Yes
American College	Yes	No

Source: Websites of the universities and the Ministry of Education and Science of the Republic of Macedonia

country, only three are accredited to organise doctoral studies in law, of which two are public institutions and one is private. Only eight of these universities offer specialised international law studies and three offer EU law as a special module, although some offer a master's programme in European studies. Some of the private higher education institutions in the Republic of Macedonia offer law studies (Table 1).

However, none of the universities deal with the application of international and EU law. This suggests that law students gain knowledge on international law, but lack the skills for its application.

3.4 Training in International and EU Law for Legal Professionals

An academy was established by the Academy for the Training of Judges and Public Prosecutors Act (OG No. 13/2006). The Academy is the main body in the judicial system that provides continuous education and training for judges, public prosecutors, and judicial and prosecution clerks, as well as the professional development of candidates for judges and public prosecutors. The Academy also contributes to the organisation and implementation of training for educators, as well as for lawyers, public notaries and other legal professionals that apply national law.

The Academy programme for initial training encompassed a total of 660 lessons in 2006–2007, and 659 lessons in 2007–2008. This figure gradually fell to 232 sessions in 2012 (Annual Reports 2006–2007; 2011–2012). The training is delivered by both domestic and foreign trainers in various legal areas. In 2007–2008, of the 659 lessons provided, 6 % were on subjects related to international law, and 5 % focused on EU law. In 2012, of 232 training sessions, almost 2 % were on international law, while interest in EU law increased up to 7 % of all training sessions provided.

However, a more detailed examination of the programme reveals that legal requirements stemming from international law and EU law in particular have been integrated into the training programme. This is especially applicable to new features introduced into the Macedonian legal system as a result of approximation with EU law in areas of material and procedural legislation in basic legal areas (criminal, civil, commercial); the fight against organised crime, corruption and human trafficking; and competition, intellectual property, consumer protection, international bankruptcy, international humanitarian law, etc. In 2012, the Academy also held workshops focusing on: 'Court Decisions within a Reasonable Period of Time'; 'Competition Law in the European Union'; 'Protection of the Environment in the EU'.

The Academy has specifically focused on the European Convention on Human Rights (ECHR) since its establishment and continuously provides training on application of the ECHR by domestic courts as well as applying the case law of the European Court of Human Rights (ECtHR) and other international courts with the aim of correctly applying international standards for a fair trial within a reasonable time (Annual Report 2007). In 2012, the strategy of the Academy turned to also providing workshops and discussions (round table discussions, conferences and seminars), including topics related to the ECHR. A good example is the round table on the topic 'Court Practice Related to Crimes against Honour and Reputation and a Review of the Practice of the ECtHR in Terms of Applying Article 10 of ECHR' (Annual Report 2012).

The Academy has contributed to a very important aspect of capacity building in the application of international and EU law since its establishment, which is by providing beginner and advanced level foreign language courses (English being the primary choice, followed by German and French). Proficiency in a foreign language is a precondition for reading decisions of the ECtHR and other international courts and applying them in domestic proceedings.

Lastly, the Academy has dedicated part of its activities to raising awareness of the work of the European Court of Human Rights in areas of Macedonian society such as the media. In 2012, it organised a study trip to the European Court of Human Rights for the highest representatives of judicial institutions in the Republic of Macedonia and also representatives of the print and electronic media in the country to familiarise them with the practice of the court in relation to Articles 8 and 10 of the ECHR. The goal was to inform the media and judiciary of the latest documents of the Council of Europe and to present an overview of the jurisprudence related to the crimes of slander and offense committed through the media. There was also a brief overview of the jurisprudence of the ECtHR through the development of standards concerning the implementation of Article 10 of the ECHR, and the degree of their implementation in national practice in terms of the conduct of judges and journalists with regard to freedom of expression and information (Annual Report 2012).

Awareness-raising activities have been further accelerated in recent years (2010–2013), with the Academy organising a number of public events such as a conference marking International Tolerance Day, as well as series of events promoting ECHR values to contribute to a renewal of the country's commitment to protection of the fundamental rights and freedoms of citizens. The target audience of these events was judges and public prosecutors, but also representatives of almost all areas of society, including journalists, politicians, academics, civil society and representatives of religious communities.

Capacity building for the application of international law does not encompass only training and awareness-raising, but also providing resources for legal professionals to use when applying international law in legal proceedings. Over the past several years, the Academy has created such resources by publishing the following publications: 'International Documents on an Independent and Efficient Judiciary: Opinions (1–6) of the Consultative Council of European Judges with the Landmark Documents and ECHR Jurisprudence' and 'International Documents on an Independent and Efficient Judiciary: Opinions (7–12) of the Consultative Council of European Judges with the Landmark Documents and ECHR Jurisprudence' (Annual Report 2012). In the course of 2013, the Academy has identified 20 out of a total of 28 relevant European Court of Human Rights decisions to be made available on the portal for international jurisprudence, which will be an integral part of the website of the Supreme Court of the Republic of Macedonia. In addition, judicial authorities in the Western Balkans recently agreed to create the WB HUDOC database, which will encompass all ECtHR decisions against Western Balkan countries translated into local languages to serve as an important resource for domestic courts when applying the ECHR (interview with Bogdanov 2013). In addition, the Supreme Court of Macedonia took a step forward by adopting a decision on setting up an editorial committee to be the main filter in the selection of national jurisprudence to which the ECHR is applied (interview with Panchevski 2013). This committee includes representatives of all four appellate regions, the Supreme Court and the Academy of Judges and Public Prosecutors.

4 Judicial Application of International and EU Law

Considering that most Macedonian judges have not been educated or trained in international law and that they have a limited knowledge of foreign languages, the level of application of international law by Macedonian courts is very limited. If we were to ask who initiates the issue of application of international law in Macedonia, we would find that it is usually the attorneys of the applicant that initiate the application. There are also a handful of judges that specialise in certain areas of international law, such as the ILO conventions or ECHR, and who use references to international law in their work (interview with Bogdanov 2013). It is rather infrequent for attorneys to initiate the application of the case law of the ECtHR and even less likely for judges to use it as a source of international law and apply it in their judgments.

For the purpose of this paper, we conducted a review of the case law of the basic and appellate courts, as well as the practice of the Constitutional Court. We used the electronic system for publishing court decisions, which is available on the websites of the courts. To detect decisions where the ECHR was applied, we used the keyword *discrimination* in the search engines of the basic, appellate and constitutional courts. As far as other international legal documents are concerned, identification was carried out using a snowball methodology and face-to-face interviewing in which legal professionals directed us to court decisions that referred to or applied international law. The cases we identified in the course of the research phase have been categorised and analysed to reveal trends in the judicial application of international law. The analysis is presented below and focuses on: (1) the application of international treaties and other legal documents; (2) the application of the case law of the ECtHR.

4.1 Application of International Treaties and Legal Documents

4.1.1 Application of the ECHR

The international legal document most widely applied and referred to by Macedonian courts has been the European Convention for the Protection of Human Rights and Fundamental Freedoms. This has been a result of the capacity-building and awareness-raising activities on the ECHR in combination with the work of the European Court of Justice, whose decisions against Macedonia have been widely reported in the media. From an analysis of the case law, three distinct strategies used by the Macedonian judiciary can be perceived: (1) reference to the ECHR indirectly through mirror provisions in Macedonian laws; (2) reference directly to ECHR provisions and use of the ECHR in the justification part of decisions; (3) application of ECHR provisions directly. Both basic and appellate courts often refer to the Convention, but rarely apply it directly. In most cases, the courts apply mirroring provisions in the Constitution of Macedonia (interview with Medarski 2013). Only one particular case was detected in the research phase. This was *Sexual Workers v. the Ministry of Interior* (no. 9-P-2605/09), where the Skopje second basic court directly applied Articles 3, 5 and 8(2) of the ECHR in its decision.

The Constitutional Court, on the other hand, leads in the number of cases in which there is a reference to this source of international law. However, in one case it did not consider the ECHR as a sufficient legal basis for its decisions. In the *Georgi Pavlov v. the Appellate Court of Shtip* case, the protection of rights enshrined in the ECHR was sought. However, the Constitutional Court of Macedonia in its decision ruled that:

> although the ECHR is encompassed in the domestic legal order it cannot be considered as a direct and independent legal basis for a court's decision. The Convention's provisions can be considered as an additional argument when deciding on the rights and freedoms the Court is entitled to protect under Article 110(3) of the Constitution of Macedonia.

4.1.2 Application of the Aarhus Convention

Implementation of the Aarhus Convention was to a large extent a result of the country's striving towards European integration. Real implementation started when the provisions from the Convention were translated into the Environment Act (Official Gazette of the Republic of Macedonia No. 53/05), adopted in 2005 as a result of the approximation of Macedonian legislation to the EU *acquis*. The following year, the country adopted another law which complemented implementation of the Aarhus Convention: the Free Access to Public Information Act (Official Gazette of the Republic of Macedonia No. 13/06). This law sets out the rules and procedures for access to information in general, including access to environmental information.

There has been only one lawsuit in the area regulated by the Aarhus Convention: *Citizens of Veles v. Republic of Macedonia* concerning long-term pollution of the city. The lawsuit was filed by seven NGOs and the municipality of Veles. However the Veles district court rejected it as unfounded.

In its decision, the court unfortunately did not apply the Aarhus Convention directly but referred to the European Charter on Environment and Health (EC 1979) and EC Directive 2004/35/E. This can also be seen in the decision of the Skopje Appellate Court concerning an appeal against the decision of the basic court in Veles. In this example, the appellate court used European Union regulations to explain how the basic court decision was based on national and international law, and rejected the appeal against this decision as unfounded.

We can conclude that Macedonian courts do not apply the Aarhus Convention but instead refer to sources of European law which mirror the Aarhus Convention and then use them as grounds for their judgments while simultaneously using Macedonian domestic laws that regulate the area.

4.1.3 Application of International Labour Law (ILO Conventions)

An analysis of case law shows that Macedonian basic and appellate courts apply international labour law parallel to domestic law regulating labour relations. This includes the conventions and recommendations of the International Labour Office. To illustrate this, we will examine Skopje Appellate Court decision no. 5943/06 of 21.09.2006 upholding the decision of the Skopje Second Basic Court no. 2357/05 of 03.04.2006. In this case, the appellate court based its decision on its interpretation of reasons for employers terminating a contract in Recommendation 166 on termination of employment, issued by the ILO in 1982. In its judgment, it noted that ILO Recommendation 166 stipulates that the termination of contracts must be regulated by law or by-laws (such as collective agreements). The judgment also stated that Article 12(1) of the Labour Relations Act stipulates that contracts and their termination should be in accordance with the Labour Act, international agreements to which Macedonia is a signatory, and other regulations such as collective agreements. 'In this respect the ILO Recommendation is compulsory and obligatory to the employer when deciding about the termination of a contract for business reasons' (no. 5943/06 of 21.09.2006). Since the decision on terminating the contract made by the employer was not in accordance with ILO Recommendation 166, the appellate court found the termination of the labour contract unlawful.

In a different case, *Avromovski v. Partner Agency for Temporary Employment*, the applicant referred to ILO Convention 111 on discrimination in employment when challenging the hiring criteria used by a temporary employment agency. The Constitutional Court also applied the Convention in its decision in this case, and ruled that the employment criteria used by the agency were in line with ILO Convention 111 and therefore non-discriminatory.

4.1.4 Application of the SAA

Application of the Stabilisation and Association Agreement has been rather limited. The review and analysis of cases only allowed us to identify a single case where the courts have applied the SAA: *Makpetrol v. Ministry of Finance Customs Office*. In this case, the First Skopje Basic Court directly applied Article 5 of the Interim Agreement and Article 18 of the SAA. In the reasoning of its judgment, which was upheld by the appellate court in Skopje, the First Basic Court referred to the SAA and Interim Agreement for Trade and Trade Issues. In this case, the applicant complained that customs duties were charged on imported goods, although the Interim Agreement and SAA annulled such charges. The defendant based the customs charges on two government decisions that have the power of by-laws in the Macedonian legal system: the Decision on closer definition of the means and conditions for importing oil and oil derivatives; and the Decision on the allocation of goods for export–import. In their judgments, the courts (both basic and appellate), besides applying the SAA and Interim Agreement directly, also gave precedence to international law rather than to domestic law (i.e. the two by-laws applied by the Customs Office and the Ministry of Finance of the Republic of Macedonia). In their decisions, the courts also concluded that the two domestic by-laws were in conflict with ratified international agreements and therefore they were no longer in force.

4.1.5 Application of the ICTY Agreement

According to the international agreement on co-operation with the ICTY, the Republic of Macedonia had to co-operate in exchanging information and documents regarding the inter-ethnic conflict of 2001. In 2005, the ICTY issued an indictment in which it stipulated that an armed conflict had occurred in Macedonia in the period from January to September 2001. On the basis of this indictment, the ICTY called upon the Macedonian government to provide all relevant information concerning the two people who had been indicted: Ljube Boshkovski (Minister of the Interior at the time of the conflict) for command responsibility and Johan Tarchulovski (inspector of the unit providing security for the President) also for command responsibility for an attack against civilians in the village of Ljuboten. In the two court cases, the accused were individually charged with war crimes in accordance with Article 7 of the ICTY Statute. The state institutions communicated well with the ICTY and provided all the relevant information and evidence, and were commended by the EC in its progress reports.

Besides this case, in accordance with the agreement on co-operation, the Government handed over jurisdiction in four more cases involving the 2001 conflict: Lipkovo Dam; the Mavrovo Workers; disappeared persons from Neproshteno; the NLA leadership. The ICTY took over the cases from the Macedonian authorities in different phases of the investigations, but due to a lack of evidence, the cases were returned to the Macedonian judicial institutions for further investigations. However, the ICTY proceeded with the cases against Boshkovski and Tarchulovski. In 2008, the ICTY judicial council decided to lift all charges against Boshkovski, whereas Tarchulovski was sentenced to 12 years in prison.

Of the four cases returned to the Macedonian authorities, only one went to trial: the Mavrovo Workers case in which 22 people were charged with war crimes, three of whom died during proceedings. However, the case was dropped by the Macedonian criminal court, as in 2012 Parliament issued its interpretation of the Amnesty Act (adopted in 2002), stipulating that

> pursuant to Article 113 of the Criminal Code (OG No. 37/96) and Article 1 of the Amnesty Act (OG No. 18/02), all those engaged in the preparation of criminal activities relating to the conflict of 2001 prior to 1 January 2001 are also subject to the amnesty provided by the Amnesty Act.

This initiated fierce discussion in the legal profession, with comments that crimes against humanity cannot be treated *ad acta*, and that the *ius cogens* norms of international law had been violated with this interpretation of the Amnesty Act. The Helsinki Committee for Human Rights criticised the interpretation as unlawful. The Council of Europe Commissioner for Human Rights in November 2012 termed the interpretation of the Amnesty Act as a political act that entrenched the 'continuity of non-punishment of the severe human rights and international humanitarian law violations during the 2001 conflict', while Amnesty International demanded justice in the cases returned by the ICTY to the Macedonian judicial authorities, stating that 'crimes against humanity cannot be subject to political bargaining and agreement'. However, the Constitutional Court of the Republic of Macedonia decided that the interpretation of the Amnesty Act did not violate basic principles of constitutionality and therefore in two instances decided on the constitutionality of the interpretation provided by Parliament.

The fact that the ICTY returned the cases to the Macedonian judicial authorities did not mean that crimes against humanity had not been committed or that there were no elements in the four cases for the criminal investigation of war crimes. The return of the cases was in accordance with Articles 25–28 of the Co-operation with the ICTY Act, which precisely regulates the instances in which the tribunal will return cases to the national judicial authorities; to which organ the case will be returned; and how the domestic judicial authorities should proceed in such cases. However, in these cases, the judicial authorities of Macedonia did not apply international law, as in three of the cases they had not acted in line with the international agreement for co-operation with the ICTY and the national legal act transforming the international law into the Macedonian legal system (the Co-operation with the ICTY Act) and had halted proceedings in the fourth as a result of the interpretation of the Amnesty Act issued by Parliament in 2012.

The application of international law (UNSCR 827) shows that the Macedonian judiciary has the capacity, willingness and track record (with the Boshkovski and Tarchulovski cases) when it comes to applying ICTY law. It can also play a political role when needed. This means that Macedonia's sovereignty has been compromised to protect human rights (as a principle of individual justice). However, as this case shows, ICTY law has not proven to be effective in the 'enforcement of universal justice norms possible on an international basis' (ibid).

4.2 Referring to the Case Law of the ECtHR

Transnational relationships between courts in this instance can be approached analytically through the framework of judicial implementation and impact (Volcansek 1989, p. 569). Impact analysis focuses on the consequences or results of judicial actions. An analysis of the case law shows that there is no commonality in the practice of the Constitutional Court when it comes to the application of the jurisprudence of the European Court of Human Rights (ECtHR). A review of all the decisions issued from 1991 to May 2013 shows that the Court chooses to: (1) ignore application of the decisions of the ECtHR; (2) apply the decisions made by the ECtHR in certain cases and uses them to justify its own decisions; or (3) explicitly refuses direct application, as the jurisprudence of the ECtHR cannot be interpreted as a source of international law. The following three cases are illustrations of these practices of the Constitutional Court of Macedonia when applying international law, particularly the jurisprudence of the ECtHR.

In the case *Nikola Gelevski v. Dragan Pavlovic Latas* (U. No. 3/2012-0-0 of 02.05.2012), which came before the Constitutional Court in an attempt to overturn a decision awarding damages on the basis of protecting freedom of expression as guaranteed under Article 16 of the Constitution, the attorney of the applicant referred to the extensive practice of the ECtHR in applying Article 10 of the ECHR. The applicant used the judgment in the *Lingens v. Austria* case of 1986 to defend themselves against the accusation of telling lies and untrue facts on the grounds that they were expressing a value judgment, which according to the ECtHR in the *Schwabe v. Austria* case of 1992 did not need to 'be proved to be true or untrue'. In the same case, the jurisprudence of the ECtHR was also used to argue that the language used by the applicant was acceptable (*Dalban v. Romania*, 1999;

Oberschlick v. Austria, 1991; *Lopes Gomes de Silva v. Portugal*, 2000) and to appeal against the basic and appeal courts in Macedonia ruling that the same was damaging and libellous.

The Constitutional Court in its decision referred to Articles 12, 19 and 29(2) of the Universal Declaration of Human Rights, to Articles 17 and 19 of the International Pact for Civic and Political Rights, and Articles 8 and 10 of the European Convention of Human Rights. It ruled that the State has the right to limit freedom of expression under Article 172(1) of the Criminal Code, which criminalises defamation. Therefore, the Constitutional Court found that the decisions of the other domestic courts were in line with the Constitution and international law, and so did not choose to apply the jurisprudence of the ECtHR.

In *Bektesh in Macedonia v. Republic of Macedonia*, which involved a religious community, the Constitutional Court chose another strategy. It again referred to international law, such as Articles 18 and 29(2) of the Universal Declaration of Human Rights; Articles 18(1), 18(3) and 26 of the International Pact for Civic and Political Rights; and Articles 9 and 12 of the European Convention of Human Rights, including Article 1 of Protocol 12 of the same. In addition, although not initiated by the applicant, the court decided to directly apply the jurisprudence of the ECtHR (the court's decision) in the (*Belgian Linguistic Case, Judgment of 23 July 1968*) and the standpoint of the UN Human Rights Committee in *General Comment No. 18*.

On the other hand, in *Ljupcho Ristovski v. Skopje Second Basic Court* (U. No. 39/2012-0-0 of 12.09.2012), the Constitutional Court decided not to accept the applicants' request to directly apply the ruling of the ECtHR in *Kraus v. Poland*. The justification the Court gave was that the ruling could not be interpreted as a source of international law and that 'domestic courts in Macedonia work in accordance with the Constitution, the law and ratified international agreements that are in conformity with the Constitution'.

Considering that change is the expected result of court decisions (Miller 1969), we may conclude that there is inconsistency in the way the international court's decisions are applied by Macedonian courts and that a consistent gap between policies to apply decisions of international courts or refer to their jurisprudence (such as the case concerning the Civil Liability for Defamation and Libel Act, which requires Macedonian courts to apply the decisions of the ECtHR) and their actual implementation.

5 Conclusion

In the hierarchy of the Macedonian legal system, international treaties and recognised principles of international law stand below the Constitution but above all other sources of law. Article 118 of the Constitution stipulates that international agreements that are ratified and which are in accordance with the Constitution are an integral part of the domestic legal order and cannot be changed or derogated with laws. Considering that ratification is needed for an international legal act to be transformed into the national legal system, it might be concluded that in Macedonia a dualistic approach to the incorporation of international law into national law is taken.

Macedonian courts have the authority to perform their adjudication function on the basis of the Constitution, the laws and international agreements ratified in accordance with the Constitution of the Republic of Macedonia. However, the application of international and EU law is related to the capacity of judicial institutions to employ provisions from international legal documents and agreements. One in six accredited Macedonian universities specialise in international law, and one in eight in EU law. Since they do not have practical education in the application of international and EU law, we can conclude that while students have knowledge they lack the skills to apply international law. The Academy for the Training of Judges and Prosecutors plays an important role in building such capacity and raising awareness, but analysis shows their strategy to be highly dependent on donor-funded projects.

To depict the level of judicial application of international law, we have reviewed the case law of both the Constitutional Court and the basic and appellate courts. Macedonia has signed the Stabilisation and Association Agreement with the European Union and is well on its way in the process of approximating domestic legislation with the EU *acquis*. The review of case law also shows that although they do so infrequently, Macedonian courts apply the SAA and use it as primary source of law. This is also the case with the International Labour Office conventions, though not so much with the ECHR and the Aarhus Convention. While for the Aarhus Convention the courts opt to apply mirroring of the Convention in the Macedonian legal system, the analysis of the case law in the application of the ECHR has shown variations in how it is done: from indirectly referring to ECHR provisions to direct application of the Convention. The practice of the Constitutional Court in this respect is not very standardised, as it often uses the ECHR to justify its reasoning in its rulings. However, the analysis has also detected cases where the Court does not recognise the Convention as a sufficient source of law for it to base its decisions upon.

Finally, the most intriguing area is the application of international court decisions. The research has shown that although the decisions of international courts are compulsory and have to be applied, an analysis of the case law related to the decisions of the ICTY and the ECtHR shows that Macedonian courts are not very aware of this requirement. The Constitutional Court in particular lacks consistency in interpreting and applying ECtHR decisions. It diverges from them, uses them as a legal basis for judgments, refers to them to justify a decision or to reject an application, or states that international court decisions are not a sufficient basis for it to make a judgment.

References

Academy for the Training of Judges and Public Prosecutors (2006) Annual report

Academy for the Training of Judges and Public Prosecutors (2012) Annual report

Amrhein-Hofman C (2003) Monismus und Dualismus in den Völkerrechtslehren. Duncker & Humblot, Berlin, pp 80–144

Birdsall A (2007) Creating a more just order: the ad hoc international war crimes tribunal for the former Yugoslavia. Cooperation Conflict: J Nord Int Stud Assoc 42(4):397–418

Blankenagel A (1996) New rights and old rights, new symbols and old meanings: re-designing liberties and freedoms and post-socialist and post-Soviet constitutions. In: Sajo A (ed) Western rights? Post-communist application. Kluwer Law, Dordrecht, p 57

Bull H (1995) The anarchical society: a study of order in world politics. Macmillan, Basingstoke

Dabovik-Anastasovska J, Janevski A, Davitkovski D, Zdraveva N, Gavrilovik N (2011) Razvojot na Pravoto na intelektualna sopstvenost. Drzaven zavod za industriska sopstvenost, Skopje, p 24

Davitkovski B (2005) Efficient judiciary, citizen's service: introducing administrative courts in the Republic of Macedonia. Paper presented at conference on judicial reforms, Skopje

Davitkovski B, Pavlovska-Daneva A (2006) The administrative dispute in the Republic of Macedonia according to the new law on administrative disputes: the legal framework of judicial reform in the Republic of Macedonia

Gelevski S (1997a) Administrative law. Prosvetno Delo, Skopje

Gelevski S (1997b) A judicial control over the legality of administrative acts. Leg Stud J

Hristov A (1981) Administrative law. Prosvetno Delo, Skopje

Kambovski V (2008) The natural and legal essence of human rights. In: Kambovski V, Treneska Deskoska R, Ortakovski V (eds) European standards for human rights and their implementation in the legal system of the Republic of Macedonia. Macedonian Academy of Sciences, Skopje

Klimovski S (2005) Constitutional law and the judicial system. Prosvetno Delo, Skopje

Miller AS (1969) On the need for 'impact analysis' of Supreme Court decisions. In: Becker T (ed) The impact of Supreme Court decisions. Oxford University Press, New York

Pelivanova N, Dimeski B (2011) Efficiency of the judicial system in protecting citizens against administrative judicial acts: the case of Macedonia. Int J Court Adm (Arlington, VA)

Risteska M (2013) The EU role in promotion of good governance in Macedonia: Between democratic policy making and effective implementation of policies. Nationalities papers, 3/2013

Treneska-Deskovska R (2008) The constitutional concept of human rights in the Republic of Macedonia. In: Kambovski V, Treneska Deskoska R, Ortakovski V (eds) European standards for human rights and their implementation in the legal system of the Republic of Macedonia. Macedonian Academy of Sciences, Skopje

Volcansek ML (1989) Impact of judicial policies in the European Community: the Italian Constitutional Court and European Community law. Polit Rev Q 42:569

Weruszewski R (1992) Human rights and current constitutional debates in Central and Eastern European countries. In: Rosas A, Helgensen J (eds) The strength of diversity: human rights and pluralist democracy. Martinus Nijhoff, Dordrecht, p 191

Laws

Co-operation with the ICTY Act, Official Gazette of Republic of Macedonia No. 73/2007

Courts Act, Official Gazette Nos. 58/06, 35/08, 150/10

Higher Education Act, Official Gazette Nos. 35/08, 103/08, 26/09, 83/09, 99/09, 115/10, 17/11, 51/11, 123/12, 15/13, 24/13

Academy for the Training of Judges and Public Prosecutors Act, Official Gazette No. 13/2006
Ratification of the Convention on Access to Information, Public Participation in Decision-Making and Access to Justice in Environmental Matters (Aarhus Convention), Official Gazette No. 40/99
Civil Liability for Defamation and Libel Act, Official Gazette No. 143/2012
Environment Act, Official Gazette No. 53/05
Criminal Code, Official Gazette No. 37/96
Amnesty Act, Official Gazette No. 18/02
Free Access to Public Information Act, Official Gazette No. 13/06
SAA FYR Macedonia OJ L 49/1

Interviews

Interview with Konstadin Bogdanov, 23 April 2013
Interview with Vladimir Panchevski, President of the First Skopje Basic Court, 5 April 2013
Interview with Zoran Mihajloski, Appeal Court in Skopje, 26 April 2013
Interview with Atanas Georgievski, March 2013
Interview with Filip Medarski, March 2013

Judicial Application of International Law in Montenegro

Dušan S. Rakitić

1 Effect Afforded to International Law by the Constitution

The Constitution of the Republic of Montenegro (the Constitution) stipulates that 'ratified and published international agreements (treaties) and generally accepted rules of international law represent an integral part of the national legal system, possess primacy over domestic legislation, as well as direct effect whenever they regulate a social relation differently from internal legislation'.[1]

The Constitution envisages also that a law must be in conformity with the Constitution and ratified international agreements, whereas all other regulations shall be in conformity with the Constitution and the laws.[2]

As noted, the Constitution formally recognises both international treaties and generally accepted rules of international law. The latter, according to some interpretations, include customary international law and general principles of law. Due to the fact that there is no reliable source for determining the scope of the concept of generally accepted rules of international law, since that concept is not widely used in the international community, the practical applicability of the provision of the Constitution mandating the effect of generally accepted rules of international law is severely limited. Further evidence for the limited applicability of the subject constitutional provision may be found in a number of other constitutional provisions, which cite only international treaties as the source belonging to the realm of international law:

[1] Constitution of the Republic of Montenegro, Official Gazette of the Republic of Montenegro No. 1/2007, Part I, Article 9.

[2] Ibid, Part V, Article 145.

D.S. Rakitić (✉)
Faculty of Law, University of Belgrade, Belgrade, Serbia
e-mail: drakitic@ius.bg.ac.rs

S. Rodin, T. Perišin (eds.), *Judicial Application of International Law in Southeast Europe*, DOI 10.1007/978-3-662-46384-0_11

Grounds and equality (Part II, Article 17)

Rights and liberties shall be exercised by virtue of the Constitution and the *ratified international treaties*.

All persons shall be deemed equal before the law, regardless of any particularity or personal feature.

Ombudsman (Part II, Article 81)

The Ombudsman of the Republic of Montenegro is an independent and autonomous authority that implements measures for the protection of human rights and liberties.

The Ombudsman exercises its duties on the basis of the Constitution, the laws and the *ratified international agreements*, observing also the principles of justice and fairness.

Principles of the judiciary (Part III, Article 118)

The courts are autonomous and independent.

A court adjudicates on the basis of the Constitution, laws and *ratified and proclaimed international agreements*.

Establishment of extraordinary courts is prohibited.

Competence of the Constitutional Court (Part VI, Article 149)

The Constitutional Court decides:

1) whether laws are in compliance with the Constitution and with *ratified and proclaimed international treaties*.... (emphasis added).

In effect, the Constitution renders international law applicable in the Republic of Montenegro either in the form of ratified and published international agreements, or if it is deemed to fall within 'generally accepted rules of international law'. Whenever international law applies, it has primacy over national legislation. However, from the enumerated operative provisions of the Constitution it is obvious that the practical significance of both the reference to the generally accepted rules of international law, as well as to the direct effect of international law, is minimal, since the Constitution is centred on the model whereby international law in the form of treaties becomes part of the national law via ratification by the national legislature in the form of a law.

1.1 Self-Executing Effect

The Constitution affords international law, i.e. both ratified and published international treaties and generally accepted rules of international law, a self-executing effect whenever they regulate a matter differently from the national legislation. However, in practice such a broad grant of self-executing effect has been relied upon by the courts primarily in the field of human rights and fundamental freedoms.

1.2 *Effect Afforded to Secondary Acts Under International Treaty Law*

Like international treaties, secondary acts adopted under international treaties may become a part of the national legal system once they are ratified and proclaimed by the Parliament of the Republic of Montenegro.

However, certain decisions taken by the Stabilisation and Association Council (SA Council)[3] are binding for the Parties when made within the scope of the Framework of the Stabilisation and Association Agreement.[4] The Parties are obliged to take measures necessary to implement a decision—which means that the binding effect of a decision does not equal direct applicability. The SA Council is authorised to supervise the implementation and enforcement of the Stabilisation and Association Agreement (SAA), as well as to review issues under the SAA or any other bilateral/international issues of mutual interest. In order to achieve the objectives of the SAA, the SA Council is thus authorised to make decisions within the scope of the SAA, as specified therein.

1.3 *Harmonisation with EU Law*

By pronouncing international agreements as an integral part of the national legal system, the Constitution not only affords international agreements legal effect, but it also makes it necessary to harmonise national legislation with international law, i.e. the necessity to enact laws and regulations to elaborate and/or implement provisions of ratified international treaties. Due to the peculiar nomotechnics of European Union law, by far the greatest need is for harmonisation with EU acts.

Activities related to the harmonisation of national legislation, including pertinent respective compliance analysis, are performed by the Directorate for Legal Harmonisation operating within the Ministry of Foreign Affairs and European Integration.

The provisions of the Montenegro Stabilisation and Association Agreement[5] mirroring the EU Founding Treaties in the Montenegrin legal system have a status

[3] The SA Council consists of the EU Council members together with the members of the European Commission, on one hand, and members of the Government of Republic of Montenegro, on the other hand.

[4] The Stabilisation and Association Agreement between the Republic of Montenegro and the European Union was signed on 15 October 2007. The Agreement entered into force on 1 May 2010, after being ratified by the 27 EU Member States at that time.

[5] The Stabilisation and Association Agreement between the European Communities and their Member States of the one part, and the Republic of Montenegro, of the other part, signed on 15 October 2007, entered into force on 1 May 2010. http://ec.europa.eu/world/agreements/prepareCreateTreatiesWorkspace/treatiesGeneralData.do?step=0&redirect=true&treatyId=7281. Accessed 10 October 2014.

identical to all other ratified and proclaimed international treaties. Examples of the judicial application of such provisions either do not exist or are very rare.

Harmonisation of national legislation is assessed continuously and the results of the assessment are publicly available via reports issued within the European integration process. Both the reports on the realisation of the EU Accession Action Plan and of the SAA, as well as analytical reports on screening results, are available on the official website of the Ministry of Foreign Affairs and European Integration.[6]

2 The Court System and Grounds for the Application of International Law

According to the Constitution, all courts are obliged to adjudicate on the basis of the Constitution ratified and proclaimed international treaties and domestic laws. The legal system of the Republic of Montenegro adheres to the continental (civil law) tradition, so that lower courts are not formally obliged to rule in line with previous *rationes decidendi* of the higher courts. In other words, precedents are not a source of law and the *stare decisis* doctrine is not abided by. However, there are two significant deviations from this express rule. The first is grounded in a statutory mechanism, and the second is caused by pragmatic considerations. Firstly, the Law on Courts[7] authorises the Supreme Court to adopt, in plenary session, and publish 'general legal holdings' and 'general legal opinions' on issues which may affect the consistent interpretation of the Constitution and of national statutes. Moreover, a plenary session of any other court is empowered to adopt 'legal holdings' and to issue 'legal opinions' on matters of interpretation of law in the field of competence of that court.[8] Secondly, the case law of higher courts has a significant impact on the decision making of lower courts in practical terms due to the vertical hierarchy of the judicial system. The probability that a decision of a lower court is upheld is far greater if that decision is consistent with the previous relevant holdings of a higher court. The percentage of judgments that have been upheld by a higher court is the single most important factor determining advancement in the career of every judge, so it is understandable that judges are motivated to adhere to the case law of the higher courts.[9]

The case law of the Constitutional Court has the potential to promote awareness of international law in the law-practising community of Montenegro, since that

[6] Ministry of Foreign Affairs and European Integration. http://www.mvpei.gov.me/rubrike/Evropske-integracije/. Accessed 10 October 2014.

[7] Law on Courts [*Zakon o sudovima*], Official Gazette of the Republic of Montenegro, Nos. 5/2002, 49/2004, 22/2008, 39/2011, 46/2013.

[8] Law on Courts, Articles 27, 28, 96-28.

[9] Law on the Judicial Council [*Zakon o sudskom savjetu*] Official Gazette of the Republic of Montenegro, Nos. 13/2008, 39/2011, 31/2012, 46/2013, 51/2013, Articles 32a and 34a.

Court regularly refers to international law, primarily to the European Convention for the Protection of Human Rights and Fundamental Freedoms (ECHR) and to other treaties promulgated within the Council of Europe, as well as to the case law of the European Court of Human Rights.[10] Entire decisions of that court, including both holdings and rationale, enacted during a calendar year are published on that court's website in the form of a single file.[11]

The Supreme Court refers regularly to international treaties as well, primarily to the ECHR[12] and to other treaties in the field of human rights and fundamental freedoms, and increasingly to the conventions enacted under the auspices of the International Labour Organization.[13]

The Supreme Court is vested with specific competence that entails a statutory duty to apply specific standards from the case law of the European Court of Human Rights. The Law on the Protection of the Right to Trial within a Reasonable Time[14] introduced two specific procedural instruments for the protection of the subject right. The second instrument introduced by that statute, which may be applied only when the first one has been exhausted, is a lawsuit for just satisfaction. The only court competent to adjudicate upon such lawsuits is the Supreme Court. In doing so, the Supreme Court needs to assess the alleged violation of the right to trial within a reasonable time, as well as the duration of the reasonable time in each particular case, by relying on the case law of the European Court of Human Rights.[15] Decisions of the Supreme Court are available online through the centralised database of the Montenegrin courts' case law.[16]

---

[10] Decision of the Constitutional Court, No. Už-III 233/10 of 27 November 2012; Decision of the Constitutional Court, No. Už-III 348/11 of 20 June 2011; Decision of the Constitutional Court, No. Už-II 12/09 of 30 September 2010; Decision of the Constitutional Court, No. U-I 17/10 of 22 September 2011.

[11] Constitutional Court of the Republic of Montenegro. http://www.ustavnisudcg.co.me/slike/ustavnisud/praksa.htm. Accessed 10 October 2014. It should be noted that as of 10 October 2014 the website contains only decisions enacted until the end of 2012, and that no decisions from either 2013 or 2014 are available.

[12] The European Court of Human Rights considers the ECHR to be in force in respect of, and binding upon, Montenegro continuously since 3 March 2004. *Bijelić v. Montenegro and Serbia*. App. no. 11890/05 (ECHR-II 28 April 2009).

[13] Decision of the Supreme Court of Montenegro, Rev. No. 490/11 of May 10, 2011; Decision of the Supreme Court of Montenegro, Rev. No. 490/11 of 10 May 2011; Decision of the Supreme Court of Montenegro, Tpz 38/13 of 20 December 2013; Decision of the Supreme Court of Montenegro, Tpz 8/2014, of 26 March 2014; Decision of the Supreme Court of Montenegro, Rev. No. 139/14, of 2 April 2014.

[14] Law on the Protection of the Right to a Trial within a Reasonable Time [*Zakon o zaštiti prava na suđenje u razumnom roku*] Official Gazette of the Republic of Montenegro, No. 11/2007.

[15] Ibid, Article 2.

[16] The database contains all the decisions of all the courts in Montenegro, except the Constitutional Court, starting from approximately 2010 or 2011. http://sudovi.me. In addition to the database, the decisions of the Supreme Court have been made available in an annual bulletin, in the form of a single file containing all the decisions from that year. Both the online database and the bulletin contain entire decisions, including both the holding and the rationale of each decision. The

Based on the case law of the past several years, which has been made publicly available, it can be concluded that the courts are acting as a progressive rather than a conservative force. Such a conclusion arises from the fact that the highest courts do not seem reluctant to refer to the international treaties and to the case law of international courts interpreting such treaties. This tendency is particularly pronounced in respect of the ECHR and the case law of the European Court of Human Rights.

The Government of Montenegro adopted in June 2013 action plans for reforms in areas covered by the *acquis* in Chapter 23—Judiciary and Fundamental Rights,[17] and Chapter 24—Justice, Freedom and Security.[18] Negotiations on these chapters commenced in December 2013.

2.1 The Court System

Courts in the Republic of Montenegro are organised on the basis of the Law on Courts, which stipulates that judicial power is exercised by the courts of general and special jurisdiction, whereas the courts of general jurisdiction are the basic courts, the higher courts, the court of appeal and the Supreme Court of the Republic of Montenegro—the highest court in the country. The courts of special jurisdiction are commercial and administrative courts.

Montenegro has 15 basic courts, two higher courts, one appellate and one Supreme Court. According to the European Commission's Progress Report for 2013, the random allocation of cases is ensured in general, with the exception of small courts where this is not possible for practical reasons.[19]

First-instance jurisdiction mostly lies with basic courts as they try all cases except criminal acts for which the punishment may be imprisonment for more than 10 years, which, together with a number of crimes enumerated in the Law on Courts, are conferred upon higher courts. Higher courts also decide on appeals against judgments of basic courts. Disputes between companies are tried by specialised commercial courts. The Court of Appeals only decides upon appeals

published texts do not contain the names of the parties and of other persons and entities, but only their initials. As of October 2014, only the bulletin edition for 2011 has been published. http://sudovi.me/podaci/vrhs/dokumenta/574.pdf. Accessed 10 October 2014.

[17] Action Plan for Chapter 23—Judiciary and Fundamental Rights, the Government of Montenegro, 27 June 2013. http://www.gov.me/ResourceManager/FileDownload.aspx?rId=138835&rType=2. Accessed 10 October 2014.

[18] Action Plan for Chapter 24—Justice, Freedom and Security, the Government of Montenegro, 27 June 2013. http://www.gov.me/ResourceManager/FileDownload.aspx?rId=138836&rType=2. Accessed 10 October 2014.

[19] Commission Staff Working Document, Montenegro 2013 Progress Report, Brussels, 16 October 2013, SWD (2013) 411 final, p. 36. http://ec.europa.eu/enlargement/pdf/key_documents/2013/package/mn_rapport_2013.pdf. Accessed 10 October 2014.

against judgments of higher courts, as well as against judgments of commercial courts.

The Administrative Court adjudicates on administrative disputes, i.e. disputes over the legality of administrative decisions, while the Supreme Court decides on extraordinary legal remedies filed against judgments of all other courts. In its plenary session, the Supreme Court, as has already been explained, also adopts general legal holdings and issues general legal opinions, with the aim of harmonising the case law.

2.2 *Ensuring Harmonised Interpretation of Law*

Harmonising case law is an obligation imposed, by virtue of the Constitution, upon the Supreme Court.[20]

As has already been pointed out, the Law on Courts contains mechanisms dedicated to securing unified interpretation of law by the judiciary, both vertically and horizontally. Vertical harmonisation is achieved by virtue of the power given to the plenary session of the Supreme Court to adopt general legal holdings and to publish general legal opinions with the aim of harmonising the practice of all the other courts. The power of each court's plenary session to adopt legal holdings and to issue legal opinions for matters falling within the competence of that court serves harmonisation at the horizontal level. The technique which the legislator applied in respect of these mechanisms is peculiar and should be noted: nowhere in the law is it expressly stipulated that adherence to the general legal holdings and opinions of the Supreme Court, and to the legal holdings and opinions of other courts respectively, is obligatory for any particular judge. The law merely posits the aim of these mechanisms: achieving a unified interpretation of law.[21] It is left to the judges to draw the obvious conclusion that if these mechanisms are to serve their purpose, they need to be followed in comparable and materially similar situations. In this way, the law does not expressly bestow the status of source of law upon court precedents, but at the same time it takes significant steps in that direction.

In addition to the described statutory mechanisms, a major factor of harmonisation of case law within the system of courts is the pragmatic reasons of pursuit of career advancement by the judges. The lower the number of cases adjudicated by a judge that are remanded by a higher court, the greater are the chances that the judge will advance in his or her career.[22] For the purpose of assessing the strength of this factor, one should consider that the European Commission's Montenegro Progress Report for 2014 contains the following assessment:

[20] Article 124 of the Constitution of the Republic of Montenegro confers the following duty upon the Supreme Court: 'The Supreme Court shall secure unified enforcement of laws by the courts'.

[21] Law on Courts, Articles 27, 28, 96-28.

[22] Law on Judicial Council, Articles 32a and 34a.

> The systems of recruitment and career development of judges and prosecutors still leave room for undue influence affecting the independence of the judiciary. Work on the legislative basis for introducing a single, countrywide recruitment system for judges and prosecutors, a system of voluntary horizontal mobility and a new system of promotion of judges and prosecutors and of periodic professional assessment of their performance is at an advanced stage.[23]

Decisions of the Constitutional Court influence the case law of all other courts both directly and indirectly. The direct impact is realised through the mechanism of 'constitutional complaint', which may be filed with that court against a decision of any public authority, including courts, infringing upon the rights and liberties guaranteed by the Constitution. The constitutional complaint may be filed only upon the exhaustion of all other legal remedies.[24] The case law of the Constitutional Court indirectly affects the practice of all other courts by virtue of the power of that court to review the constitutionality of laws and regulations.[25]

2.3 *Grounds for Review of Compliance with International Law*

The Constitution bestows upon the Constitutional Court the power to review the constitutionality of laws and regulations (bylaws) and to strike down all laws that it finds in contravention of the Constitution or of ratified and proclaimed international treaties. In line with the hierarchy of sources of law adopted by the Constitution, which assumes that international law is absorbed by the national legal system in the form of laws on ratification of international treaties, grounds for the review of bylaws and regulations below the level of laws do not encompass international law, but only national laws and the Constitution.[26]

2.4 *Preliminary References of Constitutionality*

National courts of Montenegro may not exercise a reference for a preliminary ruling of the Court of Justice of the European Union because Montenegro has not yet become a member of the EU.

A national court may resort to the mechanism of 'international legal assistance' and seek interpretation of a treaty or of another provision of international or

[23] Commission Staff Working Document, Montenegro 2014 Progress Report, Brussels, 8 October 2014, SWD (2014) 301 final, pp. 35, 36. http://ec.europa.eu/enlargement/pdf/key_documents/2014/20141008-montenegro-progress-report_en.pdf. Accessed 10 October 2014.

[24] Constitution of the Republic of Montenegro, Article 149(1).

[25] Ibid.

[26] Ibid.

national law in accordance with the procedure laid down in the appropriate international treaty (the ECHR, or usually a bilateral treaty on international legal cooperation). However, the interpretation obtained on such grounds would not be binding either upon the court that requested it, or upon other courts in Montenegro.

It should be noted that the Law on the Constitutional Court stipulates that if an issue of compatibility of law with the Constitution or with a ratified international treaty is raised before a court in the course of court proceedings, the court should suspend the proceedings and initiate a procedure for the review of constitutionality of the disputed act before the Constitutional Court.[27] There is no available data on whether and to what extent the courts abide by this obligation.

2.5 General Grounds for the Application of International Law

The Constitution proclaims supremacy of international law, consisting of both ratified treaties and generally accepted rules of international law, over national law, as well as its direct effect on all matters regulated differently by national laws.[28] However, in the operative provision of the Constitution in which the grounds on which courts adjudicate are set forth, only ratified and proclaimed international treaties are enumerated, subsequently to the national laws. This means that the operative provision on the grounds for adjudication not only disregards the constitutional declaration of applicability of generally accepted rules of international law, but that the same provision disregards the constitutional declaration of the supremacy of international law over national laws.[29]

The declaration of the supremacy of international law over national laws, including direct effect on matters regulated differently by national laws, presupposes an instruction for the courts to interpret national legislation in line with international law. However, it should be noted that an explicit order to that effect is absent from both the Constitution and the Law on Courts.

2.6 Specific Grounds for the Application of International Law

Specific grounds for the application of international law that are presently in force within the legal system of Montenegro may be grouped in two categories.

[27] Law on the Constitutional Court [*Zakon o Ustavnom sudu*] Official Gazette of the Republic of Montenegro, No. 64/2008.

[28] Constitution of the Republic of Montenegro, Article 9.

[29] Constitution of the Republic of Montenegro, Article 118(2).

Firstly, a specific statutory reference to the case law of the European Court of Human Rights was enacted in 2007 in the form of the Law on the Protection of the Right to Trial within a Reasonable Time.[30] This law provided participants in civil, criminal and administrative court proceedings affecting the protection of fundamental rights within the scope of the ECHR with two specific procedural instruments (a request for the acceleration of proceedings and a lawsuit for just satisfaction) to safeguard their right to trial within a reasonable time. The law stipulates that both the existence of an alleged violation of the subject right, as well as the duration of reasonable time in each particular case, would be determined by Montenegrin courts in accordance with the case law of the European Court of Human Rights.[31] The European Commission's Montenegro Progress Report for 2011 was the last occurrence of the negative assessment that the Law on the Protection of the Right to Trial within a Reasonable Time had not been implemented effectively. Subsequent reports, for 2012, 2013 and 2014, did not encompass that assessment.[32] Between 10 September 2014 and 10 October 2014, during a period randomly chosen for sampling purposes, the Supreme Court adopted just over 320 decisions in total. Among these, only one was taken upon a lawsuit for just satisfaction filed pursuant to the Law on the Protection of the Right to Trial within a Reasonable Time. From the beginning of 2014 until 10 October 2014, the Supreme Court adopted a total of 32 decisions upon lawsuits for just satisfaction.[33]

Secondly, statutes on civil and criminal procedure provide specific grounds for retrial if the European Court of Human Rights has determined violation of a human right or fundamental freedom guaranteed by the Convention for the Protection of Human Rights and Fundamental Freedoms, or, in the case of the statute on criminal procedure, if some other international court whose competence is recognised by Montenegro finds a comparable violation.

The Law on Civil Procedure stipulates that the request for retrial may be filed, within 3 months from the final judgment of the European Court of Human Rights

[30] Law on the Protection of the Right to a Trial within a Reasonable Time [*Zakon o zaštiti prava na suđenje u razumnom roku*], Official Gazette of the Republic of Montenegro, No. 11/2007.

[31] Ibid, Article 2.

[32] Commission Staff Working Paper, Montenegro 2011 Progress Report, Brussels, 12 October 2001, SEC (2011) 1204 final, p. 57. http://ec.europa.eu/enlargement/pdf/key_documents/2011/package/mn_rapport_2011_en.pdf. Accessed 10 October 2014; Commission Staff Working Document, Montenegro 2012 Progress Report, Brussels, 10 October 2012, SWD (2012) 331 final, http://ec.europa.eu/enlargement/pdf/key_documents/2012/package/mn_rapport_2012_en.pdf. Accessed 10 October 2014; Commission Staff Working Document, Montenegro 2013 Progress Report, Brussels, 16 October 2013, SWD (2013) 411 final. http://ec.europa.eu/enlargement/pdf/key_documents/2013/package/mn_rapport_2013.pdf. Accessed 10 October 2014; Commission Staff Working Document, Montenegro 2014 Progress Report, Brussels, 8 October 2014, SWD (2014) 301 final. http://ec.europa.eu/enlargement/pdf/key_documents/2014/20141008-montenegro-progress-report_en.pdf. Accessed 10 October 2014.

[33] Courts of Montenegro, the Supreme Court, database of decisions. http://sudovi.me/vrhs/odluke/. Accessed 10 October 2014.

finding infringement of a human right or a fundamental freedom, in contravention of the ECHR. The request should be filed with the Montenegrin court that enacted the decision that has been found to represent an infringement of a human right or fundamental freedom. The request is allowed only if the infringement established by the European Court of Human Rights may not be redressed in any other manner. The court acting pursuant to such a request is bound by the holding of the judgment of the European Court of Human Rights.[34]

The equivalent provision of the Code of Criminal Procedure[35] is of broader scope than the provision of the Law on Civil Procedure. The difference is twofold: firstly, the grounds for retrial may also be a decision of any other international court established by virtue of a treaty that has been ratified by Montenegro. Secondly, it is not necessary for the retrial to be the only remaining means by which the violation of the human right or a fundamental freedom may be redressed. It suffices that redress is possible by way of retrial. Taking into consideration that until Montenegro accedes to the European Union and thus falls under the jurisdiction of the Court of Justice of the European Union that the only international courts other than the Court of Human Rights are those that deal with criminal matters, it is evident that the identified differences are purely of theoretic significance.

It should be noted that the Law on Administrative Disputes[36] lacks a provision with an effect equivalent to the provisions of the Law on Civil Procedures and of the Code on Criminal Procedure described in previous paragraphs.

An objection may be put forth in respect of the respective provisions of both the Law on Civil Procedure and the Code of Criminal Procedure: they refer only to decisions of international courts, and thus fail to include the possibility that the findings of other bodies established under international treaties to which Montenegro is a party, e.g. decisions upon individual complaints issued by the committees tasked with monitoring implementation of human rights treaties adopted under the auspices of the United Nations,[37] serve as grounds for retrial. The significance of this objection in the case of Montenegro in practical terms is minimal, since the applicable rules of admissibility of individual complaints for all these committees deny admissibility to the complaints that have been submitted to other regional mechanisms or international bodies. Taking into account the membership of Montenegro in the Council of Europe, it would be highly unlikely for a Montenegrin entity to opt for filing a complaint with one of the UN committees instead of seeking redress from the European Court of Human Rights.

[34] Law on Civil Procedure [*Zakon o parničnom postupku*], Official Gazette of the Republic of Montenegro, Nos. 22/2004 and 76/2006, Article 428a.

[35] Code of Criminal Procedure [*Zakonik o krivičnom postupku*], Official Gazette of the Republic of Montenegro, Nos. 57/2009 and 49/2010, Article 424(1.6).

[36] Law on Administrative Disputes [*Zakon o sudskim sporovima*] Official Gazette of the Republic of Montenegro, Nos. 60/2005, 32/2011.

[37] E.g. Human Rights Committee, Committee on Elimination of Discrimination against Women, Committee against Torture, Committee on the Elimination of Racial Discrimination, etc.

3 Application of International Law in Practice

National courts apply international law mostly in the fields of human rights and fundamental freedoms. The source of international law that is predominantly applied by the judiciary is multilateral treaties, mostly those enacted under the auspices of the Council of Europe. The case law of international courts is not applied by the courts, with a major exception being the case law of the Court of Human Rights, which is relied upon for purposes of interpreting the Convention for the Protection of Human Rights and Fundamental Freedoms. Montenegrin courts, primarily the highest courts—the Constitutional Court and the Supreme Court—invoke the case law of the European Court of Human Rights not only *sua sponte* but also *ex officio*, i.e. upon their own initiative. However, in the 2012 Montenegro Progress Report, the EU Commission included the following assessment: 'Shortcomings persist in the protection of human rights by judicial and law enforcement authorities, some of them in relation to alignment with European standards and European Court of Human Rights case law'.[38]

References to the case law of other national courts, e.g. the German Federal Constitutional Court, cannot be found in practice.

Customary international law may be deemed a source of international law that is in force in Montenegro on the grounds of a declaratory provision of the Constitution, which proclaims that 'generally accepted rules of international law' are a source of law immediately below the Constitution, although constitutional provisions which would make effect of such law in the legal system are lacking. This deficiency naturally causes the courts to refrain from relying directly on customary international law, even as a tool of interpretation.

International law finds its way into the case law of Montenegrin courts also by virtue of the activity of the Supreme Court. A significant example of such activity is the issuance of guidelines for determining the level of pecuniary compensation in defamation cases commenced against the media in line with the case law of the European Court of Human Rights.[39]

---

[38] Commission Staff Working Document (2012) Montenegro 2012 Progress Report, Brussels SWD (2012) 331 final, pp. 12–13. http://ec.europa.eu/enlargement/pdf/key_documents/2012/package/mn_rapport_2012_en.pdf. Accessed 10 October 2014.

[39] Commission Staff Working Paper (2011) Montenegro 2011 Progress Report, Brussels, 12 October 2011, SEC (2011) 1204 final, p. 16. http://ec.europa.eu/enlargement/pdf/key_documents/2011/package/mn_rapport_2011_en.pdf. Accessed 10 October 2014.

3.1 *The Constitutional Court's Review of National Legislation*

As regards the application of international treaties for the purpose of *in abstracto* constitutional review, the case law of the Constitutional Court shows that in a significant number of decisions the Constitutional Court relies on an international treaty, particularly on the ECHR. Out of a total of 17 decisions it enacted in 2011 in respect of constitutionality and/or compliance with international law of statutes, the Constitutional Court assessed compliance with multilateral treaties in seven cases, and in all these cases one of the conventions of the Council of Europe served as grounds of review. Out of these seven cases, in four the review was based on the Convention for the Protection of Human Rights and Fundamental Freedoms.

An example of such practice is the Decision of the Constitutional Court No. U-I 17/10 of 22 September 2011, whereby the Court established that Article 112(4) of the Civil Servants Act allowed arbitrary conduct by administrative agencies when deciding on the rights of employed civil servants, and that this was therefore unacceptable in a democratic society and in contravention of the ECHR. The rationale of this decision included the following assessment:

> ...exclusion of the right to appeal (initiate court proceeding) against the decision of administrative authority is contrary to the right to an effective remedy prescribed by Article 13 of the ECHR.[40]

Another example of *in abstracto* constitutional review is the Decision of the Constitutional Court U-I No. 12/11 of 24 March 2011.[41] The Court adjudicated on the compliance of the Law on the Census of Population, Households and Dwellings for 2011[42] with the ECHR and with the Framework Convention for the Protection of National Minorities, finding the law compliant with both treaties.

By virtue of another decision,[43] the Court rejected a lawsuit submitted by eight Members of Parliament which challenged Article 11(1) of the General Law on Education.[44] The challenged provision categorised the Serbian language as a minority language in Montenegro. The Court found the provision to be compliant both with the Constitution and with the provisions of the European Charter for Regional or Minority Languages, the Framework Convention for the Protection of

---

[40] Decision of the Constitutional Court U-I No. 17/10 of 22 September 2011, Bulletin of the Constitutional Court for 2011. http://www.ustavnisudcg.co.me/slike/ustavnisud/Bilten%202011.htm. Accessed 10 October 2014.

[41] Ibid.

[42] Law on the Census of Population, Households and Dwellings for 2011, Official Gazette of the Republic of Montenegro, Nos. 41/10, 44/10 and 75/10.

[43] Decision of the Constitutional Court U-I Nos. 27/10, 30/10, and 34/10 of 24 March 2011, Bulletin of the Constitutional Court for 2011. http://www.ustavnisudcg.co.me/slike/ustavnisud/Bilten%202011.htm. Accessed 10 October 2014.

[44] General Law on Education, Official Gazette of the Republic of Montenegro, Nos. 64/02, 31/05, 49/07 and 45/10.

National Minorities, as well as with the Recommendations Regarding the Education Rights of National Minorities issued by the OSCE High Commissioner on National Minorities, The Hague, in 1996.

3.2 Practice of the Constitutional Court in Individual Cases

The Constitutional Court is competent to adjudicate in respect of individual cases upon individual constitutional complaints.[45]

An analysis of the case law of the Constitutional Court shows that it is common for the Constitutional Court to apply not only international treaty law but also the case law of international courts, primarily the case law of the European Court of Human Rights, primarily for the purpose of interpreting the ECHR.

In the last 2 years for which data are available—2011 and 2012—among the cases commenced by virtue of constitutional complaints against acts of state authorities with individual effect, less than 10 % did not include an assessment of compliance with a multilateral international treaty, primarily with the European Convention for Human Rights and Fundamental Freedoms.

Some of the decisions that may serve as an example of the court's practice in individual cases are the following:

- in Decision Už-III No. 348/11 of 20 June 2011, the court called upon Article 5 (unlawful deprivation of liberty) of the ECHR, a position statement of the European Court of Human Rights on the respective Article, as well as upon the relevant case law of the European Court of Human Rights in respect of the application of the Article;
- the Constitutional Court called upon Article 5 ECHR in several decisions enacted in the course of 2011: Decision Už-III No. 74/09 (infringement of Article 5(4) ECHR, Decision Už-III No. 533/10 (infringement of Article 5 (3) ECHR), Decision Už-III No. 464/11 (infringement of Article 5(1–3) and Article 6(2) ECHR);
- by virtue of its Decision Už-III No. 12/09 of 30 September 2010, the Constitutional Court found that the Supreme Court had violated the complainant's right to access the court and to an effective remedy by insisting on an excessively formal interpretation of the procedural requirements for seeking redress from the Supreme Court as the highest judicial instance;

[45] The Constitutional Court is established by virtue of the Constitution. The most important function of this court is general normative review, i.e. assessment of the conformity of legislative acts of general applicability (laws and government regulations) with the Constitution and ratified treaties. Protection of human rights, which is also within that court's competence, is no less important. All decisions of the Constitutional Court are executable, and there are no legal means for challenging them.

- in 2011 the Constitutional Court ruled favourably on several constitutional complaints which claimed violation of the rights under Article 6 ECHR (right to a fair trial). These were decisions Už-III No. 28/09, Už-III No. 112/09, Už-III No. 128/09, Už-III No. 99/10, Už-III No. 135/10, Už-III No. 155/10, Už-III No. 205/10, Už-III No. 380/10, Už-III No. 439/10, Už-III No. 462/10 and Už-III No. 291/11.[46]

The Constitutional Court has in recent years been relying extensively on the case law of the European Court of Human Rights for the purpose of interpreting the ECHR. As examples of such references, the following decisions may serve:

- Decision Už-III No. 348/11 of 20 June 2011[47]—the court relied on a number of holdings of the European Court of Human Rights for the purpose of justifying its findings in respect of alleged violation of Article 5(1 and 3) ECHR (*W. v. Switzerland,*[48] *Kemmache v. France,*[49] *Nikolova v. Bulgaria,*[50] *Trzaska v. Poland,*[51] *Yagci & Sargin v. Turkey,*[52] *Neumeister v. Austria,*[53] *Jablonski v. Poland,*[54] as well as in respect of alleged violations of the right to a fair trial and of the presumption of innocence, i.e. of Article 6(1 and 2) ECHR (*Barbera, Messegue, Jabardo v. Spain,*[55] *Matijašević v. Serbia*[56]);
- Decision Už-III No. 12/09 of 30 September 2010[57]—the court cited certain decisions of the European Court of Human Rights as sources of rules on the legality of limitations of access to the court (*Golder v. UK,,*[58] *Philis v. Greece*[59]),

[46] Bulletin of the Constitutional Court for 2011. http://www.ustavnisudcg.co.me/slike/ustavnisud/Bilten%202011.htm. Accessed 10 October 2014.

[47] Ibid.

[48] *W. v. Switzerland*, App. no. 14379/88 (ECHR 1993).

[49] *Kemmache v. France* (No. 3) App. no. 17621/91 (ECHR 1994).

[50] *Nikolova v. Bulgaria* [GC] App. no. 31195/96 (ECHR 1999).

[51] *Trzaska v. Poland*, App. no. 25792/94 (ECHR 2000).

[52] *Yagci & Sargin v. Turkey*, App. nos. 16419/90 and 16426/90, Commission decision of 10 July 1991, Decisions and Reports 71, p. 253. It should be noted that the Constitutional Court wrongly cited the date of issuance and publication details of this decision.

[53] *Neumeister v. Austria*, App. no. 1936/63, 27 June 1968, Series A no. 8. The Constitutional Court wrongly referred to a judgment issued by the European Court of Human Rights in a dispute between the same parties 6 years later, the subject of which had been the alleged violation of the applicant's rights under Art. 50 ECHR (*Neumeister v. Austria*, App. no. 1936/63, 7 May 1974, Series A no. 17).

[54] *Jablonski v. Poland* (just satisfaction), App. no. 33492/96 (ECHR 2000).

[55] *Barbera, Messegue, Jabardo v. Spain*, App. nos. 10588/83, 10590/83, 10589/83, Commission decision of 11 October 1985, Decisions and Reports 44, p. 149. The Constitutional Court wrongly stated the date of issuance and publication details of this decision.

[56] *Matijašević v. Serbia* (just satisfaction) App. no. 23037/04 (ECHR 2006-X).

[57] Bulletin of the Constitutional Court for 2011 http://www.ustavnisudcg.co.me/slike/ustavnisud/bilten2010.htm. Accessed 10 October 2014.

[58] *Golder v. United Kingdom* (just satisfaction), App. no. 4451/70, 21 February 1975, Series A no. 18.

[59] *Philis v. Greece* (just satisfaction), App. nos. 12750/87, 13780/88, 14003/88, 27 August 1991, Series A no. 209.

as well as of the rule stipulating that a party may not suffer adverse consequences of a court's failure to instruct it on the proper amount of the court filing fee (*Garzičić v. Montenegro*[60]).

3.3 Practice of the Supreme Court

The Supreme Court, as well, in its jurisdiction applies international law, mainly the law contained in human rights treaties.

The following decisions may serve as examples of the Supreme Court's application of treaty law:

- Decision Rev. No. 490/11 of 10 May 2011,[61] whereby the Supreme Court applied the UN Convention on the Rights of the Child (Article 9(3)) to issues related to a child's right to maintain personal relations and contact with both parents on a regular basis;
- by virtue of Decision Rev. No. 139/14 of 2 April 2014,[62] the Supreme Court denied the extraordinary remedy of revision against a judgment of a lower court; the request for revision alleged violation of several multilateral treaties to which Montenegro was a party on the grounds of deprivation of the right to appeal in employment-related disciplinary proceedings; the court summarily dismissed allegations that several treaty provisions had been violated: Article 2(3) of the International Pact on Civil and Political Rights, Article 7 of ILO Convention No. 158, as well as Article 24 of the Revised European Social Charter.

On both of these occasions the Supreme Court simply stated its assessment of whether or not a given treaty had been violated, without undertaking to justify such an assessment and without citing any interpretative authority.

It should be noted that the Supreme Court has shown particular deference to a judgment of the European Court of Human Rights whereby infringement of human rights and fundamental freedoms was found to have been committed by the Supreme Court itself.[63] After that judgment of the European Court of Human Rights was passed in September 2010, the Supreme Court has cited it on two occasions in which it needed to interpret the guarantee of access to the court.[64]

---

[60] *Garzičić v. Montenegro*, App. no. 17931/07 (ECHR 2010).

[61] Bulletin of the Supreme Court for 2011. http://sudovi.me/podaci/vrhs/dokumenta/574.pdf. Accessed 10 October 2014.

[62] Courts of Montenegro, the Supreme Court, database of decisions. http://sudovi.me/vrhs/odluke/. Accessed 10 October 2014.

[63] *Garzičić v. Montenegro* (n 60).

[64] Decision Rev. 422/14 of 3 June 2014; Decision Rev. 336/12 of 13 December 2012, the Courts of Montenegro, the Supreme Court, database of decisions. http://sudovi.me/vrhs/odluke/. Accessed 10 October 2014.

As has already been noted, the Supreme Court has a duty to rely on the case law of the European Court of Human Rights when it adjudicates upon lawsuits for just satisfaction submitted pursuant to the Law on the Protection of the Right to Trial within a Reasonable Time.[65] A comparison of randomly chosen decisions from 2011 and from 2014 shows marked progress in the court's reasoning. In Decision Tpz. No. 1/11 of 28 March 2011,[66] the court did not refer to the case law of the European Court of Human Rights at all, but established an infringement of the right to trial within a reasonable time solely on the basis of the applicable national statute. In contrast, two out of three randomly chosen decisions from 2013 to 2014 clearly show an evolution in the court's reasoning—express references to the case law of the European Court of Human Rights are made *sua sponte* for the purpose of justifying assessments made in the respective decisions:

- Decision Tpz. No. 38/13 of 20 December 2013[67]—the Supreme Court cited *Rezgui v. France*[68] and *Kostovski v. Macedonia*[69] as authorities for its interpretation that the time period of proceedings subject to review may not encompass the time spent by the applicant on attempting to pursue a remedy that the court finds inappropriate;
- Decision Tpz. No. 39/13 of 20 December 2013[70]—the Supreme Court limited its analysis to the assessment of whether concrete steps of the subject enforcement procedure were taken in accordance with the applicable procedural statute, and, having found that all steps were taken within statutory terms, dismissed the lawsuit without making a reference to any judgment of the European Court of Human Rights;
- Decision Tpz. No. 8/2014 of 26 March 2014[71]—the Supreme Court cited several judgments of the European Court of Human Rights as source of the rule of interpretation on the repeated remanding of a case by a higher court (*Pavlyulynets v. Ukraine*,[72] *Wierciszewska v. Poland*,[73] *Parizov v. FYROM*[74]), as well as of the position that two periods of a court's inactivity, in total

[65] Law on the Protection of the Right to a Trial within a Reasonable Time [*Zakon o zaštiti prava na suđenje u razumnom roku*], Official Gazette of the Republic of Montenegro, No. 11/2007, Article 2.

[66] Bulletin of the Supreme Court for 2011. http://sudovi.me/podaci/vrhs/dokumenta/574.pdf. Accessed 10 October 2014.

[67] Courts of Montenegro, the Supreme Court, database of decisions. http://sudovi.me/vrhs/odluke/. Accessed 10 October 2014.

[68] *Rezgui v. France* (dec.) App. no. 49859/99 (ECHR 2000-XI).

[69] No such decision may be found in the HUDOC database of the European Court of Human Rights case law.

[70] Courts of Montenegro, the Supreme Court, database of decisions. http://sudovi.me/vrhs/odluke/. Accessed 10 October 2014.

[71] Ibid.

[72] *Pavlyulynets v. Ukraine*, App. no. 70767/01 (ECHR 2005).

[73] *Wierciszewska v. Poland*, App. no. 41431/98 (ECHR 2003).

[74] *Parizov v. 'the Former Yugoslav Republic of Macedonia'*, App. no. 14258/03 (ECHR 2008).

20 months long, amount to a violation of the right to trial within a reasonable time (*Napijalo v. Croatia*[75]).

3.4 Practice of Courts of General Jurisdiction and of Commercial Courts

It is noticeable that basic, appellate and commercial courts apply international law, but almost exclusively as result of the fact that the lawsuit invoked international law. Since the protection of human rights is mostly provided through the mechanism of a constitutional complaint at the level of the Constitutional Court, partly at the level of the Supreme Court on the grounds of a lawsuit for just satisfaction, the lower courts are often faced with international law regulating fields other than human rights. The following decisions may serve as an example of such practice:

- Decision of the Basic Court in Podgorica P. No. 5341/10 of 10 May 2012[76]—the plaintiff invoked Article 11 of the ILO Convention No. 158 in respect of termination of employment at the initiative of the employer; the court found that the employer had failed to respect the right to a reasonable notice period;
- Decision of the Commercial Court in Podgorica P. No. 252/12 of 15 November 2012[77]—the court *sua sponte* applied the Madrid Agreement Concerning the International Registration of Marks, Article 4 (effects of international registration);
- Decision of the Appellate Court in Podgorica Pž. No. 729/12 of 25 December 2012[78]—the court remanded the case to a lower court on appeal, approving the appellant's claim that the Convention on the Limitation Period in the International Sale of Goods (New York, 1974) had been applicable due to its supremacy over national law.

It is difficult to find examples of a lower court applying international law in the form of holdings of international courts. Even the case law of the European Court of Human Rights as a source of rules for interpreting or even complementing the ECHR is not relied upon. This is understandable in light of the fact that lower courts in most cases do not rely on international law *sua sponte*, but only when they review claims made by the parties. The parties, however, refrain from grounding their

[75] *Napijalo v. Croatia*, App. no. 66485/01 (ECHR 2003).

[76] Courts of Montenegro, the Basic Court in Podgorica, database of decisions. http://sudovi.me/ospg/odluke/. Accessed 10 October 2014.

[77] Courts of Montenegro, the Commercial Court in Podgorica, database of decisions. http://sudovi.me/pspg/odluke/. Accessed 10 October 2014.

[78] Courts of Montenegro, the Appellate Court in Podgorica, database of decisions. http://sudovi.me/ascg/odluke/. Accessed 10 October 2014.

claims on the case law of international courts due to the fact that case law, as a matter of principle, is not a source of law in the legal system of Montenegro.

4 Availability of Case Law of National Courts

Decisions of all national courts, except of the Constitutional Court, are available free of charge in the online database on the official website of the courts of Montenegro—http://sudovi.me. It seems as though the decisions of most courts are made available starting from 2011 to 2012, whereas for the preceding 3–4 years only some of the decisions are included in the database. Entire decisions are available, including both the holdings and the rationale thereof. Names of the parties and other identifiers are reduced to initials. The database allows the categorisation of decisions by court, and further by department, the underlying procedural instrument, or by year of issuance. The database allows a search by term in the text of the decisions, as well as a search by date, court file number, etc.

The same website contains some decisions of the European Court of Human Rights in local languages—entire decisions upon applications against Montenegro, Serbia and Bosnia and Herzegovina are available, two translations of decisions of the European Court of Human Rights in cases that are not related to the region, as well as an entire book with a selection of key decisions of that court in the field of family law—the rights of the child.[79]

The case law of the Constitutional Court is available on the website of that court. It is organised in the form of annual bulletins, but individual sections of those bulletins, structured according to procedural criteria (subject of review, underlying procedural instrument, etc.), are also available on the website.[80]

All laws and bylaws, including Government decrees, in force in Montenegro are available free of charge on the website of the Official Gazette of Montenegro, in a database that is searchable by document title terms.[81] The texts of laws and regulations as amended by subsequent amendments and revisions are accessible at the same website, but only for a fee.

[79] Courts of Montenegro, the Supreme Court, Selected Decisions of the European Court of Human Rights. http://sudovi.me/vrhs/evropski-sud-esljp/odabrane-odluke/. Accessed 10 October 2014.

[80] As has been noted, the last year for which a bulletin was issued is 2012, so as of 10 October 2014 decisions issued in 2013 and 2014 are not available.

[81] Official Gazette of Montenegro. http://www.sluzbenilist.me/PAOsnPretraga.aspx. Accessed 10 October 2014.

5 Legal Education on International and EU Law

A course on International Public Law forms part of the mandatory curriculum of basic law degree studies, and is also taught within certain streams of graduate studies. Other courses that cover the area of international public law are those on International Relations, International Human Rights Law, International Law of Environmental Protection and the Law of European Integration. As for the international conventions and treaties regulating matters in the realm of private law, such as the Vienna Convention on International Trade of Goods, the Brussels Convention on Jurisdiction and the Enforcement of Judgments in Civil and Commercial Matters, the New York Convention on International Commercial Arbitration, etc., these are taught within the course on International Private Law.

The bar exam does not include an assessment of the knowledge of international law.[82]

The concept of lifelong learning was introduced in the judicial system in 2000 through the establishment of the Judicial Training Centre of the Republic of Montenegro. The main task of this centre has remained to provide training of judges and other target groups in relation to new legislation, international standards, modern methods of performing judicial tasks and court management, foreign languages, computer skills, etc. Training programmes are targeted at judges, judicial assistants and court trainees, as well as at other staff employed in the court administration. The educational programme of the Centre for 2012 primarily focuses on the specialisation and education of judges in certain areas of international and European Council law.[83] In its previous work, the Centre has developed cooperation with a number of relevant international organisations in the field of international law, such as the European Agency for Reconstruction, the Organization for Security and Cooperation—OSCE, the Council of Europe, the Open Society Institute, Checchi and Company Consulting, Inc., USAID, UNDP, etc.

In the 2012 Montenegro Progress Report, the EU Commission found that certain efforts had been made to ensure national courts' compliance with the case law of the European Court of Human Rights partly by holding training courses for judges and prosecutors.

[82] Rules of the Bar Exam of the Republic of Montenegro (2004). Courts of Montenegro. http://sudovi.me/podaci/osct/dokumenta/391.pdf. Accessed 10 October 2014.

[83] Educational programme of the Judicial Training Center (2012). Judicial Training Centre of Montenegro. www.coscg.org/test/Editor/assets/Godisnji%20program%20obuke-2012.doc. Accessed 10 October 2014.

6 Conclusion

The Constitution stipulates that both ratified international treaties and generally accepted rules of international law are an integral part of the national legal system, and that international law is qualified by supremacy over national laws and by direct effect on all matters regulated differently by national laws. However, from other operative provisions of the Constitution (powers of the Ombudsman, grounds for adjudication and for constitutional review, etc.), it is clear that the Constitution essentially deems ratification by national legislature in the form of a statute as the principal 'point of entry' of international law in the national legal system. An analysis solely based on a systemic interpretation of the provisions of the Constitution would therefore lead to the conclusion that the proclamation of the supremacy and direct effect of international law, consisting not only of international treaties but also of generally accepted rules of international law, is of a purely declaratory nature.

However, an analysis of the case law of the highest courts of Montenegro shows that a source of law that is not even mentioned in the Constitution is producing considerable effects within the national legal system—the case law of international courts, primarily the case law of the European Court of Human Rights.

The two procedural instruments provided for the protection of human rights and fundamental freedoms in individual cases before the highest courts in the country—the constitutional appeal which is judged upon by the Constitutional Court, and the lawsuit for just satisfaction for the protection of the right to trial within a reasonable time before the Supreme Court—have had a significant role in promoting international law in court practice. This is because these instruments have allowed individual claimants seeking protection of their rights to rely on the vast bodies of international law and the applicable case law of the European Court of Human Rights. It was under the pressure of such non-state actors that the courts had to look closely into the rules and standards contained not only in international treaties, but also in the case law of the European Court of Human Rights.

As a result, in recent years it can be seen that both the Constitutional Court and the Supreme Court have invoked *sua sponte* rules of international treaty law and even the case law of the European Court of Human Rights.

An analysis of the case law of the highest judicial instances, the Constitutional Court and the Supreme Court, shows that there are no substantial differences in the manner these courts interpret key principles and concepts of international law in comparison with the standards of interpretation that are generally accepted.

The fact that the case law of all the courts in the country is made publicly available in online databases, and that such databases are updated regularly, serves greatly to increase the transparency of the judicial function and to build public trust in the judiciary.

The degree to which international law permeates the case law of courts in Montenegro differs according to the functional level of the court. The greatest level of permeation is with the highest judicial institutions. There are clear signs, however, that the lower courts are starting to rely on international law as well, primarily on treaty law.

Judicial Application of International Law in Serbia

Mirjana Drenovak Ivanović and Maja Lukić

1 An Overview of Constitutional Provisions Related to the Status of International and EU Law

1.1 International Law in the Hierarchy of Legal Sources in Serbia

In the Constitution of the Republic of Serbia, international relations are regulated in Article 16. According to the Serbian Constitution, foreign policy rests on generally recognised principles and rules of international law. Ratified international treaties, as well as generally recognised principles and rules of international law, form an integral part of the legal order of the Republic of Serbia and are directly applicable.[1] In order to be a part of the legal order, a ratified international agreement must be in accordance with the Constitution of the Republic of Serbia.[2] The Constitution also stipulates the hierarchy of domestic and international general legal acts. Emphasising the unity of the Serbian legal order, Article 194 also regulates that the Constitution is the supreme legal act. To this effect, all laws and other general legal acts promulgated in the Republic of Serbia must comply with the Constitution and may not contradict ratified international treaties and generally recognised rules of international law. We may conclude that ratified international treaties and generally accepted rules have precedence in relation to domestic legislation, and only the Constitution stands above them in terms of hierarchy.

[1] Constitution of the Republic of Serbia, Art. 16(2).

[2] Constitution of the Republic of Serbia, Art. 16(3).

M. Drenovak Ivanović (✉) • M. Lukić
Faculty of Law, University of Belgrade, Belgrade, Serbia
e-mail: mirjana.drenovak@ius.bg.ac.rs; maja.lukic@ius.bg.ac.rs

S. Rodin, T. Perišin (eds.), *Judicial Application of International Law in Southeast Europe*, DOI 10.1007/978-3-662-46384-0_12

In accordance with the Constitution of the Republic of Serbia, human and minority rights guaranteed by the Constitution are directly applicable.[3] A special law may prescribe a method of exercising these rights only if it is explicitly stipulated by the Constitution or if it is necessary to exercise a specific right. If this is the case, the special law may not influence the substance of the relevant guaranteed right. Provisions on human and minority rights are to be interpreted in favour of the improvement of democratic values, pursuant to existing international standards on human and minority rights, as well as the practice of international institutions supervising their implementation.[4] In Sect. 4, we will analyse how the meaning of 'existing international standards' and 'the practice of international institutions' is understood in the Serbian legal system and jurisprudence.

1.2 The Position of the Stabilisation and Association Agreement and the Interim Agreement on Trade and Trade-Related Matters

The Stabilisation and Association Agreement between the European Communities and their Member States and the Republic of Serbia (SAA) is an international treaty signed on 29 April 2008. It was ratified by the European Parliament on 19 January 2011 and by some EU Member States, but has not yet come into force. The SAA shall enter into force after the Parties have notified each other that the approval procedures have been completed. Nevertheless, the SAA has an influence on the Serbian legal system.

The SAA foresees the commitment of the Republic of Serbia to harmonising domestic legislation with the *acquis communautaire* within the agreed schedule. As the Parties recognised the importance of the approximation of Serbian legislation to that of the Community and of its effective implementation, Serbia should not only endeavour to ensure that existing and future legislation is compatible with the *acquis communautaire*, but also proper implementation and enforcement of existing and future legislation.[5] The process of harmonisation was due to begin on the date of the signing of the SAA.[6]

The question that remains open is: what does the obligation to ensure 'that existing and future legislation will be properly implemented and enforced' mean? In the process of harmonisation, domestic legislation can be approximated to international conventions by enacting amendments to legislation. In certain cases, given the complexity and importance of addressing a certain issue, specific areas

[3] Constitution of the Republic of Serbia, Art. 18(1).

[4] Constitution of the Republic of Serbia, Art. 18(3).

[5] Stabilisation and Association Agreement between the European Communities and their Member States and the Republic of Serbia, Art. 72(1).

[6] Stabilisation and Association Agreement between the European Communities and their Member States and the Republic of Serbia, Art. 72(2).

are regulated by special laws. Under the Rules of Procedure of the National Assembly, a proposer of a bill should attach a Statement of Compliance of the Bill with the *acquis communautaire*, including a Table of Compliance of the Bill with EU regulations.[7] In some cases, the proposer may attach a statement confirming that there is no obligation for such compliance and must emphasise the impossibility of harmonisation of the bill with EU regulations. A more complex question is whether existing and future legislation is being properly enforced. In comparative theory, we find two basic approaches to this issue. One group of authors considers that, according to the SAA, domestic legislation should be interpreted in the context of EU law. Addressing the identical issue in respect of Croatia, Siniša Rodin provides three arguments for this point of view: firstly, because the Croatian Constitution, in its basic preferences, accepts a monistic view of the relationship between national and international law, and *a fortiori* between national and EU law; secondly, because the SAA stipulates the obligation to harmonise Croatian and EU law, whereby existing law must be interpreted in accordance with the principle of *favor conventionis*; and thirdly, because such interpretations, implying the Croatian public interest, are expressed in resolutions of the legislative and executive branches of government, as well as by having submitted the application for full membership of the European Union.[8] The second group of authors argues that the duty to interpret existing and future rights becomes effective only after the SAA enters into force. In this sense, Maja Stanivuković believes that the absence of a procedural and institutional mechanism for the proper interpretation of the law in 'the spirit of EU law' may lead to irregular practice by domestic courts. She further argues that the existing law does not contain the prerequisites for judges to be informed that a norm of domestic law originates from EU law.[9]

1.3 The Position of the Interim Agreement on Trade and Trade-Related Matters

When compared to the SAA, the Interim Agreement on Trade and Trade-related Matters between the European Community and the Republic of Serbia (IAT) has a different position. The Interim Agreement on Trade and Trade-related Matters came into force on 1 February 2010. The most important difference between the SAA and IAT is that the rules and interpretative instruments stipulated by the IAT are equal to the rules and instruments adopted by Community institutions. They must be enforced. An illustrative example is Article 38 of the IAT. Article 38 (1) stipulates the activities that are incompatible with the proper functioning of the IAT insofar as they may affect trade between the Community and Serbia.

[7] Rules of Procedure of the National Assembly, Official Gazette No. 31/11, Art. 151(4).

[8] Rodin (2003), pp. 591–613.

[9] Stanivuković (2012), pp. 203–221.

Incompatible activities include agreements between undertakings, decisions by associations of undertakings and concerted practices between undertakings if those activities affect the prevention, restriction or distortion of competition. The abuse of a dominant position by one or more undertakings or a distortion or a threat of distortion of competition by any State aid are also incompatible with the proper functioning of the IAT.

> Any practice contrary to this Article shall be assessed on the basis of criteria arising from the application of the competition rules applicable in the Community, in particular from Articles 81, 82, 86 and 87 of the Treaty establishing the European Community and interpretative instruments adopted by the Community institutions.[10]

This means that national courts have an obligation to enforce and interpret competition rules as they are enforced and interpreted by Community institutions. In addition, it means that national courts and the Commission for Protection of Competition[11] should directly apply interpretative instruments adopted by the Community institutions. In order to ensure full implementation of Article 38, the Commission for Protection of Competition applies criteria resulting from the application of competition rules applicable in the EU, 'which includes primary and secondary EU legislation, the practice of EU institutions, and the judgments of the Court of Justice and the Court of General Jurisdiction'.[12]

An analysis of legal texts reveals examples of direct transposition of EU law into national laws. The Customs Tariff Act in Article 3a(1) defines the classification of goods by virtue of the Customs Tariff.[13] In this regard, the Customs Tariff consists of the tariff position for goods, determined in accordance with the Customs Tariff Act and provisions laid down on the basis of this law. The application of the Commission regulations which are concerned with the classification of goods and published in the Official Journal of the European Union is obligatory.[14]

2 The Judicial System in Serbia

The basic elements of the judicial system in Serbia are established by the Constitution and the Organisation of Courts Act.[15] Judicial authority on the territory of the Republic of Serbia is unified and belongs to courts with general and special jurisdiction.[16] The specific forms of the organisation, jurisdiction and structure of

---

[10] IAT, Art. 38(2).

[11] http://www.kzk.org.rs/en. Accessed 3 February 2013.

[12] Republic of Serbia (2012), p. 3. http://www.kzk.org.rs/kzk/wp-content/uploads/2012/08/Annual-Report_2011.pdf. Accessed 6 February 2013.

[13] Customs Tariff Act, Official Gazette of the Republic of Serbia, No. 61 /2007, 5/2009, 33/2009.

[14] Customs Tariff Act, Art. 3a(3).

[15] Organisation of Courts Act, Official Gazette of the Republic of Serbia No. 116/08 of 27 December 2008.

[16] See: Constitution of the Republic of Serbia, Arts. 142(1), 143(1), 143(2).

courts are defined by law. The Organisation of Courts Act established the following courts of general jurisdiction: basic, high and appellate courts and the Supreme Court of Cassation,[17] and the following courts of specialised jurisdiction: the Administrative Court, misdemeanour courts, the High Misdemeanour Court, commercial courts and the Commercial Appellate Court.

Basic courts are established for the territory of a town, while higher courts are established for the territory of one or several basic courts. A comparison of the competences indicates that the Appellate Court is the immediately higher instance court for higher courts and basic courts. The Commercial Appellate Court is the immediately higher instance court for commercial courts, and the Higher Misdemeanour Court is the immediately higher instance court for misdemeanour courts. The Supreme Court of Cassation is the court of the highest instance. It is the immediately higher instance court for the Commercial Appellate Court, the Higher Misdemeanour Court, the Administrative Court and the Appellate Court.[18]

The Constitutional Court is established by the Serbian Constitution to protect constitutionality, legality, and human and minority rights and freedoms as an independent body.[19] Any legal or natural person has the right to institute proceedings for a review of constitutionality or assessment of legality. In addition, any person who believes that his or her human or minority rights and freedoms, as stipulated by the Constitution, have been violated or denied as a result of an action or act of the state authorities or an organisation with public authority may lodge a Constitutional appeal with this court.[20]

3 The Authority to Apply International and EU Law

The possible application of international and EU law raises many questions. Can courts in Serbia directly apply the generally accepted rules of international law and how should this concept be understood? Can courts in Serbia directly apply human and minority rights guaranteed by generally accepted rules of international law? Is there a duty for courts in Serbia to interpret provisions on human and minority rights in accordance with the practice of an international institution? Can courts in Serbia apply EU law directly? Can courts in Serbia refer to the legal principles applicable in the EU? Are courts in Serbia obliged to apply the law of the EU Court of Justice? The answers to these questions are presented below under three subheadings: general principles of international law, international treaties and human rights treaties.

[17] http://www.vk.sud.rs/. Accessed 12 February 2013.

[18] Organisation of Courts Act, Art. 14.

[19] See: Constitution of the Republic of Serbia, Art. 166(1).

[20] See: Constitution of the Republic of Serbia, Art. 170 and the Constitutional Court Act, Official Gazette of the Republic of Serbia, No. 109 /2007, Art. 83(1).

3.1 General Principles of International Law

Generally accepted rules of international law and recognised international treaties are an integral part of the legal system in accordance with the Constitution of the Republic of Serbia. Constitutional decisions stipulate that court decisions have to be based not only on the Constitution and the law, but also ratified international treaties and regulations passed on the basis of the law.[21] The question that arises is whether court decisions should be based on generally accepted rules of international law. In a decision of July 2009, the Constitutional Court indicated that generally accepted rules are an integral part of the Serbian legal order. Moreover, the Constitutional Court explained what should be regarded as generally accepted rules of international law: a source that either contains the rules of behaviour regarding subjects of international law which have emerged as an international custom and relate to the constant and uniform practice of countries in relation to general values (such as the absolute protection of one's bodily integrity, and the prohibition of genocide, slavery and racial discrimination), or a source that contains principles that should be applied if there are no detailed rules or if other standards should be interpreted on the basis of it. These rules are derived from the principles common to all or most modern democratic legal systems. In the human rights domain, the application of these principles is of particular importance due to the need to explain standards and terms included in the norms of international law without specific definitions.[22]

Therefore, it may be concluded that the courts in Serbia interpret the Constitution in such a way that an obligation for them to apply generally accepted rules of international law exists.

3.2 International Treaties

Ratified international treaties, as an integral part of the legal system in Serbia, can be directly applied by the courts. A special procedure is followed for the ratification of an international treaty. The National Assembly adopts, by a majority vote of all deputies, laws which regulate the ratification of international treaties.[23] After this, the President of the Republic of Serbia promulgates the laws in accordance with the Constitution.[24] The law on a ratified international treaty should be published in the Official Gazette of the Republic of Serbia.

[21] Constitution of the Republic of Serbia, Art. 145(2).

[22] Constitutional Court, Decision IUz-43/2009 of 09.07.2009, Official Gazette of the Republic of Serbia, No. 65/2009. The Decision is available at http://www.ustavni.sud.rs/page/jurisprudence/35/. Accessed 19 February 2013.

[23] Constitution of the Republic of Serbia, Art. 105 paragraph 2(6).

[24] Constitution of the Republic of Serbia, Art. 112 paragraph 1(2).

> The Convention on the Elimination of All Forms of Racial Discrimination (the Ratification of the Convention Act was published in the Official Gazette of SFRY-International Treaties, No. 6/67) obliges all Member States to use all appropriate means and implement, without delay, a policy that aims at eliminating all forms of discrimination and promoting understanding between races and, to that end, by all appropriate means, prohibit racial discrimination by any person, group or organisation (Article 2, item d)), and establishes that States Parties must condemn all propaganda and organisations which are guided by ideas or theories based on the superiority of one race or group of persons of one colour or ethnic origin, or who want to justify or support any form of racial hatred or discrimination, and undertake to adopt immediate and positive measures that aim to eradicate all incitement to such discrimination, or any act of discrimination, ... and to declare that participation in such organisations or activities is an offence punishable by law (Article 4, paragraph 1, item b)). The prohibition of incitement to national, racial or religious hatred encompassing calls to discrimination, hostility or violence, or the prohibition of all forms of discrimination, are contained in the International Covenant on Civil and Political Rights and the European Convention for the Protection of Human Rights and Fundamental Freedoms, which, as ratified international treaties, also form a part of the legal order of the Republic of Serbia.[25]

Does that mean that Serbian courts can directly apply any ratified international treaty? The Constitution of the Republic of Serbia does not stipulate any requirement that could be compared with the 'self-executing provisions' of an international agreement in public international law[26] or the concept of 'direct effect' of a provision developed by the EU Court of Justice.[27] Without it, the application of a ratified international treaty relies on its direct applicability. This could lead to a situation where national provisions are insufficient. When it comes to implementation of an international treaty by means of ratification, it is important to focus not only on the formal transposition, but also on the institutional capacity for identifying and applying certain standards.

3.3 Human Rights Treaties

The Constitution of the Republic of Serbia provides for the direct implementation of human and minority rights. In other words, human and minority rights, guaranteed by the generally accepted rules of international law, ratified international treaties and laws, should be directly implemented.[28] Contrary to the implementation of other international treaties, when it comes to the direct implementation of human and minority rights, the Constitution stipulates that the manner of exercising these rights may be prescribed by law if such prescription is necessary for the exercise of a specific right. It can also be stipulated by the

[25] Decision of the Constitutional Court of the Republic of Serbia, VIIУ-171/2008 of 6 June 2011.

[26] Riesenfeld (1973), pp. 504–508. Vázquez (1995), pp. 695–723. Scloss (2002), pp. 1–84.

[27] See: Joined Cases 21 to 24–72 *International Fruit Company N.V. v. Produktschap voor Groenten en Fruit* [1972] ECR 1219.

[28] Constitution of the Republic of Serbia, Art. 18.

Constitution. The law prescribing the manner of exercising human and minority rights guaranteed by the Constitution may not influence the substance of guaranteed rights.

The courts are obliged to interpret provisions on human and minority rights for 'the benefit of promoting values of a democratic society, pursuant to valid international standards in human and minority rights, as well as the practice of international institutions which supervise their implementation'.[29] The meaning of 'the practice of international institutions' is not further elaborated. The examples that follow will indicate its meaning in the practice of the Constitutional Court of the Republic of Serbia. It is also evident from the presented examples that the Constitutional Court of Serbia relies on the interpretation of the European Convention for the Protection of Human Rights by the ECtHR much more than on any other international instrument, i.e. than on any other international organisation's interpretation.

In the case law of the Constitutional Court, we find the following explanation which points to the role of the case law of international courts in interpreting the provisions of the Serbian Constitution relating to human rights protection:

> Since on 8 November 2006 the new Constitution of the Republic of Serbia entered into force, in the course of proceedings before the Constitutional Court, the sponsor amended a proposal on 24 February 2009 for assessing the constitutionality of the challenged provisions of Article 4 paragraph 1 of the Family Act. The proposed amendment states that the disputed provision was not in accordance with Article 21 of the Constitution of the Republic of Serbia of 2006, and also that, according to Article 18 paragraph 4-3 of the Constitution, the practice of international organisations must be followed in interpreting the provisions of the Constitution relating to the protection of human rights, and in assessing the constitutionality of the disputed provisions of the Constitutional Court, so that proper account should be taken of the law of the European Court of Human Rights (ECtHR), in particular the judgment in the case of *Karner v. Austria* (Application no. 40016/98, judgment of 24 July 2003), where the European Court found that unmarried partners of the same sex cannot be denied the rights provided for unmarried different-sex partners, as well as the practice of the Human Rights Committee of the United Nations.[30]

An illustrative example can be found in the reasoning of the Constitutional Court in a decision of 2009:

> In the case of the applicant's statement that the provision of Article 28 of the Act is contrary to certain statements of the Committee on Freedom of Association of the International Labour Office, and to the practice of certain international institutions that oversee the implementation of conventions and recommendations of the International Labour Organisation, the Constitutional Court has concluded that these attitudes and practices of international institutions are not formal sources of law, i.e. are not considered confirmed international agreements, in terms of Article 167 of the Constitution, and therefore there is no constitutional basis to form a consent assessment of the disputed provision of the Act on their basis. However, the Constitutional Court took into consideration that various international instruments, resolutions, recommendations, views of international organisations, charters, and other instruments that are adopted by individual authorities of universal

---

[29] Constitution of the Republic of Serbia, Art. 18 paragraph 3.

[30] Decision of the Constitutional Court of the Republic of Serbia, IУ-347/2005 of 22 July 2010.

> or regional organisations include rules that may be of importance for the protection of human rights. Therefore, the Constitutional Court considered the provisions of the instruments identified in the initiatives, but did not find them to contain special rules different from the provisions of the Constitution in respect to which the Court evaluated the challenged provisions of the Act.[31]

The following example demonstrates the meaning of various international instruments in the practice of the Constitutional Court:

> The Constitutional Court considered that the various international instruments (resolutions, recommendations, charters, etc.) adopted by some organs of universal or regional organisations, include rules that may be important for the protection of human rights. Those are not international agreements in the true sense of the word, and therefore are not subject to ratification, but their moral and political value is significant. Therefore, the Member States and international organisations recognise and respect them without any legal obligation to do so. For these reasons, the Constitutional Court considered the provisions of these instruments indicated by applicants, but has not found any special or specific rules different from the provisions of the Constitution in respect of which the disputed norms of the Judges Act have been previously evaluated.[32]

The reasoning of the decision of the Constitutional Court in the 2009 case provides the following opinion:

> In assessing claims and making decisions in this constitutional case, the Constitutional Court took into account the jurisprudence of the European Court of Human Rights in Strasbourg ... The constitutional evaluation of conducted proceedings in this legal matter, based on the practice and criteria of international institutions for the protection of human rights, confirms that, in this particular case, the right of the complainant to a trial within a reasonable time has not been infringed.[33]

Explicit reference to the case law of the European Court for Human Rights was made in a relatively recent decision of the Constitutional Court that both attracted considerable public attention and influenced the guiding principle of a law of major importance for the completion of the transition process in Serbia. The case was opened by virtue of an initiative that a law providing for the restitution in kind of property of churches and religious communities, enacted in 2006, be proclaimed unconstitutional, due to its alleged discriminatory effect towards all other natural and legal persons in Serbia which at the time had still not been granted restitution of property appropriated after World War II. Public attention was largely drawn to the case because certain officials of the Government of Serbia publicly advocated these initiatives, calling for the Constitutional Court to abrogate the law in question. These opinions alleged that had the law remained in force, and due to the fact that it provided restitution in kind to a certain category of legal persons in Serbia, the forthcoming general restitution law would need to follow the same principle, as

[31] Decision of the Constitutional Court of the Republic of Serbia, IУз-26/2009 of 3 December 2009.

[32] Constitutional Court, Decision IUz-43/2009 of 9 July 2009, Official Gazette of the Republic of Serbia, No. 65/2009.

[33] Decision of the Constitutional Court of the Republic of Serbia, Уж-408/2008 of 9 July 2009.

well as to grant compensation of the full market value of appropriated property in all cases in which restitution in kind was not possible. This argument was based on the interpretation of the non-discrimination standards and rules of the European Convention for the Protection of Human Rights and Fundamental Freedoms. The Constitutional Court rendered its judgment in 2011, when it decided to uphold the disputed law in its entirety. In its reasoning, the Court found that Serbia adopted an approach of 'crawling restitution', which encompassed gradual enactment of specific laws for different categories of natural and legal persons as beneficiaries of the restitution process. In doing so, the Court explicitly invoked:

> the case law of the European Court of Human Rights, [according to which] the Member States in principle dispose of a wide margin of appreciation in respect of the choice of means and methods for attaining a legitimate purpose, particularly in respect of substantial social and economic transformations, which in the case of denationalisation in Serbia has been done by regulating the field by virtue of several laws which were enacted in the course of a longer period of time.[34]

In line with the endorsement of the possibility of adhering to the principle of the priority of restitution in kind over compensation, a general law on restitution of property appropriated after WWII, based on this principle, was enacted in September 2011.[35]

The Constitutional Court of Serbia, according to M. Kuzman, also largely follows the ECtHR in respect of the concrete criteria for establishing the violation of the right to a trial within a reasonable time: the complexity of the case; the importance of the ruling for the applicant; the conduct of the applicant; and the actions of the competent authorities.[36]

4 Judicial Application of International Law

If we were to ask who customarily raises the issue of the application of international law in Serbia, there would be a few answers. Firstly, parties in their submissions to the court often refer to the practice of the ECtHR, the European Convention for the Protection of Human Rights and Fundamental Freedoms, and also other ratified international treaties. Secondly, the courts, regardless of whether the party itself pointed to certain sources of international law or not, sometimes often justify their decisions by referring to the case law of the ECtHR or to ratified international treaties. Finally, in certain cases the Commissioner for Information of Public Importance and Personal Data Protection, in addressing the court, bases his arguments on the law of the ECtHR. The following indicate different models of

[34] Decision of the Constitutional Court of the Republic of Serbia, IУз-119/2008 of 20 April 2011.

[35] See Rakitić (2011), pp. 212–235. http://www.ius.bg.ac.rs/Anali/A2011-2/Anali%202011-2%20str.%20212-234.pdf. Accessed 3 February 2013.

[36] Kuzman (2010), pp. 14–20.

invoking the application of international law and the procedures of courts in cases in which they make a reference to sources of international law, or when they provide an opinion in cases when a party refers to a source of international law.

According to Predrag Vasić, a judge of the High Court in Belgrade,[37] courts of general jurisdiction in Serbia rely on the European Convention for the Protection of Human Rights and Fundamental Freedoms only in respect of certain types of disputes: claims for damages resulting from defamation, family disputes, and, to a lesser extent, property disputes, in which almost always the provision of Article 1, Protocol 1 to the European Convention for the Protection of Human Rights and Fundamental Freedoms is invoked.[38]

In a case of 2010, the authorised applicant requested a review of the conformity of a disputed provision of Article 4 paragraph 1 of the Family Act with ratified international treaties that are, under the provisions of Article 16 paragraph 2 of the Constitution, an integral part of the legal order of the Republic of Serbia and apply directly. Ruling on the applicant's request, the Constitutional Court analysed Articles 8, 12 and 14 of the European Convention for the Protection of Human Rights and Fundamental Freedoms.[39] In addition to the European Convention, the Constitutional Court also analysed Article 1 of Protocol No. 12, Articles 23 and 26 of the International Covenant on Civil and Political Rights,[40] and the case law of the ECtHR. In the reasoning for its judgment, the Constitutional Court gave the following opinion:

> In its previous practice, the Court originally ruled a violation of the principle of non-discrimination based on sex under Article 14 of the European Convention in connection with the right from Article 8 of the European Convention – the right of respect for private life, expressing the view that the different treatment of persons based on sexual orientation may fall within the scope of the sphere of privacy (see the judgment of the European Court in the case of *Mata Estevez v. Spain*, No. 56 501/00). In the case of *Karner v. Austria*, the European Court ruled the conduct of the respondent State towards the applicant was discriminatory, motivated by his sexual orientation, pertaining to the right of the applicant to keep leasing the apartment after the death of a partner and in connection with the right to respect for home (see the judgment of the European Court in the case of *Karner v. Austria*, No. 40016/98). In its recent practice, in the case of *Schalk and Kopf v. Austria*, the European Court considered that the communal life of people of the same sex living in a stable *de facto* partnership may fall within the scope of the right to family life under Article 8 of the European Convention, but stated in its judgment that the issue of legal recognition of a communal life for people of the same sex belongs to the field of law where the State enjoys a margin of appreciation as to if and when it will regulate this issue (see the above judgment of the European Court on *Schalk and Kopf v. Austria*, No. 30141/04, dated 24 June 2010, paragraphs 92, 93, 94 and 105). The European Court has in several cases established a violation of the right to non-discrimination with regard to the right to respect

---

[37] Mr. Vasić is the president of the section of the court appointed to handle proceedings for the rehabilitation of persons convicted for political reasons during WWII and under communist rule.

[38] For the purpose of this study, Justice Vasić was interviewed in December 2012.

[39] European Convention for the Protection of Human Rights and Fundamental Freedoms, Official Gazette of SCG—International Contracts, Nos. 9/03, 5/05 and 7/05.

[40] International Pact on Civil and Political Rights, Official Gazette of SFRY, No. 7/71.

> for private life, because the respondent State has not proved that there was an objective and reasonable justification for different treatment (see the judgment of the European Court in the case *Salguiro Monta da Silva v. Portugal*, no 33290/96). By interpreting the provisions of the Covenant, the Human Rights Committee was tying the prohibition of discrimination to one of the rights guaranteed by this act. The Committee took the position that different treatment may not be considered discriminatory in the sense of Article 26 of the Pact as long as it is based on an objective and reasonable justification (see the decision of the Human Rights Committee in *Young v. Austria*, No. 941/2000) . . . The above-stated shows that according to the recognised international treaties and practices of international organisations for the protection of rights under such treaties, in relation to which the applicant sought a review of the disputed provisions of the Family Act, difference in treatment based on sexual orientation, besides being discriminatory, must pertain to a recognised and guaranteed law and must also transpire in a situation where the different treatment may not be objectively and reasonably justified.[41]

The following example shows the importance of the applicant presenting the case law of the ECtHR in the decision-making of the Constitutional Court.

In a case in which a constitutional complaint was filed with the Constitutional Court regarding an alleged violation of the right to a trial within a reasonable time, the applicant referred to ECtHR practice (*Klass and Others v. Germany*, Application No. 5029/71, judgment of 6 September 1978 paragraph 33 and *Dudgeon v. United Kingdom*, Application No. 7525/76, judgment of 22 October 1981 paragraph 41).[42] For the purpose of supporting the argument that the deadline for filing a constitutional appeal in accordance with Article 84 of the Constitutional Court Act was inapplicable in this particular case, since the action against which the constitutional appeal was filed had consisted of a continuous, ongoing situation, preventing the applicant from relying on his constitutional rights directly, the applicant referred to the jurisprudence of the ECtHR (*Malama v. Greece*, Application No. 43622/98, judgment of 1 March 2001, paragraph 35). The applicant substantiated in great detail the argument that the condition of exhaustion of remedies had in fact been met, i.e. that remedies were simply lacking, arguing that 'administrative remedies do not provide reasonable prospects for success in the particular case' and that 'resorting to non-contentious court proceedings, just as to administrative proceedings, would not have any legal basis' in respect of the applicant's request for change of sex in the registers. In doing so, the applicant cited the ECtHR's case-law (*Vernillo v. France*, Application No. 11889/85, judgment of 20 February 1991, *Chahal v. United Kingdom*, Application No. 22 414/93, judgment of 15 November 1996, paragraph 145, *Airey v. Ireland*, Application No. 6289/73, judgment of 9 October 1979, paragraph 23 and *Akdivar v. Turkey*, Application No. 21893/93, judgment of September 16, 1997, paragraph 68). The Constitutional Court's decision pointed out the following:

> The applicant emphasises that, apart from the constitutional complaint, Serbian legislation does not provide any remedy that would 'compel the National Assembly to act.' . . . Therefore, the Constitutional Court assessed that in this case there were no ordinary legal

---

[41] Decision of the Constitutional Court of the Republic of Serbia, IУ-347/2005 of 22 July 2010.

[42] Decision of the Constitutional Court of the Republic of Serbia, Уж-3238/2011 of 8 March 2012.

remedies, ... administrative or contentious court proceedings which would provide the applicant with reasonable prospects of success in securing the satisfaction of his demands and remedying the infringement upon his rights. In taking this position, the Constitutional Court was guided by the law of the ECtHR, which has stated several times which criteria must be met for the remedy to be considered appropriate and effective, the most important being: the remedy must be available in theory and in practice (*Vernillo v. France*, Application No. 11889/85, judgment of 20 February 1991, *Lepojic v. Serbia*, Application No. 13909/05, judgment of 6 November 2007, paragraph 51); the remedy must provide the possibility of solving essential issues related to the specific human rights which are being infringed in the case at hand, as well as adequate redress for the actual violations in the case at hand (*Chahal v. United Kingdom*, Application No. 22414/93, judgment of 15 November 1996, paragraph 145); when it appears that there are several remedies that victims of human rights violations may use, the victim is entitled to decide which remedy he or she shall rely upon (*Airey v. Ireland*, Application No. 6289/73, judgment of 9 October 1979, paragraph 23); and lastly, and most importantly, the remedy must provide reasonable prospects of success (*Akdivar v. Turkey*, Application No. 21893/93, judgment of 16 September 1997, paragraph 68). The Constitutional Court finds that the free development of a person and her personal dignity pertains primarily to the establishment and free development of her physical, mental, emotional and social life and identity. Although it does not contain an explicit provision on the right to respect for private life and is not explicitly encompassed by the constitutional right to dignity and free development of one's personality, the Constitutional Court sees the right to respect for private life as an integral part of the latter. On the other hand, the European Convention in Article 8 paragraph 1 contains a provision on every person's right to respect for private life. Although the term private life in the practice of the ECtHR has not been fully and precisely defined, the decision of that Court in *Niemietz v. Germany* provides an interpretation of the concept of private life, coupled with the notion that the Court does not consider it possible or necessary to attempt to give a final definition of the subject concept. However, the European Court concluded that it would be too restrictive to limit the meaning of that concept to the 'inner circle' within which an individual lives his life, and which has been chosen by that individual, and to entirely exclude the world outside the circle. In other words, respect for private life must, to some extent, include the right to establish and develop relationships with other human beings (Application no. 13710/88, judgment of 16 December 1992, paragraph 29). Also, in the European Court decision in the case *X and Y v. Netherlands* (Application no. 8978/80, judgment of 26 March 1985, paragraph 22), it was noted that the concept of 'private life' includes the 'physical and moral integrity of a person', including 'his or her sexual life'. Therefore, the Constitutional Court stated that the sphere of the private life of a person undoubtedly involves, among other things, her gender, sexual orientation and sexual life, and that the right to privacy includes the right to determine the details of personal identity and self-determination, and, consequently, the right to the adjustment of a person's sex to that person's gender identity.[43]

The following example indicates the activity of independent bodies in finding ECtHR practice that may be important for the decisions of the Constitutional Court. In one case, a joint proposal was submitted to the Constitutional Court by the Ombudsman and the Commissioner for Information of Public Importance and Personal Data Protection for a review of the constitutionality of the Military Security Agency and Military Intelligence Agency Act, which stipulates that the Military Security Agency has the right to demand and receive information on the

[43] See Draškić (2012), pp. 57–76.

users of telecom services from operators independently of any other institution and without the court's role. The authorised proposers pointed to the case law of the ECtHR, rendered in proceedings initiated by citizens of other countries with the aim of protecting their rights. In this case, the Constitutional Court issued the following opinion:

> The basic idea of the protection of rights to which Article 8 of the Convention is applied is that there are areas of life of each individual in which a state must not interfere, except in those situations where the conditions from paragraph 2 of that Article are met, i.e. when such interference is in accordance with the law, has a legitimate aim and is necessary in a democratic society. Starting from the claim that the provisions on human and minority rights under the Constitution of the Republic of Serbia must be interpreted in the interest of the promotion of values of a democratic society, and in accordance with valid international standards of human and minority rights, as well as with the practice of international institutions which supervise their implementation, the Constitutional Court stated that, in accordance with the views expressed in the case law of the ECtHR, the right to privacy of correspondence includes not only communications made in writing, but spoken ones as well, i.e. applies to electronically exchanged letters and messages, as well as phone calls. Also, the term 'means of communication' includes not only the immediate content of communication, but also information about who established, or attempted to establish communication with whom and, at what time, how long the conversation lasted, how often (frequently) the communication was realised through correspondence, conversations, or messages in a given period of time, as well as from which locations it was conducted. The ECtHR has in some of its judgments (e. g. *Klass and Others v. Germany*, judgment of 6 September 1978, *Malone v. United Kingdom*, judgment of 2 August 1984, and *Copland v. United Kingdom*, judgment of 3 April 2007) expressed the following views: 'The interception of telephone communications, to which a public authority resorts to, is a form of interference with the right to respect for one's correspondence. In fact, laws that allow public authorities to secretly intercept communications can, by the very fact of their existence, be treated as a "threat" and as such considered interference with the right to respect for correspondence and privacy.' One of the basic principles in a democratic society is the rule of law, which is explicitly mentioned in the Preamble of the Convention. The rule of law, among other things, prescribes that interference with the rights of the individual by the executive power must be subject to effective control, which should normally be performed by the judiciary, at least in the final instance, because judicial review provides the best guarantees of independence, impartiality and a proper procedure. The Court would reiterate its position that the phrase 'in accordance with the law' does not apply to domestic law alone, but to the property of law, requiring that it is in line with the rule of law principle ... Thus, this phrase implies that in domestic law there must be a measure of legal protection against arbitrary interference by public authorities with the rights protected by paragraph 1 of this Article, and this follows from the object and purpose of Article 8. The risk of arbitrariness is evident particularly in cases where the executive power is exercised secretly. The law must be sufficiently clear to provide citizens with adequate indications regarding the circumstances in which, and the conditions under which, the public authorities have the right to resort to this secret and potentially dangerous interference with the right to respect for private life and correspondence ... The Court states that the use of information about the date and length of phone calls, especially about dialled numbers, may raise issues under Article 8, because such information is an integral element of communication over the telephone.[44]

[44] Decision of the Constitutional Court of the Republic of Serbia, IУз-1218/2010 of 19 April 2012.

The Appellate Court in Belgrade, in the reasoning of its decision rendered in case no. Гж—1214/12, refers to the Declaration on Freedom of Political Debate in the Media, adopted by the Committee of Ministers of the Council of Europe in 2004, stating the following:

> Freedom of opinion and expression is guaranteed by the Constitution of the Republic of Serbia, as well as the freedom to ask, receive and spread information and ideas by speech, writing, in pictures or in some other form. The Constitution also allows the freedom of expression to be restricted by law, if such restriction is necessary for the protection of the rights and reputation of others . . . The Declaration on the Freedom of Political Debate in the Media, which was adopted by the Committee of Ministers of the Council of Europe, on 12 February 2004, at the 872nd Meeting of the Ministers' Deputies, *inter alia*, provides that political figures accept being exposed to the public and political debate, and are therefore subject to detailed public scrutiny and, potentially, powerful and intense public criticism, expressed in the media, of the manner in which they conduct, or have conducted their public posts. It also stipulates that political figures should not enjoy greater protection of reputation and other rights than other individuals, therefore sanctions under national law of the media for violations perpetrated in the course of criticising political figures should not be severe . . . Freedom of the press enables the public at large to become acquainted with the positions of political leaders in respect of political matters of general interest . . . The Court established that the journalist acted with due diligence and appropriately, because he faithfully interpreted and sublimated contents of already published texts about the plaintiff. By disclosing the information, no false or incomplete information was disclosed . . . [O]n the grounds of these reasons, the impugned judgment had to be reversed.[45]

Following the identical approach to freedom of the media, the Appellate Court in Belgrade also invoked Article 10 of the European Convention for the Protection of Human Rights and Fundamental Freedoms in the reasoning of its judgment upon a plaintiff's claim for damages for the mental distress caused by the publication of false news content. The reasoning, among other things, reads:

> The provision of Article 200, paragraph 1 of the Obligations Act stipulates that in the case of mental distress occurring as a consequence of injury to reputation, honour, freedom and personal rights, the court, if it finds that the circumstances of the case, in particular the strength of distress, fear and its duration, justify it, will award just monetary compensation, regardless of pecuniary damage, to the aggrieved party, even in its absence. Article 10 of the European Convention for the Protection of Human Rights and Fundamental Freedoms (ratified on 26 December 2003, and therefore an integral part of domestic law) provides in paragraph 1 that everyone has the right to freedom of expression, that this right includes freedom to have an opinion and to receive and impart information and ideas without interference by public authorities and regardless of borders, but that this article shall not prevent States from requiring a licence for broadcasting, television or cinema enterprises, and in paragraph 2 that, since the exercise of these freedoms entails duties and responsibilities, it may be subject to such formalities, conditions, restrictions or penalties as are prescribed and necessary in a democratic society . . . From the quoted provisions of the Public Information Act, as well as from the provision of the Convention, it is clear that the freedom of expression is one of the bases of a democratic society. This also means that interference with the exercise of the freedom of the press can be justified by a prevailing demand in the public interest . . . Publication of the subject article or pieces of information could not cause injury to the reputation and honour of the plaintiff that would, in

[45] Judgment of the Appellate Court in Belgrade, Гж—1214/12 of 16 July 2012.

accordance with the provisions of the cited Article 200 of the Obligations Act and the cited provisions of the Convention, justify an award of compensation for damages to the plaintiff, for which reason the judgment of the court of first instance is hereby on appeal partly reversed, and in respect of its first paragraph reversed, and the plaintiff's claim rejected as unfounded.[46]

The Appellate Court in Belgrade referred to the European Convention for the Protection of Human Rights and Fundamental Freedoms in the case in which a judgment was rendered in respect of a dispute involving the right to the protection of a family home. The reasoning of the judgment reads:

By factual change of use of an auxiliary building for residential use and the use of the building for residence for more than 40 years, the defendant acted as the occupant, or lessee. Therefore, the provisions of Article 8 of the European Convention for the Protection of Human Rights and Fundamental Freedoms grants her the right to protection of her family home.[47]

5 Judicial Application of EU Law

The Supreme Court of Cassation, in its reasoning of a judgment of 2010, referred to the Charter of Fundamental Rights of the European Union, stating the following:

The substantive law was incorrectly applied to the proper state of facts when the judgment was granted in favour of the lawsuit. According to the Charter of Fundamental Rights of the European Union, everyone has the right to respect for his private and family life. In this Charter, children's rights and child protection are particularly emphasised. Children should have the protection and care necessary for their well-being and the best interests of children should be considered primarily in all actions concerning children.[48]

In a case from 2009, the Constitutional Court presented the following opinion on formal sources of law:

The Constitutional Court has considered the initiator's allegations that the disputed provisions of the Judges Act are not in accordance with the generally accepted rules of international law which are an integral part of the legal order of the Republic of Serbia and applied directly, according to Article 16 of the Constitution and the Basic Principles of the Independence of the Judiciary, Recommendation No. R (94) 12 of the Committee of Ministers of the Council of Europe to Member States on the independence, efficiency and role of judges, and the European Charter on the Statute (law) for Judges, which are related to the independence and impartiality of judges ... In terms of the Basic Principles on the Independence of the Judiciary and Recommendation No. R (94) 12 of the Committee of Ministers to Member States on the independence, efficiency and role of judges and the European Charter on the Statute for Judges, the Constitutional Court considers that these acts are not formal sources of law in terms of Article 167 of the Constitution, and that in respect of them the constitutionality review cannot be performed.[49]

[46] Judgment of the Appellate Court in Belgrade, Гж—7983/12 of 16 January 2013.

[47] Judgment of the Appellate Court in Belgrade, Гж—1838/10 of 17 February 2010.

[48] Judgment of the Appellate Court in Belgrade, Рев. 2401/2010 of 28 April 2010.

[49] Constitutional Court, Decision IUz-43/2009 of 9 July 2009, Official Gazette of the Republic of Serbia, No. 65/2009.

In proceedings before the Administrative Court, the plaintiff made a reference to the judgment of the Court of Justice of the European Communities (*Staatssecretaris van Financiën v. Kamino International Logistics* BV C-376/07 of 19 February 2009). Upon the constitutional complaint filed against the judgment of the Administrative Court 31478/10 of 22 September 2011, the Constitutional Court gave the following opinion:

> The constitutional complaint stated: ... that the Administrative Court was required to determine whether the facts on which the final decision of Customs had been based were established beyond doubt, particularly in the context of new evidence that the constitutional complaint applicant enclosed his lawsuit in the administrative dispute proceedings (decision by the Harmonised System Committee of the World Customs Organisation on classification of subject monitors, published in the 'Official Gazette of the Republic of Serbia', No. 11 of 22 February 2011, and the judgment of the Court of Justice of the European Communities *Staatssecretaris van Financiën v. Kamino International Logistics* BV C-376/07 of 19 February 2009) ... the reference made by the complainant in the course of the administrative dispute proceedings to the judgment of the Court of Justice of the European Communities *Staatssecretaris van Financiën v. Kamino International Logistics* BV C-376/07 of 19 February 2009, had no effect on the assessment of the accepted customs declaration, because the provision of Article 3a paragraph 3 of the Customs Tariff Act provides that only decisions on the classification published in the Official Journal of the European Union are legally binding.[50]

6 Case Law on the Internet

The most important decisions of the Supreme Court of Cassation and general legal opinions deemed by that Court as capable of influencing the case law of lower courts are publicly available on the Supreme Court of Cassation website.[51] The decisions and opinions are available only in Serbian. A bulletin with general legal opinions of the General Session, conclusions of the court divisions, sentences of the decisions of courts passed at the sessions of divisions, as well as expert opinions and opinions of judges, is published by the Supreme Court of Cassation.[52] As part of additional education for judges, the Supreme Court of Cassation publishes certain decisions of the ECtHR and other international institutions of importance for the protection of human rights and fundamental freedoms.[53]

The Constitutional Court of Serbia has established a database of case law. It can be searched by the file number of the case, the type of procedure or by key words. This database is publicly available on the website of the court in Serbian. A bulletin

---

[50] Decision of the Constitutional Court of the Republic of Serbia, Уж-4787/2011 of 24 November 2011.

[51] http://www.vk.sud.rs/sudska-praksa.html. Accessed 22 February 2013.

[52] http://www.vk.sud.rs/bilten-sudske-prakse-vrhovnog-kasacionog-suda.html. Accessed 22 February 2013.

[53] http://www.vk.sud.rs/karakteristicne-presude-protiv-zemalja-clanica.html, http://www.vk.sud.rs/presude-protiv-srbije.html. Accessed 22 February 2013.

on the most important issues tackled by the Constitutional Court and the most interesting opinions of this Court is also publicly available on the same website.[54]

The relevant case law on access to information and data protection in Serbia can be found on the website of the Commissioner for Information of Public Importance and Personal Data Protection.[55] The cases include the basis for some of the Commissioner's decisions and opinions, the most important decisions of domestic courts, and decisions of international and foreign courts and other bodies.[56] Some cases are available only in Serbian, while others are available in English as well.

7 Legal Education on International and EU Law

The process of initial and ongoing training of judges is regulated by the Judicial Academy Act.[57] The Academy is responsible for organising and conducting training through lectures, mentoring and professional training of judicial staff and establishing co-operation with international institutions concerning its activities. In order to be admitted to a position in the judiciary, a candidate has to take an entrance exam set by the Steering Committee of the Academy.[58] The candidates with the highest overall mark, which represents the sum of a grade point average from their studies and the mark given at the entrance exam, are employed as judicial interns. During their internship, they are trained by experienced judges, *inter alia*, in the fields of European law, human rights law and international law. This training should provide interns with advanced knowledge of the judicial practice of the ECtHR, and basic principles and standards of European law and the case law of the EU Court of Justice.[59]

As a matter of principle, the continuous training of judges is voluntary. However, the High Judicial Council is authorised to organise compulsory training,[60] and there are laws that stipulate the compulsory training of judges, such as the Juvenile Offenders and Criminal and Legal Protection of Minors Act.[61] The Judicial Academy organises short-term training, as well. Since 2009, the Judicial Academy has organised over 20 seminars for judges on the Convention on Human Rights and on

[54] http://www.ustavni.sud.rs/page/view/sr-Latn-CS/83-100208/bilteni-suda. Accessed 25 February 2013.

[55] http://www.poverenik.rs/en.html. Accessed 26 February 2013.

[56] http://www.poverenik.rs/en/cases.html, http://www.poverenik.rs/en/cases-di.html. Accessed 22 February 2013.

[57] Judicial Academy Act, Official Gazette of the Republic of Serbia, No. 104/2009.

[58] Judicial Academy Act, Art. 49 paragraphs 1 and 2.

[59] The training programme is available at: http://www.pars.rs/active/sr-cyrillic/home/pocetna_obuka.html. Accessed 3 March 2013.

[60] Judicial Academy Act, Art. 43.

[61] Juvenile Offenders and Criminal and Legal Protection of Minors Act, Official Gazette of the Republic of Serbia, No. 85/05, Art. 165.

standards of application, ECtHR case law and cases dealt with by the UN Human Rights Committee, with a special emphasis on the application of relevant standards in the case law of national courts, including direct application in judgments of the highest courts, in particular the standards of Council of Europe bodies and the ECtHR in respect of the application of Articles 5, 6, 7, 8 and 14 of the European Human Rights Convention, including Protocol 12 to the Convention, and the standards and practices of the UN Human Rights Committee in respect of application of the UN conventions against discrimination.[62] Records on participants in these training events are used in judicial advancement procedures.

A judge is not allowed to rule on family matters without first obtaining a certificate on having completed training on international law standards applicable in such matters.

8 Conclusion

In the hierarchy of sources of law in the Serbian legal system, ratified international treaties and recognised principles of international law stand below the Constitution, but above all other sources of law. Moreover, the fact that human and minority rights guaranteed by the Constitution are directly applicable is directly related to the applicability of international law, not only because several international instruments are regarded as undisputed authoritative sources for interpreting contents of human rights standards and guarantees within the legal systems that have acceded to such instruments, but also by virtue of a rule of interpretation expressly imposed by the Constitution of Serbia.

Serbia has signed the Stabilisation and Association Agreement with the European Communities and their Member States, but this agreement has still not come into force (as of 1 April 2013). A dilemma exists in respect of the point in time at which certain provisions of the SAA, namely the obligation to harmonise its law with the *acquis communautaire*, as well as to 'ensure proper implementation and enforcement of existing and future legislation', would become binding for Serbia. Strong arguments may be identified in favour of the view that these obligations have already come into force. Contrary to the SAA, the Interim Agreement on Trade and Trade-Related Matters, executed between the European Community and Serbia, entered into force in February 2010. This treaty in effect obliges Serbian administrative, regulatory and judicial bodies to review Serbian legislation and administrative and court decisions in terms of certain rules and interpretative instruments of EU law.

Analysis of the case law of the Constitutional Court of Serbia has shown substantial deference of this court towards the standards that the European Court

[62] More information about these seminars is available at: http://www.pars.rs/active/sr-cyrillic/home/vesti.html. Accessed 5 March 2013.

of Human Rights has established in terms of the application of the relevant standards for the purpose of interpreting the human rights provisions of the Serbian Constitution, the right to a trial within a reasonable time, the direct application of the provisions of the European Convention for the Protection of Human Rights and Fundamental Freedoms, reviews of restitution legislation, interpretation of the right to respect for private life, etc.

While the Constitutional Court may from time to time be faced with application of a ratified international treaty other than the European Convention for the Protection of Human Rights and Fundamental Freedoms, the courts of general jurisdiction in Serbia limit themselves to applying only that particular convention. The disputes in respect of which the European Human Rights Convention is applied by courts of general jurisdiction are almost solely those based on claims for damages resulting from defamation (interpretation of the freedom of opinion and expression), as well as those involving family matters, children's rights and child protection, and certain aspects of property rights.

Since the Constitutional Court has in effect become the principal authority for interpreting the European Human Rights Convention within the legal system of Serbia, sources of knowledge about the case law of the Strasbourg court are of prime importance for the final effect of the application of Convention provisions. Independent bodies, such as the Ombudsman of the Republic of Serbia and the Commissioner for Information of Public Importance and Personal Data Protection, have proved to be instrumental in providing knowledge about the relevant case law.

In general, the courts in Serbia, including the Constitutional Court, have been reluctant to give any deference to the provisions of the founding treaties of the EU or to the case law of EU courts. One notable exception is the reference made by the Supreme Court of Cassation, made in a judgment of 2010, to the provisions of the Charter of Fundamental Rights of the EU in respect of the rights to respect for private and family life, children's rights and child protection.

In general, an assessment may be made that the case law of higher Serbian courts is not sufficiently publicly accessible, with the exception of the Constitutional Court, whose decisions are fully and freely accessible on its website. The Supreme Court of Cassation only publishes its own selection of anonymous opinions on judgments and sentences. By the same token, the training of judges in respect of international law does not seem to be sufficient, particularly in respect of the case law of the European Court of Human Rights. One notable exception is the field of family matters and children's rights, in respect of which appropriate additional training of judges is mandatory.

The conducted analysis shows that in addition to enhancing institutional capacity for the application of international law, as well as increasing the transparency of established interpretative standards of Serbian courts, the application of international law in Serbia would greatly profit from raising awareness of the direct applicability of the European Human Rights Convention before courts of general jurisdiction.

References

Draškić M (2012) Evolution in the jurisprudence of the European Court of Human Rights concerning transsexual persons: evolution in Serbia. In: Lilic S (ed) Perspectives of implementation of European standards in Serbian legal system. Pravni fakultet Univerziteta. Belgrade, pp 57–76

Kuzman M (2010) Pravo na sudjenje u razumnom roku u praksi Ustavnog suda [Right to trial within reasonable time]. Izbor sudske prakse 7–8:14–20

Rakitić D (2011) Analysis of principal elements of the general restitution statute of Serbia from the perspective of the European Court of Human Rights case-law. Ann Fac Law Belgrade 2:212–235

Republic of Serbia (2012) Commission for the protection of competition. Annual report for 2011, Belgrade

Riesenfeld SA (1973) The doctrine of self-executing treaties and community law: a pioneer decision of the Court of Justice of the European Community. Am J Int Law 3:504–508

Rodin S (2003) Sporazum o stabilizaciji i pridruživanju u pravnom poretku Europske zajednice i Republike Hrvatske. Zbornik Pravnog fakulteta u Zagrebu 3–4:591–613

Scloss D (2002) Non-self-executing treaties: exposing a constitutional fallacy. UC Davis Law Rev 1:1–84

Stanivuković M (2012) Pravo Evropske Unije i sudovi u Srbiji. Zbornik radova Pravnog fakulteta u Novom Sadu, 1/2012, pp 203–221

Vázquez CM (1995) The four doctrines of self-executing treaties. Am J Int Law 89:695–723

Judicial Application of International and EU Law in Slovenia

Janja Hojnik

1 Introduction

The Republic of Slovenia, as an independent state, acquired its Constitution on 23 December 1991,[1] i.e. 6 months after adopting documents on independence and 6 months after adopting the Foreign Affairs Act,[2] which regulates substantive and procedural issues related to international treaties. The Constitution in its preamble derives from three principles that are *per se* principles of international law, i.e. respect for human rights and fundamental freedoms, the right to self-determination and the right of sovereign equality of states.[3] The compatibility of the Slovenian Constitution with international law standards was confirmed by the Arbitration Commission of the International Conference on the Former Yugoslavia (known as the Badinter Commission) in its arbitration opinion No. 7 of 11 January 1992.[4]

The legal status of international law in Slovenia is predominantly determined by the Constitution and by the Foreign Affairs Act,[5] but also by the Constitutional Court Act[6] and the case law of the Constitutional Court.

[1] Official Gazette No. 33/91 (as am.).

[2] First published in the Official Gazette No. 1/91 as of 25 June 1991.

[3] Pogačnik (1996), p. 365.

[4] International Legal Materials (1992), pp. 1512–1517.

[5] Zakon o zunanjih zadevah, Official Gazette of the Republic of Slovenia, official consolidated version, 113/03. The Act includes provisions on concluding international treaties.

[6] In Slovenian: *Zakon o ustavnem sodišču*, consolidated version published in the Official Gazette of the Republic of Slovenia, No. 64/2007.

J. Hojnik (✉)
Faculty of Law, University of Maribor, Maribor, Slovenia
e-mail: janja.hojnik@um.si

S. Rodin, T. Perišin (eds.), *Judicial Application of International Law in Southeast Europe*, DOI 10.1007/978-3-662-46384-0_13

By obtaining independence, Slovenia became a member of the international community and as a consequence domestic courts increasingly have to deal with issues concerning the application and interpretation of international law.[7] International law has considerably developed in the last decades and now covers numerous fields, from classical issues of international law (e.g. state sovereignty, etc.) to extremely specific issues (e.g. air transport, intellectual property, etc.); it not only concerns relations between states, but more and more the position of individuals (e.g. issues of human rights, international criminal law, international trade and investment law).[8] Considering the increase in the amount of secondary international law and in the number of self-executing provisions, the impact of international law upon the work of domestic courts is significant.

In this respect it is important that in 2004 Slovenia became a Member State of the European Union (EU), and its courts (as well as its administrative authorities) had to start applying 'a new legal order of international law'[9] with many specifics in comparison to 'traditional' international law.

This chapter examines the application of international law by Slovenian courts—to a large extent by the Constitutional Court. Emphasis is given to 'traditional' international law, although the last part of the chapter also considers the application of EU law.

2 Constitutional Status of International Law in Slovenia

The constitutional foundation determining the relationship between the international and Slovenian legal order can be found in Article 8 of the Slovenian Constitution.[10] In the first paragraph it provides the overall position of the generally accepted principles of international law and international treaties in the hierarchy of the Slovenian legal order—by placing them above the laws and other provisions, whereas the Constitution is the highest and basic act of the state.[11] It derives from this that international law has a similar position in the hierarchy of Slovenian law as in the hierarchy of EU law. The Court of Justice of the EU ruled that EU secondary acts must be applied and interpreted in line with international treaties, whereas the position of the founding treaties is comparable to the Slovenian Constitution. The

[7] Sancin (2012), p. 1214.

[8] Sancin (2012), p. 1214.

[9] See Case 26/62 *Van Gend en Loos* [1963] ECR 3.

[10] Article 8 states that '(l)aws and regulations must comply with generally accepted principles of international law and with treaties that are binding on Slovenia. Ratified and published treaties shall be applied directly'.

[11] Umek (2011), p. 132. See also Škrk (2009), p. 53.

competences of the Court of Justice of the EU to review international treaties are comparable to the competences of the Slovenian Constitutional Court.[12]

In this respect, it must be emphasised that Article 153(2)[13] of the Constitution more precisely stipulates that ratification of international treaties is to be performed in two forms: by acts of the Parliament (called the National Assembly) and by government regulations (decrees). It derives from this provision that international treaties ratified by a government regulation should be hierarchically placed below the laws.

It is true that according to the Slovenian Constitution the generally accepted principles of international law hold a sub-constitutional status (they are also considered in the case law of Slovenian courts as part of domestic law, unless in contradiction with the Constitution).[14] Nevertheless, considering that many generally accepted principles of international law protect fundamental legal and societal values, much the same as the Slovenian Constitution, it is hard to imagine a conflict between them and fundamental constitutional principles.[15]

The second paragraph of Article 8 states that international treaties apply directly. For formal and substantive reasons, not all provisions of international treaties are, of course, capable of direct application, but only so-called 'self-executing' treaty provisions—i.e. provisions that concern individuals and contain sufficiently clear and precise rights and obligations for the parties to invoke them before the courts (and this must be determined by the national courts on a case-by-case basis).[16]

3 Slovenian Courts' Structure and Accessibility of Case Law

The judiciary is one of three independent branches of government and its role is outlined in the Constitution. According to the Constitution, judges are independent and are not permitted to belong to political parties. They are elected by the National Assembly from nominees provided by the Judicial Council. Article 126 provides that the organisation and jurisdiction of courts are determined by law.[17] It also

[12] See e.g. Case C-402/05 P and C-415/05 P *Kadi and Al Barakaat v. Council and Commission* [2008] ECR I-6351.

[13] Article 153(2) provides: 'Laws must be in conformity with generally accepted principles of international law and with valid treaties ratified by the National Assembly, whereas regulations and other general legal acts must also be in conformity with other ratified treaties'.

[14] See judgment of the Supreme Court of the RS, VSRS II Ips 55/98.

[15] Umek (2011), p. 133.

[16] Ibid.

[17] I.e. the Courts Act *(Zakon o sodiščih)*, consolidated version published in the Official Gazette of the Republic of Slovenia, No. 94/2007.

states that extraordinary courts may not be established, nor may military courts be established in peacetime.

The court structure is arranged hierarchically with 44 local[18] and 11 district courts,[19] as well as four courts of appeal[20] and a supreme court.[21] These courts deal primarily with civil and criminal cases. Additionally, there are four specialised courts of the first instance competent for the determination of labour disputes, and one of them also for the determination of social security disputes. The Administrative Court of the Republic of Slovenia has the status of a higher court and deals with administrative matters (actions against the state).

Special status is given to the Constitutional Court, which is provided for by the Constitution and governed by the Constitutional Court Act of 1994. Its nine members are appointed by the National Assembly from nominees recommended by the president. Members of the Constitutional Court serve 9-year terms. The primary concern of this court is to safeguard the constitution by monitoring the constitutionality of laws passed by the National Assembly. The Constitutional Court also decides on the conformity of laws and other regulations with ratified treaties and with the general principles of international law. It also deals with cases involving possible infringements of individual rights.

There are three main websites to access the case law of Slovenian courts.

a) http://www.sodisce.si/
   This is the website of the Slovenian Supreme and High Courts. It is only available in Slovenian and offers a variety of information, e.g. office hours, a calculator for default interest, etc. Additionally, it refers to the website http://www.sodnapraksa.si/, which allows for a case-law search in the following fields:

[18] Local or county courts (in Slovenian: *okrajna sodišča*) are courts of the first instance and are vested with jurisdiction over less serious criminal cases: civil cases concerning claims for damages or property rights up to a certain value; all civil cases concerning disturbance of possession, tenancy relations etc.; probate and other non-litigious matters; keeping of land registers and civil enforcement.

[19] District courts (in Slovenian: *okrožna sodišča*) are courts of the first instance as well. They are vested with jurisdiction over criminal and civil cases which exceed the jurisdiction of county courts; juvenile criminal cases; execution of criminal sentences; family disputes, except maintenance disputes; recognition of rulings of a foreign court; commercial disputes; bankruptcy, forced settlements and liquidation; copyright and intellectual property cases and keeping of the company register.

[20] High Courts or Courts of Appeal (in Slovenian: *višja sodišča*) are courts of appellate jurisdiction, which determine appeals against decisions of the local and district courts in their territories and disputes of jurisdiction between local and district courts.

[21] See Article 127 of the Constitution. It is the highest appellate court in the state; it functions as a court of cassation—a court of appellate jurisdiction in criminal and civil cases, in commercial lawsuits, in cases of administrative review and in labour and social security disputes. It is the court of the third instance. The grounds of appeal to the Supreme Court (defined as extraordinary legal remedies) are limited to issues of substantive law and to the most severe breaches of procedure.

- Supreme Court
- High Courts
- Higher Employment and Social Tribunal
- Administrative Court
- Court of Justice of the European Union
- Calculation of immaterial damage
- Professional articles
- Legal opinions

b) http://www.us-rs.si/odlocitve/vse-odlocitve/
This website provides access to the case law of the Constitutional Court of the Republic of Slovenia. It has published all decisions of the Constitutional Court since Slovenian independence. The website also has an English version: http://www.us-rs.si/en/. The Case-Law Section of the website is updated periodically. The aim of the website is to allow the foreign public to be informed of the most important Constitutional Court decisions since 1992. The decisions are presented in the following manner: Registration Number, Date of the Decision, Challenged Act, Keywords, Legal Basis, Abstract, and Full-Text. In addition, decisions and certain orders (if the Constitutional Court so decides) are published in the Official Gazette of the Republic of Slovenia, local official gazettes, on CD-ROM, in the IUS-INFO databases (in Slovene), as well as in the Collected Decisions and Orders of the Constitutional Court (in Slovene along with abstracts in the English language).

c) http://www.iusinfo.si/Judikati/Kazalo.aspx
IUS-INFO is Slovenia's leading online portal for legal and business information. Over the past 20 years, IUS-INFO has become the focal point of legal developments in Slovenia, where all current legal and other information converges into the biggest interconnected collection of legal knowledge. The portal comprises:

- consolidated texts of complete legislation in the Republic of Slovenia
- IUS-INFO Register, a directory of legal acts in force classified by subjects, which contains useful information and references
- the largest collection of case law from all Slovenia's courts
- legislation and case law of the European Union
- comprehensive collection of legal publications, professional articles and legal opinions
- official notices and calls for public tender
- schematic collection of preparatory acts named 'Poročevalec Državnega zbora RS'
- daily updated information on legal matters (news, commentaries and columns).

Document cross-referencing enables users to navigate through substantially connected collections and provides an intuitive method to search for an answer to specific legal problems. The search engine uses advanced filtering to classify found documents according to several criteria so that the more important information is presented at the top of the search results. The page MOJ IUS-INFO (MY IUS INFO) allows favourite documents to be saved, which enables faster access to frequently used content, the management of settings for the daily information tool, IUS Alert, and the management of users' accounts.

4 Application of International Law by the Slovenian Courts

4.1 Introduction

The authority to apply international law by the judiciary is determined by the Constitution, which in Article 125 states that judges are independent in the performance of the judicial function; however, they are bound by the Constitution and laws. In this respect, Article 3 of the Courts Act provides more precisely that when performing his judicial profession a judge shall be bound by the Constitution and laws, and that according to the Constitution he is also bound by the general principles of international law and by ratified and published international treaties. This means that all judges, at ordinary and specialised courts of all instances, are under the obligation to apply international law. Nevertheless, the most important role in this respect is given to the Constitutional Court[22] as the highest judicial authority for the protection of constitutionality and legality as well as of human rights and fundamental freedoms.[23]

International law is part of the legal education of judges and other legal professionals, as it is included as a mandatory course at undergraduate level in all three law schools in Slovenia, whereas specific international law courses (e.g. diplomacy law) are offered as optional courses. Additionally, international law courses are also offered at the masters and PhD level. Nevertheless, the bar exam does not include examination of international law, apart from its constitutional aspects, discussed in this chapter. Further, the bar exam centre for education in the judiciary[24] offers various seminars for judges, e.g. on the recent case law of the European Court for Human Rights, cross-border judicial co-operation, etc.

4.2 Application of Article 8 of the Constitution by the Constitutional Court

Article 8 of the Constitution which provides for the status of international law within the Slovenian legal order is applied by the Constitutional Court in two ways. Firstly, as a subject of interpretation—when the Constitutional Court defines its

[22] Škrk (2007), p. 275.

[23] See Article 1(1) of the Constitutional Court Act.

[24] Center za izobraževanje v pravosodju (CIP).

content by interpreting certain words and concepts mentioned therein, the conditions for the application of international treaties, etc., and secondly, as a legal basis for the application of international legal sources. Additionally, there are three aspects of the application of international law:

as a standard of review of laws and other provisions;
as a subject-matter of constitutional review;
as an interpretative instrument to substantiate its rulings.

4.2.1 Interpretation of Article 8

4.2.1.1 Dualism with Elements of Monism

The Constitutional Court asserts in its rulings that Article 8 at a general level determines the relationship between international law and the legal order of the Republic of Slovenia.[25] International law and domestic law are therefore considered as two separated systems. This view is also shared by Slovenian legal theory,[26] which means that a dualistic approach towards the relationship between international and national law has been adopted. Nevertheless, there are some elements of monism, which can be noticed in the way international treaties are endorsed in the domestic legal order. This endorsement does not require specific legislation, but only confirmation of an act of ratification and the consequent direct application of the provisions of international treaties.

In addition to Article 8, Article 15 of the Slovenian Constitution, which concerns the exercise of human rights and fundamental freedoms, relates to the status of international law in Slovenia. Article 15(5) provides that 'no human right or fundamental freedom regulated by legal acts in force in Slovenia may be restricted on the grounds that this Constitution does not recognise that right or freedom or recognises it to a lesser extent'. The Constitutional Court ruled that 'Article 15 (5) gives human rights and fundamental freedoms, recognised by ratified international treaties, constitutional rank'.[27]

4.2.1.2 Application of Generally Accepted Principles of International Law

Generally accepted principles of international law are not often used as a standard of review in the case law of the Slovenian Constitutional Court.[28] It has, however, defined their meaning. The Constitutional Court says that generally accepted

[25] See e.g. Case U-I-274/02; Case U-I-245/00.
[26] See e.g. Sancin (2012) and Pogačnik (1996).
[27] See e.g. case Up-42/96, para 8.
[28] See Škrk (2012a), pp. 1224–1234.

principles of international law include general legal principles recognised by civilised nations, as well as rules of international customary law. Therefore, in the case concerning military courts, the Court found:

> The provisions of the Decree on Military Courts of 24 May 1944, which even at the time of issuing and application conflicted with the general legal principles recognised by civilised nations as well as the Constitution of the Republic of Slovenia, shall not be applied in the Republic of Slovenia.[29]

Furthermore, in the case concerning 'stolen kids' the Court found that '(j)udicial state immunity has developed on the basis of state practice to become international customary law'.[30]

The Court is competent to review the consistency of legislative and executive acts with generally accepted principles; it cannot, however, present a standard of review of international treaties in the procedures of *a priori* references of constitutionality.[31]

Many generally accepted principles of international law concern relationships between states (e.g. peaceful resolution of conflicts, principle of equality of states, principle of non-intervention, etc.) and are therefore rarely applied in domestic judicial procedures.[32] The exceptional situation concerns *ex post* review of acts of ratification of international treaties. In this respect, the Constitutional Court in the case concerning the Agreement between the Republic of Slovenia and the Republic of Croatia on Border Traffic and Cooperation interpreted the principle *uti possidetis* and ruled that it is 'a generally accepted principle of international law and as such

[29] Case U-I-6/93. The Court held in para 4 (part B-1) that: 'The extent of Constitutional Court control over substantive criminal regulations as defined by the Constitutional Court with the views expressed in this ruling, raises the question of what criteria are used to judge the constitutionality of pre-constitutional regulations. Considering the fact that, in terms of time, the possibility of assessing such regulations is virtually unlimited, they have to be assessed in view of their usefulness in proceedings based on extraordinary legal remedies from the point of view of their conformity with the constitutional and general legal principles in effect at the time and recognised by civilised nations, their applicability in new trials and their conformity with the Constitution'. See also Case U-I-266/04.

[30] Case Up-13/99. The Court ruled in this case that: 'Since there is demonstrated a rational link between the complainant's case – the action for compensation for the damage caused during the Second World War (for the period of time spent in a concentration camp, for mental anguish due to the death of his parents and destroying happiness in his life and for the property destroyed by the occupier's authorities) – and the Republic of Slovenia, the exclusion of judicial protection before a Slovenian court would entail an interference with the right to judicial protection (Art. 23 of the Constitution). The rejection of the action against the Federal Republic of Germany due to the activities performed during the Second World War by its armed forces is an allowed interference with the right to judicial protection'. More on this in Škrk (2007, 2012b), pp. 290–292, 321–350.

[31] See the section on *A Priori* Reference of Constitutionality below.

[32] Umek (2011), p. 136.

applies also to Slovenia'.[33] When applying these principles it is particularly difficult to decide whether a certain rule or principle actually is a generally accepted principle of international law. In this respect, in its older case law, the Constitutional Court did not allow references to the General Declaration on Human Rights, explaining that it did not have the power and nature of an international treaty, whereas later it started to treat it as part of international customary law.[34]

In general, the Constitutional Court has applied generally accepted principles of international law mostly in relation to the regulation adopted during World War II and immediately afterwards. In Case U-I-23/93,[35] it reasoned from the fact that after WWII the international legal order was established on the basis of the condemnation of the Nazi and Fascist regimes and the persecution of the perpetrators responsible for the crimes committed, which was confirmed by the entire international community of that time. In the mentioned decision, the Constitutional Court took the position that certain activities of an individual during the war can be a reason for such a person not to be entitled to Yugoslav citizenship. In the case concerning the Victims of War Violence Act,[36] the Court ruled that:

> Legislation which recognizes the status of victim of war violence to persons who collaborated with the occupying forces would be inconsistent with the generally valid principles of international law, and thereby also inconsistent with the Constitution.[37]

In this respect, it should also be mentioned that in the case concerning the Convention against Torture,[38] Judge Škrk stated in her concurring opinion that:

> we cannot overlook the fact that the Convention against Torture, which defines torture as an offence under criminal law, was adopted on 10 December 1984. Today, the prohibition of torture, alongside the prohibition of genocide and grave massive breaches of human rights, is among the absolutely binding (peremptory) norms of customary international law (*ius cogens*), which have *erga omnes* effects. It is thus the case of norms in international law

[33] Case Rm-1/00, para 24. The Court continued by saying that '(a)pplying the *uti possidetis* principle, the Constitutional Court established that at the moment of the establishment of the sovereign and independent Slovenia, its former republic border with Croatia "within the framework of the former SFRY" became its internationally recognized State border'.

[34] Case Up-490/03.

[35] In Case U-I-23/93 the Constitutional Court reviewed the statutory regulation by which the post-war Yugoslav authorities had denied persons of German nationality who during the occupation had been loyal to the German Reich the possibility to acquire Yugoslav citizenship. It established that such a regulation was not inconsistent with the general legal principles which were already then recognised by civilized nations.

[36] Case U-I-266/04.

[37] Ibid, para. 20. Nevertheless, the Court ruled that 'it does not follow from the Constitution that the concept of victim of war violence should be restricted to only those civilian persons who had been subject to violent acts or forcible measures by the armed forces of the occupier. Therefore, it is inconsistent with the Constitution that the legislature excluded from the circle of civilian victims of war violence all those persons who had been subject to violent acts or forcible measures by the armed forces of the other warring side'.

[38] Up-555/03 Up-827/04, para 8.

which in the hierarchy of legal norms are above other norms and principles of international law.[39]

4.2.1.3 What Is an 'International Treaty'?

What constitutes an international treaty is at an informal level left to the Ministry for Foreign Affairs. In line with the Vienna Convention on the Law of Treaties, the Slovenian Foreign Affairs Act defines an international treaty in Article 69.[40] The second paragraph of the same provision states that an opinion on whether an international instrument is an international treaty shall be given by the Ministry of Foreign Affairs before the commencement of the procedure for the conclusion of an international treaty. This is a soft-law provision, as in the case of dispute the Constitutional Court is competent to define what constitutes an international treaty.[41]

The Constitutional Court has adopted a broad interpretation of international treaties, so that Article 8 of the Constitution also encompasses treaties *sui generis* (e.g. Vatican accords, concordats, pacts, etc.). In its ruling concerning the Agreement between the Republic of Slovenia and the Holy See, the Court had to determine whether the Agreement was an international treaty, as it would otherwise not be competent for its review. The Court found:

> The Agreement is being reached by the Republic of Slovenia as an independent and autonomous State and the Holy See as a *sui-generis* subject of international law. Treaties that the Holy See enters into as the highest and sovereign authority of the universal Catholic Church refer to the issues that are directly connected with the Catholic Church in States – treaty parties (...). Irrespective of the special character of agreements between the States and the Holy See (known as concordats, conventions, covenants, modus vivendi, protocols or agreements) the prevailing theory of international law treats them as real treaties, which do not only confirm the existing rights of treaty parties (e.g. the free activities of the Church), but can also create new rights and obligations for both sides. What applies to the interpretation of these agreements as well as to treaties entered into by States are the rules of the Vienna Convention on Contract Law (...), which was also signed and ratified by the Holy See.[42]

It should also be emphasised that in the case concerning the Act on the Reestablishment of Agricultural Communities and Restitution of their Property

---

[39] On the basis of this, Judge Škrk concluded that '(c)ertainly there exists an obligation under international law for Slovenia to incriminate in (the Criminal Code) the criminal offence of torture, as defined in Article 1 of the Convention against Torture, on the basis of the obligations assumed by acceding to this Convention in 1993'—ibid, para 10.

[40] The first paragraph of Article 69 provides: 'An international treaty shall be understood to be an agreement that the Republic of Slovenia has concluded in writing with one or more states or international organisations and to which international law applies, regardless of the number of instruments of which it is composed and regardless of its particular name'.

[41] Škrk (2009), pp. 51–52.

[42] Case Rm-1/02, para 9, footnotes omitted.

and Rights, the Constitutional Court stated that legislation, which would condition enforcement of a ratified and published international treaty binding upon Slovenia with the adoption of a new international treaty, would contravene Articles 8 and 153 (2) of the Constitution.[43]

4.2.1.4 The Role of Ratification and Publication

Ratification and publication of international treaties are of paramount importance for their application.[44] In the Case Rm-1/97 concerning the European Association Agreement, the Court held:

> Article 8 of the Constitution provides that proclaimed and ratified international agreements shall apply directly. From the viewpoint of international law, ratification is unilateral declaration of intention of one contracting party addressed to the other contracting party, to the effect that it accepts the content of a signed agreement as binding. Such declaration of intention is delivered by the State on the occasion of exchanging instruments of ratification. According to the provision of indent 5 of article 107 of the Constitution, such instruments are published by the President of the Republic.
>
> However, the President of the Republic may publish such instrument of ratification after the National Assembly has passed the law on ratification of an international agreement. The instrument of ratification is an international act, and the law on ratification is an act under internal law, whose importance is twofold. On the one hand, it is a sort of authorization granted to the President of the Republic, allowing him to publish an instrument of ratification and, on the other hand, it is a normative act by which obligations under international law are transformed into internal law of the State (...).
>
> Thus, provisions of an international agreement are integrated in the internal legal system of the Republic of Slovenia with the coming into force of such agreement on condition that they have been ratified in accordance with the internal law of the Republic of Slovenia. By an international agreement, rights and obligations are created for the State.
>
> When the international agreement has been approved by the law on ratification, it can create rights and obligations also for natural and legal persons in the country if its provisions

---

[43] Case U-I-308/02, para 18.

[44] Article 77 of the Foreign Affairs Act provides: 'International treaties shall be published in the Official Gazette of the Republic of Slovenia in the Slovene and a foreign language. If the Slovene language does not feature among the languages in which an international treaty is concluded, the treaty shall be published in a foreign language and in the Slovene translation.

An international treaty shall be published in the Official Gazette of the Republic of Slovenia prior to its entry into force under international law. Information regarding entry into force and termination shall be published in the Official Gazette of the Republic of Slovenia.

Following a decision by the Government, instruments referred to in Article 75, paragraph 8 of the present Act may also be published in the Official Gazette of the Republic of Slovenia, and following a decision by the National Assembly or the Government, international instruments that are not international treaties may also be published in the Official Gazette of the Republic of Slovenia'.

> are by their nature such that they make this possible (in the case of the so called 'self-executing treaty').[45]

This subject-matter has also been explored by the Constitutional Court in the case concerning the Agreement between the Republic of Slovenia and the Republic of Croatia on Border Traffic and Cooperation. In relation to the effects of ratification the Court held[46]:

> Ratification[47] creates internal legal effects of an international treaty; the latter becomes a part of the domestic legal order. This does not change the international obligation of the state. Quite to the contrary, with ratification of an international treaty the state upholds international obligations covered by international law (. . .) Non-fulfilment of the obligation is a breach of the treaty – it means that the court has made an international tort.

If a treaty is not ratified and published in the Official Gazette, it does not apply in Slovenia.[48] This was clarified by the Constitutional Court, e.g. in the case concerning the Israeli Agreement, which was signed by army officials only.[49] However, it is sufficient if the act of ratification is only published in the Slovenian language.[50]

From the point of view of ratification, two groups of treaties must be distinguished:

a) Treaties ratified by an act of the National Assembly; and
b) Treaties ratified by a Government regulation (decree).

The former are considered to be hierarchically above laws, whereas the latter are considered to be below laws, adopted by the National Assembly.[51] The internal hierarchy of legal acts *per se* does not affect the fulfilment of international treaties. Problems could therefore arise if the provisions of such a treaty are inconsistent with a national act of a higher rank (the Constitution, a law), as the constitutional demand for consistency of legal acts requires primacy of the constitution over all international treaties and primacy of parliamentary acts over international treaties ratified by the Government—whereas the principle of international law '*pacta sunt servanda*' requires respect of international treaties *bona fide*.[52] It should also be

---

[45] Case Rm-1/97, paras 16–19, footnotes omitted.

[46] Case U-I-376/02, para 10.

[47] The Court added in footnote 1 that the substance of an international treaty becomes part of the Slovenian legal order through an act of ratification; one can therefore talk about adoption (endorsement) and not about transformation, whereby every rule of international law needs to be expressly transformed into the domestic legal order—thereby referring to Andrassy et al. (1995), p. 6.

[48] Article 154(1) of the Constitution provides: 'Regulations must be published prior to coming into force. A regulation comes into force on the fifteenth day after its publication unless otherwise determined in the regulation itself'.

[49] Case U-I-128/98.

[50] Case U-I-376/02, para 14.

[51] This has been confirmed by the Constitutional Court—Case U-I-147/94.

[52] In the case of inconsistency, Article 87 of the Foreign Affairs Act provides that 'If the provisions of an international treaty do not conform to the law or other regulations, the Government shall initiate a procedure for amending the law or other regulation, or for amending or terminating the

emphasised that the Government may not ratify a treaty if this requires the adoption of new laws or the changing of existing ones.

4.2.1.5 Self-Executing Effect of International Treaties

The second paragraph of Article 8 of the Slovenian Constitution provides that international treaties apply directly. Direct application, however, is possible only of so-called 'self-executing' treaty provisions—i.e. provisions that concern individuals and contain sufficiently clear and precise rights and obligations for the parties to invoke them before the courts.[53] Whether a treaty provision is self-executing must be determined on a case-by-case basis by the national courts.[54] When this is not the case, the treaties oblige the authorities to adopt further regulation.

So, for example, the Constitutional Court decided in a case concerning the Convention on Children's Rights that the Convention is directly applicable and overrides a provision of Slovenian law on the right of a child to keep contacts with his parents. The Court claimed that the principle '*lex posterior derogate legi priori*' does not apply in the relation between the Convention and national legislation, but that the former is hierarchically higher than the latter. On the other hand, as regards some procedural rights of children guaranteed by the European Convention on the Exercise of Children's Rights, the Court decided that they are not directly applicable and cannot be assured without appropriate legislative action of the national authorities:

> If treaties are not directly applicable, such ratified and published treaties create international obligations for the state to adopt in its national legal order appropriate national legal acts by which it ensures compliance with such obligations.[55]

In this respect also the Constitutional Court's ruling on the Convention against Torture is illustrative. The Court found therein that:

> Most certainly, the Convention against Torture does compel the legislature to incriminate torture in (the Criminal Code) and such in a form as the aforementioned criminal offence is defined in Article 1 of the same. The Convention against Torture leaves it to the national legislature to determine the penalties for such, while it compels the legislature to define torture as regards the prescribed penalties as a grave criminal offence. Thus, such requirements of the Convention against Torture cannot be ascribed the nature of self-executing provisions or provisions that can be applied directly before Slovenian criminal courts. The impediment to the direct application of the Convention against Torture in the prosecution of alleged offenders of torture is the requirement to respect the principle of legality (*nullum crimen nulla poena sine lege praevia*), which is a universally recognized general principle

---

treaty concerned. Pending the decision of the competent body, the international treaty shall be applied'.

[53] Buergenthal (1992), p. 317. See also Škrk (2007), pp. 298–300.

[54] Umek (2011), p. 133.

[55] Case U-I-312/00.

> of law, recognized by civilized nations and determined in Article 28 of the Constitution. However, the obligations accepted by means of treaties bind the state to comply with such obligations. (. . .) As regards the discussed issues, the Constitutional Court refers to the generally recognized treaty law principle of *pacta sunt servanda*, which compels contracting states to perform treaties in good faith.[56]

When an international treaty provision is in conflict with a domestic law provision, the question arises whether a national judge may adopt a ruling that is faithful to international law. If the conflicting national law was adopted prior to the applicability of an international treaty in Slovenia, judges should follow the Constitutional Court position that the hierarchically higher provisions of the treaty override the contrary provisions of national legislation. However, when contrary national legislation was adopted after the international treaty started to apply in the domestic legal order, it is disputable whether a judge may apply the international treaty provision or whether he should start a procedure for a constitutionality review of the conflicting law before the Constitutional Court. The Slovenian Constitutional Court has still not decided on this matter. However, on the basis of its human rights case law, Umek concludes that judges may deliver a ruling themselves if consistent interpretation of domestic law in the light of the treaty is possible. In the opposite situation, however, they should ask the Constitutional Court for a constitutionality review.[57]

4.2.2 Application of International Law as a Standard of Review of National Law

4.2.2.1 Applicable Approaches

The Constitutional Court has developed several approaches to the review of national regulation in the light of international treaties and generally accepted principles of international law.

When interpretation of a right under an international treaty is comparable to the interpretation of a right under the Slovenian Constitution, the Court considers the asserted breach of the right on the basis of the Constitution only. Consequently, the Court ruled that Article 6 of the European Convention on Human Rights (ECHR) does not assure a broader right to effective judicial protection than the Constitution and therefore reviewed the challenge only in light of Article 23 of the Constitution.[58] Similarly, the Court reviewed the requirement that courts in civil

[56] Case Up-555/03 Up-827/04, para 6, footnote omitted, KZ (Kazenski zakonik) replaced by 'Criminal Code'. See also the Constitutional Court ruling in the Case Rm-1/97.

[57] Umek (2011), p. 140. Cf. Case 106/77 Simmenthal [1978] ECR 629.

[58] Case Up-610/05, U-I-100/07, para 5.

proceedings should enable parties to use a language which they understand only in the light of Article 62 of the Constitution,[59] whereas the Court only reviewed the asserted procedural mistakes, which also breached Article 6 ECHR, in light of Articles 22 and 23 of the Constitution.[60] The Court noted that these two provisions 'guarantee at least such extent of protection as the first paragraph of Article 6 ECHR'.[61] Another example in this series of cases concerned the right to property as assured by Article 1 of the First Protocol to the ECHR, but which is also regulated by Article 33 of the Constitution. For this reason the Court reviewed the asserted breach of this right only in view of the constitutional provision.[62]

When, on the other hand, the substance of international treaty provisions does not overlap with similar provisions of the Constitution or when the latter does not contain any similar provision, the Court reviews the contested provision of national law directly in the light of the relevant international treaty. In this respect, the Court usually uses the Vienna Convention on the Law of Treaties and legal doctrine as well as the case law of international courts and other institutions.

Consequently, in the case concerning the Lipica Stud Farm Act, the Constitutional Court reviewed the Act in the light of the Aarhus Convention and ruled:

> The provision of the Act on the Amendment to the Lipica Stud Farm Act which with regard to the spatial regulation plan excludes a procedure for the preparation and adoption of such a plan in accordance with general spatial regulations although the plan is considered to be a state detailed area plan, and thereby also prevents the public from participating in such, is inconsistent with the Aarhus Convention.[63]

4.2.2.2 References to the European Convention on Human Rights

Particular importance is given to the case law of the European Court of Human Rights (ECtHR), which is binding upon Slovenia. For example, in a case concerning the right to a trial, the Slovenian Constitutional Court emphasised:

> Irrespective of its positions mentioned in the previous paragraph of the reasoning, in the review of the challenged Administrative Dispute Act's provisions the Constitutional Court must consider the case law of the ECtHR, according to which the effective judicial protection of the right to a trial within a reasonable time is ensured only if it also encompasses protection which affords appropriate satisfaction. The Constitutional Court must consider this case law irrespective of the fact that it was adopted in a case in which

[59] Article 62 protects the right to use one's language and script and provides: 'Everyone has the right to use his language and script in a manner provided by law in the exercise of his rights and duties and in procedures before state and other bodies performing a public function'.

[60] Article 22 protects equal protection of rights, and Article 23 protects the right to judicial protection.

[61] Case Up-1378/06, para 8.

[62] Case U-I-90/03, para 8.

[63] Case U-I-406/06. See also Case U-I-312/00 in which the Court found a provision of the Marriage and Family Relations Act inconsistent with the International Convention on Exercise of Children's Rights.

> Slovenia itself did not participate in proceedings before the ECHR. It namely concerns a clear and well established practice of the ECtHR, according to which conditions which must be fulfilled are determined in abstract so that concerning the ECHR it is possible to consider that the legal system of any contracting state contains an effective legal remedy against the violation of the right to a trial within a reasonable time also in cases in which a violation has already ceased.[64]

Furthermore, in a case concerning the Housing Act, the Constitutional Court stated that although the Slovenian Constitution does not recognise the right to a home, this does not mean that such a right is not guaranteed by international treaties that are binding upon Slovenia, and consequently relied on Article 8 ECHR and the ECtHR ruling in *Larkos v. Cyper*.[65] It derives from here that the Constitutional Court relies on the case law of the ECtHR in all relevant cases, not only when reviewing the compatibility of a law or decree with the ECHR or when considering a breach of a right guaranteed by the Convention—irrespective of whether the parties rely on the Convention or not.[66]

It is true, however, that the Court often does not expressly use international law as a standard for review of the national law, but it is evident only from its reasoning that the Court also used international law when reviewing a provision. For example, in its ruling concerning the Criminal Procedure Act, the Court found that '(t)he regulation determined in the Criminal Procedure Act (. . .) according to which the President of the court appoints a legal representative without obtaining the prior opinion of the defendant, is not inconsistent with the Constitution.' However, from its reasoning it follows:

> Neither the Constitution nor the ECHR and International Covenant on Civil and Political Rights grant a defendant the right to require the right to choose a legal representative also in cases in which a legal representative is appointed ex officio. (. . .) It does not follow from the text of the above-mentioned provisions of ECHR or from the case law of ECtHR that a defendant should be guaranteed the right to a particular legal representative in cases in which a legal representative is appointed ex officio.[67]

Furthermore, in the case concerning the Non-litigious Civil Procedure Act, the Constitutional Court reviewed compulsory detention in closed wards of psychiatric hospitals and in this respect in its reasoning relied on the case law of the ECtHR:

> The European Court of Human Rights (hereinafter ECtHR), deciding in the case *Winterwerp v. The Netherlands*, determined three fundamental requirements that must be met for the detention of mental patients to be lawful. According to the ECtHR, involuntary commitment is allowable only if the mental disorder has been reliably demonstrated based on objective medical expertise, and if the patient's mental disorder is of such a kind or such a gravity as to make him an actual danger to himself or to others. The third demand refers to

---

[64] Case U-I-65/05, para 12, footnote omitted.

[65] Case U-I-172/02.

[66] Umek (2011), p. 141.

[67] Case U-I-204/99, para 15, footnotes omitted.

the duration of commitment. Commitment may last only as long as the mental disorder justifying it persists.[68]

4.2.2.3 References to the International Law Within the Scope of a Constitutional Complaint

A constitutional complaint is a legal remedy by which a constitutional complainant in proceedings before the Constitutional Court claims a violation of human rights or fundamental freedoms.[69] A constitutional complaint cannot be lodged due to the erroneous application of substantive or procedural law or due to an erroneously established state of the facts in proceedings before courts. A constitutional complaint may, as a general rule, be lodged against a judicial decision only after all (ordinary and extraordinary) legal remedies in the Republic of Slovenia have been exhausted.[70] As such, it cannot be used to claim breaches of Article 8 as a fundamental constitutional principle.[71] Nevertheless, the complainants may challenge breaches of rights that have been made by wrongful interpretation or application of international treaties and generally accepted principles of international law under the same conditions as are imposed for a review of wrongful interpretation or application of domestic regulation. Further, the complainants may directly challenge breaches of human rights guaranteed in international treaties that are binding upon Slovenia. In practice, the most frequent document of reference is understandably the ECHR, but also the International Covenant on Civil and Political Rights and the General Declaration on Human Rights that is considered as international customary law in Slovenia and as such directly applicable. With the entering into force of the Lisbon Treaty, the Charter of the EU on Fundamental Rights also gained binding force and as such needs to be applied by the Slovenian Courts.

There are some cases where the Constitutional Court reviewed a human rights breach only from the perspective of an international treaty, mostly concerning the right to examine incriminating witnesses.[72] For example, in decision Up-207/99 the Constitutional Court examined a constitutional complaint against the decision of the Supreme Court, thereby referring to the third paragraph of Article 6 of the

[68] Case U-I-60/03, para 11, footnotes omitted.

[69] See e.g. Kaučič and Grad (2003), pp. 318–319.

[70] Before all extraordinary legal remedies have been exhausted (however, not before all appeals, which have the nature of an ordinary legal remedy, have been exhausted), the Constitutional Court may exceptionally decide on a constitutional complaint if two conditions are met: (1) the alleged violation is manifestly obvious, and (2) irreparable consequences for the complainant would result from the implementation of the individual act—see Guide through the Constitutional Court. What is a constitutional complaint and in what instances may one be lodged? http://www.us-rs.si/en/about-the-court/institution/frequently-asked-questions/4-what-is-a-constitutional-complaint-and-in-what-i/. Accessed 21 March 2013.

[71] See Cases Up-123/05 and Up-605/05.

[72] Umek (2011), p. 143.

ECHR. It stated that the defendant must be allowed to challenge incriminating statements, either in the investigation phase or at the main hearing, and to examine the author thereof with respect to such statements. In that case, it decided that the right to examine witnesses against the defendant was not violated, as the defendant had had the opportunity to examine the injured party in the investigation phase but did not use the opportunity for reasons he was responsible for. In this decision, the Constitutional Court took into account the positions of the ECtHR in *Kostovski v. The Netherlands* (1989), in which the ECtHR explained the substance of the right to examine witnesses against the defendant.[73]

4.2.3 References of Constitutionality

International law is also applied by the Constitutional Court in a different role, i.e. as a subject-matter of review in the ratification procedures of international treaties, when the Constitutional Court reviews their consistency with the Constitution.

4.2.3.1 A Priori Reference of Constitutionality

According to Article 160(2) of the Constitution, 'In the process of ratifying a treaty, the Constitutional Court, on the proposal of the President of the Republic, the Government or a third of the deputies of the National Assembly, issues an opinion on the conformity of such treaty with the Constitution. The National Assembly is bound by the opinion of the Constitutional Court'. A similar provision is also contained in Article 21 of the Constitutional Court Act[74] as well as in Article 70 of the same act, which also states that 'the Constitutional Court adopts such opinion at a closed session'.[75]

In the above-mentioned case concerning the European Association Agreement, the Constitutional Court held that an opinion of the Constitutional Court is not a consultative opinion:

> Regardless of a different designation, what is involved is a decision of the Constitutional Court whose legal character is, with respect to its effects, identical with other decisions of the Constitutional Court. It differs from decisions in that it cannot be used by the Constitutional Court in a manner which will interfere with the international agreement itself, so as

[73] See also Case Up-1378/06.

[74] Paragraph (2) of this Article states: 'In the process of ratifying a treaty, the Constitutional Court issues an opinion on the conformity of such treaty with the Constitution in the manner provided by this Act'.

[75] See Škrk (2009), pp. 54–61.

> it can interfere with acts of internal law – which are abrogated retrospectively or prospectively whenever a nonconformity has been identified.[76]

The Court also emphasised that in the case of assessing the conformity of an international agreement with the Constitution, it acts as a State body governed by internal law. For this reason it will carry out a review of an international agreement from the viewpoint of its conformity with the Constitution, but not also from the viewpoint of international law.[77] The Court made clear that an opinion concerning conformity with the Constitution as established does not bind just the National Assembly but, to an equal degree, with regard to the scope of and the reasons for the review, it also binds the Constitutional Court itself—and thus has the effect of a matter adjudged *(res iudicata)*.[78]

In the same case, the Court confirmed that a proposal for the evaluation of constitutionality can only be filed by three petitioners who are defined as such by the Constitution: the President of the Republic, the Government, or one third of the Deputies of the National Assembly.[79] It can be lodged only during the ratification procedure, that is, at the time when an international agreement has already been signed and after a proposed law on ratification has been submitted for consideration but has not yet been adopted by the National Assembly.[80] As the Constitution provides that the National Assembly shall be bound by any such opinion of the Constitutional Court, the National Assembly can, after a motion for constitutional review has been filed, decide concerning the ratification only after the opinion of the Constitutional Court has been delivered to it.

The Constitutional Court also explained that it evaluates the conformity of provisions of an international agreement with the Constitution at the time of reaching the decision, and regardless of when (if at all) the agreement will become effective.

It should also be mentioned that in the case concerning the Agreement between the Republic of Slovenia and the Republic of Croatia on Border Traffic and Cooperation, the Court found:

> The Agreement of the Presidents of the Governments of the states parties (...) is not a regulation as it was neither ratified nor published, and thus did not become a part of the internal law. Therefore, according to Art. 160.1 of the Constitution, the Constitutional Court does not have jurisdiction to review it.[81]

In the case concerning the Nuclear Power Plant Krško,[82] the Court explained that the purpose of the preventive constitutional review of treaties is to prevent the

---

[76] Case Rm-1/97, para 15, footnotes omitted.

[77] This is under the competence of the International Court of Justice in The Hague and other international courts and tribunals. See Škrk (2009), p. 53.

[78] More on this in Škrk (2009), p. 59.

[79] Ibid, p. 58.

[80] Ibid, p. 57.

[81] Case U-I-376/02, abstract. Umek (2011), p. 138.

[82] Case Rm-2/02, a review of the Treaty between the Government of the Republic of Slovenia and the Government of the Republic of Croatia on the Regulation of Status and Other Legal Relations Connected with the Investments in the Krško Nuclear Power Plant, its Use and Decommissioning.

State at the moment of ratifying a treaty from assuming an obligation under international law that would be inconsistent with the Constitution.[83] It continued by holding that when the Constitutional Court issues an opinion that the individual provisions of a treaty are inconsistent with the Constitution, the effect of such a decision can be double:

(1) if the treaty can be ratified with a proviso, the National Assembly can ratify such only provided that it uses its proviso concerning those provisions for which the opinion on inconsistency was issued;
(2) if the treaty does not allow a provision or if such is not admissible according to the provisions of the Vienna Convention on the Law of Treaties, given the valid constitutional system, the National Assembly must not ratify such a treaty or can ratify such only after it appropriately amends the Constitution. When the Constitutional Court issues an opinion that a treaty is not inconsistent with the Constitution, the decision on adopting an act of ratification is a matter of the political decision-making process of the National Assembly. Similarly, as when it reviews regulations, the Constitutional Court may not embark on the issue of the appropriateness of certain solutions when it decides on the consistency of a treaty with the Constitution; even less so can it review the issue of whether certain solutions are favourable for the State, or not.[84]

As already mentioned, the Constitutional Court is competent to review the consistency of legislative and executive acts with generally accepted principles of international law; however, it cannot present a standard of review of international treaties in the procedures of *a priori* references of constitutionality. In the case related to the Agreement between the Republic of Slovenia and the Holy See on Legal Issues, the Constitutional Court ruled:

> On the basis of Art. 160.2 of the Constitution, the Constitutional Court is vested with a special power of the preliminary (a priori) constitutional review of treaties. This power only refers to the review of conformity with the Constitution, not with ratified treaties and the general principles of international law. The purpose of the preliminary constitutional review of treaties is to prevent the State, at the ratification of a treaty, from assuming an international-law obligation that would be inconsistent with the Constitution, or from being compelled, after the ratification, to adjust the treaty with the Constitution, what could cause serious complications.[85]

Additionally, the Constitutional Court emphasised that it does not have jurisdiction to review the mutual consistency of treaties.[86]

---

[83] Ibid, para 19.
[84] Ibid, para 21.
[85] See e.g. Case Rm-1/02, para 8.
[86] Case Rm-1/97.

4.2.3.2 A Posteriori Reference of Constitutionality

Although *a posteriori* reference of constitutionality is not foreseen in the Constitution, the Constitutional Court in its opinion Rm-1/97 already declared it was competent to review already ratified treaties,[87] although this is rare in practice.[88] This concerns indirect review of the legality of international treaties—through reviewing the act of ratification and can be both substantive and procedural. In this respect, the Court may review acts of ratification adopted both by the National Assembly and by the Government.

In the case concerning the Agreement between the Republic of Slovenia and the Republic of Croatia on military pensions, the Court held:

> Since on the basis of article 160 of the Constitution, the Constitutional Court is competent to assess the constitutionality and legality of statutory regulations, the subject of assessment of constitutionality and legality is the Decree on ratification of the Agreement. With the assessment of the constitutionality and legality of this Decree, the Constitutional Court also of course indirectly judges the constitutionality of the Agreement itself. Such an indirect assessment of the constitutionality of international agreements is also validated in the practice of the Italian Constitutional Court and the German Federal Constitutional Court.[89]

A specific question related to *a posteriori* reference of constitutionality is whether the Constitutional Court is also competent to review the legality of international treaties ratified by a decree of the Government. The Court decided in the case concerning the Code of Conduct for Fishermen on the border with Croatia that a review of a decree of the Government by which a treaty was ratified cannot justify the jurisdiction of the Constitutional Court to review the legality of a treaty. This means that a statute and a treaty ratified by a decree may be inconsistent, but the Constitutional Court does not have jurisdiction to review such inconsistency.[90] The Constitutional Court will review inconsistency between a statute and a treaty ratified by a decree of the Government only if the inconsistency is a violation of the principle of the rule of law. In such a case, the question of the legality of the decree on ratification (for which the Constitutional Court has jurisdiction) could be raised. The question of the constitutionality of a decree is also raised in the case of the unconstitutionality of one of the provisions of a treaty.

---

[87] See also Case U-I-128/98 concerning the Israeli Agreement.

[88] Umek (2011), p. 144. See also Škrk (2009), pp. 66–67.

[89] Case U-I-147/94, para 9.

[90] According to Škrk (2009), p. 70; and Škrk (2007), pp. 308–310, this changes the position the Court implied in Case U-I-147/94 (the pensions case), where it left at least the hypothetical possibility to review the legitimacy of international treaties ratified by a governmental decree.

In such a case, the decree would violate the Constitution, as it would incorporate an unconstitutional legal norm into the internal legal order.[91]

4.2.4 Application of International Law as an Interpretative Instrument

In practice, international law is often used as an instrument when interpreting certain provisions of the Constitution and defining the scope of certain constitutional rights. For example, in the case concerning the Act on the Census of the Population, Households, and Housing,[92] the Constitutional Court declared that collecting data on the religious beliefs of citizens by the state is not inconsistent with the principle of the separation of religious communities and the state, as the Act on the Census of the Population ensures that the persons counted freely declare their religion, or decide whether at all to answer such a question. Thereby, it emphasised that the Universal Declaration of Human Rights of the United Nations ensures everyone the right to freedom of thought, conscience and religion (Art. 18). The Court explained that pursuant to the Universal Declaration of the UN, this right includes the freedom to change one's religion or belief, and the freedom, either alone or in community with others and in public or private, to manifest one's religion or belief in teaching, practice, worship and observance. The Court also found that, in compliance with the Universal Declaration of the UN, the right to the freedom of thought, conscience and religion is also ensured by Art. 9 ECHR and Article 18 of the International Covenant on Civil and Political Rights and concluded that the freedom of religion arises from the provisions of the Constitution and the binding instruments of international law (Art. 8 of the Constitution).

Further, in the case concerning the Enforcing the Public Interest in the Field of Culture Act,[93] the Court held that the particularities of the work and profession of theatre actors follow from the nature of the matter and therefore this is not like any other type of work. It said that the legislature could thus regulate their fixed-term employment relations differently from other workers, given that ensuring a quality cast is a sound reason for the different regulation of the employment relations of theatre actors and for the greater possibility to apply fixed-term employment relations. In this respect, the Court also referred to the European Social Charter, which provides for the right to work, which should, however, be defined by statutory legislation.

[91] Case U-I-376/02. Thus, the Constitutional Court did not review whether the Code of Conduct for Fishermen during Fishing is inconsistent with the law. The petitioners did not assert that a manifest inconsistency of this Code with the stated laws would be a violation of Art. 2 of the Constitution. The allegations on inconsistency with other constitutional provisions were general; therefore the Constitutional Court did not review them.

[92] Case U-I-92/01.

[93] Case U-I-278/07.

4.3 *References to International Law by Ordinary Courts*

As mentioned above, the Constitutional Court is not the only court bound to apply international law in Slovenia, but also ordinary courts of all instances.[94] Concluding from the case law of the Supreme Court, they most often refer to and apply the ECHR. This is necessary if the state wants to avoid condemnation by the ECtHR. Employment tribunals also often refer to the conventions of the International Labour Organisation (ILO). A few examples of applying the ECHR by the Slovenian Supreme Court are presented in this section.

As stated above, the Constitutional Court often applies the ECHR—both when reviewing the legality and constitutionality of the Slovenian legislation, as well as of executive acts and when considering constitutional complaints. Additionally, the Supreme Court of the Republic of Slovenia has referred to the ECHR and the case law of the ECtHR in numerous decisions.[95] Betetto[96] found that the civil law department of the Supreme Court directly referred to the ECHR in at least 63 cases, whereas it referred to the case law of the ECtHR in at least 224 cases. The number of references is rapidly increasing.[97] The impact of the ECHR and the case law of the ECtHR extends to various fields:

(a) The right to a fair trial (including the right to access to court,[98] the right to be heard,[99] the right to a hearing within a reasonable time[100]);
(b) The right to respect for private and family life[101];
(c) The right to freedom of expression[102];

[94] In the past years this has become increasingly accepted by judges at all instances. There were cases in the past, however, when judges claimed that the parties may not refer to the ECHR before the national courts, but only before the ECtHR—see e.g. Case P 166/06. For a comment, see Knez (2012), p. 104.

[95] Betetto (2012), pp. 1235–1248.

[96] Judge and vice-president of the Supreme Court.

[97] From about five cases a year in 2001–2004 to about 50 cases a year in 2010 and 2011.

[98] This is the most common ground to refer to the ECHR—see e.g. the following decisions of the Supreme Court: VSRS II Ips 996/2006, VSRS II Ips 367/2008, VSRS II Ips 868/2009 and VSRS II Ips 64/2010.

[99] See e.g. VSRS II Ips 288/2009, VSRS II Ips 908/2007, VSRS II Ips 431/2010, VSRS II Ips 410/2010, VSRS II Ips 133/2011 and VSRS II Ips 134/2011.

[100] See e.g. VSRS II Ips 477/2008, VSRS II Ips 362/2010, VSRS II Ips 198/2010, VSRS II Ips 232/2008 and VSRS II Ips 297/2008.

[101] In the Case VSRS II Ips 462/2009, the Supreme Court referred to Article 14 ECHR when considering the rights of same-sex couples. In the case VSRS II Ips 706/2009, the Supreme Court was deciding on the right to contact children after divorce and was in this respect critical of the ECtHR ruling in *Hokkanen v. Finland* (Case 19823/92).

[102] In Cases VSRS II Ips 274/2005 and VSRS II Ips 275/2005, the Supreme Court referred to *Malone v. United Kingdom* (ECtHR Case 8691/79) and *Roemen and Schmitt v. Luxembourg* (ECtHR Case 51772/99). In Case Cp 8/2004, the Supreme Court referred to Article 10 ECHR

(d) The right to receive information.[103]

In contrast, there are provisions of the ECHR, which, according to the Supreme Court decisions, are not directly applicable as they are not sufficiently clear and precise in defining rights and obligations to enable application by the national courts. An example of such a provision is Article 13 ECHR on the right to effective legal remedy.[104] In relation to this provision of the ECHR, the ECtHR ruled in *Kurić and others v. Slovenia*[105] that Slovenia violated Article 13 ECHR. On 26 February 1992, the date on which the Aliens Act became applicable, the municipal administrative authorities removed those who had not applied for or obtained Slovenian citizenship from the Register of Permanent Residents and, according to the Government, transferred them into the Register of Aliens without a Residence Permit (the so-called erased case). However, since the Supreme Court considers Article 13 ECHR directly inapplicable, a 'systematic solution' by the National Assembly was necessary.[106] The Supreme Court similarly declines that national courts would be granting damages on the basis of Article 41 ECHR guaranteeing just satisfaction, as, according to the Supreme Court, this is limited to procedures before the ECtHR and concerns international liability for damages of states.[107]

5 References to the Case Law of Foreign Courts

In decisions of the Slovenian Constitutional Court, one can also find references to the case law of foreign courts. This case law is understandably not binding upon the Court; however, it gives a comparative law perspective to the reasoning of the Court and serves as an interpretative instrument that strengthens the arguments of the Court. The courts to which the Slovenian Constitutional Court most often refers include the German *Bundesverfassungsgericht*, the French *Conseil Constitutionnel*, the Italian *Consiglo dello Stato* and the US Supreme Court. A few examples are given as follows.

In the case concerning the Restrictions on the Use of Tobacco Products Act,[108] the Court ruled that a statutory regulation which prohibits smoking in indoor public places and indoor working places does not breach the right of assembly. It

when declining the appeal against a decision of a lower court to fine the appellant for contempt of court.

[103] See Cases VSRS II Ips 274/2005 and VSRS II Ips 275/2005.

[104] See Cases VSRS II Ips 591/2008 and VSRS II Ips 470/2009.

[105] ECtHR Case 26828/06.

[106] See the Act Regulating the Legal Status of Citizens of Former Yugoslavia Living in the Republic of Slovenia, Official Gazette of the Republic of Slovenia, No. 76/2010, as well as the Supreme Court's decision in VSRS II Ips 315/2010.

[107] Betetto (2012), p. 1248.

[108] Case U-I-218/07.

explained *inter alia* that the 'right of assembly requires assembly with the intention of common expression with the objective of participating in a public expression of opinions'.[109] In this respect, the Court referred to the German Federal Constitutional Court decision in the Loveparade Case.[110]

In the case concerning the Organization and Financing of Upbringing and Education Act,[111] the Court reviewed the question of whether the exclusion of denominational activities from the premises of public and licensed kindergartens and schools, outside the scope of performing their public service, admissibly interferes with the positive aspect of the freedom of conscience of an individual. In paragraph 13, the Court interpreted the meaning of negative religious freedoms and in this respect referred to the case law of the German Federal Constitutional Court[112] and of the US Supreme Court.[113]

In the case concerning the Rules of Procedure of the National Assembly,[114] the appellant referred to the German Law, and the Constitutional Court found:

> In German law (...) the budget is adopted in the form of a law, since the German Constitution explicitly determines this in the first paragraph of article 110. In the practice of the German courts and in German legal theory, the standpoint has been formed that the budget (act) is a law only in the formal sense, and that it does not have external effect, that it does 'not provide grounds for and does not remove rights (claims) and obligations' (decision of the Federal German Constitutional Court – BVerfGE, 38, 125 and following). It is thus possible to find a firm basis in German legal theory and court practice (quite contrary to what the appellant states) for concluding that the budget does not contain legal norms which would have to be adopted in the form of a law in compliance with article 87 of the Constitution.[115]

In the case of the Agreement between the Republic of Slovenia and the Holy See on Legal Issues,[116] the Court referred to the French Conseil Constitutionnel and stated:

> An interpretative decision (*la décision de non-contrariété sous réserve*) was introduced in the constitutional review of treaties by the French Conseil constitutionnel. Instead of finding that a treaty provision is inconsistent with the constitution, it interprets such in a manner such that makes possible a review that it is not inconsistent with the constitution.[117]

---

[109] Ibid, para 20.

[110] The Loveparade Case, BVerfG, 1 BvQ 28/01, dated 12 July 2001, para 16.

[111] Case U-I-68/98.

[112] BVerfG, judgment dated 16 May 1995—1 BvR 1087/91 in BVefGE 93, 1 and BVerfGE, judgment dated 16 May 1995—1BvR 1087/91.

[113] *Stone v. Graham*, 449 U.S. 39 (1980) and *Lee v. Weisma*, 505 U.S. 577 (1992).

[114] Case U-I-40/96.

[115] Ibid, para 12.

[116] Case Rm-1/02.

[117] Ibid, footnote 41.

As the last example, in the case concerning the Quality, Labelling, and Packing of Feedingstuffs,[118] the Court referred not only to the decision of the Court of Justice of the European Union,[119] as the case concerned Directive 2002/02/EC, but also to the *Conseil d'État* and *Consiglio di Stato*:

> As the reasons due to which it established serious doubt as to their validity, the (CJEU) mentioned lack of a legal basis in Art. 152(4)(b) of the EC Treaty, the violation of the fundamental right to property, and the violation of the principle of proportionality. The temporary suspension of regulations of member states issued on the basis of the disputed Directive was for similar reasons also adopted by the French State Council (Conseil d'État) and the Italian State Council (Consiglio di Stato). Concerning the above-said, the Constitutional Court established that there was a serious doubt as to the validity of the mentioned Directive. In view of the fact that the request for preliminary ruling as submitted to the EC Court by the English court entirely covers the reasons which also in the petitioners' opinion point to the fact that the disputed provisions of the mentioned Directive are invalid, and due to which also the Constitutional Court found a serious doubt as to their validity, it is not necessary that the request for preliminary ruling as regards the validity of the disputed Directive provision is also submitted by the Constitutional Court.[120]

6 Association Agreement: Towards the '*New Legal Order of International Law*'

In May 1992 the Agreement on the Establishment of Diplomatic Relations between the EEC and Slovenia entered into force. On the basis of this agreement, the so-called Co-operation Agreement was signed in April 1993, introducing the Most-Favoured Nation principle and covering commercial, technical and financial cooperation, as well as trade issues, which were then under the exclusive competence of the EEC. In January 1997 the so-called Interim Agreement on Trade[121] started to apply, which began the process of gradual liberalisation of trade between the parties. This agreement was repealed by the Association Agreement,[122] which entered into force on 1 February 1999 and served as a legal basis for intense integration of the EU legal order into Slovenian law. When the Association

[118] Case U-I-113/04.

[119] Case C-453/03 *ABNA Ltd and Others v. Secretary of State for Health and Food Standards Agency* [2005] ECR I-423.

[120] Case U-I-113/04, para 10, footnotes omitted.

[121] The Interim Agreement on Trade and Trade-Related Affairs between the Republic of Slovenia of the one part and the European Community, European Steel and Coal Community and European Atomic Energy Community of the other part—ratification act published in the Official Gazette of the Republic of Slovenia, No. 8/1997.

[122] The Europe Agreement Establishing an Association between the European Communities and their Member States, acting within the Framework of the European Union, of the one Part, and the Republic of Slovenia, of the Other Part, ratification act published in the Official Gazette of the Republic of Slovenia, No. 13/1997.

Agreement was signed in June 1996 Slovenia also officially applied for membership.[123]

The Association Agreement was considered as an ordinary international treaty and has been applied by the Slovenian Constitutional Court in three cases.

Firstly, the Association Agreement was the subject of an *a priori* constitutional review, which was requested by the Government in the procedure of ratification.[124] The Court ruled that the following provisions were consistent with the Slovenian Constitution:

a) the provision according to which subsidiaries of Community companies shall have the right to acquire and sell real property and, as regards natural resources, agricultural land and forestry, the same rights as enjoyed by Slovenian nationals and companies, where these rights are necessary for the conduct of the economic activities for which they are established in so far as a subsidiary of a Community company shall be deemed to be a company established, registered and operating on the territory of Slovenia and in accordance with the law of the Republic of Slovenia;
b) the provision according to which foreigners shall, in accordance with international agreements, enjoy all those rights which are guaranteed by the Constitution, with the exception of those rights which only citizens of Slovenia may enjoy pursuant to the Constitution or the law, in so far as interpreted in the sense that the citizens of the Member States of the European Union shall have the right to purchase real property in Slovenia under conditions equal to those applying to the citizens of the Republic of Slovenia.

In contrast to this, the Court found the following provisions inconsistent with the Constitution:

a) the provision of the Association Agreement according to which Slovenia shall grant to Community nationals and branches of Community companies the right to acquire and sell real property and, as regards natural resources, agricultural land and forestry, the same rights as enjoyed by Slovenian nationals and companies, where these rights are necessary for the conduct of economic activities, in so far as the right to acquire and sell real property refers to land as Article 68 of the Constitution at that time provided that foreigners may not acquire title to land except by inheritance subject to reciprocity;
b) the provision according to which Slovenia shall take the measures necessary to allow the citizens of the Member States of the European Union, on a reciprocal

[123] Ilešič et al. (2000), pp. 30–31.

[124] Case Rm-1/97 as of 6 May 1997 concerning the Ratification of the Europe Agreement Establishing an Association between the Republic of Slovenia, of the one part, and the European Communities (hereinafter: the Community) and their Member States, Acting within the Framework of the European Union, of the other part. The whole opinion is accessible at: http://odlocitve.us-rs.si/usrs/us-odl.nsf/o/920B1846747C32CCC12571720029D449. Accessed 3 April 2013.

basis, the right to purchase real property on a non-discriminatory basis (. . .) in so far as the right to purchase real property refers to the purchase of land;

c) the provision according to which Slovenia shall grant to the citizens of the EU Member States, having permanently resided on the present territory of the Republic of Slovenia for a period of 3 years, on a reciprocal basis, the right to purchase real property (. . .) in so far as the right to purchase real property refers to land.

The Court also emphasised that a competent State body may not approve any such commitment of the Republic of Slovenia under international law that would be in disagreement with the Constitution. A commitment under international law would be in disagreement with the Constitution if, by the coming into force of an international agreement, it created directly applicable unconstitutional norms in internal law, or if it bound the State to adopt any such instrument of internal law as would be in disagreement with the Constitution. It also held that by passing a law on ratification of the Association Agreement, the Republic of Slovenia would bind itself to adopt legal instruments which would guarantee the rights to purchase land, in particular a statute for amending the applicable constitutional provision according to which foreigners may not acquire title to land.[125]

In addition to the constitutional review, the Constitutional Court later referred to the Association Agreement in two other cases.

In the case concerning the conditions for leasing areas beside motorways for the construction of facilities for associated activities,[126] the Court ruled that the Association agreement does not apply, as the disputed Order preceded its application:

> The European Agreement on Association (. . .) did not enter into validity with the concluding document signed on 10 June 1996 in Luxembourg (hereinafter: EA). It came into effect, namely, on the first day of the second month of the date on which the contract parties informed each other that the internal procedures for approving the agreement in Slovenia, on the one hand, and in all member states on the part of the European Union on the other (article 131 EA) were completed. The positive opinion of the European parliament is also required (. . .). The impugned provision of the Order also ceased to apply prior to the introduction (8.8.1997) of the Ratification Act (. . .), with final documents and protocols with which is adopted the European Agreement (. . .), whereby the National Assembly approved that the State of Slovenia binds itself in international law to fulfilling the EA. The impugned provision of the Order also ceased to apply prior to the Ratification Act of the Interim Agreement (. . .), which covered only the trade part of the (association) agreement. This provision of the Order even ceased to apply prior to 1.1.1997, that is prior to the date from which this Temporary Agreement which was signed in Brussels on 11 November 1996, was temporarily used even prior to its ratification in the National Assembly. So an investigation in the sense of whether the impugned provision of the Order was in conflict

---

[125] The Constitutional Act amending Article 68 of the Constitution was proclaimed by the National Assembly on 14 July 1997, so that since then it provides: ‘Foreigners may acquire ownership rights to real estate under conditions provided by law or a treaty ratified by the National Assembly’.

[126] Case U-I-296/96.

> with adopted international obligations which derive from the EA was unnecessary, even if the initiator were to have introduced it.[127]

In the case concerning the method and conditions by which non-residents buy securities in the Republic of Slovenia,[128] the Court rejected the petitions of companies Publicum and Catalia for the commencement of proceedings to review the constitutionality and legality of the Order on Cross-Border Payment and to review the constitutionality and legality of the Order on the Method and Conditions by which Non-residents Buy Securities in the Republic of Slovenia. The Court held:

> The challenged regulation does not regulate legal relations between a stock exchange broker and an alien. It has only an indirect impact on these relations, and insofar as the stock exchange broker must obey these regulations when entering into transactions for an alien. Therefore, the stock exchange broker does not have a legal interest for challenging thereof. The Europe Association Agreement (EAA), to which the second petitioner refers to does not relate to it, as it is not a resident of Slovenia neither a resident of the Community. Therefore, it does not have a legal interest to challenge the regulation, which is alleged to be inconsistent with EAA.[129]

The Association Agreement has also been applied by the Slovenian Supreme Court, although rarely. However, in most cases when the parties relied on it the Court decided the Agreement does not apply. For example, in Case X Ips 13/2010 the appellant invoked the Agreement by requiring the application of a preferential customs duty. Nevertheless, the Supreme Court held that the imported goods could not be considered as goods having origin that is required for the Association Agreement to apply.[130] In Case X Ips 845/97, the Court denied the application of the Association Agreement to mutually recognise a customs information document issued by the Austrian customs authorities. Courts that quite often relied upon the Association Agreement include the Administrative Court. Relevant cases concern duty-free shops,[131] competition law,[132] patents,[133] etc.[134] It has generally been accepted that the provisions of the Association Agreement apply directly on the basis of Article 8 of the Slovenian Constitution and that national courts may, if they

---

[127] Ibid, para 14.

[128] Case U-I-94/97.

[129] Ibid, abstract.

[130] See also Cases I Up 147/2004, I Up 969/2004, I Up 1282/2004, I Up 1441/2004, I Up 83/2005, X Ips 77/2009, X Ips 375/2009, X Ips 63/2010 and X Ips 65/2010. Most of these cases concern situations where goods were initially recognised of appropriate origin for the Association Agreement to apply, but then falsification of the relevant documents on origin was proven and the customs procedures were renewed by denying the application of the Associational Agreement.

[131] Case I-U-700/2010.

[132] Case U 1286/2003.

[133] Case U 706/2001.

[134] In Case I-U-82/2009, the Administrative Court also referred to the Stabilisation and Association Agreement with Croatia.

consider specific provisions self-executing, grant rights to individuals directly on the basis of such a provision of the Agreement.[135] It has in this respect also been accepted that they should *mutatis mutandis* apply the case law of the Court of Justice of the European Union in cases concerning mirror provisions of the Treaty establishing the European Community. This was important to catalyse delay in the work of the executive and legislative authorities in bringing the Slovenian law in line with the EU law.[136]

For the application of EU law to come into practice, it was important to introduce various seminars on EU law for those judges and others under duty to apply EU law, who did not have EU law courses at university level. Courses on EU law had already been gradually introduced since 1992, first as one semester optional courses of general EU law, then as an obligatory course of two semesters. After accession, Slovenian law faculties introduced more specialised courses on EU law (e.g. institutions and principles of EU law, internal market law, judicial protection in the EU, EU competition law, European civil procedure, European environmental law, etc.). An examination of EU law is also included in the bar exam.[137]

7 Application of EU Law After Accession

With Slovenian membership in the EU, it was no longer sufficient to grant EU law a subconstitutional status as for traditional international law. If Article 8 was being applied also in relation to EU law, the principle of supremacy of EU law as defined by the Court of Justice of the European Union in the cases *Van Gend en Loos*[138] and *Costa/ENEL*[139] could not have full effect. There were intense discussions about whether the Constitution should be changed for this purpose. The decision was taken to amend the Constitution in order to pave the way for a limited transfer of sovereignty to EU institutions, as otherwise the Accession Treaty would on the basis of Article 8 of the Constitution be below the Constitution, and the Slovenian Constitutional Court could hold primary and secondary EU law inapplicable in Slovenia for reasons of its conflict with the Slovenian Constitution.[140] As this is not

[135] Professor Mirko Ilešič prepared an overview of the Agreement's provisions in terms of their direct effect. See Ilešič (1997), pp. 1323–1351.

[136] See e.g. Ilešič (1999), pp. 3–4.

[137] See Ilešič (1995), pp. 26–27.

[138] In the Case 26/62 *Van Gend en Loos* [1963] ECR 3, the CJEU held: 'the Community constitutes a new legal order of international law for the benefit of which the states have limited their sovereign rights, albeit within limited fields'.

[139] In Case 6/64 *Flaminio* Costa *v ENEL* [1964] ECR 585, it was held: 'the law stemming from the Treaty, an independent source of law, could not, because of its special and original nature, be overridden by domestic legal provisions, however framed, without being deprived of its character as Community law and without the legal basis of the Community itself being called into question'.

[140] See Cerar (2011), pp. 83–84.

in accordance with the principle of supremacy of EU law, various solutions were proposed to amend the Slovenian Constitution—from abstract (to enable a transfer of sovereignty to international organisations in general) to concrete (to mention the EU expressly, and potentially some other organisations, e.g. NATO). A combined solution was also proposed, but the abstract approach prevailed. Consequently, by a Constitutional Law of 2003,[141] the Constitution was amended, so that a new Article 3a was added[142] which recognises that EU law actually is a different kind of international law and that it can produce effects which override the highest Slovenian law—the Constitution.

As to the application of EU law by the Slovenian courts, a conclusion can be made that in the first few years EU law was relatively rarely applied—mostly by administrative courts, but gradually also other courts started to apply it more regularly.[143]

Most EU-related cases of Slovenian courts concern public law: asylum cases, issues concerning indirect and direct taxation (including excise duties), environmental protection, health services (e.g. cost reimbursement), recognition of professional qualifications, free movement of goods, the European arrest warrant, etc. Civil law cases related to EU law, on the other hand, mostly concern competition law, employment law and recognition of judgments. Despite initial passiveness by the Slovenian courts as to referring questions for a preliminary ruling to the Court of Justice of the EU, in the past few years some questions have been referred.[144]

---

[141] Official Gazette of the Republic of Slovenia, No. 24/03.

[142] Article 3a of the Slovenian Constitution provides: 'Pursuant to a treaty ratified by the National Assembly by a two-thirds majority vote of all deputies, Slovenia may transfer the exercise of part of its sovereign rights to international organisations which are based on respect for human rights and fundamental freedoms, democracy and the principles of the rule of law and may enter into a defensive alliance with states which are based on respect for these values.

Before ratifying a treaty referred to in the preceding paragraph, the National Assembly may call a referendum. A proposal shall pass at the referendum if a majority of voters who have cast valid votes vote in favour of such. The National Assembly is bound by the result of such referendum. If such referendum has been held, a referendum regarding the law on the ratification of the treaty concerned may not be called.

Legal acts and decisions adopted within international organisations to which Slovenia has transferred the exercise of part of its sovereign rights shall be applied in Slovenia in accordance with the legal regulation of these organisations.

In procedures for the adoption of legal acts and decisions in international organisations to which Slovenia has transferred the exercise of part of its sovereign rights, the Government shall promptly inform the National Assembly of proposals for such acts and decisions as well as of its own activities. The National Assembly may adopt positions thereon, which the Government shall take into consideration in its activities. The relationship between the National Assembly and the Government arising from this paragraph shall be regulated in detail by a law adopted by a two-thirds majority vote of deputies present'.

[143] See Knez (2012).

[144] Case C-403/09 PPU Detiček—concerning recognition of foreign judgments (referred by the High Court in Maribor); Case C-536/09 Omejc—concerning the Common Agricultural Policy (referred by the Administrative Court); Case C-603/10 Pelati—concerning taxation (again referred

8 Conclusion

Slovenia has adopted nearly 3,000 bilateral international acts and nearly 1,500 multilateral international acts,[145] although Slovenian courts do not often apply them. The Constitutional Court is to a certain extent an exception in this regard as it often applies international treaties—much more often than customary international law.[146] Reservations as to its application also stand for EU law, although to a lesser degree, particularly because of the directly applicable EU regulations. Regardless of the increasing application of EU law by Slovenian courts, some systemic problems can still be noticed, e.g. distinguishing between direct applicability and direct effect, the relationship between the Constitution and EU law, the applicability of EU law *ratione temporis*, etc.[147] Notwithstanding this, however, there is a legal basis, as well as a duty, to apply international and EU law in situations provided for by law. What is needed is for judges to become increasingly aware of the provisions covered by their duty enshrined in the maxime '*iura novit curia*', and for parties before Slovenian courts to become better informed about their rights recognised by international and EU law, as then they can also claim these rights before national courts.

References

Andrassy J, Bakotić B, Vukas B (1995) Međunarodno pravo I. Školska knjiga, Zagreb, p 6

International Legal Materials (1992) Arbitration opinion of the Arbitration Commission of the International Conference on the Former Yugoslavia No. 7 of 11 January. Int Legal Mater 6:1512–1517

Betetto N (2012) Vpliv Evropske konvencije za človekove pravice na slovensko sodno prakso. Podjetje in delo 38(6–7):1235–1248

Buergenthal T (1992) Self-executing and non-selfexecuting treaties in national and international law. Recueil des Cours, Académie de droit Int 235:317

Cerar M (2011) Komentar člena 3a. In: Šturm L (ed) Komentar Ustave Republike Slovenije, dopolnitev – A. Fakulteta za državne in evropske študije, pp 83–84

Drenik S (2009) Praksa sklepanja mednarodnih pogodb v Republiki Sloveniji. Javna uprava 45 (1/2):127–129

Ilešič M (1995) Uvajanje evropskega prava v študijske programe v Sloveniji. Univerzitetna revija Maribor 2(3):26–27

Ilešič M (1997) Pridružitveni sporazum in njegovi učinki v notranjem pravnem redu. Podjetje in delo 23:1323–1351

Ilešič M (1999) Pridruženi smo... kaj pa zdaj? Pravna praksa 3:3–4

by the Administrative Court); and Case C-541/11 Grilc—concerning insurance (referred by the Supreme Court).

[145] Drenik (2009), pp. 127–129.

[146] Sancin (2012), p. 1220.

[147] Knez (2012), p. 109.

Iləšič T, Jug P, Pogačnik M, Prek M, Vehar P (2000) Pravni vidiki pridružitvenega procesa. Gospodarski vestnik, Ljubljana, pp 30–31
Kaučič I, Grad F (2003) Ustavna ureditev Slovenija. GV Založba, Ljubljana, pp 318–319
Knez R (2012) Analiza prakse uporabe prava EU v sodnih postopkih v Sloveniji. Gospodarski subjekti na trgu. Zbornik, Pravna fakulteta Univerze v Mariboru, p 104
Pogačnik M (1996) Veljavnost mednarodnih pogodb v Republiki Sloveniji. Pravnik 51(6–8):365
Sancin V (2012) Uporaba mednarodnega prava pred slovenskimi sodišči. Podjetje in delo 38 (6–7):1214
Škrk M (2007) Odnos med mednarodnim pravom in notranjim pravom v praksi Ustavnega sodišča. Pravnik 62(6–8):275
Škrk M (2009) Ustavnosodna presoja mednarodnih pogodb. Javna uprava 1–2:53
Škrk M (2012a) Običajno mednarodno pravo v slovenski sodni praksi. Podjetje in delo 38 (6–7):1224–1234
Škrk M (2012b) 'Ukradeni otroci' in sodna imuniteta držav. Pravnik 67(5/6):321–350
Umek U (2011) Komentar 8. člena. In: Šturm L (ed) Komentar Ustave Republike Slovenije, dopolnitev – A. Fakulteta za državne in evropske študije, Ljubljana, p 132

Part IV
Conclusions

Judicial Application of International and European Law in Southeast Europe

Steven Blockmans

1 United in Diversity

History does not move in a straight line. And yet, while there are obvious differences in their political, economic and social constructs, the countries of Southeast Europe (SEE)[1] share—by and large—a common trajectory: one of transformation from authoritarian communist rule and centrally planned economies to liberal democracy and capitalism. With the exception of Albania, all countries of the Western Balkans were part of a single jurisdiction until the violent implosion of the Socialist Federal Republic of Yugoslavia. For almost half a century, they shared the same body of law, judicial system and legal culture. The new structures that have taken shape following the collapse of communism in the region in the early 1990s are largely the same. And like the countries of Central and Eastern Europe before them, the transformation of the countries of Southeast Europe has been driven by a desire to join the European Union. Whereas legal transition has so far been fairly swift on paper, the process remains incomplete in most parts of the region when measured against the standards applied by the European Commission.

Indeed, differences do exist, for instance in the speed of transformation. This is partly due to the diverging impact of the wars in the first half and at the end of the 1990s. In part, regional differences are also due to varying levels of political will to look beyond electoral cycles, break vested interests, curb corrupt trends during

[1] The loose geographical concept employed in this volume applies to the successor states of the Socialist Federal Republic of Yugoslavia + Albania. It does not encompass Greece, Bulgaria, Romania and Turkey.

S. Blockmans (✉)
Professor of EU External Relations Law and Governance, University of Amsterdam, 1012 WX Amsterdam, The Netherlands

Head of EU Foreign Policy, Centre for European Policy Studies, Brussels, Belgium
e-mail: steven.blockmans@ceps.eu

S. Rodin, T. Perišin (eds.), *Judicial Application of International Law in Southeast Europe*, DOI 10.1007/978-3-662-46384-0_14

transition, and implement tough reforms for ulterior gain. Even if some results appear shaky, Slovenia and Croatia have realised the dream shared by all. They acceded to the EU in 2004 and 2013, respectively. All of the other countries of the region are locked into the Stabilisation and Association Process (SAP), the pre-accession process for the countries of the Western Balkans. They are parties to the Central European Free Trade Agreement (CEFTA) which, as a precursor to joining the Union's internal market, liberalises trade between them. And they have all concluded Stabilisation and Association Agreements (SAAs) with the EU,[2] even if the one with Bosnia and Herzegovina has entered into force only partially pending full ratification,[3] and the one with Kosovo has only been initialled.[4]

2 Constitutional Status of International Law

All SEE countries covered by the research in this volume have a monist approach to the relationship between national and international law. The Constitutions of Albania (Art. 122), Croatia (Art. 141), Kosovo (Art. 19), Macedonia (Art. 118), Montenegro (Art. 9), Serbia (Arts. 16 & 194) and Slovenia (Art. 8) state that international agreements which have been properly ratified and published in the official journal are an integral part of the country's legal order and enjoy primacy over national laws.

The latter phrase concerning primacy of ratified treaties over national law is not always as clear cut. This is the case, for instance, in the Constitution of Macedonia. In their contribution to this book, Marija Risteska and Kristina Miševa adhere to the formal distinction between monism and dualism and argue that given the fact that ratification is needed for an international legal act to become an integral part of the domestic legal order, the Macedonian system is to be described as a dualist one. In practice, however, the monist and moderate dualist approaches give rise to the same

[2] Stabilisation and Association Agreement between the European Communities and their Member States, of the one part, and the former Yugoslav Republic of Macedonia, of the other part [2004] OJ L84/1-197; Stabilisation and Association Agreement between the European Communities and their Member States, of the one part, and the Republic of Croatia, of the other part [2005] OJ L26/3-220; Council of the European Union, Stabilisation and Association Agreement between the European Communities and their Member States, of the one part, and Bosnia and Herzegovina, of the other part (6.6.2008) 8226/08; Stabilisation and Association Agreement between the European Communities and their Member States, of the one part, and the Republic of Albania, of the other part [2009] OJ L107/116-502; Stabilisation and Association Agreement between the European Communities and their Member States, of the one part, and the Republic of Montenegro, of the other part [2010] OJ L108/3-254; Stabilisation and Association Agreement between the European Communities and their Member States, of the one part, and the Republic of Serbia, of the other part [2013] OJ L278/14-471.

[3] Interim Agreement on trade and trade-related matters between the European Community, of the one part, and Bosnia and Herzegovina, of the other part, [2008] OJ L169/13–807.

[4] The EU and Kosovo chief negotiators initialled the SAA in Brussels on 25 July 2014.

results.[5] In keeping with widely accepted views on the relationship between international and national law,[6] one could therefore ascribe a monist status to the Constitution of Macedonia. After all, Article 118 stipulates that 'international agreements that are ratified and in accordance with the Constitution are an integral part of the domestic legal order and *cannot be changed or derogated with laws*'.[7]

Although the Constitution of Bosnia and Herzegovina (BiH) is silent on the legal status of international agreements in general, it is based on a treaty (the 1995 Dayton Peace Agreement) and its Article 2(2) states that the European Convention on Human Rights (ECHR) is directly applicable and hierarchically superior to national law.[8] Furthermore, Annex I to the Constitution of BiH lists other human rights agreements which also appear to be self-executing.

Some constitutions literally incorporate provisions of international agreements ratified by the SEE countries. The Slovenian, Croatian and Kosovo constitutions, for instance, borrow directly from the language of the ECHR.[9] The Constitution of Macedonia, which was developed incrementally on the basis of the 2001 Ohrid Framework Agreement, is founded on a long list of treaties and includes many a provision of the ECHR, the International Convention on Civil and Political Rights (ICCPR) and the International Convention on the Elimination of All Forms of Racial Discrimination (ICERD).[10] As such, international and EU law has to a great extent been domesticated in the basic law of the lands of Southeast Europe. The same applies, albeit to a lesser extent, to the jurisprudence of international courts and tribunals. In Kosovo, the Constitution demands respect for the jurisprudence of the European Court of Human Rights (ECtHR), even if—or rather, exactly because—the country is not a member of the Council of Europe.[11] Slovenia and Croatia adopted constitutional amendments so as to secure the supremacy of EU law, as developed in the *Van Gend en Loos* and *Costa v. ENEL* judgments of the Court of Justice of the EU (CJEU).[12]

---

[5] See also Janja Hojnik's interpretation about the views held in Slovenian legal theory in the chapter Judicial Application of International and EU Law in Slovenia.

[6] See Denza (2006), p. 429; Stein et al. (2012), p. 58.

[7] Emphasis added.

[8] The Albanian Constitution also refers directly to the ECHR (Art. 17). See the chapter by Gentian Zyberi and Semir Sali, The Place and Application of International Law in the Albanian Legal System.

[9] See, e.g., Arts. 22, 23 and 33 of the Slovenian Constitution, Art. 3 of the Croatian Constitution and Arts. 25 and 31 of the Kosovo Constitution. See also the chapters by Janja Hojnik, Judicial Application of International and EU Law in Slovenia; Ivana Božac and Melita Carević, Judicial Application of International and EU Law in Croatia; and Kushtrim Istrefi and Visar Morina, Judicial Application of International Law in Kosovo.

[10] See the chapter by Marija Risteska and Kristina Miševa, Application of International Law in Macedonia.

[11] Art. 53 of the Kosovo Constitution. See also the chapter by Kushtrim Istrefi and Visar Morina, Judicial Application of International Law in Kosovo.

[12] See Art. 3a of the Slovenian Constitution and Art. 145 of the Croatian Constitution. See also the chapters by Janja Hojnik, Judicial Application of International and EU Law in Slovenia; and Ivana

All this confirms that the treaties and international agreements to which the SEE countries are parties (e.g. ECHR, WTO treaties,[13] Aarhus Convention,[14] etc.) are part and parcel of their domestic legal orders and that they are hierarchically superior to national laws. This finding gives rise to the central question of this volume: to what extent is international law in fact applied by the judiciaries of the eight SEE countries under review?

3 Judicial Attitudes: The Soul Travels on Foot

As Sanja Bogojević points out in her contribution to this book, the judiciary in each country of the region typically consists of a three- or four-tier court system with the Supreme Court and the Constitutional Court on top. The judicial architecture of Slovenia and Croatia has been supplemented since accession to the EU: the CJEU has the monopoly to decide on the interpretation and validity of EU law, and as such binds Slovenian and Croatian courts and tribunals in their domestic application of EU law. The judicial system in BiH and Kosovo is different still, with foreign judges (and prosecutors) being part of the composition of higher court structures like the War Crimes Chamber of the State Court in Sarajevo and the Constitutional Court in Pristina, precisely in an effort to help the local judiciary attain higher standards and get to know international law better. While, as Bogojević observes, it is important to bear these institutional differences in mind when assessing *how* the judiciary functions in Southeast Europe, there is more than just the judicial architecture that explains national courts' relatively poor track record in the implementation of international law.

Unlike the—sometimes lightning—speed with which the governments and parliaments of SEE countries have been blazing the paper trail, the legal culture in the judiciaries has been far slower to adapt. The shadow of the authoritarian and communist legal mind-set, whereby judges were supposed to follow—not to interpret—the will of the legislature,[15] still looms large over Southeast Europe. Whereas older generations of judges are gradually retiring from the bench, a positivist approach to adjudication still prevails whereby the role of the judge is restricted to the objective application of the law and the act of legal interpretation amounts to nothing more than 'a process of deduction, void of any contextual considerations'.[16] As Zdenek Kühn has argued elsewhere for the countries of Central

Božac and Melita Carević, Judicial Application of International and EU Law in Croatia. More generally, see Albi (2005) and Kellermann et al. (2006).

[13] See the chapter by Tamara Perišin, Judicial Application of WTO Law in Southeast Europe.

[14] See the chapter by Lana Ofak, Application of the Aarhus Convention in Southeast Europe.

[15] Rodin (2009). http://www.pravo.unizg.hr/_download/repository/13_Rotterdam.pdf. See also Kühn (2006), p. 19; and Bobek (2011), p. 4: Legislative sovereignty was put on a pedestal, and law 'operated with the notion of unity of state power, not the separation of powers'.

[16] Rodin (2009), p. 2.

Europe, most post-communist judges still adopt a formalist understanding of the law, although their discourses are 'often clothed in a new legal vocabulary'.[17] The national reports compiled in this volume show that the situation in the countries of Southeast Europe is not much different. It will probably take another generation before legal education and culture catch up with the Europeanisation of the other branches of the *trias politica*.

The same applies to the reduction of corruption levels in the judiciaries of Southeast Europe, a matter which has remained outside the scope of the current research. The situation is rather bleak, as evidenced in a report prepared for the European Commission in 2013:

> The independence of the court system is a particular concern throughout the Western Balkans. The threat to this independence comes from several sides. From the state it is primarily through the control of the budget for the court system, and/or the appointment or termination of judges and prosecutors and finally in exerting political pressure in specific court rulings. From the private sector it is through the buying or influencing of legislation and/or outcomes in court cases, though this issue seems to be of much less concern in the region than the threat of state interference and influence.[18]

Subsequent progress reports issued by DG Enlargement have confirmed this sorry state of affairs.

4 Judicial Application of International Law

4.1 Introduction

One of the main features of a monist relationship between national and international law is the obligation of the authorities of a contracting party to a treaty to interpret and apply domestic legislation in conformity with the international obligations entered into by the state. In Albania, Croatia, Kosovo, Macedonia, Montenegro, Serbia and Slovenia, ratified rules of international law are applicable by the domestic courts and other public authorities without the need for any additional regulatory activity of the parliament or the government.[19] Recognition of the direct application of international agreements in Bosnia and Herzegovina arises from the interpretation of Articles 28 and 29 of the Law on the Procedure for the Conclusion and Execution of International Treaties.

---

[17] Kühn (2004), p. 550.

[18] Berenschot and Imagos, 'Final main report: thematic evaluation of rule of law, judicial reform and fight against corruption and organised crime in the Western Balkans – Lot 3', IPA Service Contract Ref. No 2010/256 638, February 2013, p. 26.

[19] See Article 122(1) of the Albanian Constitution; Article 118(3) of the Croatian Constitution; Article 22 of the Kosovo Constitution; Article 98(2) of the Macedonian Constitution; Article 9 of the Montenegrin Constitution; Article 16(2) of the Serbian Constitution; Article 8(2) of the Slovenian Constitution.

4.2 Track Record (I): International Law

Reflecting judicial attitudes prevalent throughout the region, the national reports compiled in this volume show that courts in Southeast Europe are generally reluctant to apply international law, in spite of the institutional structures that have been established to facilitate the judicial consideration of ratified international law.[20] Insofar as higher courts are concerned, the focus is primarily on the direct application of rights codified in the ECHR, as exemplified by the reports on BiH, Kosovo and Macedonia. Contrary to lower courts elsewhere in Europe, which tend to be less conservative than superior—let alone last—instances, junior courts in the Western Balkans do not have a tendency of referring to international law, restrained as they are by the authority of their judicial hierarchy.

It transpires from all national contributions to this volume that the most frequently applied source of international law is the ECHR. Paraphrasing Sanja Bogojević: in Kosovo, 90 % of the case law referring to international law is related to rights and freedoms derived from the ECHR. Similarly, in Slovenia, BiH and Macedonia, the ECHR and the jurisprudence of the ECtHR are the main international sources of law referred to. In Serbia, Strasbourg case law (mainly relating to damages for defamation, family and property disputes) has been extensively used to interpret national law and, although it may not have any legally binding force, it is deemed to carry great moral and political value.[21] Along similar lines, the Albanian judiciary has in almost all human rights-related cases pointed to the ECHR. The same applies to Croatia.[22]

At the other end of the spectrum, Tamara Perišin and Lana Ofak in their contributions to the volume find that WTO law, environmental law and the Aarhus Convention have only rarely been applied in SEE countries.

With respect to the WTO, the membership picture is rather different from that of the ECHR: Montenegro joined the WTO only in 2012 and can thus not be expected to have produced a lot of practice; Bosnia and Herzegovina and Serbia are still in the pre-accession phase (but have observer status); and Kosovo has yet to apply. In

[20] As explained by Sanja Bogojević in her contribution to this book, 'Europeanisation' of the Judiciary in Southeast Europe, several SEE countries have also established special institutions and judicial pathways to facilitate the application of international law. In Serbia, for instance, a Commission for Information of Public Importance and Personal Data Protection has been set up to help litigators in making the necessary international law references. In BiH, litigants have the right to appeal to the provincial Human Rights Commission after they have exhausted all access to the domestic judiciary. This system is understood to help ensure that judicial decisions are in line with European and international principles of human rights. Similarly, the lower courts may refer to constitutional court issues concerning the ECHR or matters of public international law. See Gould (2002), pp. 178–179.

[21] See the chapter by Mirjana Drenovak Ivanović and Maja Lukić, Judicial Application of International Law in Serbia.

[22] Extensive citation of ECtHR case law by the Constitutional Court has become commonplace, but it remains very rare for other courts, even the Supreme Court, to do so. See Ćapeta (2005), p. 23, at 37.

the other four SEE jurisdictions there are hardly any cases where a national court has relied on WTO law or where parties have cited WTO law to support their claims. For Slovenia and Croatia, one could perhaps raise the argument that, with their accession to the EU, a large share of the competence in the field of WTO law has been conferred on the EU and that the status of WTO law is now largely governed by EU law. Yet, these countries had been WTO members for a decade prior to EU accession and so their courts could have been expected to cite or even apply WTO law.[23] Croatian courts stand out as the most active in the region, even if the total number of publicly available decisions referring to WTO law can be counted on two hands. The most prominent case concerns a foreign law firm wanting to set up a branch in Croatia on the basis of the General Agreement on Trade in Services (GATS). Slovenia comes second in the ranking, with regular courts and the Constitutional Court being exercised only by the Agreement on Trade-Related Aspects of Intellectual Property Rights (TRIPS). The picture in the other two WTO countries is depressing. In Albania (a member since 2000), WTO law has been invoked once before the Constitutional Court. But the Court established that there had been a breach of the SAA and did not go on to analyse the compatibility of the measures with WTO rules.[24] In Macedonia (a member since 2003), there has been no court practice with WTO law whatsoever.

As Perišin surmises, the dearth of application of WTO law by national courts can be explained mainly by the small size of the SEE markets, making it too costly for other WTO members wanting to export to a country in the region to go through a WTO dispute in order to improve market access. What is worse, perceptions of endemic corruption, outdated laws, red tape and an ineffective and corrupt judiciary render many a Western Balkan country an unfriendly place for foreign investment. Whereas Western European companies expanded their businesses in Central and Eastern Europe prior to the EU enlargement waves to those countries, they now tend to look past Southeast Europe to more lucrative markets in Southeast Asia and the Far East. Insofar as foreign companies do try to get a foothold in the Western Balkans, they tend to resolve their issues and disputes out of court. Another explanation for the unpopularity of WTO law before national courts in SEE countries lies in the lack of education in the field,[25] making it unlikely for practising lawyers to invoke WTO law and for judges to rely on it. This is not helped by the fact that the WTO Agreement, its annexes and WTO case law are mostly unavailable in the official languages of SEE countries. On a brighter side, SEE countries have achieved trade liberalisation with each other and with their major trading partners through CEFTA and the SAAs, thus making adherence to and enforcement of WTO law less pertinent.

---

[23] Croatia (since 2000) and Slovenia (since 1995).

[24] See the chapter by Gentian Zyberi and Semir Sali, The Place and Application of International Law in the Albanian Legal System.

[25] Croatia stands out as the single exception.

With respect to international environmental law, all of the SEE countries (except Kosovo) are party to the 1998 Aarhus Convention.[26] Yet, there exists only one case of a SEE court (i.e. the Constitutional Court of Slovenia) repealing domestic legislation due to its incompatibility with the Aarhus Convention, *in casu* the omission by the national legislature to prescribe procedural rules for effective public participation in the preparation of implementing regulations for the Convention. As Lana Ofak points out, the ruling of 2008 exposes the duty which rests on all parties' shoulders to adopt detailed provisions in their national legislation to render full effect to the Aarhus Convention. Seizing the opportunity, the Constitutional Court in Ljubljana even went as far as to gold-plate Article 8 of the Aarhus Convention by turning the obligation of intent into one of result in the Slovenian national legal order.

Apart from this flagship judgment in which a national court set aside national law so as to give full effect to the Aarhus Convention, only the national reports of Slovenia and Croatia mention cases in which the Convention was referred to.[27] Since the Aarhus Convention came into force in respect of Croatia, there has only been one judgment of the Administrative Court of the Republic of Croatia in which the provisions of the Aarhus Convention were directly applied.[28] Ofak offers a host of explanations for the rare application of the Convention. The most important of those is no doubt that many rules of the Convention and other acts of international environmental law have been absorbed by the *acquis* of the EU,[29] domesticating them in the national legal orders of SEE countries which approximate their legislation so as to meet pre-accession requirements:

> In situations where the Aarhus Convention could be applied, courts would rather apply the rules of domestic legislation that are relevant to the merits of the case, or the provisions of the EU directives that regulate access to information, public participation in decision-making and access to justice in environmental matters. In addition, in many environmental

[26] All have also signed up to the 2003 Protocol on Pollutant Release and Transfer Registers (BiH and Montenegro still need to ratify the latter). Slovenia is the only country that has ratified the GMO amendment. These acts remain beyond the remit of the current research though.

[27] In Slovenia: Judgment of the Administrative Court, I U 2/2010; in Croatia: Judgment of the Administrative Court, Us-7555/2004-5, Judgment of the Misdemeanour Court in Zagreb, VI-G-2047-09). Ofak also mentions that out of 83 communications by individuals to a designated Committee which deals with cases of non-compliance under the Aarhus Convention, only four cases have been triggered by citizens of Western Balkan countries (two from Albania and two from Croatia). This harks back to the point made by Perišin, namely that the lack of education in the field partly explains the absence of attempts to invoke or refer to international environmental law.

[28] Judgment of 23 October 2009, Us-5235/2009-5, in a case in which the Croatian Society for Bird and Nature Protection appealed against a decision by the Ministry of Environmental Protection refusing to allow the Society to make copies of an environmental impact assessment study for the project 'Control works on the River Drava' over alleged breach of the intellectual property rights of the author of the study.

[29] There exist several EU Directives, binding on the Member States, that include rules on access to information, public participation in decision-making and access to justice in environmental matters: e.g., Directives 2003/4/EC, 85/337/EEC, 2001/42/EC, 2003/35/EC, 2004/35/EC.

cases the Aarhus Convention [would] not be applicable, since it does not contain any substantive rules regarding the right to a healthy environment.[30]

4.3 Track Record (II): SAA and EU Law

When it comes to EU law, Slovenia and Croatia, in their capacities as Member States, are under a legal obligation to apply EU law. Slovenia, however, has reported little EU-law activity before the national courts since its accession in 2004; the few cases that deal with this body of law concern mainly asylum and taxation.[31] It is too early to detect any post-accession pattern in the Croatian courts.

A pertinent pre-accession period case in which EU law was taken into account and discussed as if it were binding on Croatian courts is that of the Zagreb County Court dealing with a collective claim raised by a group of NGOs against the discriminatory statements of a football official about homosexuals.[32] The Albanian Constitutional Court has made direct references to EU law,[33] as has the Supreme Court of Cassation in Serbia,[34] raising issues relating to the EU Charter of Fundamental Rights.

Prior to EU accession, the CJEU-developed doctrines of primacy, direct effect and state liability obviously do not apply in the legal orders of aspirant states. However, it seems reasonable to argue, as Mislav Mataija does in his contribution to this book, that there is nothing stopping national judges from interpreting the

[30] Ofak claims that the procedural rules of the Convention which were not incorporated into EU law remain irrelevant for the adjudication of disputes. Examples from Slovenia and Macedonia include Judgment of the Administrative Court, I U 2/2010, and *Citizens of Veles v. Republic of Macedonia*, respectively.

[31] See the chapter by Janja Hojnik, Judicial Application of International and EU Law in Slovenia.

[32] Zagreb County Court, judgment 15 Pnz-6/10-27 of 6 April 2011. The plaintiffs invoked the CJEU judgment in case C-54/07 (*Firma Feryn*) in which an executive's general statements against hiring immigrants were considered discriminatory.

[33] See, e.g., the Constitutional Court's judgment in *Instituti i Ekspertëve Kontabël të Autorizuar*, in which the Court invoked Directive 2006/43 on statutory audits of annual accounts and consolidated accounts as support in order to reject a claim that the national law on auditing was unconstitutional. It found, for example, that State supervision of auditors did not violate the independence of the profession, *inter alia* because such supervision is required by the Directive. Thus, hypothetical conformity with EU law was used as an argument for the actual conformity of the law with the Albanian constitution, though without clarifying the precise basis on which EU law was taken into account. See the chapter by Gentian Zyberi and Semir Sali, The Place and Application of International Law in the Albanian Legal System.

[34] Judgment of the Appellate Court in Belgrade, Rev. 2401/2010 of 28 April 2010. The Supreme Court supported its findings in a family law dispute by referring, in general terms, to the provisions on the right to family life and children's rights of the EU Charter of Fundamental Rights—again, without explaining why the Charter was a relevant legal source. See the chapter by Mirjana Drenovak Ivanović and Maja Lukić, Judicial Application of International Law in Serbia. See further Blockmans and Mihajlovic (2011), pp. 65–94.

already approximated domestic law and provisions of the SAA in the light of the *acquis*, in effect creating a 'back door' for the application of EU law prior to accession. In the countries which joined the European Union in the past decade this was not an everyday practice but there were notable examples whereby the Europe Agreements served as a back door to the application of EU law *avant la lettre*.[35]

In view of their content, the fact that some provisions are capable of having direct effect, and the inclusion of approximation clauses that could be read as imposing a duty on SEE courts to interpret national law in the light of EU law, one would assume that the SAAs concluded with the countries of the Western Balkans should provide at least as much material for judicial application as the Europe agreements did for the countries that joined in 2004 and 2007. However, as Mataija points out, despite these similarities, the evidence compiled in this volume shows that:

(i) the SAAs have not been relied upon to impose broad interpretative duties in the SEE states, such as the duty to interpret national law in the light of EU law (including CJEU jurisprudence);
(ii) [even if the first cases are now surfacing in Albania[36] and Macedonia,[37]] the SAAs have rarely been relied upon directly before national courts in order to disapply or annul conflicting measures of national law; but that
(iii) they have had a more practical effect in areas where the SAA makes a specific reference to the EU *acquis* – notably in competition law.[38]

---

[35] See, e.g., Łazowski and Wentkowska (2009), pp. 277–323 at 293–298. See also the chapter by Janja Hojnik, Judicial Application of International and EU Law in Slovenia. See further the national reports in Kellermann et al. (2006).

[36] The Albanian Constitutional Court found a violation of the SAA standstill clause, prohibiting the introduction of new or more restrictive quantitative restrictions on imports and measures having equivalent effect, against a decision of the Albanian Council of Ministers which treated domestically produced diesel oils more favourably than imports. The Constitutional Court not only found fault with the SAA standstill clause but also the SAA provision on measures that 'constitute a means of arbitrary discrimination or a disguised restriction on trade'. See the chapter by Gentian Zyberi and Semir Sali, The Place and Application of International Law in the Albanian Legal System. See further Caka and Blockmans (2010), pp. 511–530.

[37] In *Makpetrol v. Ministry of Finance Customs Office*, the First Skopje Basic Court similarly disapplied two by-laws imposing customs duties in violation of the Macedonian SAA and interim agreement. This judgment is the only example found for the purposes of this book of an ordinary court disapplying a provision of national law on the basis of the SAA. The court even made a declaratory finding that the provisions were 'no longer in force' because they conflicted with the SAA and the interim agreement. See the chapter by Marija Risteska and Kristina Miševa, Application of International Law in Macedonia.

[38] See, e.g., the 2006 case law of the Croatian Administrative Court, as well as the 2010 judgment of that court that again refuses the application of EU law, in contrast to the Constitutional Court. See also the chapter by Ivana Božac and Melita Carević, Judicial Application of International and EU Law in Croatia. Apart from Croatia, there is only one such case in the national reports: Court of BiH, decision No. S1 3 U 005412 10 Uvl of 15.3.2012, M.R.M. Ljubuški/ASA Auto d.o.o. Sarajevo (*ASA Auto*). See the chapter by Zlatan Meškić and Darko Samardžić, Application of International and EU Law in Bosnia and Herzegovina.

> The conclusion is that an SEE court disinclined to apply an SAA provision would be more likely to find it wholly inapplicable or not to have direct effect rather than to contrast it with CJEU case law and show why the SAA contextually warrants a lower level of protection, because the latter strategy would require a shift in the usual mode of argumentation applied by those courts.[39]

In sum, there is little evidence of the pre-accession use of EU law, whether directly or on the basis of an interpretative duty imposed by the SAAs. The key question, of course, is to what extent the judges in Southeast Europe can be expected to be *au courant* with EU law and use it in their daily practice. Issues of translation and education again play up in this context. As Adam Łazowski and I have argued elsewhere, one of the main weaknesses of the current candidates and potential candidates for EU membership is the poor shape of their national public administrations and judiciaries.[40] In the pre-accession context, human capacities are limited and due to budgetary restraints it remains a major challenge to create and to staff all national authorities which are necessary for the successful transposition and enforcement of SAA and EU law.

5 Final Remarks

The Southeast European countries examined in this book share a similar recent legal history and a future strategic goal. With the aim of acceding to the EU, itself a community of law, a general political will exists to abide by international and European law. This will has even been translated in more or less clear terms in the constitutions of the SEE countries, enabling the direct applicability of ratified international agreements to run supreme over national legislation.

However, as argued by Michal Bobek, what is important is not the creation of constitutional and institutional frameworks *per se*, but the degree to which the judiciary is able to critically assess and apply various, sometimes conflicting, laws.[41] Unfortunately, practice has shown that, unless provisions have been explicitly incorporated into national law, the domestic courts of EU aspirant countries are

[39] See the chapter by Mislav Mataija, The Unfulfilled Potential of Stabilisation and Association Agreements Before Southeast Europe Courts: "There are a number of examples of SEE courts refusing to interpret domestic law in the light of EU sources. One of them is the Serbian Constitutional Court judgment in *ERC Commerce Computers*, a customs classification case". The Croatian Constitutional Court, too, rejected a complaint related to a customs procedure during which imported goods were reclassified under a higher tariff heading. Another example concerns the High Commercial Court in Croatia, which in a 2007 ruling rejected a party's attempt to use the SAA as a basis for relying on the Treaty rules on free movement of goods and the corresponding ECJ case law in a case on parallel imports and the trade mark exhaustion of rights principle.

[40] Łazowski and Blockmans (2014), pp. 108–132.

[41] Bobek (2008), p. 99.

generally reluctant to apply international law. The national reports compiled in this volume show that most SEE courts follow an all-or-nothing logic: international and EU law is either followed to the letter, or not at all. The prevailing legal culture is one characterised by high levels of formality, whereby '[a]dapting the interpretation of a similarly worded legal instrument, depending on the context, is an unnatural exercise for SEE courts, which are accustomed to viewing legal texts either as binding "sources of law" or as largely irrelevant'.[42] Paradoxically, this judicial conservatism tightens when plaintiffs invest in explaining why 'foreign' sources should be used.

Arguably, this legal culture can be transformed through education which embraces critical thinking, problem-based learning and twinning, and endorses a more dynamic interpretation of the law such as that espoused in the community of law that the SEE countries wish to join.[43] Renewed investment in the modernisation of legal education is key to the creation and maintenance of a progressive judicial system and to the application of international and European law in Southeast Europe.

References

Albi A (2005) EU enlargement and the constitutions of Central and Eastern Europe. Cambridge University Press, Cambridge

Blockmans S, Mihajlovic M (2011) Ensuring the correct implementation of the Stabilisation and Association Agreement in Serbia: a case study on the imports of second-hand vehicles. Revija za evropsko pravo 13:65–94

Bobek M (2008) The fortress of judicial independence and the mental transitions of the Central European judiciaries. Public Eur Law 14:99

Bobek M (2011) Judicial transformations in post-communist societies: a study in institutions, administration and interpretation. CAS Sofia working paper series 4, pp 1, 4

Caka F, Blockmans S (2010) Implementing the Stabilisation and Association Agreement in Albania: avoiding discriminatory practices in the free movement of goods. Eur J Law Reform 11:511–530

Ćapeta T (2005) Courts, legal culture and the enlargement of the EU. Croatian Yearb Eur Law Policy 1:23

Denza E (2006) The relationship between international and national law. In: Malcolm DE (ed) International law, 2nd edn. OUP, Oxford, p 429

Gould J (2002) Bosnia and Herzegovina. In: Kritzer H (ed) Legal systems of the world. ABC-CLIO, Santa Barbara, pp 178–179

---

[42] See the chapter by Mislav Mataija, The Unfulfilled Potential of Stabilisation and Association Agreements Before Southeast Europe Courts.

[43] The reform of curricula should not be limited to the judicial academies but should also be implemented at graduate and undergraduate levels at university. See Malleson (1997), pp. 655, 667. See the chapter by Sanja Bogojević, 'Europeanisation' of the Judiciary in Southeast Europe.

Kellermann A, Czuczai J, Blockmans S, Albi A, Douma W (eds) (2006) The impact of EU accession on the legal orders of new EU member states and (pre-)candidate countries. Asser Press, The Hague

Kühn Z (2004) Worlds apart: Western and Central European judicial culture at the onset of the European enlargement. Am J Comp Law 52:531

Kühn Z (2006) The authoritarian legal culture at work: the passivity of parties and the interpretational statements of supreme courts. Croatian Yearb Eur Law Policy 2:19

Łazowski A, Blockmans S (2014) Between dream and reality: challenges to the legal rapprochement of the Western Balkans. In: Van Elsuwege P, Petrov R (eds) Legal approximation and application of EU law in the eastern neighbourhood of the European Union: towards a common regulatory space? Routledge, London, pp 108–132

Łazowski A, Wentkowska A (2009) Poland: constitutional drama and business as usual. In: Łazowski A (ed) The application of EU law in the new member states: brave new world. Asser Press, The Hague, pp 277 323

Malleson K (1997) Judicial training and performance appraisal: the problem of judicial independence. Mod Law Rev 60(655):667

Rodin S (2009) Functions of judicial opinion: a view from a post-communist European state. http://www.pravo.unizg.hr/_download/repository/13_Rotterdam.pdf

Stein T, Von Buttlar C, Seidel-Hohenveldern I (2012) Völkerrecht. Heymanns, München, p 58

> The conclusion is that an SEE court disinclined to apply an SAA provision would be more likely to find it wholly inapplicable or not to have direct effect rather than to contrast it with CJEU case law and show why the SAA contextually warrants a lower level of protection, because the latter strategy would require a shift in the usual mode of argumentation applied by those courts.[39]

In sum, there is little evidence of the pre-accession use of EU law, whether directly or on the basis of an interpretative duty imposed by the SAAs. The key question, of course, is to what extent the judges in Southeast Europe can be expected to be *au courant* with EU law and use it in their daily practice. Issues of translation and education again play up in this context. As Adam Łazowski and I have argued elsewhere, one of the main weaknesses of the current candidates and potential candidates for EU membership is the poor shape of their national public administrations and judiciaries.[40] In the pre-accession context, human capacities are limited and due to budgetary restraints it remains a major challenge to create and to staff all national authorities which are necessary for the successful transposition and enforcement of SAA and EU law.

5 Final Remarks

The Southeast European countries examined in this book share a similar recent legal history and a future strategic goal. With the aim of acceding to the EU, itself a community of law, a general political will exists to abide by international and European law. This will has even been translated in more or less clear terms in the constitutions of the SEE countries, enabling the direct applicability of ratified international agreements to run supreme over national legislation.

However, as argued by Michal Bobek, what is important is not the creation of constitutional and institutional frameworks *per se*, but the degree to which the judiciary is able to critically assess and apply various, sometimes conflicting, laws.[41] Unfortunately, practice has shown that, unless provisions have been explicitly incorporated into national law, the domestic courts of EU aspirant countries are

[39] See the chapter by Mislav Mataija, The Unfulfilled Potential of Stabilisation and Association Agreements Before Southeast Europe Courts: "There are a number of examples of SEE courts refusing to interpret domestic law in the light of EU sources. One of them is the Serbian Constitutional Court judgment in *ERC Commerce Computers*, a customs classification case". The Croatian Constitutional Court, too, rejected a complaint related to a customs procedure during which imported goods were reclassified under a higher tariff heading. Another example concerns the High Commercial Court in Croatia, which in a 2007 ruling rejected a party's attempt to use the SAA as a basis for relying on the Treaty rules on free movement of goods and the corresponding ECJ case law in a case on parallel imports and the trade mark exhaustion of rights principle.

[40] Łazowski and Blockmans (2014), pp. 108–132.

[41] Bobek (2008), p. 99.

generally reluctant to apply international law. The national reports compiled in this volume show that most SEE courts follow an all-or-nothing logic: international and EU law is either followed to the letter, or not at all. The prevailing legal culture is one characterised by high levels of formality, whereby '[a]dapting the interpretation of a similarly worded legal instrument, depending on the context, is an unnatural exercise for SEE courts, which are accustomed to viewing legal texts either as binding "sources of law" or as largely irrelevant'.[42] Paradoxically, this judicial conservatism tightens when plaintiffs invest in explaining why 'foreign' sources should be used.

Arguably, this legal culture can be transformed through education which embraces critical thinking, problem-based learning and twinning, and endorses a more dynamic interpretation of the law such as that espoused in the community of law that the SEE countries wish to join.[43] Renewed investment in the modernisation of legal education is key to the creation and maintenance of a progressive judicial system and to the application of international and European law in Southeast Europe.

References

Albi A (2005) EU enlargement and the constitutions of Central and Eastern Europe. Cambridge University Press, Cambridge

Blockmans S, Mihajlovic M (2011) Ensuring the correct implementation of the Stabilisation and Association Agreement in Serbia: a case study on the imports of second-hand vehicles. Revija za evropsko pravo 13:65–94

Bobek M (2008) The fortress of judicial independence and the mental transitions of the Central European judiciaries. Public Eur Law 14:99

Bobek M (2011) Judicial transformations in post-communist societies: a study in institutions, administration and interpretation. CAS Sofia working paper series 4, pp 1, 4

Caka F, Blockmans S (2010) Implementing the Stabilisation and Association Agreement in Albania: avoiding discriminatory practices in the free movement of goods. Eur J Law Reform 11:511–530

Ćapeta T (2005) Courts, legal culture and the enlargement of the EU. Croatian Yearb Eur Law Policy 1:23

Denza E (2006) The relationship between international and national law. In: Malcolm DE (ed) International law, 2nd edn. OUP, Oxford, p 429

Gould J (2002) Bosnia and Herzegovina. In: Kritzer H (ed) Legal systems of the world. ABC-CLIO, Santa Barbara, pp 178–179

[42] See the chapter by Mislav Mataija, The Unfulfilled Potential of Stabilisation and Association Agreements Before Southeast Europe Courts.

[43] The reform of curricula should not be limited to the judicial academies but should also be implemented at graduate and undergraduate levels at university. See Malleson (1997), pp. 655, 667. See the chapter by Sanja Bogojević, 'Europeanisation' of the Judiciary in Southeast Europe.